Why is nominalism rampant within the church? Could it be that it has to do with deficient preaching that fails to expound God's word in a faithful and challenging way to his people? Johnson Raih has set out to explore the connection in relation to the Baptist churches in Imphal, Manipur, in northeast India, an area with a long Christian tradition. Taking care to situate his findings in a wider biblical and contemporary framework concerning preaching, he is, above all, concerned with listening to the voice of the people. They reveal why much preaching fails to produce mature and holy Christians and what can be done about it. If his findings are given the seriousness they deserve, it could revolutionize the quality of Christian living not only in Imphal but well beyond it too.

Derek Tidball, PhD
Adjunct Lecturer and Research Supervisor,
South Asia Institute of Advanced Christian Studies (SAIACS), Bangalore, India
Former Principal, London School of Theology, UK

This is an extensive and elaborate work, perhaps a premier for the region of northeast India. There is elaborate and in-depth research – it is refreshing to go through the analytical discussions on the expository preaching in chapter 6, and in chapter 7, the pragmatic task is very relevant for all. Raih rightly points out that "effective preaching must ultimately lead people to encounter God, and experience him personally in their lives, thus bringing spiritual vitality" (pg. 268). After a thorough examination on the works of some of the Western and Oriental practitioners of homiletics, Raih's research recommends that "preaching a clear expository and biblical gospel will impact the spiritual lives, ethics, and commitment of the people positively, thus combating nominalism" (pg. 299). This monograph is a must-read for all preachers and is worthy of a space in your library.

Rev. A. K. Lama, DMin, PhD
Former General Secretary,
Council of Baptist Churches in North East India (CBCNEI)

Good preaching packs a punch. Probing the disarray that nominalism has brought to the church in northeast India, Johnson Raih's fine qualitative research explores the evangelical intuition that systematic expository preaching strengthens the church and combats nominalism. His study confirms better preaching will have impact. Every northeast Indian Christian leader needs to read it.

Ian Payne, PhD
Former Principal,
South Asia Institute of Advanced Christian Studies (SAIACS), Bangalore, India
Executive Director, Theologians Without Borders

This book reveals the long-time experience of Johnson Raih with the Baptist churches in Manipur, their preaching, and its impact on the lives of the congregation. Many people get frustrated when preaching is unrelated and unimpressive. Johnson Raih's writings in this book are a great guide to effective preaching in times of spiritual lethargic attitude. He fills the gap between the pulpit and the pews through his conclusions. If pastors want to move their congregation from nominalism to spirituality, through an effective method of preaching, this book is the right book to read.

Rev. Prof. Alfred Stephen, DTh
Professor of Homiletics,
Tamilnadu Theological Seminary, India

Expository Preaching in a World of Spiritual Nominalism

Exploring the Churches in India's North East

R. T. Johnson Raih

© 2021 R. T. Johnson Raih

Published 2021 by Langham Academic (Previously Langham Monographs)
An imprint of Langham Publishing
www.langhampublishing.org

Langham Publishing and its imprints are a ministry of Langham Partnership

Langham Partnership
PO Box 296, Carlisle, Cumbria, CA3 9WZ, UK
www.langham.org

ISBNs:
978-1-83973-223-2 Print
978-1-83973-599-8 ePub
978-1-83973-601-8 PDF

R. T. Johnson Raih has asserted his right under the Copyright, Designs and Patents Act, 1988 to be identified as the Author of this work.

All rights reserved. No part of this publication may be reproduced, stored in a retrieval system or transmitted, in any form or by any means, electronic, mechanical, photocopying, recording or otherwise, without the prior written permission of the publisher or the Copyright Licensing Agency.

Requests to reuse content from Langham Publishing are processed through PLSclear. Please visit www.plsclear.com to complete your request.

Unless marked otherwise, Scripture taken from the New American Standard Bible®, Copyright © 1960, 1962, 1963, 1968, 1971, 1972, 1973, 1975, 1977, 1995 by The Lockman Foundation. Used by permission.

Scripture quotations marked (ESV) are taken from The Holy Bible, English Standard Version® (ESV®), copyright © 2001 by Crossway, a publishing ministry of Good News Publishers. Used by permission. All rights reserved.

Scripture quotations marked (NIV) are taken from the Holy Bible, New International Version®, NIV®. Copyright © 1973, 1978, 1984, 2011 by Biblica, Inc.™ Used by permission of Zondervan.

British Library Cataloguing-in-Publication Data
A catalogue record for this book is available from the British Library

ISBN: 978-1-83973-223-2

Cover & Book Design: projectluz.com

Langham Partnership actively supports theological dialogue and an author's right to publish but does not necessarily endorse the views and opinions set forth here or in works referenced within this publication, nor can we guarantee technical and grammatical correctness. Langham Partnership does not accept any responsibility or liability to persons or property as a consequence of the reading, use or interpretation of its published content.

Contents

Foreword xiii

Acknowledgements xvii

Abstract xxi

Abbreviations xxiii

Chapter 1 1
Introduction
    1.1 Introduction 1
    1.2 Rationale 3
        1.2.1 Personal Rationale 3
        1.2.2 Academic Rationale 3
    1.3 Statement of Purpose 3
    1.4 Objectives 4
    1.5 Significance of the Study 4
    1.6 Scope and Limitation of the Study 5
    1.7 Statement of the Problem 5
    1.8 Research Questions 6
        1.8.1 Primary Research Question 6
        1.8.2 Subsidiary Research Questions 6
    1.9 Definition of Key Terms 7
    1.10 Structure of the Study 7
    1.11 Research Design for the Study 8
    1.12 Selected Strategy of Inquiry 9
        1.12.1 Qualitative Method: Practical Theology and Social Sciences 9
    1.13 Philosophical Worldview of Phenomenological Approach: Social Constructivist Worldview 14
    1.14 Research Methods 17
        1.14.1 Method of Data Collection 17
    1.15 An Analysis of Various Research Models 20
        1.15.1 Rambo and Leh 21
        1.15.2 Kevin Gary Smith's Model 21
        1.15.3 Richard R. Osmer's Model 22

Chapter 2 29
   Literature Review
      2.1 Introduction 29
      2.2 The Effect of Preaching 29
         2.2.1 A Theological-Homiletical Survey 29
         2.2.2 The Situation of Preaching in India's North East 48
         2.2.3 Previous Research 50
      2.3 Nominalism 58
         2.3.1 Lausanne Movement Discussions 58
         2.3.2 World Council of Churches (WCC) and Council of
             Baptist Churches in North East India (CBCNEI) 62
      2.4 Nominalism and Preaching 63
         2.4.1 Regional Survey 63
      2.5 Working Definition of Nominalism 71

Chapter 3 75
   Christianity in Manipur: Arrival, Growth, and the Early Preaching Movement
      3.1 A General Background of Manipur and Imphal City 75
      3.2 Religious Background 76
      3.3 Arrival of Christianity in Manipur 77
      3.4. The Early Preaching Movements in North East India
         (CBCNEI) 78
      3.5 Christian Mission and Preaching in Manipur through the
         American Mission Society (AMS) 80
         3.5.1 William Pettigrew's Mission Work and the
             Formation of Manipur Baptist Convention (MBC) 80
         3.5.2 Preaching, Persecution, and Church Growth in
             Manipur 84
      3.6 Effect of Christian Preaching in Manipur: The First Half of
         the Twentieth Century 88
      3.7 Health of the Baptist Church and Preaching in Manipur:
         The Second Half of the Twentieth Century 94
         3.7.1 The Ministry Focus of MBC Leadership in Different
             Eras of Its History 95
         3.7.2 Eras of the MBC Leadership: An Analysis from a
             Homiletical Point of View 99
         3.7.3 The Role of Preaching for Church Growth:
             Y. L. Mingthing 102
         3.7.4 An Analysis of Y. L. Mingthing's Voice on the Role
             of Preaching for Church Growth 103
      3.8 Conclusion 106

Chapter 4 107
Description of the Data
- 4.1 Introduction 107
- 4.2. Data Coding and Analysis... 109
- 4.3. Description of the Data 112
  - 4.3.1 Church Members' Understanding of the Word of God ... 112
  - 4.3.2 Spiritual Vitality... 121
  - 4.3.3 Nominalism.. 125
  - 4.3.4 Preaching.. 147
  - 4.3.5 Reading of the Scripture Inspired by Preaching.............. 173
  - 4.3.6 General Challenges to the Spirituality of the Members in Baptist Churches of Imphal 174
  - 4.3.7 Observation of the Data and Connection with the Research Questions 176
- 4.4 Conclusion 176

Chapter 5 177
Interpretation of the Data
- 5.1 Introduction 177
- 5.2 The Task of Interpretation... 177
- 5.3 Theories and Literature Review vis-à-vis the Interpretative Task.. 180
- 5.4 Interpreting the Impact of Preaching in the Church................ 181
  - 5.4.1 Interpreting the Positive Impact of Good Preaching........ 181
  - 5.4.2 Interpreting the Negative Impact of Bad Preaching 185
- 5.5 Interpreting the Impact of Preaching on Society..................... 189
- 5.6 An Engagement between Research Findings and Literature Review.. 190
  - 5.6.1 The Advantage of Qualitative Approach 190
  - 5.6.2 The Effect of Preaching: The Homiletical-Theological Survey 191
  - 5.6.3 Preaching and Spiritual Vitality....................................... 192
  - 5.6.4 Preaching and Nominalism 193
  - 5.6.5 Nominalism: Description and Definition 201
- 5.7 Interpreting the Believers' Poor Understanding of the Word of God 205
- 5.8 Goals and Themes in Preaching.. 207
- 5.9 Methods of Sermons Preached in the Baptist Churches......... 211
- 5.10 An Analysis of the Methods of Sermons................................. 211
- 5.11 Conclusion 216

Chapter 6 217
   Normative Task
     6.1 Introduction..217
     6.2 Spiritual Lethargy in the Bible and a Homiletical Response 217
        6.2.1 Spiritual Lethargy in the Old Testament: Malachi............220
        6.2.2 Malachi's Homiletical Response 225
        6.2.3 Spiritual Lethargy in the New Testament:
            1 Corinthians 240
     6.3 The Role of Charisma in Topical and Expository
        Preaching: An Evaluation..251
     6.4 The Theology and Method of Expository Preaching..................253
        6.4.1 John Stott...254
        6.4.2 Timothy Keller...257
     6.5 Critique against Expository Preaching.......................................261
        6.5.1 Critique against Expository Preaching by the
            Proponents of New Homiletic (NH)...................................261
        6.5.2 Critique against Expository Preaching by Some
            Evangelicals..263
        6.5.3 Challenges of Expository Preaching in Terms of
            Its Homiletical Method in Comparison to Topical
            Preaching Method 264
     6.6 Rebuttal against the Criticisms of the New Homiletic on
        Expository Preaching..267
     6.7 Evaluation of Stott and Keller and a Response to the
        Critique against Expository Preaching..268
     6.8 Recommendation of Expository Preaching for the Baptist
        Churches of Imphal..270
     6.9 Conclusion 271

Chapter 7 273
   Pragmatic Task
     7.1 Introduction..273
     7.2 Discussions and Recommendations to Revitalise the
        Preaching Ministry in Order to Combat Nominalism................274
        7.2.1 Love the Word of God... 274
        7.2.2 Preach the Biblical Gospel Faithfully.................................279
        7.2.3 Preach as a Shepherd with Love to God's People 280
        7.2.4 Pastors Should Be Humble, Prayerful, and Preach in
            the Power of the Holy Spirit, because They Hold
            the Key 283
        7.2.5 Pastors Should Preach to the Believers' Context...............284

- 7.2.6 Pastors Should Put Personal Integrity above Their Sermon 285
- 7.2.7 The Church Should Provide Formal and Non-Formal Preaching Training for the Pastors 286
- 7.2.8 Pastors Must Extend Their Preaching Ministry Beyond the Pulpit 288
- 7.2.9 Deacons Must Play a Pro-Active Role in the Pastor's Preaching Ministry 289
- 7.3 Conclusion 290

Chapter 8 293
Conclusion
- 8.1 Introduction 293
- 8.2 Summary 293
- 8.3 A Critical Self-Evaluation and Critique 295
  - 8.3.1 Weaknesses 295
  - 8.3.2 Strengths 296
- 8.4 Contribution to the Field of Practical Theology 298
  - 8.4.1 Baptist Churches in Imphal 299
  - 8.4.2 Practical Theology 299
- 8.5 Further Recommendations for Future Research 299
- 8.6 Summary and Conclusion 300

Appendix 1 301
The Spectrum of Preaching

Appendix 2 331
Open-Ended Research Questionnaire

Appendix 3 337
Some Other Ways to Address Nominalism

Appendix 4 339
List of Some Theologically Trained MBC Leaders

Appendix 5 341
Political Map of Manipur in the Context of Global Map

Appendix 6 343
A Political Map of India

Appendix 7 345
Manipur Map

Appendix 8 347
    Imphal Map

Appendix 9 349
    Semi-Structured Interview Questions

Appendix 10 353
    Pilot Survey Questionnaire

Appendix 11 359
    Pilot Survey Interview Questions

Appendix 12 361
    General Challenges to the Spirituality of the Members

Bibliography 367

List of Figures

Figure 1: A Framework for Design – The Interconnection of Worldviews, Strategies of Inquiry, and Research Methods 9
Figure 2: Four Worldviews 15
Figure 3: Theoretical Generalisation 16
Figure 4: Kevin Gary Smith's Practical Theology Research Model 21
Figure 5: Richard R. Osmer's Model 22
Figure 6: A Graphic Map for the Literature Review 31
Figure 7: A Spectrum of Effect of Preaching on Spiritual Life 32
Figure 8: Holistic Ministry of Pastor 175
Figure 9: Sequence of Bad Preaching and Nominalism 199
Figure 10: Sequence of Good Preaching and Spiritual Vitality 201
Figure 11: Equipping Preachers Has an Exponential Impact 288
Figure 12: A Spectrum of Theology of Preaching 328

Foreword

It was a question I had never been asked before. Having just finished preaching on salt and light and the importance of living distinctive lives in the world, I was greeting people at the back of the church. Someone came up and asked me, "How does this work when everyone in the world around you is already Christian?" Momentarily, the question took me by surprise, and then I remembered where I was – Nagaland, the most Baptist area in the world, yet, ironically, an area with a reputation in India for corruption, widespread social issues, and poor infrastructure. With this in the back of my mind, I mumbled a response – "Well, you probably need to start by imagining that they are *not* Christian" – because the evidence seems to suggest that the salt and light is not having its intended impact on the world.

Johnson Raih was with me on that day but, sadly, his thesis was not. His thesis would have helped me as I found myself face-to-face with the challenge of nominalism – the problem of Christians being Christian "in name" only, rather than in reality. It does such damage to the cause of Christ in so many places across the world.

Johnson Raih and I have enjoyed a friendship that stretches back a decade. He participated in the first round of Langham Preaching training in Northeast India, coming to be with us from his job as the principal of a high school in Imphal, Manipur. Quite independently, we found ourselves arriving at the South Asia Institute of Advanced Christian Studies (SAIACS), Bangalore, at roughly the same time – he as a student, me as a teacher. After he graduated with his MTh, he went back to a grassroots training ministry in the Northeast with his family, but then returned to SAIACS, convinced of God's call to complete doctoral studies in homiletics. Our friendship took new turns and deepened, now fueled by him becoming my Teaching Assistant in the MA, MTh, and DMin courses in homiletics.

In the week prior to that Sunday in Nagaland, we had been in Imphal visiting churches and pastors in the Manipur Baptist Convention, as well as his parents in their home outside Senapati. As Raih affirms in his thesis, nominalism, or spiritual lethargy, is "an open secret" in these churches. While the Lausanne Movement has had a working group engaging the topic for some years, there has been a dearth of specific contextual studies of nominalism that can contribute to the academic discussion around the world.

Raih's work helps fill this gap as he examines the role of preaching, as both a cause and an effect of nominalism. At its worst, preaching can be "an incubator of nominality" (pg. 62, Eddie Gibbs) while, at its best, it can subvert the lethargy and vitalize spirituality. This book is a crucial study for the church in India as well as the church in the USA, among other countries. Take the Indian context for a moment. Raih references research which demonstrates that evangelistic work by Indian Christians is not vibrant because two-thirds of the Christians in India need themselves to be evangelized. This is a tragic consequence of nominalism, and this is the world into which Raih steps.

Raih's study sparkles with engaging features. First, there is the *nuance*. The Lausanne working group settled on twelve "varieties of nominality." That sounds comprehensive. One would expect that further examples would fit somewhere within their classification. But such is the care with which Raih engages his research that three further varieties, gathered from his review of the literature, are drawn into the conversation: the impact of mass conversion within a family decades earlier; liberal theology from the pulpits; and the phenomenon of "the prayer warrior" where believers outsource their prayer requests, weakening their own intimacy with God.

Second, there is the *depth*. So prevalent is nominalism that it can become the air people breathe, the water in which they swim, and the lens through which they look. It becomes hard to recognize because it is everywhere. This is an issue of worldview, as the "-ism" at the end of the word suggests, just as it is with syncretism, dualism and animism – each of which Raih discusses. The air, the water and the lens need to be exegeted. These things are not turned around merely by more evangelism, or by increased ministries of compassion and justice. It takes a jolt to disturb a worldview like nominalism. Without that jolt, conversion stories can be compared to turning around on a train that is still travelling in the same direction. There is no lasting change or impact. The train *itself* needs to be turned around, and this is what Raih is attempting here.

Third, there is the *data*. I had no idea that reading through information emerging from questionnaires could be so fascinating. I expected to scan them as I fast-tracked through to the conclusions; however, I became engrossed in the data. As I listened to people speak, I was struck by the depth of their insight regarding both the problem of nominalism and its solution. And I imagine their wisdom and insight is readily transferable to other contexts. Raih listens, lingers, and learns from those he surveys, and it is laudable.

Fourth, there is the *restraint*. Preachers, together with teachers of preaching, so easily succumb to a besetting sin, which is that they have their favoured approach, painting it in its best light, while depicting other approaches in their worst light. This is such a missed opportunity for their own further development. The battle lines tend to be drawn, most frequently, around topical and expository preaching. Raih's work in this regard is admirable. He offers a critique of both types of preaching, and articulates a place for both, but only when represented by the best version of each one. By the end, there is a tilt towards exposition – at its best, not its worst – but for sound reasons and without disparaging topical preaching. As Raih writes, "expository preaching is not a ready-made automatic remedy to address spiritual lethargy in churches, nor can nominalism be unfailingly neutralized by expository preaching"(pg. 215). The situation is more subtle. The restraint is refreshing.

Finally, there are the *outcomes*. A masterstroke was the decision to open up the Old Testament book of Malachi, with its post-exilic context, and the New Testament book of 1 Corinthians, with its conflictual context, and frame them as responses to nominalism. In both communities there is a lethargy needing an infusion of vibrancy and vitality. While central to the academic argument that Raih is building, this decision to indwell these two biblical books demonstrates how both preacher and listener, professor and student, can come together, with benefit, in this research, because it provides such a practical way forward into a different reality.

Over three decades of teaching preaching, I've observed how the most strident critique of preaching can come from *within* the church, not beyond it. The scepticism and cynicism can be surprising, even shocking. Might this not be another symptom of nominalism's seepage into communities of God's people? If so, there is reason to engage with Johnson Raih's thesis, using it to help us shape a warm, confident and winsome theology and practice of preaching today.

Paul Windsor
Programme Director, Langham Preaching
Auckland, New Zealand — July 2021

Acknowledgements

"This is the LORD's doing; it is marvellous in our eyes."
(Ps 118:23)

"But by the grace of God I am what I am . . ." (1 Cor 15:10), acknowledged Paul. This is also my testimony – a sinner justified and forgiven, loved and saved, called and kept by his grace! Right from the beginning, when the conversation began almost four years ago about this research journey, up to this moment of completion, it is the love of God, the gracious hand of Christ, and the enabling power of the Holy Spirit that has made this dream a reality. Thank you, Lord, for providing all our family's needs, healing our sicknesses, allaying all our doubts, and guiding each step forward.

But God works through his people, and he blessed us through the Windsors (Rev. Dr. Paul and Barby), and the friends of Langham Partnership New Zealand. Thank you for generously sharing with us the blessings of God. As a teacher, coach, well-wisher and friend, Paul, you have poured your life into mine (and Barby into Dinny's) without holding back – you dreamed with us, believed in us, and accepted four of us (including Joel and Julian) just the way we are. Only our Father in heaven can repay you for all your sacrifices. The trips and training we did together, including the "smilingly scary" landslide episode at Karong in 2017, on our way back from Kohima, will remain in my memory for a lifetime.

As the intelligent design argument implies, my dissertation in its final shape did not spin out of a carrel in the SAIACS library. With the patience and sacrifice of a father, the compassion of a pastor, the precision of a surgeon, and the critical mind of a scholar, Dr. Derek Tidball meticulously guided me. With encouragement, you always pushed me beyond what I thought I could possibly achieve, and today it is both humbling and delightful to look back at the footprints of the journey. Despite several challenges confronting you and your family, you made sure that my drafts were always back on time. I am truly honoured and thankful for your labour of love.

I am also deeply grateful to Dr. Ian Payne (previous principal) for stepping in when I needed to re-work my research proposal. Despite the pressure of transition, you gave me your time and invested in my work. The positive impact of those six tutorial sessions with you (between 1 March and 24 April 2018) is far-reaching in terms of cultivating a pattern of critical thinking and so far beyond merely clearing the proposed work.

I am grateful to the library staff for helping me locate important resources: Dr. Arun for helping me with the methodology chapter during the thesis proposal stage; Dr. E. D. Solomon and Mr. Yesan for praying with me and encouraging me as cell group mentors; Dr. Varghese Thomas, the HoD of PTC, for his constant encouragement and valuable feedback; Dr. Nigel Ajay Kumar for his valuable comments both during the thesis proposal and defence stages; and Dr. Prabhu Singh (Principal, SAIACS) for his encouragement, advice, and prayers. I also thank the MBC leaders and Manipur Theological College authorities, for helping me access some valuable resources from their respective libraries.

As helium gas floats balloons, the prayers, support, and encouragement of my parents, parents-in-law, brother, brothers-in-law, sisters, sister-in-law, extended families, and well-wishers have kept my family afloat, especially for me during a researcher's lonely journey. Thank you, brother Poudi and sister Hatmuanting for your warm hospitality and lending me your bike during my empirical research trips. Thank you, brother Manoj Sonam and sister Sunita for your open home, hospitality, and enduring friendship. Thank you, brothers Daniel Peshai and Nehemiah Rong, for your partnership and support that enabled me to get the *NVivo* software for my data analysis. Thank you, brother David Zote, uncle Hepuni and aunty Rashmi, for your friendship and generosity. Thank you, brother Wantson, for assisting me in collecting and sending the questionnaires. Your support is deeply appreciated.

Thank you Dinny, my beloved wife, for your incarnational heart and for walking with me during the entire research journey, despite several health challenges coming your way. Thank you also for editing and proofreading the entire manuscript. As you sacrificed as unto the Lord, may God's promise of an abundant life be yours in full measure in the years to come. Kaikai (Joel Hokaiho Raih) and Juju (Julian Tsangvang Raih), you constantly pulled me into your evolving world, and I find myself always refreshed and energised as I played and studied with you. You rejoiced that Saturday nights don't have library hours, and so did I, for our father-son time. Thank you for your love and sacrifices, for which I dedicate this book to the three of you!

Abstract

This research explores the impact of preaching on the spiritual lives of the members in the Baptist churches of Imphal, between 2000 and 2015, particularly focusing on the relationship between preaching and nominalism, guided by the research question, "What do people perceive to be the effects of preaching on the spiritual life of the members of the Baptist churches of Imphal, 2000–2015?" The study revealed that not many had academically engaged with the issue of nominalism and preaching in relation to the members' spiritual life in India's North East region. Although some research work had already explored nominalism in the context of church membership globally, studied nominalism with a pastoral-theological response, and considered how discipleship could address nominalism among the youth of MBC, none had explored how nominalism could be addressed homiletically. On the other hand, while there had been a discussion of how preaching had developed the church and impacted the members' spiritual lives from a quantitative research viewpoint, none had examined the effect of preaching in members' spiritual lives using a qualitative methodology.

The methodology employed is eclectic in design as it followed the phenomenological approach and integrated the four steps of practical theology research method of Richard R. Osmer. The research data was collected through twenty semi-structured interviews and seventy open-ended questionnaires from the pastors, church leaders, and lay members of fifteen selected Baptist churches in Imphal.

The empirical research yielded a rich data. Most participants expressed their awareness of the existence of nominalism in the churches, irrespective of whatever method of preaching the pastors and preachers employed. The data also provided some information to understand nominalism from a contextual viewpoint and revealed that not many pulpits preached a biblical gospel. Further, it showed that although there were exceptions where preaching had a positive impact on the spiritual lives of the members, and especially on society at large, there was more evidence of the negative impact of bad preaching in many churches, leading to a growing spiritual lethargy and a weak understanding of the Scriptures. The findings further revealed that topical preaching was the most common form of preaching in the churches and some pastors effectively used it to revive their members' spiritual health. However, it was found that the impact of preaching characterised by topical sermons was largely dependent on the exceptional skills and charisma of some gifted pastors and therefore it cannot become the norm for everyone. Although some participants endorsed topical preaching, more participants recommended expository preaching to effectively counter nominalism and to bring about spiritual vitality.

The research then scripturally and theologically engages with the issue of spiritual lethargy among God's people in the Bible by showing how Malachi and Paul engaged with the spiritual problems of the people homiletically, through prophetic and expository sermons. We also discuss the theology and methodology of two homileticians who endorsed the expository preaching method, and consequently address the critiques and challenges levelled against this method, and then recommend the same for the Baptist churches in Imphal to combat nominalism. The research concludes with ten recommendations to counter nominalism homiletically in the Baptist churches of Imphal.

Abbreviations

1. Bibles

ESV: English Standard Version
NASB: New American Standard Bible
NIV: New International Version

2. Commentaries

BST: The Bible Speaks Today
HOTC: Holman Old Testament Commentary
MOBS: Message of Biblical Spirituality
NCBC: New Century Bible Commentary
NIGTC: The New International Greek Testament Commentary
NTS: New Testament Studies
TOTC: Tyndale Old Testament Commentaries
TOTL: The Old Testament Library
TNICOT: The New International Commentary on the Old Testament

3. Journals

BS: *Bibliotheca Sacra*
CAM: *Cultural Anthropology Methods*
CPQ: *Counselling Psychology Quarterly*
ER: *Educational Researcher*
ET: *Expository Times*

FM: Field Methods
FQSR: Forum Qualitative Social Research
HTR: Harvard Theological Review
IJQM: International Journal of Qualitative Method
JAET: Journal of Asia Evangelical Theology
JAN: Journal of Advanced Nursing
JSOT: Journal for the Study of the Old Testament
JSNT: Journal for the Study of the New Testament
MAS: Modern Asian Studies
NCRMRP: National Centre for Research Methods Review Paper
PSB: The Princeton Seminary Bulletin
QHR: Qualitative Health Research
RRR: Review of Religious Research
SJT: Scottish Journal of Theology
SSI: Social Science Information

4. Others

AAM: Arthington Aboriginese Mission
ABC: Assam Baptist Convention
ABFMS: American Baptist Foreign Mission Society
ABM: American Baptist Mission
AMC: American Mission Society
BMM: Baptist Mid-Mission
BMS: Baptist Missionary Society
CBCNEI: Council of Baptist Churches in North East India
CNBC: Council of Naga Baptist Churches
FMS: Frontier Mission Society
IPS: Indian Police Service
LBCI: Liangmei Baptist Church Imphal
MBC: Manipur Baptist Convention
MBC CCI: Manipur Baptist Convention Centre Church Imphal
MBI: Manipur Bible Institute
MCA: Manipur Christian Association
MCBS: Manipur Central Bible School
MTC: Manipur Theological College

NH: New Homiletic
PNBA: Poumai Naga Baptist Association
SAIACS: South Asia Institute of Advanced Christian Studies
SBLDS: Society of Biblical Literature Dissertation Series
TBCI: Tangkhul Baptist Churches Imphal
TGC: The Gospel Coalition
TTGST: Torch Trinity Graduate School of Theology
UESI: Union of Evangelical Students India
UMS: Ukhrul Mission School
UPS: Upper Primary School
WCC: World Churches Council
WEA: World Evangelical Alliance
WUNT: Wissenschaftliche Untersuchungen zum Neuen Testament

CHAPTER 1

Introduction

1.1 Introduction

This research seeks to explore the impact of preaching on the spiritual life of the people in the Baptist churches of Imphal, the capital city of the Indian state of Manipur. Preaching is assumed to bring about spiritual vitality, from new birth to spiritual maturity. However, we have heard that certain types of preaching have contributed to spiritual lethargy or nominalism. There are voices who claim that "nominalism is widespread" in Manipur, including the Manipur Baptist Convention (MBC),[1] even as MBC celebrates the quasquicentennial advent of Christianity in Manipur.[2] The literature review will further confirm this presupposition. Nominalism could be due to a result of multiple factors, but this research primarily focuses on its relationship to preaching.

The subject of spirituality interests almost every religious group.[3] Below, we discuss some definitions of spirituality before we arrive at our own. Richard

---

1. Mandryk, *Operation World*, 433. The following Baptist pastors and church leaders in Manipur support this view: Mathiudinbou (Pastor, LBCI), interview by researcher, 16 September 2017; Rev. Simon Raomai (Pastor, MBC CCI) interview by researcher, 16 September 2017; Rev. Ngamlei Zimik (Pastor, TBCI) interview by researcher, 16 September 2017; Poudikhon Pamei (State Secy., UESI Manipur) interview by researcher, 16 September 2017; Rev. R. L. Tennyson (Former Ex. Secy., PNBA) interview by researcher, 20 September 2017; P. G. Singsit (IPS Officer) interview by researcher, 20 September 2017; Wahengbam Lokendro Meitei (President, UESI Manipur) interview by researcher, 17 September 2017.

2. Parratt, *Wounded Land*, 61; see also Dena, *Christian Mission and Colonialism*, 33; Raih, "Mighty Acts," 16.

3. *Contra*, Benner, *Care of Souls*, 89.

Foster, representing the evangelical tradition, to which I belong, defines spirituality in terms of "a life founded upon the living Word of God, the written Word of God, and the proclaimed Word of God."[4] Because of the word of God, "we experience the knowledge of God that grounds our lives and enables us to give a reason for the hope that is in us."[5] Here, spirituality is to be measured by whether one puts into practice that which one already knows from the word of God – to be in sync both in words and deeds.[6] Foster here is clearly stating a biblical truth, because knowing and having faith in God's word and then doing it is scriptural.[7] Benedict J. Groeschel argues, "The center of Christian spirituality is the Incarnate Word of God. He is the center, not as a point of gravity, but as a single source of light in an utterly dark and lifeless universe."[8] Alister McGrath also declares, "Christian spirituality concerns the quest for a fulfilled and authentic Christian existence, involving the bringing together of the fundamental ideas of Christianity and the whole experience of living on the basis of and within the scope of the Christian faith."[9]

Hence, our working definition is that *Christian spirituality* centres on the incarnate, proclaimed, and written word of God, on the integration of the knowledge of Christian faith and practice, and on the quest for authentic Christian living through the power of the Holy Spirit, for one's growth towards maturity, to glorify God.[10] By this definition, *spiritual lethargy* would mean a life inconsistent with the teaching of the word of God and a life with a discrepancy between confession and deeds.

---

4. Foster, *Streams of Living Water*, 233.
5. Foster, 233.
6. Foster, 232.
7. See Jas 1:22–25; 2:17; 4:17; Rom 2:12–13; Prov 3:21.
8. Groeschel, *Spiritual Passages*, 17.
9. McGrath, *Christian Spirituality*, 2. There are several others who engaged with this subject, but for our purpose, the above discussion will suffice. For more see Westerhoff and Eusden, *Spiritual Life*, 2; Keating, *Heart of World*, 13; Groeschel, *Spiritual Passages*, 4; Cully, *Education for Spiritual Growth*, 15, 17; Schaeffer, *True Spirituality*, 28; Benner, *Care of Souls*, 95.
10. If one begins to critically analyse what the Bible teaches, it will touch the other five traditions of spirituality as well (The Contemplative Tradition; The Holiness Tradition; The Charismatic Tradition; The Social Justice Tradition; The Incarnational Tradition). To narrow down to certain aspects of spirituality would be unbiblical because the Bible teaches a holistic understanding. Foster, *Streams of Living Water*, passim.

1.2 Rationale

1.2.1 Personal Rationale

As a follower of Christ, I have personally experienced phases of spiritual dryness in my life. I have also wondered how preaching in the churches has impacted my own spiritual life. This has made me personally curious to explore the subject of nominalism, especially its relationship to preaching.

1.2.2 Academic Rationale

In academic circles, there is an ongoing discussion on good preaching and spiritual vitality and on bad preaching's role in incubating nominalism,[11] thus the need to further this discussion even in the Baptist churches of Imphal under the Manipur Baptist Convention (MBC).[12] Moreover, this research seeks to encourage preachers to re-examine their preaching in terms of theology and methodology. Further, it will enable pastoral trainers to identify the needs of pastors, and this will then help them to intelligently prepare their training materials.

1.3 Statement of Purpose

The purpose of this research is to explore whether the pastors, church leaders, and members in fifteen selected Baptist churches of Imphal are aware of the effect of preaching on the spiritual lives of the people – both spiritual vitality and nominalism. Although the data will ultimately shape and determine the outcome of the research, an assumption can be made, and will be verified, that this research could contribute to a generalisation or a functional theory that clear expository and biblical gospel preaching will improve the spiritual vitality, ethics, and commitment of Christians, thus reducing nominalism.[13]

---

11. This issue will be addressed in the Literature Review.

12. MBC is the umbrella Baptist church body in Manipur. According to its General Secretary, Wungnaoting Konghar, MBC comprises "29 Associations, 1407 local churches and Fellowships with 206,257 baptized members." Konghar, "Word of Welcome," 10.

13. Max Weber is regarded as the founder of the "structural-functional theory." Bretton, *Power of Money*, 209; Weber, *Protestant Ethic*, 127–45; "Max Weber's 'The Protestant Ethic'"; explained further in 1.12.1; see also Swinton and Mowat, *Practical Theology*, 47.

1.4 Objectives

i. To explore if there is a significant relationship between preaching and spiritual vitality, and preaching and spiritual lethargy, especially nominalism.
ii. To explore if there is a sufficient understanding of God's word[14] through preaching in the Baptist churches of Imphal.
iii. To explore if there is an insufficient understanding of God's word through preaching in the Baptist churches of Imphal.
iv. To explore if an insufficient understanding of the word of God contributes to a life of dichotomy (between sacred and secular), thus breeding nominalism.
v. To explore the impact of a right understanding of the word of God through preaching in the various situations of listeners' lives.
vi. To explore the methods of preaching that generate vibrancy and spiritual vitality, and those that contribute to nominalism.

1.5 Significance of the Study

First, this research, although confined to the Baptist churches in Imphal, presents a new in-depth study of the relationship between preaching vis-à-vis spiritual vitality, and preaching vis-à-vis nominalism. This research will add depth to the discussion concerning these issues in preaching by examining local churches.[15]

Second, most pastors seldom take the time to investigate if their sermons over a period have been spiritually vitalising to the congregation. This research will help pastors to realise the importance of evaluating their sermons regularly.

Third, the research will conscientise the congregations to become more intentional in their quest and receptivity of God's word.

Fourth, this research will help pastoral trainers in identifying strategic areas in the training of pastors in preaching.

---

14. By "sufficient understanding of God's word," I mean a clear understanding of the four epochs in Christian theology and history – Creation, Fall, Redemption and Second Coming. Some argue there are other important doctrines of the Bible; however, it can be argued that all other doctrines in the Bible fall within one of the four epochs in biblical history.

15. Cameron, "How to Study," 36; cf. Davies, "Why Study," 4.

1.6 Scope and Limitation of the Study

The city of Imphal has many churches affiliated with various Christian groups and denominations.[16] However, this research will focus on the Baptist churches under MBC in Imphal, 2000–2015. Although the issue of nominalism may not be absent in other denominations and Baptist churches in Manipur, an in-depth study of the fifteen selected Baptist churches belonging to and representing various ethnic groups under MBC in Imphal is preferred. This period enables a contemporary exploration where primary data collection may be more feasible.[17]

Further, Christian spirituality could be linked to many factors, but this research will examine preaching and its effect on the spiritual life of church members: what types of preaching lead to spiritual vitality and what types of preaching lead to spiritual lethargy, even nominalism.

Moreover, while there may have been studies done on nominalism in other religious groups this research will be confined to Christianity, specifically within the boundary of the Baptist denomination MBC.

1.7 Statement of the Problem

There have been claims and assertions of widespread nominalism and lack of spiritual vitality in the Baptist churches of Imphal City as the literature review will reflect under the regional survey section on India's North East state of Manipur. Although research had been done on preaching's role in the church development under MBC and addressing nominalism among the youth in MBC through discipleship, as the literature review will evidence, none has explored the effect of preaching in the spiritual lives of the MBC church members in Imphal, with special reference to nominalism. Despite a variety of views on the effect of preaching, there is no consensus on whether preaching can be said to have any observable results. It is reasonable to explore whether

---

16. Some of the denominations are: Roman Catholic; Christian Revival Church; Fundamental Baptist; Presbyterian; Seventh-day Adventist; Evangelical Free Church of India; Evangelical Church of India; Reformed Presbyterian Church; Evangelical Congregation Church; Independent Church of India; Kuki Christian Church; Manipur Baptist Convention; The Pentecostal Mission; etc.

17. Although the researcher will focus on these fifteen years, a section on the waves of preaching movement in Manipur will be included.

spiritual lethargy or nominalism in the Baptist churches of Imphal could be linked to poor preaching. The quality of preaching in the Baptist churches of Imphal may well have had a measurable impact on the spirituality of the current members between 2000 and 2015. In this research work, I will explore how preaching vitalises spirituality or alternately incubates nominalism, by examining the effects of preaching on the members of the Baptist churches of Imphal, 2000–2015, and the impact it has had on society at large.

1.8 Research Questions

The research questions are categorised as follows.

1.8.1 Primary Research Question

The primary research question is, "What do people perceive to be the effects of preaching on the spiritual life of the members of the Baptist churches of Imphal, 2000–2015?"

1.8.2 Subsidiary Research Questions

i. To what extent are the pastors, church leaders, and members in the Baptist churches of Imphal aware of the effect of preaching on the spiritual vitality of the members in the church?

ii. To what extent are the pastors, church leaders, and members in the Baptist churches of Imphal aware of the effect of preaching on the spiritual lethargy, nominalism, in the church?

iii. Are the pastors, church leaders, and members in the Baptist churches of Imphal aware of the existence or non-existence of nominal Christians in the churches?

iv. How plausible is the claim that Christian nominalism thrives when the "biblical gospel"[18] is not preached clearly?

---

18. So, what is the biblical gospel? There is debate between N. T. Wright and John Piper on what constitutes the gospel. While Piper emphasises the idea of justification, Wright gravitates towards the kingdom of God by moving away from the reformed position of imputed righteousness. Wax, "Justification Debate." It is argued that their "dispute lies in whether or not the gospel (to be *the gospel*) must include justification by faith *through* the imputed righteousness of Christ." Orendorff, "Gospel According to N. T. Wright"; cf. Wright, *What Saint Paul*, 60–61. On the possibility of reconciling his differences with Piper on the issue of justification, Wright says, "No, not an equilibrium. A lot of confusion, rather." Wax, "Interview N. T. Wright." For

v. In the city of Imphal, where the preaching ministry is considered vibrant, how valid is the claim that there is a relationship between preaching and nominalism?

vi. What effect does preaching have on the society at large?

1.9 Definition of Key Terms

1.9.1 Impact: The effect a certain variable (preaching) has on something (spirituality).

1.9.2 Preaching: The verbal proclamation of the Christian message based on the Bible.

1.9.3 Nominalism: A Christian who is one in name only.

1.9.4 MBC: The Manipur Baptist Convention. It consists of more than 1,407 Baptist churches and fellowships under its umbrella. It is affiliated with BWA (Baptist World Alliance) through CBCNEI (Council of Baptist Churches in North East India).

1.10 Structure of the Study

The study is comprised of the following chapters:

The first chapter is a general introduction of the thesis, where the rationale, the statement of purpose, objectives, significance of the study, scope and limitation of the study, and statement of the problem are discussed. It also includes the research design and methodology.

The second chapter consists of the literature review, surveying literatures related to the effect of preaching, nominalism, and nominalism and preaching, beginning from the Lausanne discussion in 1974 to the North East Indian context, especially Manipur.

The third chapter introduces Manipur Christianity in general, and the Baptist denomination in particular, exploring the waves of preaching ministry

---

more see Piper, *Future of Justification*; N. T. Wright, *Justification*; N. T. Wright, *Simply Good News*. Choosing one voice over the other would be taking a binary position which is not helpful. Therefore, this research will find a working definition of a biblical gospel (in chapter 5), without discarding their voices. For further discussion see, 5.6.4.2.

of the pioneers, their early struggles, and the growth of the preaching movement over time.

The fourth chapter deals with the description of the data emerging from the interviews and questionnaires, steered by the question, "What is going on?"[19] Here, we will also listen to the research participants' interpretation of their own experiences.

In the fifth chapter the researcher stands back from the trees to look at the forest, interpreting the responses and analysing the data. The researcher also tries to make sense of why this is happening – bringing other theories and disciplines[20] of scholarship to comprehend the situation at hand.

The sixth chapter focuses on the normative task. The researcher engages the situation with biblical examples and theological interpretations guided by the question, "What ought to be going on?"[21]

The seventh chapter focuses on the pragmatic task guided by the question, "How might we respond in ways that are faithful and effective?"[22] Here, several recommendations will be made for pastors and churches to combat nominalism.

The eighth chapter includes a summary, a critical self-evaluation and critique, and recommendations for future research.

1.11 Research Design for the Study

A research design, by definition, strategizes one's research work to accomplish it according to one's choice and purpose within the research approach one has chosen. A research design consists of three components: Philosophical Worldviews; Research Methods and Selected Strategies of Inquiry.[23] Below is a framework that elucidates this.

---

19. Osmer, *Practical Theology*, 4.
20. Osmer, 6–8.
21. Osmer, 4.
22. Osmer, 4, 10.
23. Creswell, *Research Design*, 5.

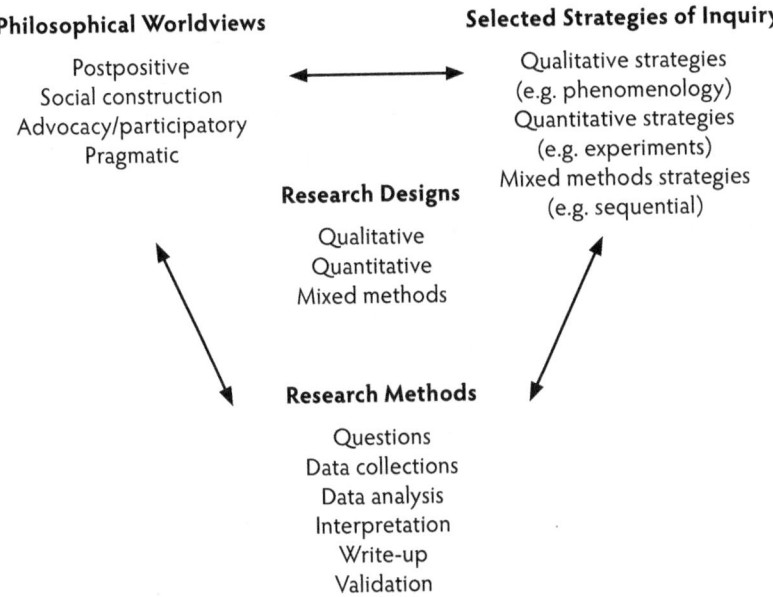

Figure 1: A Framework for Design – The Interconnection of Worldviews, Strategies of Inquiry, and Research Methods[24]

In what follows, we will discuss these three aspects as recommended by John W. Creswell. For our convenience, we begin with selected strategies of inquiry.

1.12 Selected Strategy of Inquiry

1.12.1 Qualitative Method: Practical Theology and Social Sciences

A Practical Theology research work uses the methodological approach of social sciences because "social science has offered practical theologians necessary access to the nature of the human mind, human society and culture, the wider dimensions of church life . . ."[25] Although Practical Theology research could use the varieties of methods of social sciences in this research we will employ the qualitative research method.

A qualitative method is different from quantitative research as the former deals with "words" and "open-ended questions" for interviews, while the

---

24. Adapted from Creswell, 5.
25. Swinton and Mowat, *Practical Theology*, xii.

latter deals with "numbers" and "closed-ended questions" for "quantitative hypotheses."[26] Some argue that a qualitative method has five very crucial elements: "seeing through the eyes of research participants; description and context; process; flexibility and lack of structure; and concepts and theory as outcomes of the research process." Moreover here, understanding of the phenomenon under investigation is arrived at through interpretation by the participants.[27] Some others consider the chief task of qualitative research as "identifying and developing understandings" of human beings' "struggle to make sense of their experiences."[28]

I have chosen the qualitative method rather than the quantitative method because in this research, the focus is neither on finding out the percentage, numbers, and figures of how many people are nominal Christians in the church, nor to quantify any information related to preaching and spirituality. Rather, it aims to explore people's real-life experiences through in-depth interviews, questionnaires, and other means regarding their spiritual life as a result of listening to preaching over the years; in what ways has good preaching stirred their spiritual vitality or in what way has bad preaching led to spiritual lethargy, even nominalism? It is argued that "if a concept or phenomenon needs to be explored and understood because little research has been done on it, then it merits a qualitative approach."[29] This research merits a qualitative method because few studies have examined preaching in the Baptist churches of Imphal in relation to its effect on the spiritual life of the people.

Creswell recommends five methods under the overall umbrella of qualitative research: "narrative, phenomenology, ethnography, case study, and grounded theory."[30] This study will adopt the phenomenological approach which is recognised as an important approach for Practical Theology.[31]

There are several reasons why the phenomenological approach has been chosen. First, unlike the narrative approach which only listens to a

---

26. Creswell, *Research Design*, 3; Crotty, *Foundations of Social Research*, 93–99.
27. Bryman, *Social Research Methods*, 202, 380.
28. Swinton and Mowat, *Practical Theology*, 28–29.
29. Creswell, *Research Design*, 18.
30. Creswell, 187; see also Hsieh and Shannon, "Three Approaches," 1278.
31. Swinton and Mowat, *Practical Theology*, xv; see also Osmer, *Practical Theology*, 52.

participant's story or experience and then constructs a story out of it,[32] phenomenology takes the "thick descriptions" of the participants seriously and gives priority to bracketing of one's presuppositions.[33] Second, phenomenology does not aim to engage with the research subjects over a long period of time, as in ethnography, but only during the limited time of the interviews, questionnaire, and gathering of other documents.[34] In this research, the main focus is not on knowing the cultural and behavioural pattern of the people, but to hear their experiences and reflections through interviews, questionnaires, and other forms of data collection. Third, phenomenology allows for a wider range of contact with the participants, and there is comparatively more data to work with, unlike case studies.[35] Fourth, a phenomenological approach does not launch out with the sole intention to "generate or discover a theory"[36] like grounded theory but to hear the stories and interpretations of the people's experiences. Then it moves to propose a functional theory where, "while not statistically generalizable," it has "the theoretical potential to move beyond the particularities of the situation being examined."[37] Below is a more elaborate discussion of the phenomenological approach I have chosen for this research.

1.12.1.1 Phenomenology

Although Quentin Lauer calls Edmund Husserl the "father of phenomenology,"[38] Moran states that even before Husserl, philosophers like "Lambert, Herder, Kant, Fitche, and Hegel" made use of the term "phenomenology" in different ways.[39] But, phenomenology as a philosophical and scientific research approach was developed by Edmund Husserl who was inspired by Franz Brentano, and it was from Brentano, says Moran, that Husserl's thinking on "empiricism" and "description" developed.[40]

---

32. Lieblich, Tuval-Mashiach, and Zilber, *Narrative Research*, 2.
33. Shapiro and Bentz, *Mindful Enquiry*, 96.
34. O'Reilly, *Ethnographic Methods*, 2.
35. Hage, *Stakeholders Concern*, 124.
36. Urquhart, *Grounded Theory*, 4.
37. Swinton and Mowat, *Practical Theology*, 47.
38. Lauer, "Introduction," 1.
39. Moran, *Introduction to Phenomenology*, 6.
40. Moran, 7.

As Clark Moustakas explains,

> the researcher following a . . . phenomenological approach . . . launch[es] the study . . . free of preconditions, beliefs, and knowledge of the phenomenon from prior experience . . . to be completely open, receptive, and naïve in listening to and hearing research participants describe their experience of the phenomenon being investigated.[41]

Phenomenology seeks for truth and knowledge from previously overlooked and even mundane objects or phenomena of life experiences. Often, knowledge and information of various kinds are presumed to be stored only in books and articles. But people and their experiences are the real storehouse of knowledge when it comes to the field of social sciences, including Practical Theology. In the context of this research, the listeners' experience, understanding, perception, and opinions are valuable assets to formulate a better understanding of what is happening in our churches, as to people's spirituality in relation to the preaching they have heard.

Real-life experiences with their thick correlates have taken centre stage in the search for knowledge, all due to the emergence of phenomenology, although it has different strands of thoughts.[42] In this research, I will try to "bracket" my presuppositions,[43] as Husserl says, and listen to the participants' "thick description" (i.e. understanding their experiences of listening to preaching "as it is experienced by the person herself,"[44] and the interpretation of their experiences,[45] relating it with their own spiritual life). Others will judge how successful I have been in doing so.

1.12.1.2 Advantages and Disadvantages of Phenomenology

Here are some advantages and disadvantages of phenomenological approach and the justification for why I have chosen it for this research. On the

---

41. Moustakas, *Phenomenological Research*, 22; see also Creswell, *Research Design*, 13; Swinton and Mowat, *Practical Theology*, 53, 100.

42. More will be discussed below, especially under Interpretive Phenomenological Analysis (IPA).

43. Husserl, *Phenomenology*, 76; see also Merleau-Ponty, *Husserl Limits*, 44, 51.

44. Shapiro and Bentz, *Mindful*, 96; see also Grady, *Qualitative and Action Research*, 8; Hopewell, *Congregation*.

45. Heidegger, *Being and Time*, 222.

advantages, first, it "seeks to find the universal nature of an experience" which can shed light for better knowledge. Second, all "the themes and meanings of an experience" come from the people. Third, it "helps to understand a lived experience and brings meaning to it." Fourth, it could correct a stereotyped "misconception" of an experience, by bringing to light a different narrative.[46]

The criticisms levelled against phenomenology are: First, there is a doubt about the participants' ability to clearly and appropriately express their own experiences. Many fear that "language barriers, age, cognition, embarrassment and other factors" may be an obstacle. Second, "researcher bias is difficult to determine or detect." Third, "results are not statistically reliable, even with a larger sample size. It does not produce generalizable data." Fourth, "it may be difficult to gain access to participants." Fifth, "presentation of findings may be difficult. The subjectivity of the data may lead to difficulty in establishing reliability and validity." Sixth, "policymakers may give less credibility to phenomenological study." Seventh, "gathering data and data analysis may be time consuming and laborious."[47]

1.12.1.3 Evaluation and Justification for Choosing Phenomenological Approach

Without minimising the reality of the criticisms the phenomenological approach faces, these are the reasons I have chosen this approach.

First, only those who volunteer and are fluent enough in English and the Manipuri language to express their feelings and experiences will be considered as participants. Second, it is true that the bias of the researcher is difficult to detect. But the researcher will make efforts to employ data triangulation,[48] once the interviews have been transcribed, for authentication. Third, although coming up with a functional theory to address the issue through the research is a part of the goal, another important objective is to listen to the individual experiences of the people through the thick descriptions and interpretations of the phenomenon under investigation. Fourth, as this research will employ the snowball sampling method, the researcher will have the advantage of

---

46. Grand Canyon University, "Strength and Limitations," online.
47. GCU, "Strength and Limitations."
48. Bryman, *Social Research*, 386. (A process of going back to the participants to clarify and validate the data collected in case of confusion.)

finding other participants by word of mouth and recommendation from fellow participants. Fifth, human experiences are subjective and dissimilar to others in many ways. What one person experiences may be different from the others, although they are located in the same context. So, subjectivity should not be a problem. Moreover, as the aim is to present the findings of the phenomenon under investigation as they are, the question of unreliability does not arise, particularly as the researcher plans to refer back to the participants for validation. Sixth, it can be counter-argued that any empirical research done well, including the phenomenological approach, which engages with the grassroot situation of the people's spirituality, will be of significant interest to the policymakers in the church who will then influence the way preaching is taught and practised. Moreover, the intent of this research is also to engage with the academic discussion on the phenomenon of preaching and its relationship with spiritual life. Seventh, it is true that data analysis demands time and energy. One cannot gloss over these challenges as if they are absent. But if other researchers have been successful in employing this approach in the past, this researcher will also make a similar attempt with much hard work and dedication.

1.13 Philosophical Worldview of Phenomenological Approach: Social Constructivist Worldview

The next thing to consider while designing an empirical research is the philosophical worldview. This research will follow the constructivism worldview, which is also called the "social constructivist worldview . . . often combined with interpretivism."[49]

On the next page is a figure of the four worldviews.

---

49. Getz and Page, *Event Studies*, 412; cf. Childers, *College Identity Sagas*, 58.

Four Worldviews	
Postpositivism	**Constructivism**
• Determination • Reductionism • Empirical observation and measurement • Theory verification	• Understanding • Multiple participation meanings • Social and historical construction • Theory generation
Advocacy/Participatory	**Pragmatism**
• Political • Empowerment issue-oriented • Collaborative • Change-oriented	• Consequences of actions • Problem-centred • Pluralistic • Real-world practice oriented

Figure 2: Four Worldviews[50]

It is believed that the "interpretivist worldview allows for an examination of the construction of diverse identities." People who hold this worldview are convinced that "interpretivism allows for individual perspectives to be heard . . . from the perspective of those involved."[51] So, the researcher will listen to the participants' responses, the interpretation of their own experience of the preaching event and its impact in their lives.

Then the process of analysis will be undertaken, where the researcher will merge meanings emerging from the individual experiences of the listeners, towards a probable theorisation of the issue studied, through an inductive method. J. Sim affirms this approach of theoretical generalisation and states, "the data gained from a particular study provide theoretical insights which possess a sufficient degree of generality or universality to allow their projection to other contexts or situations which are comparable to that of the original study,"[52] which could lead to a theorisation.

Below is a figure about theoretical generalisation by J. Sim.

---

50. Creswell, *Research Design*, 6.
51. McMillan, "Theory in Healthcare," 19.
52. Sim, "Collecting and Analysing," 350; cf. Creswell, *Research Design*, 8, 64; Swinton and Mowat, *Practical Theology*, 33–34, 43, 46. *Contra*, generalisation may not always be possible but the research can add knowledge for future researchers who may study similar issues.

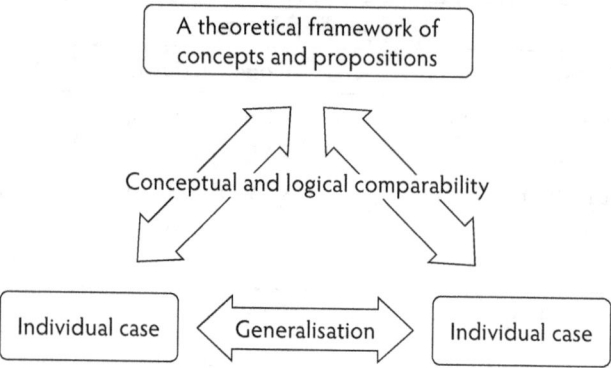

Figure 3: Theoretical Generalisation[53]

The research aims to explore the description and interpretation of the experiences of the individuals' spiritual life in relation to the preaching they have heard. Although the data will finally shape the outcome of the current research, an assumption can be made that this research could contribute to this functional theory: that clear, biblical gospel preaching in the Baptist churches of Imphal city will improve the ethics, spiritual vitality, and commitment of the Christians, thus reducing nominalism.

Beyond interpretivism, there has been recent discussion on interpretive phenomenological analysis (IPA) within the phenomenological approach. Initially in my research work, I had reasoned that within phenomenology, IPA could be a good and improved phenomenological method, because IPA's strength lies in the in-depth interviews with the participants. So, I shifted my methodological affiliation towards it for a while. However, I discovered that IPA leans solely on a few in-depth interviews,[54] whereas, I wanted to have more participants in the interviews and include the tools of questionnaires and other documents for my data collection. So I reverted to the phenomenological approach for my research, because a multiple way of collecting "empirical materials, perspectives and observers in a single study" as a "strategy . . . adds rigor, breadth, complexity, richness, and depth to any enquiry."[55]

---

53. Adapted from Sim, 47.

54. Jonathan A. Smith and others recommend that for a PhD, the number of IPA interviews could range from four to ten. Smith, Flowers, and Larkin, *Interpretive Phenomenological Analysis*, 52.

55. Swinton and Mowat, *Practical Theology*, 49.

1.14 Research Methods

1.14.1 Method of Data Collection[56]

1.14.1.1 Sampling

Sample is a small specimen of a larger quantity.[57] According to Hycner, "the phenomenon dictates the method (not vice-versa) including even the type of participants."[58] The research was done with the fifteen Baptist churches in Imphal[59] who have experienced the phenomenon under investigation.[60] Arksey and Knight, Bloor, and Holloway state that diverse sample groups help contrast and ensure validity.[61] The characteristics of the participants, especially interview participants, are roughly laid out here: Those who demonstrate considerable seriousness in listening to sermons, demonstrating it by discussing the content, method, and application of the sermons they have heard from the preacher; those who carry their spirituality to the work place;[62] those who have preached in these churches during the chosen period of research; those who have served in these churches as leaders; and those who already confessed their born-again experience.

1.14.1.2 Pilot Study

A pilot survey[63] was needed to answer the query, "Will it work?"[64] Thirty questionnaires were sent out and in the light of that pilot survey, the questionnaire was revised before finalising and despatching it. Moreover, five pilot

---

56. While "method of data collection" is used for qualitative research, "instrument" is the term generally used for quantitative research. Lodico, Spaulding, and Voegtle, *Methods in Educational Research*, 112, 375.

57. Ahuja, *Research Methods*, 155.

58. Hycner, "Some Guidelines," 143–64.

59. MBC Centre Church Imphal; Tangkhul Baptist Church Imphal; Poumai Colony Baptist Church; Chingmeirong Baptist Church; Thangmeiband Baptist Church; Rongmei Naga Baptist Churches Association Baptist Church (RNBA); Kuki Baptist Convention (KBC) Church Checkon; Kakhulong Baptist Church; Mao Baptist Church, Dewlahland; Namdunlong Baptist Church; Tangkhul Langol Baptist Church; Lamphel Baptist Church; Anal Baptist Church; Chongthu Baptist Church; Vaiphei Baptist Church.

60. Kruger, *Introduction to Phenomenological*, 50.

61. Arksey and Knight, *Interviewing for Social Scientists*, 56, 58. Bloor, "Techniques of Validation," 37–50. Holloway, *Basic Concepts*.

62. Locating such people came through the snowball sampling method.

63. Ward, "Methodological Approaches," 34; see also Helen Cameron, "Research Process," 38.

64. Phillips and Pugh, *How to Get a PhD*, 76.

interviews were also conducted which aided in finetuning the questions to address the experiences of the people.

1.14.1.3 Procedure

As the researcher had previously worked with the MBC,[65] the leaders and pastors of the churches were known to him. As such, they were cooperative and supportive of the research. Nonetheless, the researcher went to all the fifteen churches and met the pastors and leaders and sought their permission for an empirical study on the subject. Each church provided a member for questionnaire disbursement and collection. For the interview, this research first employed the purposive sampling method and initially identified six pastors and three church members. The rest were found through snowball sampling method.[66] The samples were selected "based on my (the researcher's) judgment and the purpose of the research."[67] During the interviews, the researcher made use of modern electronic devices to record the conversations after obtaining due permission.[68]

1.14.1.4 Research Participants

For the interviews, the researcher made two trips to Manipur (October and December 2018) from Bangalore and interviewed twenty participants, in addition to the five pilot interviews. These were all done with prior appointments and permission, and the participants' identities were not disclosed in the research. Rather, pseudonyms were given to each person.

For the semi-structured interviews, twelve pastors along with eight members of the Baptist churches in Imphal formed the epistemic base. The former were those who regularly preached while the latter were those who listened to their preaching between 2000 and 2015. The data from these two groups provided contrasting perspectives on the subject of the discussion.

---

65. He worked as the principal of the MBC Hr. Sec. School, Imphal (2008–2012).
66. Bryman, *Social Research*, 204.
67. Groenwald, "Phenomenological Research," 45.
68. McComish, Greenberg, and Easton, "Avoid Common Pitfalls," 703–8.

1.14.1.5 Interviews

The semi-structured interviews[69] were conducted with open-ended questions.[70] The interview began with some introductory questions. The major questions were memorised and based on the environment and responses of the participants, the secondary interview questions were asked. For example, two major questions were, "To what extent are you aware of the effect of preaching on the spiritual life of a listener?"; and "How far is there an adequate understanding of God's word in your church?"[71] Although the interviews were not structured with fixed questions, nevertheless, they were in line with the researcher's objectives and were "directed to the participant's experiences, feelings, beliefs, and convictions about the theme in question."[72]

There is no clear consensus on how many interviews are enough following a qualitative research method, as there are some who recommend twenty interviews,[73] while others argue for twelve in-depth interviews.[74] However, Mark Mason and others say that for "qualitative PhD studies using interviews," the number could range from ten to thirty or more.[75] In this research, twenty participants were interviewed.

1.14.1.6 Questionnaire

The researcher sent out 170 questionnaires for the non-interview participants. The questionnaires were arranged in an "open-ended-survey"[76] style guided by the objectives of the research.[77] The researcher trained a co-researcher who helped in filling the questionnaires and in collecting and sending the questionnaires back to the researcher.[78] In total, seventy questionnaires were returned to the researcher.

---

69. Creswell, *Research Design*, 182.
70. Kvale, *Doing Interviews*, 12.
71. Cf. "Interview Questions" in Appendix 9.
72. Welman, Kruger, and Kruger, *Research Methodology*, 196.
73. Crouch and McKenzie, "Logic of Small Samples," 483.
74. Boyd, "Phenomenology," 93–122; Guest, "How Many Interviews," 59–82; Creswell, *Qualitative Inquiry*, 65, 113.
75. Baker and Edwards, "How Many Qualitative," 8–11; Mason, "Sample Size," 13.
76. Rubin and Babbie, *Essential Research Methods*, 94.
77. The sample of the questionnaire is found in Appendix 2.
78. The co-researcher was unable to help everyone though.

1.14.1.7 Coding and Analysis

The data was analysed with the help of a computer-assisted qualitative data analysis (CAQDAS), the "NVivo 12 Plus" software. The software provided the tools to structure the codes and themes, although the textual materials were manually coded and interpreted by the decisions of the researcher.[79] Then, the researcher employed Richard R. Osmer's four-steps method of Practical Theology data analysis.

1.14.1.8 Ethical Code of Consent

The interviewees were chosen based purely on their "informed consent,"[80] their willingness to voluntarily be a part of this research project. As Bailey advised, the researcher did not deceive the participants but showed them the purpose of the research; the steps of the research; a clear statement of voluntary participation; the possible positive and negative outcome of the research; and the precautions made to protect the identity and security of the participants.[81] After going through these disclosures, each consented to be a part of the research work.

1.15 An Analysis of Various Research Models

Apart from employing the three important aspects of research design recommended by Creswell as mentioned above (selected strategy of inquiry, philosophical worldviews, and research methods) for a qualitative research, because practical theologians endorse "an eclectic and multi-method approach" to get the "best of what is available within the accepted models of qualitative research,"[82] this research also employs a Practical Theology model. Below, we will discuss three models[83] and justify why a particular model was chosen.

---

79. Cf. Bryman, *Social Research*, 591; Weitzman and Miles, "Choosing Software," 1–5.
80. Bailey, *Guide to Field Research*, 11.
81. Bailey, 11.
82. Swinton and Mowat, *Practical Theology*, 48.
83. There may be more than three models used for Practical Theology research, but for our purpose, these three will suffice.

1.15.1 Rambo and Leh

Initially I had chosen the six steps recommended by Rambo and Leh, as quoted in Joshua Iyadurai's book, as the structure for my research design.[84] These steps are: Observation; Description; Empathy; Understanding; Interpretation; and Explanation.[85] Then I came across two more models of doing Practical Theology research by Kevin Gary Smith and Richard R. Osmer. Because of the suitability of Osmer's model, I decided to adopt his method and abandon that of Rambo and Leh's model. Before explaining why Osmer's model is preferred to Smith's, it will be appropriate to first discuss Smith's Practical Theology research model.

1.15.2 Kevin Gary Smith's Model

Kevin Gary Smith's method is adopted by the Loyola Institute of Ministry as a model for Practical Theology research.[86] His four steps are: Introduction; Present Situation; Preferred Scenario; and Practical Suggestions. Below is a figure of his four steps.[87]

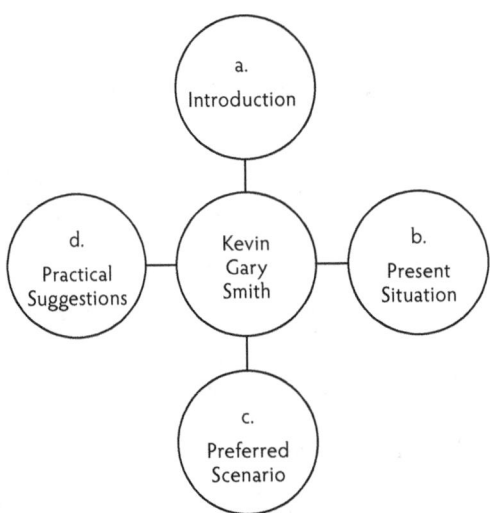

Figure 4: Kevin Gary Smith's Practical Theology Research Model

---

84. Apparently, the primary source is unavailable.
85. Iyadurai, *Transformative Religious Experience*, 4.
86. Smith, *Writing and Research*, 206-210. A PhD thesis was done using this methodology. Edre, "Christian Nominalism."
87. Smith, *Writing and Research*, 154–56.

The first stage is the "introduction." Here, the real-life problem and its background is stated by reviewing the relevant literature. The second stage describes the "current situation" of the problem one is investigating.[88] It also helps in interpreting[89] the situation one has been presented with. The third stage deals with the "preferred scenario" over the present situation. The fourth stage is developing a strategy and plan of action so that the situation no longer remains as it is, but transitions into the preferred future. Below, we look at Osmer's model.

1.15.3 Richard R. Osmer's Model

Osmer's methodology comprises four stages: Descriptive-Empirical Task; Interpretative Task; Normative Task; and Pragmatic Task.[90] Below is a figure that demonstrates it.

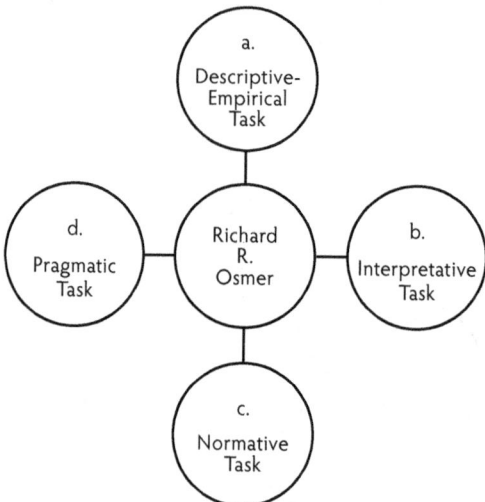

Figure 5: Richard R. Osmer's Model

The first stage is the descriptive-empirical task, where we listened to and described the church members' experiences, feelings, and interpretation of

---

88. Smith, 206.
89. Smith, 206.
90. Osmer, *Practical Theology*, 4. Noel Woodbridge agrees that "the Osmer model is currently one of the most widely used models for doing research in practical theology"; Woodbridge, "EDNA Model," 90.

their own spiritual life in relation to listening to sermons from the churches. Here we answered the question, "What is going on?"[91] In this stage, we collected information that helped us make sense and "discern patterns and dynamics" of the phenomenon under investigation.[92] We also asked the pastors about the spiritual lives of their church members resulting from preaching in the churches and about their own experiences as preachers. Here, the data was simply described as received, without any interpretation by the researcher as his presuppositions had been bracketed.

The second stage is the interpretative task, to make sense of why this is happening – bringing other theories and disciplines[93] of reasoning to comprehend the situation at hand. This is guided by the question, "Why is this going on?"[94] by interpreting the "living human documents"[95] and present situations[96] as described by the participants, and by finding a link between the present situation and the reason for it to have happened. At this juncture, the researcher stepped back from the trees to look at the forest to ask why the pastors expressed themselves the way they did, about people's spirituality and their own preaching ministry, and also why the people were facing these spiritual situations in the context of the preaching going on in the churches.

The third stage is the normative task, guided by the question, "What ought to be going on?"[97] Here, the focus is finding: ethical principles to "guide strategies of action";[98] scriptural and Christian tradition that helps "in shaping the patterns of the Christian life" towards reforming "a congregation's present actions";[99] and a theological guideline to interpret situations[100] that

---

91. Osmer, 4.
92. Osmer, 5.
93. For example, we could ask, could it be because of a psychological, economic, or political issue? Osmer gives some examples through his case study by asking if the situation could have been because of the issue of tradition and culture (of treating elders with respect); the congregational context (new and young members coming in); or psychological line of interpretation. Osmer, 6–8.
94. Osmer, 4.
95. Gerkin, *Living Human Document*, 200.
96. Osmer, *Practical Theology*, 32–33.
97. Osmer, 4.
98. Osmer, 8.
99. Osmer, 8.
100. Osmer, 8.

"focuses on good practice."[101] This can help in knowing "God, the Christian life, and social values beyond those provided by the received traditions."[102] This particular theological reflection step is different from other social sciences research which may include the ethical dimension in some cases, but will not "develop normative *theological* perspectives to interpret research" nor "attempt to shape the field they are investigating."[103]

The normative task in the research explored the ethical and spiritual situation of God's people in the Scripture. We looked at one example from the OT (Malachi) and another one from the NT (1 Corinthians) and saw how Malachi and Paul addressed and tried to shape the peoples' spiritual lethargic situation homiletically. Moreover, we engaged with two homileticians analysing their theology and methodology of preaching. This task was not only a model but epistemic because it gave us guidance on how to bring about change.[104]

Finally, the fourth stage is the pragmatic task, where we were driven by the question, "How might we respond in ways that are faithful and effective?"[105] This stage talks about strategies and recommendations that could be followed "to shape events towards desired goals."[106] In this stage we asked, "How might we respond?" to the prevailing scenario of spiritual nominalism in the context of the present preaching situation among the churches. We then came up with several plans of actions and recommendations to combat nominalism, by developing the suggestions and recommendations of the participants.

1.15.3.1 A Critique of Richard R. Osmer's Model by Kevin G. Smith and Noel Woodbridge

Osmer is not without his critics. Kevin G. Smith and Noel Woodbridge make the following critiques of Osmer's model. We will first discuss them and then respond to their critiques and justify why we ultimately chose Osmer's model.

Some of the strengths that Smith notices in Osmer's model are, first, Osmer's treatment of the first of the four steps is highly recommended as it

---

101. Osmer, 152.
102. Osmer, 152.
103. Osmer, 10–11; cf. Swinton and Mowat, *Practical Theology*, 24.
104. Osmer, 153.
105. Osmer, 4, 10.
106. Osmer, 10, 176.

gives a good introduction to "empirical research for theological students."[107] Second, Osmer's call for "a more integrated model of theological interpretation" among theological educators and practitioners, so that they may exegete the "world and the word" better, has value.

Following are some of the weaknesses of Osmer's model, according to Smith. First, Smith avers that Osmer does his practical theology from "a liberal Protestant perspective," whereas Smith prefers "a conservative evangelical approach." Second, Smith thinks that Osmer leans more towards "theological concepts and on theories from the arts and sciences to guide theological interpretation than on in-depth study of Scripture."[108] Third, Smith critiques Osmer's view that "all theories and theologies are fallible and perspectival, so such new understandings would be held lightly." Fourth, Smith considers Osmer's fourth step to be weak, as it does not help find a "system for developing a theological theory of action based on the three foundational tasks."[109]

According to Noel Woodbridge, first, although Osmer's method has value, "it needs to be adjusted to meet the requirements of doing theology optimally and scripturally."[110] Second, he critiques that Osmer's second step, "Interpretive Task," should actually take place with the literature review, before the initial "Empirical-Descriptive Task," because this reversal would help in gaining a "better understanding of (1) what is the nature and extent of the present situation, and (2) what led to the present situation."[111]

1.15.3.2 A Rebuttal to the Critiques of Kevin G. Smith and Noel Woodbridge, and Justification for Preferring Richard R. Osmer's Model

Here are some responses to the criticisms of Smith and Woodbridge, and the justification for choosing Osmer's method. Smith affirms that one of the strengths of Osmer's model is the "more integrated model of theological

---

107. Smith, "Review of Richard Osmer," 111. *Contra*, although Woodbridge agrees with Smith in critiquing some features of Osmer's model, he contrasts Smith's view and says that the Interpretive step should precede the Empirical step. Woodbridge, "EDNA Model," 92. More discussion follows.

108. Smith, "Review of Richard Osmer," 112.

109. Smith, 112.

110. Woodbridge, "EDNA Model," 90.

111. Woodbridge, 92.

interpretation" which helps a researcher to exegete the "world and the word" better. Osmer's method allows a researcher to objectively investigate a situation or experience from various fields of human knowledge and reality by making use of various theories of arts and sciences, and Scripture. To call the knowledge emanating from the studies of arts and sciences unscriptural is to dichotomise between the spiritual and the material world. As it is widely accepted that all truth is God's truth, because God is the author of both his word and his world, any holistic study must be integrative. Had Osmer rejected a theological and scriptural engagement with the issue under investigation in his Normative method, then labelling his method as leaning towards liberal Protestant position as Smith claimed,[112] could be justified; but that is not the case. Hence, being a conservative evangelical does not mean detachment from the subjects and experiences of the world. On the contrary, these other theories can serve as handmaidens to theology.

On the issue of fallibility and perspectivalism in Osmer's method, as raised by Smith, we must clarify that Osmer's aim is towards epistemic humility as a researcher, as one's interpretation and perspective may not always be correct. However, this does not question the infallibility of God's word.

Perhaps Smith is right to say that Osmer's fourth step, seen in isolation, is weak as it does not provide a system towards developing a theory of action. However, in reference to the current research, this supposed weakness of Osmer's method will not hinder it, because as it is shaped by an eclectic design, the research has come up with a functional theory as the phenomenological approach has recommended,[113] along with ten recommendations.[114]

Second, let us respond to Woodbridge's criticism of Osmer's model, in relation to the methodology of the current research. As the research design I have chosen is eclectic, which includes phenomenology alongside Osmer's model, the critique of Woodbridge that "Interpretative Task" should come before "Empirical-Descriptive Task" does not arise, because I wanted to listen to people's real-life experience first, before coming to know why such a situation in their lives had happened. Besides the logical inappropriateness

---

112. Woodbridge also alleged that Osmer does not prioritise scriptural engagement in his method. Woodbridge, "EDNA Model," 90.

113. Cf. 8.4.2.

114. Cf. 7.2 and 8.4.1.

of asking "Why is this going on?" before asking "What is going on?," another disadvantage is that the researcher's thinking risks being influenced, even before hearing the status quo of the situation. Thus, a fair assessment of the situation by primarily listening to people's experiences first may be absent during the collection of the data.

1.15.3.3 A Justification for Preferring Richard R. Osmer's Model in Comparison to Rambo and Leh, and Kevin Gary Smith's Models

The reasons why Osmer's model is preferred over the other two are set out here. First, although the six-steps model of Rambo and Leh correctly talks about how the participant observes and describes a phenomenon, how a researcher must empathise with the participants and understand them, and how the researcher must interpret the data received and explain them from some theoretical framework, there is no provision in the model for a preferred future situation where the researcher can, within a framework, talk about "what ought to be going on" and what the future course of actions should be.[115] This is because one of the goals of a Practical Theology research work is to "examine . . . current forms of practice" "in the light of fresh questions that emerge from particular situations" and then "contribute to the development and reshaping of new theories which are then fed back into the practices of church and world."[116] Perhaps it is appropriate here to elaborate and interject the unique aim of Practical Theology. It is a discipline where "practice" is "studied theologically" and it aims to build from the current understanding of theology towards its praxis dimension.[117] It theologically explores the critical situations of humankind which are not easily identifiable[118] and "provide[s] insights and strategies that will enable the movement towards faithful change."[119] Thus, it moves beyond a mere accumulation and understanding of a situation towards changing[120] and shaping a God-oriented lifestyle.[121]

---

115. Osmer, *Practical Theology*, 4.
116. Swinton and Mowat, *Practical Theology*, 25.
117. Cameron and Duce, *Researching Practice*, 12.
118. Swinton and Mowat, *Practical Theology*, xv.
119. Swinton and Mowat, 24.
120. Swinton and Mowat, 26.
121. Swinton and Mowat, 25.

Second, Smith's and Osmer's models are very similar in their structural design. Smith has both the "preferred future" and "practical suggestions" steps which we have seen are absent in Rambo and Leh. However, the reason why Osmer's model is preferred is because unlike Smith's method, Osmer clearly categorises "description" and "interpretation" in different categories as prescribed by the phenomenological research approach.

CHAPTER 2

Literature Review

2.1 Introduction

In this chapter, we will review and examine current literature related to the topic of this research work. Then we will be able "to identify a gap in knowledge" that this research can fill by referring to previous research related to this topic.[1] Keeping in mind the topic of the research, figure 6 is given on page 31 as a representation of the structure of this chapter. Here, we will discuss the available literature under three headings – The Effect of Preaching, Nominalism, and Preaching and Nominalism.

2.2 The Effect of Preaching

2.2.1 A Theological-Homiletical Survey

Here, the main task is to examine what various homileticians and theologians of preaching think about "the effect of preaching." Therefore, the main focus is on "what preaching does." There are different views on "what the sermon does"; these viewpoints are categorised in figure 7 on page 32 to provide more fluidity. After laying out and analysing the various viewpoints, I will then locate myself under one of them. Then, I will, in my practical research, examine what the members in the Baptist churches in Imphal think preaching does in their pulpits.

The aim is to choose some voices of homileticians or theologians of preaching to represent each category and era. Although there may be other voices, the chosen voices from different eras suit our purpose as their works

---

1. Cameron and Duce, *Researching*, 64. See also Hart, *Doing Literature Review*; Ridley, *Literature Review*.

and writings clearly demonstrate "what preaching does." However, there are some categories where a general discussion would be more helpful. The first section is on the minimal effect of preaching on spiritual renewal.

2.2.1.1 *Good Preaching May Have Minimal Effect on Spiritual Renewal*

There are some scholars who claim that personal spiritual vitality is not necessarily brought about by preaching. In Europe, Robin W. Winks thinks that the fertility of the soil, the presence of waterways for trade, the opening up of mountain routes, the increase in mining, technological advancement, border security against external invasion, etc., brought about "general economic prosperity that peaked in the late thirteenth century." This "demographic expansion and agricultural prosperity" ushered in a Christian spiritual renewal.[2] What is interesting here is that Winks does not connect spiritual renewal to the primary role of preaching or other spiritual activity but puts other factors first. There are other religious and social groups who also claim the same, that some general societal improvements through economic and political or social factors usher in spiritual renewal.[3]

Marvin Perry also affirms that in Europe, "accompanying economic recovery and political stability in the High Middle Ages was a growing spiritual vitality . . . The common people showed greater devotion to the church."[4] Going by these arguments then, there may be some who would argue that economic, political, and social, even class or caste reforms, adequately determine the response of people in revival or to preaching, and therefore influence the growth of spiritual renewal. Klaus Fiedler, supporting this view, argues differently saying that the two world wars America was in brought economic instability and as a result there was a steep decline of spirituality in the country. He says, "Between two wars, no far-reaching spiritual renewal occurred in Europe or America, and any hope that the material depression would usher in a spiritual revival, as it had done in 1858–59, proved futile."[5]

---

2. Winks, *World Civilization*, 174–75.

3. Cf. Fan and Whitehead, "Spirituality in Modern Chinese," 27; Campanini, "Abu Hamid," 217, 221. *Contra*, Milward, *War, Economy*, 6.

4. Perry, *Western Civilization*, xxxi.

5. Fiedler, *Story Faith Missions*, 84.

Literature Review 31

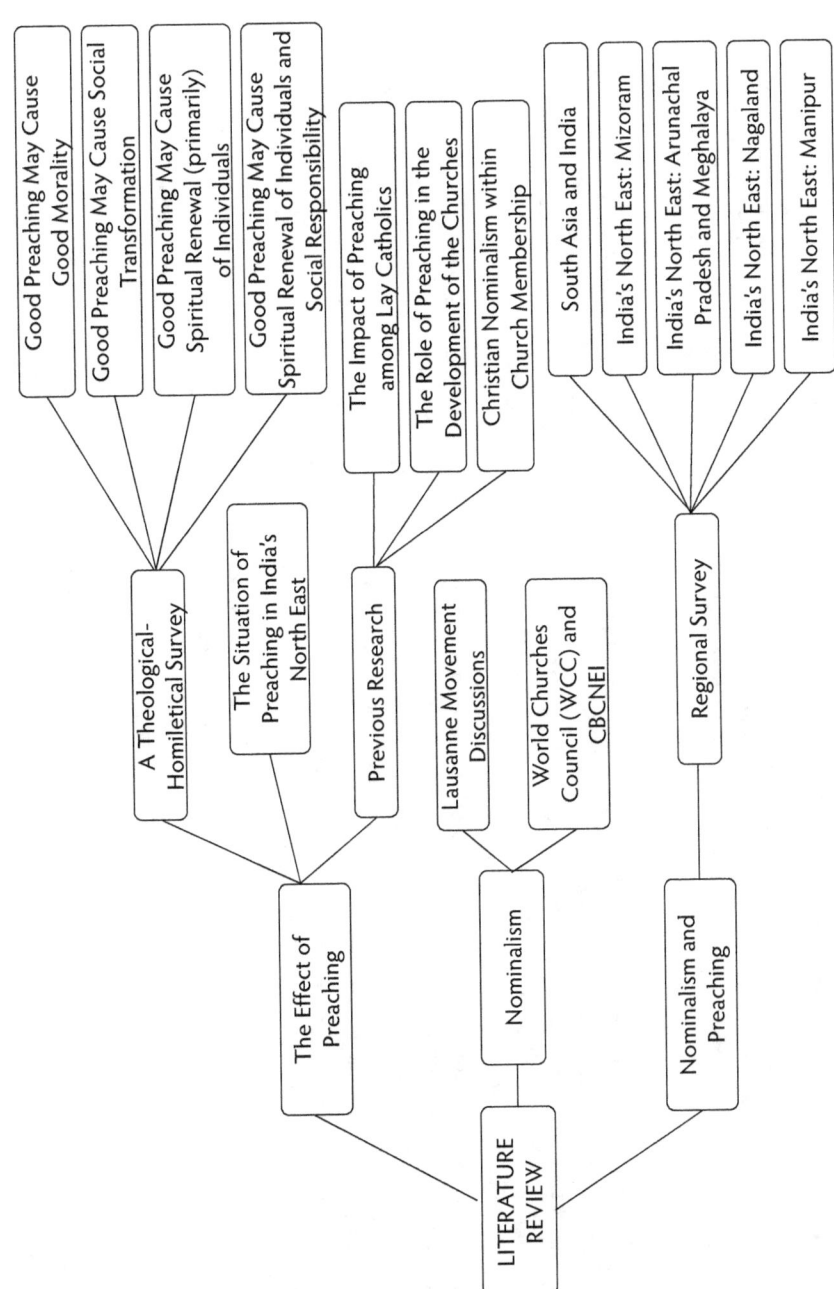

Figure 6: A Graphic Map for the Literature Review

THE SPECTRUM OF THE EFFECT OF PREACHING ON SPIRITUAL LIFE

	Good preaching may have minimal effect on spiritual renewal.	Good preaching may cause good morality.	Good preaching may cause social transformation.	Good preaching may cause spiritual renewal (primarily) of individuals.	Good preaching may cause spiritual renewal of individuals and social responsibility.
What does good preaching do?	Preaching may be irrelevant as a cause of spiritual renewal or it may have a minimal effect.	Morality, ethics, and behavioural change is the goal of preaching.	Social action is the primary purpose of preaching.	Proclamation is the primary purpose of preaching.	Proclamation and social responsibility are the purposes of preaching.
What is the tool/ factor used to bring about the effect?	Factors like "Economic prosperity; Transport and communication; Technological advancement; Border security; Political liberation" etc., may usher in spiritual renewal.	*Reason* is used as a tool (during the Enlightenment period) by the preachers to effect moral rectitude and dispel wrong beliefs.	*Human effort* without reference to any divine help is the basis of bringing forth social transformation.	*Holy Spirit* is the only being who has "power over men's minds" and can regenerate the human heart.	"Sovereign work of the Holy Spirit" alone brings spiritual renewal and inspires an individual and the church as a community of believers to be responsible in their social affairs and duties.
			Theologians of Preaching	**Theologians of Preaching**	**Theologians of Preaching**
			Walter Rauschenbusch (1861-1918)	Charles Haddon Spurgeon (1832-1892)	John Stott (1921-2011)
			Gnana Robinson (1935-)	John Wesley (1703-1791)	Darrell Johnson (1948-)

Figure 7: A Spectrum of Effect of Preaching on Spiritual Life

However, there are people who disagree with this claim and argue that much revival is explained in terms of people being economically depressed and therefore using religion as a compensation.[6] Then there are those who opine that religion becomes a channel, especially for people's emotions, and a vehicle to articulate and advocate change to their social situation. Mary Beth Norton and others argue that "religious revival movements lead to social reform" in North America, during the years 1815–1880. They claim that preachers "preached that there was a direct link between how people lived and whether they would enter God's kingdom, and in so doing, inspired social and moral reform."[7] Technically, religion then becomes an epiphenomenon rather than a phenomenon in itself. So, although these various factors are not the phenomena that invigorate Christian spirituality, they become the channels to host preaching that ultimately revitalise spirituality.

The proponents of this section do have a case, given their unique historical contexts and their points of argument. Nevertheless, this view is problematic because there are equally valid contrasting opinions based on historical evidence. However, this view has been included as a category in our present study because it serves to identify and acknowledge that various factors can bring spiritual renewal.

While it may be true that several external factors are important in their supportive roles in ushering in spiritual renewal, it is arguable that Christian spirituality is also significantly nourished or impacted by the good preaching of God's word. Below is the second viewpoint where the goal and purpose of preaching is to cause good morality, which will be introduced by a general discussion as it will benefit the purpose of the study better.

2.2.1.2 *Preaching as the Cause for Good Morality*

Preaching in the Enlightenment period digressed from the gospel to a moralistic preaching. During this period, preaching tried to eliminate "superstitious" "misconceptions from the minds of the faithful and instil a sense of moral rectitude and social responsibility."[8] Preachers like Archbishop Tillotson of England (1743), Principal Robertson of Scotland (1812) and Johann Lorenz

---

6. Herzog, *Spiritual-Industrial Complex*, 32.
7. Norton, *People and Nation*, 298.
8. Schmidt, *What Is Enlightenment?*, 7; cf. Birstsch, "Christian as Subject," 317–26.

Mosheim of Germany (1832) tried to rationalise the Christian message to fit into Enlightenment ideology.[9] And many believed that "in the final analysis, the decisive proof for faith is to be found in an upright conduct of life. For them the moral aspect was superior to the religious."[10] However, some felt that their efforts compromised the authentic gospel and their brilliant efforts bore no fruit, except some applause for their fluent articulation.[11] The preachers of this era were critiqued as brilliant in presentation but devoid of biblical content.[12]

Evaluating this viewpoint, preaching which is aimed to effect good morality is a praiseworthy endeavour. In fact, the Bible exhorts Christians to demonstrate kingdom values through their attitudes and behaviours. However, the point of divergence is simply that the Enlightenment era's glorification of morality was for the sake of good morality and not out of a transformed and thankful response due to the gift of salvation through the birth, death, burial, and resurrection of Jesus Christ. So, despite every good intention to bring about behavioural change, this type of preaching fails in its effort because it ignores the gospel. Labouring to impact the external behaviours without focusing on inner transformation through the gospel, will not lead to the germination of good behaviour in a person, as the Bible teaches.

2.2.1.3 Good Preaching May Cause Social Transformation

The proponents in this category identify social issues and social transformation as the driving force in their preaching to effect change in society. Below are two homileticians who could be categorised within this group.

2.2.1.2.1 Gnana Robinson[13] (1935–)

Gnana Robinson claims, "Christian homiletics has the task of leading straying Christians back to truth, enabling them to understand that truth in relation to the situations of their daily lives, which Christ came to redeem."[14] He also believes that preaching should speak to the "existential situation of

---

9. Tillotson, *Works*; Robertson, *Works*; Mosheim, *Institutes Ecclesiological History*; cf. Van Eijnatten, "Reaching Audiences", 135.

10. Younis, "Chapter 32 – Enlightenment," online.

11. Larsen, *Company*, 348.

12. Garvie, *Christian Preacher*, 199; see also Ker, *Lectures*, 242.

13. He is the former Principal of the United Theological College, Bangalore, and President of the Peace Trust, Kanyakumari, Tamil Nadu, India.

14. Robinson, "Homiletics Today," 59.

those addressed" based on several biblical passages.[15] He then argues that "every homily should have in it the twofold dimensions of *admonition* against people's alliance with the forces of evil and death and *exhortation* inviting members to align with the forces of good and life."[16] Robinson argues that the preacher must be vocal and prophetic against evil structures in society like injustice and corruption,[17] and should convict and help the listeners "to realize their weaknesses, failures, and shortcomings, which we call 'sins,' and helping them to amend their ways and return to God."[18] Unless this is done, he laments, it will be "homiletics of convenience, where we preach to the convenience and comfort of both the preacher and the hearers."[19]

Operating from these two key words (admonition and exhortation), he advises that our preaching must admonish the Indian churches against "mammon, the idol of wealth," "injustice," and "prosperity cult." Then he recommends that theological colleges should encourage their "homiletics students to do their dissertations on the types of sermons preached in churches, revival meetings, and television shows these days – the texts preached on, and the focus of the messages given."[20]

Expressing his concern for social transformation, he argues that the church's preaching must address corruption if we want India to be free of it. Further, he claims that the preaching must focus on the struggles of the people in society brought about by "unjust, corrupt structures, and powers rather than on superstitious niceties such as heavenly bliss and solace."[21]

Robinson rightly emphasises that preaching must include both admonition and exhortation. He is right that the church must address societal concerns by preaching prophetically. His position on the propagation of justice and truth in the society is also commendable. However, his arguments are not without problems. First, while Robinson points out that preaching is for the purpose of correcting and straightening Christians who have walked

---

15. 2 Sam 12:1; 1 Kgs 21:17; Amos 5:21; Mic 6:1–8; Luke 3:2; Matt 5–7. Robinson, "Homiletics Today," 59.
16. Robinson, 60.
17. Robinson, 61.
18. Robinson, 62.
19. Robinson, 63.
20. Robinson, 63.
21. Robinson, 63–64.

away from the good ancient path of God, he excludes the role and effect of preaching on people who are not Christians. It is too Christian-centric. The Bible never says nor exemplifies that the preaching of God's word must be focused only on Christians. Rather, we see examples from the preaching of Jesus,[22] Peter,[23] and Paul,[24] to mention just a few, that it must be directed towards every human being, irrespective of their theological or ideological affiliations. Second, Robinson's concept of redemption which Christ brings is on the "situations of their daily lives." Perhaps this is so because he undermines the gravity of "sins." The Bible never claims that Jesus primarily came to make our temporal lives better, but that he first came to die for our sins and redeem us.[25] By having this truth firmly anchored, we can agree that he also promised to give us abundant life.[26] Third, Robinson does not point out that preaching should effect a spiritual renewal and inner transformation, where the convert changes camp from the clutches of Satan and hell to the kingdom of God. He is more interested in describing this as a behavioural amendment to the "forces of good and life." The idea which this phrase conveys, points to aligning to a neutral impersonal force, whereas the Bible always talks about a personal relationship between God and human beings. Although this phrase sounds objective and inclusive, unfortunately it is not biblical. Fourth, Robinson wrongly elevates the role of a human being as the one who should "convict" the listeners and not the Holy Spirit.

In the light of the evaluation made above, although Robinson is right that the church's preaching must combat evil social realities, his belief that preaching causes social transformation in measurable and temporal ways and downplaying it in the realm of eternal spiritual realities lacks biblical mandate.

2.2.1.2.2 Walter Rauschenbusch[27] (1861–1918)

Walter Rauschenbusch is famously known for authoring the book *Christianity and Social Crisis* (1924). He is believed to have "merged the

---

22. Luke 5:32; 19:10
23. Acts 2:14–42.
24. Acts 17:22–31.
25. 1 Pet 2:21–25; 3:18; Heb 9:28; 10:12.
26. John 10:10.
27. He served as the professor of New Testament and Church History in Rochester Theological Seminary. He also pastored a church in New York City. See Fant and Pinson, "Walter Rauschenbusch," 127–28.

heat of evangelicalism and the rationality of socialism into the Social Gospel movement."[28] His voice is one of reaction against his Baptist context with its emphasis on individual soul competency and over-emphasis on "soul winning."[29] Some consider him as one who preaches to the needs of the human body and their "social situation," however not at the expense of avoiding preaching directed at "saving people's souls" (personal salvation).[30] On personal salvation, Rauschenbusch states, "salvation of the individuals is, of course, an essential part of salvation."[31] And in another instance he avers, "our discussion cannot pass personal salvation by."[32]

It is claimed that in his search for a theological and ministerial basis for his enterprise, he found a useful direction to "the ethical teaching of Jesus" in the works of "Horace Bushnell, Friedrich Ritschl, Julius Wellhausen, and Adolf Harnack."[33] On his newfound theological position, Rauschenbusch expresses:

> When the kingdom of God dominated our landscape, the perspective of life shifted into a new alignment. I felt a new security in my social impulse . . . I found that this new conception of the purpose of Christianity was strangely satisfying. It responded to all the old and all the new elements of my religious life. The saving of the lost, the teaching of the young, the pastoral care of the poor and frail, the quickening of starved intellects, the study of the Bible, church union, political reform, the reorganisation of the industrial system, international peace – it was all covered by the one aim of the reign of God on earth.[34]

Elaborating his theological position, he argues,

> The Kingdom of God is still a collective conception, involving the whole social life of man. It is not a matter of saving human atoms, but of saving the social organism. It is not a matter of

---

28. Lischer, *Preacher King*, 54.
29. Bush and Nettles, *Baptists and Bible*, 294.
30. Edwards, *History of Preaching*.
31. Rauschenbusch, *Christianity*, 95.
32. Rauschenbusch, 96.
33. Edwards, *History of Preaching*.
34. Rauschenbusch, *Christianizing the Social Order*, 93.

getting individuals to heaven, but of transforming life on earth into the harmony of heaven.[35]

Here, Rauschenbusch explains that the main task of preaching is to effect social change, not necessarily save the human individual. Further, he is said to have come "under the influence of the Ritschlian emphasis on the ethical kingdom of God" and preached it as "the heart and soul of the gospel."[36] Defining the preacher's role, Smith states that for Rauschenbusch,

> the priorities, the sacrifices that Moses made represent the kind of action in which the preacher must engage. Social crisis preaching for Rauschenbusch was not merely a matter of the proclamation of the Word, though that was vital. It was surrounding that proclamation with a life that participates with God in correcting social evils and institutes social justice.[37]

Here, we find Smith describing Rauschenbusch's understanding of the role of a preacher to be one that advocates social transformation not only with words but with deeds and even life itself.

Rauschenbusch must be appreciated for his significant contribution to transforming the oppressive society of his time. He believed that good preaching can effect change, although his priority leans heavily towards social transformation. With exceptions, an individual is a child of its time – socially, culturally, economically, and politically. Rauschenbusch's context shaped his preaching and his understanding of the kingdom of God.[38] Although many would categorise him as a prominent "liberal theologian" and preacher,[39] there are others who say that he was not a "typical liberal" theologian and preacher[40] but, Olson claims that "because of his Ritschlian influence and leanings he is usually put there."[41] Critiquing Rauschenbusch's sermon on "The Kingdom of God in the Parables of Jesus," Edwards points out that his focus was more

---

35. Rauschenbusch, *Christianity*, 65.
36. Olson, *Journey*, 164.
37. Smith, *Social Crisis Preaching*, 59.
38. Kindell and Demers, *Encyclopedia of Populism in America*, 2:594–96; Fant and Pinson, "Walter Rauschenbusch," 129, 131.
39. Long, *Against Us*, 62.
40. Suttle, *Evangelical Social Gospel*, 74–75.
41. Olson, *Journey*, 163.

on the "Brotherhood of the kingdom, a fellowship of socially involved Baptist clergy that was an important support group."[42] Moreover, in another sermon from Isaiah 1, Edwards again shows that Rauschenbusch's focus was to address "poverty . . . Rauschenbusch calls upon his audience to overthrow poverty by the abolition of privilege and by association . . . The methods recommended are thought and agitation."[43]

Further, Tim Suttle has critiqued Rauschenbusch for his theology on personal salvation because he is perceived to have made it "intentionally vague" to avoid conflict between various denominations of his time. His only interest, Suttle argues, was to "add . . . social dimension" to whatever view of personal salvation a person understands according to one's denomination, and he did not expound from the Scripture. Suttle elaborates that Rauschenbusch did not care "about the mechanics of personal salvation, but to argue for the addition of the social aspect of salvation to whatever form of personal salvation one was committed to."[44]

Rauschenbusch must be credited for sensitising the conscience of the society from soul centrism to social transformation. He is right that a truly born-again Christian (with the assurance of personal salvation) will demonstrate his inner spiritual transformation by his ethical conduct and by working towards social change as well. However, in his case, the balance tilted heavily towards social concern and issues, so much so that he was unconcerned to define what personal salvation means from the Scripture. Although he mentions that personal salvation and spirituality are important, he downplays it, as his focus in preaching was social transformation. Although the kingdom of God coming to earth and bringing kingdom values and ethics is the prayer and wish of a Christian, the primacy of heaven and its otherness for a sinner to hope for cannot be equated with anything else, and here Rauschenbusch misses the mark.

In this section, the homileticians we engaged with focused their attention on social transformation. Their earnestness and passion to see a society with Christian values and ethics through their preaching and theological engagement deserve appreciation. However, when the foundational truth of eternity

---

42. Edwards, *History of Preaching*, 653.
43. Edwards, 653.
44. Suttle, *Evangelical Social Gospel*, 75.

regarding personal salvation and individual spirituality becomes redundant for the sake of temporal realities, the priority becomes self-defeating: we are putting the cart before the horse. Nevertheless, it must be clarified here that I agree with these homileticians that preaching for social change can have some visible external effects, although such outcome may be rare. But on the other hand, I do believe that preaching can also influence and transform society, without disregarding the eternal realities of Christ's cross and of the individual's saving appropriation of that work today.

2.2.1.3 Good Preaching May Cause Spiritual Renewal (Primarily) of Individuals

In this category, the focus of the effect of preaching is soul winning. The lifeboat imagery[45] that focuses on a person's salvific escape from the prison of sin and hell to heaven undergirds this category. Let us consider two homileticians in this category.

2.2.1.3.1 John Wesley (1703–1791)

John Wesley is famously known as the preacher on horseback,[46] who preached "over forty thousand sermons" as a "grand itinerant" preacher for over five decades,[47] and who later founded Methodism.[48] Although he initially experienced doubts about his salvation,[49] once his conviction and faith was established, he became a fierce ambassador of soul winning. Pouring his entire energy into it and declaring soul winning as the priority, Wesley said, "all at it and always at it."[50] Demonstrating the gravity of his soul winning urgency, he appeals:

> Friend, stop! you have the form of a man still. . . . Think a little for once. What is it you are doing? Why should you destroy yourself? . . . Why would you murder yourself inch by inch? Why should you burn yourself alive? O spare your body at least, if you have no pity for your soul! But you have a soul then?

---

45. This imagery is essentially credited to D. L. Moody; Moody, *Gospel Awakening*, 667.
46. See Wellman, *John Wesley*.
47. Wesley, *Works*, vol. 1, 248; Leonard, "Preaching," 31.
48. Poxon, *Through the Year*, 227.
49. Rice, *Golden Path*, 13.
50. "Pastoral Office," 879; Hutson, *Great Preaching*, 12.

Do you really believe it? What, a soul that must live forever! O spare thy soul! Do not destroy thy own soul with an everlasting destruction! It was made for God. Do not give it into the hands of that old murderer of men![51]

Following Wesley's teachings, the Wesleyan Methodist believes that soul winning is the chief priority of the missionaries and they are "required to renounce every other business; to leave all things else behind; and devote all their energies to the work of evangelizing a lost world . . . be wholly separated from secular business, and devoted exclusively to the work of saving souls from death."[52] It is also said that he taught his students, "you have only one business, and that is the salvation of souls."[53]

Although Wesley preached from several themes and doctrines in the Bible, it is argued that his most favoured ones were the doctrines of salvation by faith, assurance of salvation, and sanctification in grace.[54] His core message is summed up in: "Christ has reconciled us to God. Sinners can be restored to fellowship with God and experience assurance of salvation. Salvation is not limited to an elect spiritual or economic elite. All who come to Christ by faith may receive God's grace."[55] A lay preacher under Wesley confessed that Wesley's preaching "made my heart beat like the pendulum of a clock and when he did speak, I thought his whole discourse was aimed at me. When he had done, I said, 'This man can tell the secrets of my heart.'"[56]

On the other hand, Leonard clarifies that through his preaching, Wesley "sparked . . . social reform throughout Great Britain."[57] Wesley was vocal against drinking alcohol and drunkards in his preaching. An alcoholic convert remarked, "When you was [sic] at Bolton last, I was one of the most eminent drunkards in all town; but I came to listen . . . God struck me to the

---

51. Wesley, *Miscellaneous Works*, 306.

52. "Pastoral Office," 757.

53. Although the primary source could not be ascertained, this statement is credited to John Wesley. As quoted in Olford and Olford, *Secret of Soul Winning*, xi.

54. Doughty, *John Wesley*, 85.

55. Leonard, "Preaching," 31.

56. Pudney, *John Wesley*, 71.

57. Leonard, "Preaching," 31–32.

heart. I then earnestly prayed for power against drinking; and God gave me more than I asked: he took away the very desire of it."[58]

Thomas C. Oden comments on John Wesley's contribution to social reform:

> There is little evidence that Wesley was a "political activist" in the modern sense of being actively engaged in influencing legislation or administrative law. Rather, he was focused on the formation of character and habits that would benefit society wherever they were applied. People whose hearts have been redeemed have a capacity to make the realm of legislation, law, jurisprudence, and political administration healthier. Wesley's vocation as a minister of the gospel and pastoral caregiver called him to focus on the heart but also to show the relevance of the renewed heart to public policy questions.[59]

Oden mentions the following writings by Wesley: "The Reformation of Manners"; "Public Diversion Denounced"; "National Sins and Miseries"; "A Group of Essays on Wars and the Search for Peace during the American Revolution"; and "Thoughts upon Slavery."[60]

Evaluating Wesley, one must recognise that he was not blind to the social problems of his day. His writings on various social issues are evidence of his engagement with society. However, it would be unfair to Wesley's legacy if we consider him as a preacher who had any other priority than soul winning. Perhaps the title of a book by Thomas E. Pool, *John Wesley the Soul Winner*, is a fitting tribute to his life and legacy as a preacher.

2.2.1.3.2 Charles Haddon Spurgeon (1834–1892)

Famously known as the "Prince of Preachers," Charles Haddon Spurgeon was a Baptist pastor of the Metropolitan Tabernacle and the founder of Spurgeon College.[61] Spurgeon is known for his resolute focus on the priority of soul winning as a preacher. In his *Lectures to My Students*, he exclusively deals

---

58. Wesley, *Journal*, 217.
59. Oden, *John Wesley's Teachings*, 109.
60. Oden, 170.
61. Harmon, *Charles Haddon Spurgeon*.

with the noble duty of a preacher to win souls in the chapter "On Conversion as Our Aim."[62] He writes:

> God has sent us to preach in order that through the gospel of Jesus Christ the sons of men may be reconciled to him. . . . the work of preaching is intended to save the hearers. It is ours to sow even in stony places, where no fruit rewards our toil; but still we are bound to look for a harvest, and mourn if it does not appear in due time . . . Our great object of glorifying God is, however, to be mainly achieved by the winning of souls. We must see souls born unto God. If we do not, our cry should be that of Rachel, "Give me children, or I die." If we do not win souls, we should mourn as the husbandman who sees no harvest, as the fisherman who returns to his cottage with an empty net, or as the huntsman who has in vain roamed over hill and dale. . . . The ambassadors of peace should not cease to weep bitterly until sinners weep for their sins.[63]

Spurgeon also claims, "soul-winning is the chief business of the Christian minister; indeed, it should be the main pursuit of every true believer."[64] And what is soul winning? He answers, "its main operation consists in instructing a man that he may know the truth of God,"[65] and "to impress him so that he may feel it."[66] On the role of the Holy Spirit in conversion, he states, "Since conversion is a divine work, we must take care that we depend entirely upon the Spirit of God, and to look to him for power over men's minds . . . Should we not in preaching give more scope for his operation?"[67]

On the other hand, he believed that whoever had been redeemed should "be on the side of peace and justice . . . on the side of everything that is according to the mind of God, and according to the law of love."[68] He also founded the Stockwell orphanages for both boys and girls, and Spurgeon's

---

62. Spurgeon, *Lectures*, 179.
63. Spurgeon, 179–80.
64. Spurgeon, *Soul Winner*, 15.
65. Spurgeon, 21.
66. Spurgeon, 25.
67. Spurgeon, *Lectures*, 180.
68. Spurgeon, "Present Crisis," 391.

Child Care, its contemporary expression, continues to be an important social agency today.[69]

Spurgeon was also vocal against the practice of slavery and racism.[70] Recognising the dual dimensions in his preaching,[71] Ernest Bacon quotes an article in *The Times* in 1884:

> Mr. Spurgeon laid his foundation in the Bible, his utterances abound with Scriptural text, figure, metaphor, and allusion . . . He cannot be accused of not being a man of the world, or of not knowing the ways of the world, for he reads the Book and the book of nature too.[72]

Here is a homiletician who firmly believed and exemplified that good preaching has an effect on soul winning. Spurgeon cannot be branded as a single lens preacher, who focused entirely on soul winning, with no interest in the temporal affairs of the world. Nevertheless, none will disagree that he gravitated towards soul winning and the weight he gave to it in his preaching and teaching is undeniable. While some may argue that Spurgeon had multiple interests and goals in preaching, it is indisputable that soul winning was his primary goal and therefore for our purposes he has been categorised accordingly. This viewpoint is heavily driven by the eternal destination of the soul.

2.2.1.4 Good Preaching May Cause Spiritual Renewal of Individuals and Social Responsibility

Homileticians in this category believe that preaching that is faithful to the text and sensitive to the context will,[73] through the power of the Holy Spirit, renew individual and corporate spirituality, and promote a focus on both soul winning and social transformation.[74] Below are two such homileticians.

---

69. Drummond, *Spurgeon*, 427. See also Johnson, *What Will*, 109.

70. Spurgeon, *New Park Street*, 155.

71. For example, Spurgeon's sermon, "1857 Day of Humiliation" (in Mackrell, *Evangelical Times*) is social preaching from a theologically puritan and conservative perspective.

72. Bacon, *Spurgeon*, 79.

73. The brand of preaching I am referring to is the "Contextually Applied Theodramatic View" of preaching. See Appendix 1.

74. Social transformation can also happen through the believers' responsible stewardship of resources and responsibilities, as a response to their encounter with God during the

2.2.1.4.1 John Stott (1921–2011)

Apart from being an evangelical scholar and author of many books, John Stott was the Rector and then the Rector Emeritus of All Souls' Church, Langham Place, London.[75] On the effect of preaching on the spiritual renewal of believers, Stott declared that the moment of spiritual revival, where "sinners are convicted, repenters converted, backsliders restored, enemies reconciled, believers transformed, and dead churches brought back to life" happens through the "sovereign work of the Holy Spirit" in the context of a church where there is a faithful exposition of the word of God.[76] He further stressed that a faithful exposition of the Word through the power of the Holy Spirit "cuts out cancerous growths from the body of Christ" and brings spiritual vitality and renewal in the church.[77] Stott believed that darkness disappears from us as the light of the gospel shines forth through preaching.[78] Stott is also convinced that preaching transcends bringing mere individual spiritual vitality,[79] but also encompasses societal concerns.[80]

Alister Chapman states that by the early 1960s, Stott began to see social issues as an "integral part of God's mission for the church."[81] And consequently, based on Jesus saying, "As the Father has sent me, even so I am sending you,"[82] he played an important role in framing the famous 1974 Lausanne Congress statement that Christian mission encompasses the realms of both spiritual redemption (proclaiming the good news) and bodily wholeness (healing the sick).[83] From here on, points out Alister Chapman, "Social action became a prominent theme in Stott's preaching ministry."[84] It must also be noted that in his book *Basic Christianity* (1971 edition) there is a new section not in

---

preaching event.

75. Stott was also the founder of the London Institute for Contemporary Christianity and Langham Partnership and one of the main architects of the Lausanne Covenant document in 1974. John Stott, "Lausanne Covenant."
76. Stott, *God's Word*, 42.
77. Stott, 42.
78. Stott, *I Believe*, 93–94.
79. Stott, *The Preacher's Portrait*, 16.
80. For examples of the breath of these concerns see: Stott, *Issues Facing*.
81. Chapman, "Evangelical or Fundamentalist," 203.
82. John 20:21.
83. Stott, "Biblical Basis," 65–78. Cf. Stott, "Lausanne Covenant"; Ott, "Introduction," xxiv.
84. Chapman, "Evangelical or Fundamentalist," 203.

the original 1958 edition, under the heading "Our Duty to the World," that emphasises Christian responsibility to the needy world.[85] Moreover, Stott established the London Institute for Contemporary Christianity[86] which focuses on "empowering Christians to make a difference for Christ in our Monday to Saturday lives"[87] and authored some prominent books focused on this concern.[88]

Although Stott's initial understanding of preaching was confined to matters of the soul and spiritual welfare, the shift in his theological formulation is apparent in his later work both in setting up an institute to engage with contemporary issues Christians face, and in his books after 1974. He showed that preaching should transcend mere focus on churchly congregation and soul-related issues, that it should engage with the worldviews of the times, and spur believers to be salt and light in society. Stott passionately believed that good preaching has valuable effects.

2.2.1.4.2 Darrell Johnson (c. 1948-)

Darrell Johnson served as a Senior Minister of First Baptist Vancouver and as a professor of preaching at Regent College, Vancouver, Canada. Johnson's understanding of preaching the word of God is closely intertwined with the work of the Holy Spirit. According to him, God's word "not only informs, it performs, it transforms. The Spirit who breathes the text breathes his power into us to live the text."[89] So, on the effect of preaching,[90] he declares that expository preaching is "the place, the venue, where the miracle of divine transformation takes place. For in expository preaching the preacher is participating with what the risen Jesus, through the Holy Spirit is doing in and with and through a text."[91] Johnson also demonstrates his high view of the authority of God in the preaching event by stating, "in the preaching moment, the risen Jesus himself (through the person and ministry of the Holy Spirit)

---

85. Stott, *Basic Christianity*, 140. Compare with the first edition of the same book, page 142. There the emphasis is only on evangelism, not social concerns.

86. Stott and Wright, *Christian Mission*, 121.

87. "Vision," accessed 10 March 2019, https://www.licc.org.uk/about/.

88. Stott, *Issues*; Stott and Wright, *Christian Mission*; Stott, *Balanced Christianity*.

89. Johnson, *Glory of Preaching*, 75.

90. Johnson believes expository preaching alone brings spiritual transformation. See Johnson, 75.

91. Johnson, 75.

takes a text of Scripture in hand and opens it in such a way that confused and dejected men and women find their hearts 'burning within.' Jesus is at once the one who is preached and the one who is preaching."[92] Thus, Johnson believes that individual transformation happens in the context of preaching.

Although Johnson is deeply committed to the supremacy of God's authority and has a high view of revelation in the preaching event towards spiritual renewal and individual transformation, he does not limit the goal and impact of preaching there. His concern covers earthly realities as well. He categorically states:

> I believe the preaching of the Word of God changes the world. I believe individuals, neighbourhoods, cities and nations are changed by the preaching of the gospel of Jesus Christ. For in preaching the good news of Jesus Christ (which is ultimately what any biblical text preaches), it turns out that we are participating with the living God in God's ongoing transformation of the world."[93]

As we have seen, Johnson's high view of God's role in transforming an individual believer through expository preaching does not end with the matters of the soul, restricted to the spiritual dimension alone. His belief is that true preaching transforms the individual who eventually will help change the world by participating in its affairs. In this way, Johnson amplifies the role and effect of preaching by integrating both spiritual and worldly aspects.

Summarising this section then, we must acknowledge the holistic goal of preaching effecting both individual spirituality and impacting the world humankind lives in with multi-dimensional issues. As a person is made up of physical, emotional, and social aspects as well as his spiritual being, preaching that focuses on only one aspect misses the whole truth about God's lordship over human beings and everything in this world. Further, and most importantly, homileticians in this section undeniably depend on the work of the Holy Spirit for transformation.

The indispensable role of the Holy Spirit in transforming people's lives goes unsaid in the preaching event. Johnson T. K. Lim argues that "what creates

---

92. Johnson, 53.
93. Johnson, 7.

faith or change in the listeners is not our skill, nor eloquence or lack of it."[94] He quotes Marquart's statement that whoever contradicts this position is like "the foolish rooster [which] thinks he causes the sun to rise, and the foolish preacher [who] thinks he causes faith to grow."[95]

I agree with this last viewpoint for the obvious reason that, as God spoke life into the world during creation (Gen 1), his Word must speak life (Prov 3:1; Ps 119:25, 43, 50) into the spiritual lives of individuals and the affairs of this world again (John 1:13) from the pulpits and through the changed lives of the believers (1 Pet 1–5). Moreover, to bring any change in the minds and hearts of the listeners is purely the prerogative of the Holy Spirit (Zech 4:6; 1 Cor 2:4; Titus 3:5) through the medium of the human preacher (Rom 10:14–16). Therefore, preachers cannot play God, although they are capable of preaching powerful sermons. Furthermore, I believe that preaching must not be disconnected from the lived-out realities of the listeners' lives if it is to be holistically transformational.

Although I believe that preaching should vitalise an individual's spirituality, and consequently spur them to become socially responsible, in this research work, the aim is to listen to the experiences of the people in selected Baptist churches in Imphal and know what they think preaching does, especially to their spiritual life.

2.2.2 The Situation of Preaching in India's North East

In the article "Interpreting Scripture in Northeast India," A. K. Lama[96] brings to light the contemporary scenario of the pulpit ministry in the churches of North East India and its impact on those in the pews. These issues can be discussed under two categories. First, he raises the issues of the listeners as they listened to the sermons in the churches, and the plight of the pastors and preachers expressing their difficulties in sermon preparation. Second, he deliberates on the issues of exegeting the text and contexts well for good and relevant preaching.

---

94. Lim, *Power in Preaching*, 21.

95. Lim, 21. See also Marquart, *Quest*, 151. For more on Holy Spirit's role in preaching, see Robinson, *Biblical Preaching*, 20; Addo, *Principles of Transformation*; Issler, "Practicing the Elements," 251; McQuilkin, "Spiritual Formation"; Jensen, "Preaching," 141.

96. He is the former General Secretary of the CBCNEI (2010–2015).

In his engagement with the first category, he recounts how the church members expressed to him their response to his question, "How was the sermon?":

> Well, the sermon was not grounded in the biblical text; preached without interpreting the text; preached interpreting the text incorrectly; preached expounding the text inadequately; preached with the right theology from the wrong text; based on personal subjective experiences; too theoretical, with no practical applications; too emotional, with very poor content; too much focused on miraculous healing; focused on the false hope of the prosperity gospel; preached with a theological slant that undermines the whole counsel of God; and preached without addressing the issues we face today.[97]

Then he narrates how the pastors and preachers confided to him about their struggles and situations.

> I have never been to any seminary; I am not a full-time pastor – the church only pays me to work on Sundays; my seminary never taught me how to do exegesis; in my seminary we had only two courses on exegesis; in my 30 years of ministry, this is the first training in exegesis that I have received; I wish I had learned exegesis earlier in my ministry... I will retire in two years; I wish I could do exegesis, but I have no time for research and writing sermons; my congregation prefers stories rather than exegesis; I feel inadequate; I am not gifted for this; all the exegetical sermons I have heard were boring; I do not know how to make my exegesis interesting; I did not do well in biblical languages, so I am struggling; my senior pastors discourage me from using exegetical tools in my preaching; the era of exegetical preaching has passed – this is the era of narrative preaching; my church's members are oral learners – reading a sermon text puts them off; my church's members do not bring their Bibles; my church's members watch televangelists and want similar preaching from

---

97. Lama, "Interpreting," 23.

me; people are living in a high-tech era – they prefer an audio-visual presentation; exegetical preaching is outdated.[98]

On the second category of exegeting both the text and contexts well to make one's preaching effective, Lama argues that a weak exegesis and interpretation of the biblical text leads to weak preaching and that a weak exegesis of the listeners' contexts leads to an incorrect, weak, and even "dangerous" application of a biblical text, although it had been exegeted and interpreted well.[99] He also argues that it is because the two ends of the spectrum (text and contexts) are not respected in the homiletical exercise of the North East Indian churches, that we suffer from a weak and irrelevant pulpit. This gives rise to the need for relevant and prophetic preaching in the churches.

Considering these issues Lama has generically raised in the churches of India's North East, it is pertinent to ask if his claims are indeed relevant and true among the Baptist churches in Imphal. Moreover, he reveals that many church members considered their pastors' preaching as unfulfilling and dissatisfactory, and the pastors themselves confessed their inability to exegete and prepare their sermons properly. Thus, it is reasonable to explore the effect of pastors' preaching in the spiritual lives of their members, especially how it addresses the problem of nominalism in the Baptist churches in Imphal.

2.2.3 Previous Research

In this section, we will review some work which has been done in relation to the current research and find out what gaps exist, in order to show how this research could help push forward new discussions on the subject.

2.2.3.1 *The Effects of Sermons among Lay Catholics: An Exploratory Study*

William M. Newman and Stuart A. Wright did research to explore "the effects of sermons among lay Catholics."[100] They asked two research questions: "To what extent do sermons have an effect on their intended audiences?" and

---

98. Lama, "Interpreting," 24–25.

99. Lama uses the term "dangerous" because the cultural, social, economic, religious, and political situation of India's North East is so diverse and complicated, that if one does not know the people's context, the sermons will be counterproductive. Lama describes this potential danger by the phrase, "stepping on [a] live cobra"; Lama, "Interpreting," 29–32.

100. Newman and Wright, "Effects of Sermons," 54–59.

"What kinds of social variables explain the differential effects of sermons on laypersons?"[101] Some of their findings are: They felt that the questionnaires in the quantitative method they employed were too abstract and so it was easier for "theologians and other religious professionals" to understand it, while the lay people found it elusive. They remarked that as the lay participants were required to tick the "forced-choice questions," the lay participants responded ticking the "middle, rather than high or low, response categories." The respondents seemed unsure of certain things.[102] They recommended that future research on such a topic requires a "more comprehensive evaluative research." This statement can be interpreted in more than one way, but the disadvantage of the quantitative method in addressing this kind of topic is evident because people are unable to explain what they feel because the provision to express with their words and language is absent in a quantitative method. Moreover, Newman and Wright discovered that a question that related to the problem of their lives "received one of the most positive ratings," and so they are convinced that the existential issues of human life in relation to sermons are "worth exploring."[103] Furthermore, they confessed that "questionnaire items should exhibit greater specificity than those used here,[104] and should encompass a wider range of religious and secular consequences of sermons."[105]

Evaluating this section, we can conclude that the phenomenological approach (qualitative method) can provide both the educated and semi-literate the space to freely express their experiences and also clarify their doubts on certain questions through interviews and open-ended questionnaires.[106]

---

101. Newman and Wright, 54.
102. Newman and Wright, 58.
103. Newman and Wright, 58.
104. The questions are: "Have you ever read the Bible because of a sermon you heard?"; "Have you ever changed your attitude toward another person because of a sermon you heard?"; "Do sermons provide you with a sense of God's love?"; "Has a sermon made you want to praise and thank God?"; "After a sermon, do you feel like telling the world about God's love?"; "Do sermons relate the Message of Christ to the problems of your own life?"; "Do sermons answer your important questions about God and religion?"; "Do you feel your knowledge of Jesus Christ has improved due to sermons?"; "In reality, do sermons affect the way you see God?"; "Do the guidelines in sermons actually change the way you live?"; Newman and Wright, "Effects of Sermons," 56.
105. Newman and Wright, 58.
106. As mentioned in the Research Methodology section.

Moreover, Newman and Wright's research validates the importance of asking about the effect of preaching on believers' individual lives.

Thus, the findings of this research further strengthen the need for the current research to be undertaken, particularly from a phenomenological approach where the participant's voice, language, and experience can lend more depth to the research.

2.2.3.2 *The Role of Preaching in the Development of the Church*

Here we discuss Y. L. Mingthing's findings and recommendations through his research done in the 1970s.[107] First, Mingthing discovered that the early preachers "had little knowledge of the historic role of preaching in the life of the church, or theological and textual explanation or any special forms of preaching . . . The Bible was their only source while preaching."[108]

Second, he found that the preferred themes in preaching among the first converts were the second coming, life after death, revival, and then others,[109] and that, "except those who were born in Christian families, preaching was the main factor in converting people."[110]

Third, he claims that "early preaching reflected the theological biasness [sic] of the missionaries who brought the preaching themes with them from the West and applied them to the Naga situation."[111]

Fourth, he learned that the most important factor for the people to soften their aggressive stance and accept the preaching and teaching of William Pettigrew, the first missionary in Manipur, was his "personal presence, his interest in them, his sincerity, humility, and concern for them."[112]

Fifth, Mingthing claims that although preaching is defined by different people in different ways, "true Christian preaching cannot go away from proclaiming the good news that was announced by Jesus Christ"[113] – that

---

107. Mingthing, "Role of Preaching." Mingthing comes from Ukhrul, the region where the first Baptist missionary William Pettigrew set up his first mission centre in Manipur. Mingthing's research work is probably the earliest, and the only one done so far in this subject from Manipur.
108. Mingthing, 70.
109. Mingthing, 72.
110. Mingthing, 87.
111. Mingthing, 127.
112. Mingthing, 83.
113. Mingthing, 89.

preaching cannot be severed from the gospel,[114] or else it "ceases to be a Christian preaching."[115]

Sixth, Mingthing observes that one of the reasons for the church not growing is because the villagers are unable to pay a trained pastor; they choose a person who is a leader among them who can read and write. Since they are not paid enough, they are more occupied by their family work in the fields. This weakens the administration of the church and fails to keep the church growing. Pastoral care, the sacramental acts, and the proclamation of the word of God are totally lacking.[116]

Seventh, Mingthing also found that "the Tangkhul Naga Churches have not had leaders who have had adequate training on Christian preaching, which is really necessary."[117]

Eighth, Mingthing points out the pertinent danger in the gap between what a preacher thinks the people need and the actual need and desire of the people.[118] Mingthing warns that "if the church expects to attract people by the old traditional methods" and choice of themes as in the missionary era, then "she will fail in this present situation."[119]

Ninth, he has argued that in the post-missionary era there must be a new direction for preaching. Preachers must engage with the people in the Baptist churches with intentionality, they must bridge the expectation of the second and third generations after the early missionary period, because people have become "more educated and more acquainted with modern industrial society where social, political, and economic conditions have become much more complex." If not, there will be gaps and people will look for help in other places. He argues:

> If the church fails to convince these people that the Gospel continues to be good news even today and it will be forever, they will withdraw from the faith and confidence they have in the religion. The church has to get along with the present society

---

114. Mingthing, 90.
115. Mingthing, 92.
116. Mingthing, 100.
117. Mingthing, 102.
118. Mingthing, 112.
119. Mingthing, 112.

with all its complexities. If so, the church needs to preach a relevant message to the people. Its method, its theme, and its approach have to be re-thought in accordance with the context.[120]

Tenth, Mingthing states that the church had been impacted by the revival movement wave coming from the neighbouring states.[121] He describes the characteristics of revival preaching as,

> Emotional; concerned with regeneration and renewal of life; characterised by a strange emphasis upon second coming and life after death; judgement to all who do not come into the movement; critical of the existing church structures; given to misinterpretation of the Bible; exclusivist, intolerant, and cliquish; condusive [sic] to abnormal behaviour; an excessive expression of sorrow and joy; ecstatic; escapist; concerned with unnecessary imaginary burdens; puritanical against commonly accepted social pleasures and practices; condusive [sic] to strange teachings based on dreams and visions.[122]

Mingthing evaluates such revival preaching by saying that such a movement's "motives and concepts . . . are peculiar and difficult to understand. The characteristic (of revival preaching) shows a poor relation with the Scripture. The revelation of God to mankind has been confusing." The appeal for "confession, repentance, and salvation become [sic] strange and misleading" and it "has become diverted from the true Christian preaching,"[123] because according to Mingthing, "preaching for confession, repentance, and salvation should be in relation to the Good News proclaimed. Always the Good News preached must prevail."[124]

Mingthing then analyses revival preaching as follows:

> It is a serious matter to be careful enough that one does not go astray from the given truth and the ultimate reality. Thus, to preach for revival, which is of course, necessary, must take a

---

120. Mingthing, 112–13.
121. Mingthing talks of the revival movements of 1923 and 1973. Mingthing, 115.
122. Mingthing, 118–19.
123. Mingthing, 118.
124. Mingthing, 118.

right course. The church leaders today need to think and take cautious action to renew the revival guided by the Scriptures and by the spirit of Christ through whom the church receives the gospel and the authority to extend the kingdom of God. Revival preaching needs to be critically examined in the light of contemporary human need, as well as the biblical revelation. While it may play a useful role in bringing a person to an awareness of his sinfulness and need of divine grace, it needs to be radically modified if the "sinner" is to enter into the fullness of life in Christ and so become fully human.[125]

Eleventh, Mingthing makes the following recommendations:

1. Themes for preaching and methods of presentation can be developed in relation to local situation. The social, cultural, and economic condition of the locality should be surveyed and preaching themes formalised according to the local needs.

2. The Eastern Theological College at Jorhat and Manipur Bible Institute[126] at Kangpokpi should inaugurate courses on preaching to cover in extension the untrained pastors. Since language is a great problem in using other programmes, training must be given to the local leaders in the vernacular. Along with the casual routine, classes, correspondence courses in the vernacular can be done.[127]

He warns that,

Unless some steps are taken immediately, the situation will continue to deteriorate. Dissatisfaction among the masses, especially young men and women, will increase. Pastors who are not trained have not realised the danger. They find it difficult to understand the minds of the people and their problems. Therefore, it is possible that they will go on preaching in an irrelevant way.[128]

---

125. Mingthing, 120.
126. Now, Manipur Theological College (MTC).
127. Mingthing, "Role of Preaching," 120–21.
128. Mingthing, 121.

Due to the lack of documentation and materials related to preaching and church growth during this period, the lack of wider academic conversations with Mingthing's work and the lack of access to Mingthing's files, we will evaluate his work in relation to the current research and see how it lends impetus for further research.

First, Mingthing talks about a limited homiletical understanding on the form and genre of preaching among the early pastors. Moreover, he mentions that the themes they preached were also selective and unholistic, influenced by the missionaries' own presuppositions. His observation opens the way for us to investigate how much things have changed since his work and explore what themes of preaching occupy the pulpits of the Baptist churches in Imphal, and if these themes and sermons have had a visible impact on the people's spirituality.

Second, Mingthing points out the indispensability of preaching the gospel for the church to grow and for preaching to be called "Christian preaching." This is another area which the current research will investigate to probe if the pulpits of the Baptist churches in Imphal preach the gospel or other content.

Third, Mingthing talks about the low quality of preaching in the churches because of the kind of pastors the congregation preferred to have, influenced by the church's weak economic situation. Moreover, he says that the churches do not have leaders who have been trained to preach as such; many preachers resort to prooftexting. Even more serious is the claim that some pastors do not interpret the text correctly. This finding justifies an investigation as to whether the situation is the same today or if there are other factors apart from financial incapacity that are hindering the appointment of good preachers in the church.

Fourth, Mingthing points out a gap between preachers and the pews, particularly in relation to the complex issues of life faced by the younger generation. This supports the value of the research and gives voice to its legitimacy, to explore if pastors today know what the people need, or if the people are being fed well spiritually. Mingthing's findings justify exploring whether our preaching is any different from that of the missionary days and what changes we have made, if any.

Fifth, Mingthing warned of the need to examine the content and relevance of revival preaching, and it opens the way for the current research to explore if a spirituality sparked off and sustained by revival or a similar movement is enduring and has any visible impact on society. It further lends impetus to explore the conditions of churches' spirituality that had neglected holistic gospel biblical preaching or the Scripture and whether the contemporary pulpits of the Baptist churches in Imphal are holistic in their homiletical theology or still otherworldly, and what their impact is.

2.2.3.3 Christian Nominalism within Church Membership

This section discusses Enosh Anguandia Adia Edre's thesis, by briefly examining his findings and recommendations.[129] Edre's "purpose of this [his] study was to understand the extent of [sic] to which Bunia churches know the problem of nominal Christianity within their memberships."[130]

Under the heading "Relationship between the research findings and the purpose of the study," he states that "the pastoral leadership may be to blame for, among other things, not preaching the biblical gospel clearly."[131] He elaborates, "preaching of the gospel in many churches omits important elements, whether by ignorance or deliberately by fear of losing adherents."[132] He also remarks that spiritual lethargy in the church could be "traced back to failure in preaching this [the] biblical gospel of repentance and saving faith in Jesus."[133] He then asserts that "the pastoral ministry is not only about preaching and teaching God's Word. It is also a question of who is preaching and the content of what is being preached and taught."[134] In his recommendation to preach biblical content, Edre concludes,

> The preaching and the teaching of the gospel should be carried out in the power of the Holy Spirit. More attention needs to be given to aspects of the proclamation of the Gospel that are overlooked or ignored. These are: God's sovereign rule, his holy character and just wrath against sin; man's rebellion against God

---

129. Edre, "Christian Nominalism."
130. Edre, 227.
131. Edre, 227. Mandryk also argues that many believers do not have a sound understanding of "repentance and faith in Christ nor of salvation by grace not works" and that one of the "major causes of Christian nominalism . . . is an inadequate preaching of the gospel in many church denominations." See Mandryk, *Operation World*, 271; cf. Gibbs, "Introduction," 17.
132. Edre, "Christian Nominalism," 180.
133. Edre, 189.
134. Edre, 205.

and its consequences; the necessity of repentance from sin and faith in Jesus for salvation; holiness of life as the evidence of being a true Christian.[135]

Edre's primary research goal was to find out if the Bunia churches were aware of Christian nominalism in their church membership. One of the findings in his research was about whether the relationship between preaching and spirituality leads towards growth or nominalism. This was a new direction for research work. His discovery and recommendation strengthen the need to explore in-depth, in what way and to what extent, *not* preaching the "biblical gospel clearly" leads to nominalism.[136] Edre also confirmed the need to examine the content of preaching in relation to the members' spiritual health. Although Edre's research was done among Christians in the Democratic Republic of Congo, his research is relevant for the global church. In this research, I will include and explore Edre's findings and recommendations in relation to the Baptist churches in Imphal.

2.3 Nominalism

2.3.1 Lausanne Movement Discussions

This section will survey the problem of Christian nominalism and discuss the definitions, characteristics, and possible reasons for its incubation. Many church bodies have contributed to the discussion on nominalism but one of the major contributors is the evangelical Lausanne Movement.[137]

2.3.1.1 Lausanne Definition on Nominalism

The issue of nominalism is not a stranger in the history of the church nor is the study of it a recent development. Its existence and instances have been mentioned in various parts of the world and by many church denominations.[138]

---

135. Edre, 229.
136. Edre, 227.
137. As we will see below, the WCC through its member CBCNEI also states that among others, it faces the challenge of Christian nominalism in its churches, without elaborating on it. "There's Need," *World Council of Churches*; cf. Rongpi, "Challenge of Nominalism," 94–96. Baptist churches in Imphal city are under MBC which is affiliated to CBCNEI.
138. See Qualben, *History of the Christian Church*, 131, 329; Torrey, *General History*, 223–26; Stokes, *History of the Church*, 349; Browne, *Julian's Reply*, 20–21; Milner, *History of the Church*, 243.

In recent times, a working group of the 1980 Lausanne Congress in Thailand investigated and defined nominalism among Protestant Christians in the following way:

> A nominal Protestant Christian is one who, within the Protestant tradition, would call himself a Christian, or be so regarded by others, but who has no authentic commitment to Christ based on personal faith. Such commitment involves a transforming personal relationship with Christ, characterised by such qualities as love, joy, peace, a desire to study the Bible, prayer, fellowship with other Christians, a determination to witness faithfully, a deep concern for God's will to be done on earth, and a living hope of heaven to come.[139]

Elaborating further that a nominal Christian is a Christian "in name only," Eddie Gibbs, one of the experts on this subject in the Lausanne Movement, in his 1998 paper during the Lausanne consultation in England states,

> the term "nominal Christian" refers to those who are non-practicing members of Christian churches. Some may have originally been practicing but then became inactive, whereas others have simply been baptized in infancy as a "rite of passage," with their only subsequent contact being their wedding and funeral. A further category relates to those people who insist on calling themselves Christian but who do not identify with any local congregation or denomination. These persons are referred to by Peter Brierley as "Notional"[140] Christians.[141]

---

139. "Christian Witness to Nominal Christians among Protestant Christians," 5. Quoted by Gibbs, *In Name Only*, 21.

140. Peter Brierley breaks down the traditional understanding of "nominal" Christians into two categories: nominal and notional. Narrowly defined, while "nominal Christians" are "those who are members of a church but who do not regularly attend," "notional Christians" are "those who are neither members nor regular attenders of a church but who would say they are Christians." See Brierley, "Numbering the Nominals," 73.

141. Gibbs, "Introduction," 10.

2.3.1.2 Twelve Varieties of Nominality

The Lausanne consultation in 1998 in England came out with twelve varieties of nominality and argued that "a person may be considered nominal for (one) or more than one of these reasons."[142]

They are:

- "Ethnic-religious identity," which means "those whose religious commitment is closely tied to ethnic or national identity."
- "Second generation" refers to "people who have distanced themselves from their parents' faith, or the faith of their parents' church."
- "Ritualistic" are those "worshippers whose outward acts of devotion are not accompanied by an inner reality of faith."
- "Syncretistic" are "those who retain some dimensions of Christianity but have embraced aspects of spirituality and moral values from other religions or worldviews."
- "Disillusioned" are "people for whom Christianity has not worked."
- "Burned-out" are "professional or lay people who have given all they could to the church to their own personal detriment and thus have either opted out or remained in as a duty."
- "Bifurcated" refers to "people who live dual, compartmentalised lives so that their faith is not integrated into everyday life."
- "Compromised" are "those with a primary commitment to a spiritual, intellectual, or organisational system of values which takes priority over their Christianity."
- "Disobedient" are "those who have left the church because they are not prepared to live up to the moral standards of their particular Christian tradition."
- "Secularised" encompasses "people who uphold Christian values and principles without embracing Christian beliefs."
- "Socially distanced" refers to "people who have never attended church regularly, but who want it to be there when they need it" and,

---

142. Wraight, "Varieties of Nominality," 5.

- "Alienated" are those "people who feel that they do not fit culturally or socially within the church."

2.3.1.3 The Nature of Nominalism

Gibbs warns that nominalism should not be considered as a static and "fixed state" without any room for movement, because it is a "complex condition which takes on many aspects."[143] Brierley substantiates this argument as he affirms, "what has become clearer in the last decade . . . is that nominalism is often less of a 'state' (that is, a position which a person permanently holds) than a time of transition (that is, a position which is undertaken for a period), sometimes over many years."[144] Therefore, as Gibbs points out, "it is a progressive, spiritually-degenerative condition" while in the situation of others "it is a fluctuating state in which they blow spiritually hot and cold."[145] Looking at the issue of nominalism this way, several questions arise: "Are nominal Christians in the process of becoming real or actual Christians, that is, are they moving towards something?"; "Are nominal Christians those who have left an intensity, an involvement, an interest, that is, are they moving away from something?"; and "Are nominal Christians those who have accepted an inadequate, or misrepresented form of belief and have no opportunity to move towards something, and are therefore truly static?"[146] These are helpful questions for this research work.

2.3.1.4 Lausanne Movement Consultation on Nominalism and Preaching

During the Lausanne consultation in 1998, Gibbs mentioned that many churches have become "an incubator of nominality"[147] because of several factors, including preaching. He observed, "The congregation has never had the gospel clearly presented in the power of the Holy Spirit"; "The authority of the Bible has been undermined"; and "The Word of God has been proclaimed in a cold, abrasive, and judgemental manner."[148] Gibbs rightly affirmed in

---
143. Gibbs, "Introduction," 10.
144. Brierley, *Leaders Briefings*, 1.
145. Gibbs, "Introduction," 10.
146. Brierley, *Leaders Briefings*, 2.
147. Gibbs, "Introduction," 17; Gibbs, *In Name Only*, 16.
148. Gibbs, "Introduction," 17.

his presentation at the same consultation, that his work on nominalism may become "a starter and stimulus to further research,"[149] concerning a relationship between preaching and spiritual life including nominalism, for the global church. It remains to be further explored if what he expressed is true in the other parts of the world, including the Baptist churches in Imphal.

2.3.2 World Council of Churches (WCC) and Council of Baptist Churches in North East India (CBCNEI)

The CBCNEI, a member of the WCC acknowledged that one of its churches' main challenges is the problem of nominalism. Solomon Rongpi,[150] its General Secretary, acknowledged this predicament to Robert Bartram in 2016.[151] Rongpi, speaking for all the CBCNEI fraternity, acknowledges that today, we follow in our churches the Assamese[152] maxim, *Nam hole Khristan, Kam hole Soitan*, which in English means "the name is Christian but the actions are Satan's!"[153] He points out that the lack of sound biblical teaching both at home and in the church has led to this nominal situation.[154] He grieves that many pastors have compromised the gospel and have become people pleasers, preaching only "what is pleasing to hear."[155] Such a pastor, he warns, "will produce more nominal members."[156] Rongpi's argument that ear-tickling preachers will only produce more nominal Christians aligns with the current discussion on the relationship between preaching and nominalism.

Rongpi must have come to this conclusion out of his ministerial experience with the churches he had previously worked with. However, Rongpi's argument does not seem to be based on any empirical data nor a church context, because exceptions could exist in such a large church council. This

---

149. Gibbs, 16; Similarly, Heather Wraight writes, "The debate about nominality has only just begun." See Wraight, "Foreword: The Consultation," 4.

150. Solomon Rongpi is the General Secretary (2015–2019) of the CBCNEI and its headquarters is in Guwahati Assam. It is the largest protestant group in India's North East.

151. Bartram, "There's Need for a United Voice."

152. *Assamese* is the language of the people of the state of Assam, where the headquarters of CBCNEI is located.

153. Rongpi, "Challenge of Nominalism," 94.

154. Rongpi, 94–96.

155. Rongpi, 96.

156. Rongpi, 97.

current work will therefore explore if what he has said resonates with the Baptist churches under MBC in Imphal.

2.4 Nominalism and Preaching

2.4.1 Regional Survey

In this section, we will conduct a regional survey of the issue of nominalism. Nominalism could thrive because of several factors, but whether preaching and nominalism are related or if their relationship has been explored is a different issue. This survey will help us understand if there is a gap in the study of nominalism and preaching, and if research on their relationship could be a significant work.

2.4.1.1 South Asia and India

On nominalism in South Asia, particularly in India, Saphir P. Athyal claims, "By the time the second or third generation of believers comes along, Christian faith may appear to be little more than a set of rituals, prayers, and traditions, that is, a form of religion without any personal deep convictions or inner power." He argues, "this condition also seems to breed internal disunity and quarrels." Athyal makes the above reflection in connection with Christian nominalism vis-à-vis the poor returns of missions.[157] It is recorded that right from the time of the missionaries in India, the existence of nominalism among Indian Christians had been a problem.[158] Jonathan Lewis laments that although the Indian churches have 25 million (2.5 crores) Christians, evangelistic work among the non-Christians by Indian Christians is not vibrant because,

> two-thirds of the Christians in India need themselves to be evangelised ... The real shocker is that according to one study, 98 percent of the evangelism in India is devoted to rewinning nominal Christians rather than to penetrating the frontiers that effectively wall off 500 million (50 crores) people.[159]

---

157. Athyal, "Southern Asia," 59–61.
158. "Great Britain: Parliament House of Commons," 19–20; Smith, *Missionary Appeal*, 44; "A Short View," 325.
159. Lewis, *World Mission*, 27.

Although the discussions made by Athyal and Lewis are in the context of missions, these discussions perhaps reflect the spiritual situation of the churches in India. It is therefore only appropriate to explore the factors that have crippled the spiritual growth and renewal of the Christian churches. This problem could be explored from various angles, but this current research will examine nominalism in the context of preaching in the Baptist churches of Imphal city. Below, we will set the research in the wider context of nominalism in India's North East.

2.4.1.2 *India's North East: Mizoram Churches*

P. C. Lawmkunga[160] reveals that because of the missionaries' arrival in 1894,[161] and the subsequent Christianisation in Mizoram, the once "irreclaimable savages"[162] transformed into "staunch believers who abided by the teachings in the Bible in its forms and substance."[163] However, Lawmkunga laments that today, many Mizo Christians have become seekers of "worldly pleasures" and "material prosperity," subsequently, their "spiritual life . . . suffered a serious setback."[164] Although it is true that "while there are many true Christians among Mizos," many have chosen to become "nominal Christians giving no serious thought to God's words."[165] Fanai Hrangkhuma agrees that many Mizos in Mizoram are "nominally Christians," affiliated to either one of the Christian denominations.[166] Looking then at the contemporary scene as captured by Lawmkunga, what is intriguing lies in the irony of his comment that "today's Mizo Christian can preach louder . . . and pray more passionately, yet their adherence to God's commandments does not show a corresponding

---

160. P. C. Lawmkunga is a retired Indian Administrative Service (IAS) officer from Mizoram. See "PC Lawmkunga to Relieve." The reason his voice is chosen is because he is neither a clergy nor a theological scholar, and so he can give an assessment of the church and her spirituality from a very different perspective.

161. The first two missionaries were H. Lorrain and F. W. Savidge from the Arthington Mission. Nunthara, *Mizoram*, 103.

162. Lawmkunga, *Welcome to Mizoram*, 25.

163. Lawmkunga, 32.

164. Lawmkunga, 33.

165. Lawmkunga, 32. See also Zawngia, "Christianity in Mizoram," 47. For a historical discussion on Mizo nominalism, see Lalsawma, "Shaking of Foundations," 13–17; Hminga, "Life and Witness," 276–77; Hrangkhuma, "Mizoram Transformational Change," 318–19.

166. Hrangkhuma, "Mizo Spirituality," 403.

growth."¹⁶⁷ Hrangkhuma too points out the failure of "practical spirituality," among the Mizos "in families, in offices, in business, in politics, and in public life in general."¹⁶⁸ What is interesting here is Lawmkunga's admission that the decadence of Mizo spirituality is happening in the context of a preaching ministry that is thriving. This provokes one to think about the kinds of preaching happening in the pulpits of the Mizo churches and correspondingly in the other North Eastern churches.

2.4.1.3 India's North East: Arunachal Pradesh Baptist Churches and Meghalaya Churches

Molem Ronrang, writing for the Tangsa Baptist churches in the state of Arunachal Pradesh reveals, "today many Christians are stagnant" and many pastors "can neither preach an inspirational sermon . . . Even though many people attend church, they do not get any message from the pulpit" and "so they are spiritually weak and dry in the Word of God."¹⁶⁹ Although Ronrang made these statements about the spiritual situation of a single tribe among many in the state in 1997, a later discussion in 2010 made by Jason Mandryk in "Operation World" points out that many other tribes also consider nominalism as "an issue in many churches."¹⁷⁰

Jason Mandryk notes that Meghalaya is a state dominated by Christians right from "the 19th and early 20th centuries." Apart from citing traditionalism as a problem, Mandryk points out that "the younger generation are drifting away from the Church, nominalism is a concern." What is interesting in his evaluation is that this problem of nominalism is thriving at a time when "the churches suffer from lack of pastoral care and lack of strong biblical teaching, especially in rural areas, since most pastors are based in cities."¹⁷¹

The discussions on the churches in Arunachal Pradesh and Meghalaya point to a relationship between the presence or absence of good preaching and spiritual vitality or nominalism.

---

167. Lawmkunga, *Welcome to Mizoram*, 32.
168. Hrangkhuma, "Mizo Spirituality," 408.
169. See Ronrang, *Emergence and Growth*, 118.
170. Mandryk, *Operation World*, 419.
171. Mandryk, 434.

2.4.1.4 India's North East: Nagaland Baptist Churches

A discussion on Naga Christianity,[172] spirituality, and preaching had begun as early as the 1970s. I. Ben Wati[173] remarked that sermons were broadcast from the *All India Radio* accompanied by tribal songs to strengthen the Christians and also to win over the animists.[174] In the 1980s, a wave of holy discontent was evident in the writings of many Naga church leaders including V. K. Nuh.[175] Nuh poignantly paints the spiritual depravity of Nagaland with grief:

> Our streets are filled with violence. Our homes are filled with crime. Our villages are filled with confusion. Our systems are filled with corruption. Our worship places are filled with apostasy and indifferences. Alcoholics and drug addictions are rampant; they kill not only the body but the soul too. Our society has become immoral.[176]

Nuh further laments,

> We have three thousand strong Naga churches. Today the Naga population is about three million people, out of which 90% of them are Christians. There will [be] no less than ten thousand Naga theological graduates. But despite of all these claims [we] have failed to give any meaningful impact on the Naga society. All the beautiful church buildings on the hill tops are just the outward beauty. The invisible church have [sic] become almost non-existence [sic].[177]

---

172. "Christianity" in this section refers to the Baptist denomination to which most of the scholars I am referring to belong.

173. Lovingly known as Uncle Ben, Rev. Dr. I. Ben Wati was a renowned church leader and President of the International Council of the World Evangelical Fellowship (as it then was known) in 1968–1974. "WEA Pays Tribute." He belonged to the Ao Naga tribe. "A Tribute to Dr. I. Ben Wati."

174. Wati, "Music of Ten Thousand Hills," 35.

175. V. K. Nuh is a respected senior church leader of the Naga churches. His voice is esteemed even by the political leaders of the society.

176. Nuh, *Revive Us Again*, 42; Dozo, "Unique Role," 105; Hattaway, *From Head-Hunters*, 110–12. *Contra*, Roger E. Hedlund also states that "Christianity is vigorous and growing in Nagaland"; Hedlund, *World Christianity*, 155. Although it is true that statistics evidence the growth of Christian population in numbers, Nuh and the others are here talking of deeper Christian commitment and spiritual vibrancy.

177. Nuh, "Theological Reflection," 118; see also Sema, unpublished report quoted by Paul Hattaway in *From Head-Hunters*, 109.

Nuh also warns that a church that has a well streamlined administrative system may not have a systematic biblical doctrine "preached or taught" from the pulpits of the church.[178] Nuh rues the spiritually sick Naga society and church[179] and asks, "Why have the preachings in the pulpit become so irrelevant? Why have churches become so powerless and lost their credibility?"[180] On preaching, he elaborates, "the watch dog, the prophets are sleeping silent [sic] in the lap of the devil"[181] and "our pulpit has no prophetic message for sinners. This is the reason why Naga people are going through such catastrophe and crisis one after another."[182]

Several decades after Nuh's evaluation, a breakthrough in Naga spirituality remains elusive.[183] In a panel discussion on "Nominalism and Christianity," Kevi Meru, a respected Christian leader from Nagaland, concedes that the absence of good preaching might have bored people to spiritual stagnation, even nominalism, but envisions that good preaching can transform the church.[184]

In his MTh dissertation, Imsungnungsang Pongen came up with ten common factors[185] that opened the door for nominalism to set in among the Ao tribe in Nagaland. One very important dimension was the "lack of sound biblical teaching" in the church. He pointed out that many believers do not even know "the meaning of 'Christian,' 'Bible' and 'Church,'"[186] not to mention other basic doctrines of Scripture. Another important factor is the "over depend(ence) on 'prayer-warriors' to run their lives."[187]

---

178. Nuh, "Theological Reflection," 120.
179. Nuh, *Struggle for Identity*, 71.
180. Nuh, 72.
181. Nuh, "Theological Reflection," 129.
182. Nuh, 128.
183. See Crossroads International, "Indigenous Missions"; Richter, "Teaching Former Head-Hunters"; Mandryk, *Operation World*, 436; see also Singh, "Soul Hunters."
184. Kevi Meru does not explain what is "good preaching." North East Cornerstone TV, "Nominalism in Christianity."
185. They are: "Lack of personal commitment"; "Lack of sound biblical teaching"; "Lack of disciple-making"; "Over-familiarity with Christian activities"; "Depend(ence) on 'prayer-warriors' to run their lives"; "Compromise of values and ethics"; "Questionable lifestyles of church leaders"; "Lack of proper guidance during childhood"; "Emphasis on religiosity rather than spirituality," and "No proper teaching on water baptism"; See Pongen, "Nominalism among Christians," 36–41.
186. Pongen, 38.
187. Pongen, 39. This phenomenon will be elaborated in the subsequent section.

The spiritually impoverished situation faced by the church is real. However, this does not mean a complete absence of uncorrupted gospel truth in the pulpits and lives of the Naga churches. An analysis of the above discussion points in the direction that better preaching, both in its theological content and its form, may reverse the downward spiral of the church's fate. This discussion therefore legitimises the need for research to examine the relationship between preaching and the believers' spirituality.

2.4.1.5 India's North East: MBC

Jason Mandryk confirms that "nominalism is widespread" in Manipur also.[188] Ringphami Kengoo in his research, "Effective Strategies for Discipling the Nominal Baptist Youth of the Manipur Baptist Convention," concedes that "the issue of nominalism is prevalent in the Baptist Churches of Manipur as well as the whole North Eastern states in India."[189] He states the following as factors that contribute to nominalism:[190] mass conversion; liberal theology in the church; church management; lack of biblical discipleship; lack of leadership; lack of spiritual programmes;[191] insurgency problems; economic instability; lack of educational prospects; low moral standard;[192] and cultural influence. Due to the constraint of space, only a few of them will be discussed here.

First, Kengoo talks about the phenomenon of "mass conversion." He argues that in the face of persecution and social excommunication, mass conversion is a great option to avoid personal conflict; however, it is not without its disadvantages. In the case of individual conversion, a person often knows the "what" and "why" of the new faith one is embracing,[193] while in the case of mass conversion, it is often following the decision of the village chief or the head of the clan or family or joining with the majority in the "wave

---

188. Mandryk, *Operation World*, 433; cf. page 1.
189. Kengoo, "Effective Strategies," 3, 6.
190. As the focus of his thesis is among the youth, these reasons are not exclusive for the situation of nominalism among the other age groups or members of the church.
191. Under this, Kengoo lists the following activities: triennial conference; evangelistic youth camp; discipleship youth camp; Bible study; small group; praise and worship, mission trips; and counseling centre. See Kengoo, 22–30.
192. Under this category, Kengoo lists the following: drug abuse; premarital sex; and co-habitation. See Kengoo, 34–38.
193. Kengoo, 12–13.

of the gospel,"¹⁹⁴ and rarely because of a personal conviction of the gospel. Consequently, Kengoo concludes that if good nurturing does not follow conversion then nominalism will set in, within the church.¹⁹⁵ Mathai believes that in the context of mass conversion many Christians fail to understand the "cardinal Christian doctrine from the Word of God,"¹⁹⁶ and therefore, potentially, the next generation of Christians will also be weak in their knowledge of Christian doctrine. This reality is acknowledged by Kengoo who affirmed that "the first generation of mass converted Christians (in Manipur) were illiterate and so most of the evangelists, lay pastors and church leaders had no theological background."¹⁹⁷ Amidst all this, it must be clarified that "the missionary, [sic] with their best effort, trained as many converts to carry on the good news to various hills in Manipur." However, as the wave of mass conversion was colossal in its breadth, it was impossible to either authenticate true conversion or teach the gospel in depth.¹⁹⁸

After more than a hundred years, the situation should have been reversed with many theological graduates and pastors taking care of the churches in Manipur today.¹⁹⁹ But it is tragic to see that authentic Christian commitment based on the word of God seems to still be lacking today. Perhaps the absence of proper preaching and teaching of basic Christian doctrines from the pulpits during the mass conversion movement has had a far more consequential results than we imagine. Indeed, the shaky spiritual foundation during the mass conversion in Manipur cannot withstand the test of time and the onslaught of unspiritual forces. Biological Christianity will beget nominalism.²⁰⁰ We can agree with Donald G. Bloesch that, "the reason why many of the great Christian doctrines are not understood by the lay people of the

---

194. Kengoo, 15.

195. Kengoo, 12; See also Mathai, "Would God Transform," 338; McGavran, *Understanding Church Growth*, 231.

196. Mathai, "Would God Transform," 339.

197. Kengoo, "Effective Strategies," 15–16.

198. Kengoo, 15.

199. See some of the church leaders of MBC who have been theologically trained in Appendix 4.

200. This is the conviction Taimaya Ragui shares (Research Scholar at SAIACS, Bangalore); discussion with the researcher, 17 January 2018. Ragui comes from Ukhrul, the birthplace of Manipur Baptist Christianity; his voice adds weight to the discussion because of his wide interaction with elderly people (first- and second-generation Christians) in Ukhrul.

church is that doctrinal matters are often avoided in sermons. . . . Doctrine safeguards the message of faith and also serves to communicate it."[201] Herein then lies a close relationship between Christian nominalism and the absence of good biblical, gospel-centred preaching, which thereby provides a further compelling reason for this research. This research will also explore whether the poor preaching (that is not aimed at eliciting authentic personal commitment) that exists in Manipur today is also an outcome of nominalism, that is, whether nominalism is a source as well as an effect of poor preaching.

Second, he argues, "as most theologians were exposed to liberal theology, their shallow teaching could not reach the hearts of the people." Further, he laments at the miserable lifestyle and behaviour showcased by "some of the liberal Christian leaders in Manipur."[202] Liberal preaching then, may have incubated nominalism in Manipur, and this enhances the need for this research.

The other crucial issue in the context of Manipur is to discuss Christianity in the context of the phenomenon of "prayer-warrior."[203] Pongen, in his research work in Nagaland, also pointed out this factor.[204] One can argue that the result of a past Christianity poorly based on the word of God, for example in or through the mass conversion movement, is being harvested today in the over-dependence on prayer warriors[205] to orchestrate believers' lives.[206] Pongen considers this culture of Christians running "to these well-paid 'seer' and prayer centers for quick answers" during "sickness, decision making, (and for) general guidance" as an aspect of nominalism.[207] He laments that Christians are almost committing idolatry because "they consider these

---

201. Bloesch, *Reform of the Church*, 21.

202. Kengoo, *Effective Strategies*, 17; Morris, *High Impact Church*, 44–45; Seamands, *Tell It Well*, 50; Nuh, "Theological Reflection," 120–22. *Contra*, one can ask, "Are evangelical leaders free from this accusation?" Perhaps the answer is "no."

203. This will be substantiated in the descriptive chapter.

204. Pongen, "Nominalism," 39.

205. The indispensability and inseparability of prayer in a believer's life goes without saying. However, if the emphasis on prayer leads to the undermining of the authority of God's word in a believer's life, we are faced with a serious problem of priorities, for how can one even pray correctly without knowing the truth of God's word?

206. This trend of dependence was already warned against by Dr. E. W. Clark, the first missionary to Nagaland: "Christianity was going to the *Arasentzur* (soothsayer). Whenever there was sickness, a soothsayer was employed to get a revelation from a deity. For instance, in Molung village, Subonglemba was excommunicated from active church membership for a month because of employing a soothsayer for a sick child"; See Clark, *Naga Mission*, 5.

207. Pongen, "Nominalism," 39.

prayer warriors as god for their family."²⁰⁸ The situation is similar with the Christians in Manipur too. If one observes carefully, one can see a cyclical pattern: a poor foundation of the word of God leading to nominalism, and nominalism leading to dependence on the prayer warriors, which is again a non-dependence on the word of God. One only wonders if poor preaching in the churches has failed to teach congregations how to seek God's guidance in practical matters, which has led them to visit prayer-warriors, a practice that resembles old pagan shamanism and soothsayers. Thus, the great need for the examination of preaching in the Baptist churches, especially in Imphal city.

We have established there is evidence, in the view of many, that Christianity in North East India and in Imphal, especially among the members of the Baptist churches, is greatly affected by nominalism. Initial indications suggest that field research should seek to explore whether preaching is aimed at authentic personal commitment within a healthy view of tribal corporate solidarity, whether preaching is liberal in its approach to Scripture's authority and Christ's saving uniqueness, and whether preaching addresses practical issues of discipleship such as prayer and guidance.

2.5 Working Definition of Nominalism

It is easier to describe what nominalism looks like than to define what it is; however, a working definition will be proposed for the purpose of this research. To arrive at that, we will begin by making a critical evaluation of the definitions and criteria given by the various Lausanne Congresses mentioned above, along with the discussions emerging from India's North East.

First, the content of the definition of nominalism during the 1980 Lausanne Congress in Thailand can be endorsed[209] for this research, with some additional nuancing, as this definition is scriptural, transcending any cultural particularities. Second, the discussion of Christians "in name only" by Gibbs during the Lausanne consultation in 1998 needs some contextual re-construction. Nominal Christians in the Baptist churches of Imphal comprise two groups – those who are Christians because they are born to Christian parents, or as a result of mass conversion. Going by this criterion,

---
208. Pongen, 39.
209. Cf. 2.3.1.1.

most so-called Christians will fall into the nominal Christian category. The other category is those who have accepted Jesus Christ as their Saviour and Lord at one point of time but have failed to grow towards maturity. Third, the twelve varieties of nominality that came out of the 1998 Lausanne consultation need to be contextually scrutinised to identify their relevance and applicability to the Baptist churches of Imphal city. Out of twelve varieties, the following eight varieties are relevant to the churches under discussion: second generation; ritualistic; syncretistic; disillusioned; burned-out; bifurcated; disobedient and socially distanced.[210] Fourth, it is seen that from the literature of India's North East, the following factors influence Christian nominalism in the Baptist churches of Manipur: mass conversion, liberal theology, and the prayer warrior phenomenon.

Here then is the working definition of nominalism which will be employed in this research:

> A nominal Christian is one who is a Christian in name only and lacks the corresponding reality of a personal conviction associated with authentic Christian experience. It may either be defined as one whose relationship with God is characterised by lethargy after a genuine personal encounter and walk with God or a false optimism of salvation because of one's Christian heritage and ritualism.

Elaborating on this, nominalism has two sides as a coin does. First, it is a condition of spiritual lethargy in a person's relationship with Jesus Christ, whom the believer at one point in time acknowledged and accepted as his or her personal Lord and Saviour and has also publicly testified to this inward change with the rite of water baptism and public confession of faith. This spiritual lethargy is evident in the lack of the fruit of the Spirit, the diminishing passion and enthusiasm for spiritual disciplines (worship, prayer, fellowship, growing in the knowledge of the Scripture, and fasting),[211] indifference to evangelism, lack of commitment to pursue God's will in all matters of

---

210. Although the other four varieties (ethnic-religious identity, compromised, secularised, and alienated) cannot be written off, these eight varieties are more directly related to the context under examination.

211. Due to medical reasons some people may not be able to fast and keep themselves physically hungry, but there can be other forms of fasting, for example fasting from electronic gadgets or other routine activites to focus on God and be in a spirit of prayer.

life, carelessness in personal character, an absence of the fear of hell, and no anticipation for heaven and the personal return of Jesus Christ.[212] Second, it is also the state of false optimism of salvation built upon a wrong perception that being a Christian and the attainment of salvation is a matter of simply belonging to a Christian family and heritage,[213] by following routine rituals of prayer, church attendance, tithing, taking water baptism for church membership and also to get a church marriage or be a member of the choir, without an inner conviction and a personal relationship with Jesus Christ.[214]

Keeping in focus Lausanne's "varieties of nominality" and the context of the Baptist churches in Imphal as described in the literature, I will elaborate on how the first and second categories of nominal Christians may have been influenced by the following one or more factors towards nominalism.

a. For a few of them, the authority of the Scripture is not final and binding, because, for example, they will not hesitate to be syncretistic in subscribing to the animistic worldview in matters of agriculture[215] and healing from sickness.[216]

b. For others, they will not hesitate to live a bifurcated life, to become like one of the counterparts in various life situations,[217] without any distinctiveness as salt and light in society. They simply become chameleonic in their expression of faith.

c. For some, the consequence of mass conversion in the family decades ago might still be affecting their unholistic understanding of Christian faith.

d. For others, the theology and Christian doctrinal teaching from the pulpits of proponents of liberal theology may have stunted their spiritual growth.

---

212. The following varieties would come under the first side of the coin: syncretistic, disillusioned, burned-out, bifurcated, disobedient, and socially distanced.

213. "Second generation" Christians would be in this category.

214. "Ritualistic" Christians would fall into this category.

215. "Major decisions pertaining to the activities of the villages are carried out under the auspices of the animistic authority" . . . for example, "choosing the official day for 'seed sowing.'" Raih, "Critical Reading," 1.

216. There are instances where many physically sick Christians do not hesitate to go to traditional animistic healers, who are called *maibas* and *maibis* (sorcerer or shaman).

217. For example, their attitude towards corruption, bribery, nepotism, purchase of government jobs, etc.

e. Still for some others, the phenomenon of "the prayer warrior" could have sabotaged their personal devotion, Christian discipline, and individual responsibility in seeking the face of God. Dependence on the prayer warriors tends to encourage Christians to outsource their prayer requests, discourage them from seeking God's guidance in practical matters of life, and weaken their desire to grow intimate with God out of love. Instead, prayer warriors in some instances issue threats and warnings so that the believers become easy prey to blackmailing.[218]

Furthermore, in the process of the research, if the researcher discovers new trends of nominalism emerging from the context-specific political, social, economic, and spiritual dimensions of the churches under investigation, which are relevant to the present study, they will be identified, analysed, and the working definition will be revisited.

---

218. There are instances when the prayer warriors will warn that if a particular family does not fast and pray for twenty or forty days, tragedy will happen to them (the researcher speaks from personal experience).

CHAPTER 3

Christianity in Manipur: Arrival, Growth, and the Early Preaching Movement

3.1 A General Background of Manipur and Imphal City

Manipur, elegantly described as the "Jewel of India,"[1] is one of twenty-nine states[2] in India's North East,[3] bordering with Myanmar in the east, Nagaland in the north, Mizoram in the south, and Assam in the west.[4] It has sixteen districts[5] covering around "22,327 sq. km., which constitutes only 0.7% of the total land surface of India" and "a population of 28,55,794" people according to the 2011 Census.[6] The state is home to thirty-four tribes[7] who mostly

---

1. A title given by India's first Prime Minister, Jawaharlal Nehru; Kumar, *People of India*, 1.
2. India also has nine union territories; "9 Beautiful Union Territories of India."
3. Political maps of India are included in appendixes 5 and 6.
4. Prasain and Singh, *Industrial Sickness*, 28.
5. They are: Bishnupur, Chandel, Churachandpur, Imphal-East, Imphal-West, Senapati, Tamenglong, Thoubal, Ukhrul, Kangpokpi, Tengnoupal, Pherzawl, Noney, Kamjong, Jiribam and Kakching; "Districts in Manipur."
6. Singh, "Impact of NRC," 22. For political maps of Manipur and Imphal, see appendixes 7 and 8 respectively.
7. They are: "Aimol, Anal, Angami, Chiru, Chothe, Gangte, Hmar, 'Kabui, Inpui, Rongmei,' 'Kacha Naga, Liangmai, Zeme,' 'Koirao, Thangal,' Koireng, Kom, Lamkang, Mao, Maram, Maring, Any Mizo, Monsang, Moyon, Paite, Purum, Ralte, Sema, Simte, Suhte, Tangkhul,

occupy the hill regions,[8] and the Meitei,[9] Meitei Pangals, and other groups who are settled in the valley.[10] Today, most of the tribal groups, also known as "hills-men," have their settlements in several pockets of the valley.[11] Imphal is the capital city of the state.[12] It is located "790 metres above sea level"[13] and its administrative jurisdiction comes under the districts of Imphal East and Imphal West. It has a population of around two hundred and fifty thousand people.[14] The city is centrally located[15] and one must pass through it to go to almost all the other districts in the state.

3.2 Religious Background

Before the arrival of Christianity, the people followed either the tribal or the Meitei religious practices. In the Meitei religion, people worshipped *Lamlai*, the aquatic deity (especially of rain) and *Umanglai*, the benevolent household god. The Meiteis worshipped ancestor spirits. They also recognised the spirits of various geographical spaces, of mountains, valleys, or bodies of water. Further, they recognised the creator god as the chief god and this deity is associated with "the Snake ancestor of the royal family."[16]

On the other hand, the tribal religious belief was more animistic, having no "fixed place of worship and never worship idols."[17] The tribal sacrifices were randomly performed in any convenient natural surrounding: house, road, under a tree, on a rock, river side, paddy field, etc., where spirits were expected to visit.[18] Although the names that the tribal people used to address

---

Thadou, Vaiphei, Zou, Poumai, Tarao, Kharam, Any Kuki Tribe and Mate"; see, "Tribes of Manipur."

8. "Tribes of Manipur."
9. McDuie-Ra, "Borders, Territory, and Ethnicity," 98.
10. Hatzaw, *Christianity in Manipur*, 4.
11. Singh, *Elections*, 4.
12. Imphal simply means "a large collection of houses"; Brown, *Statistics*, 2.
13. Sen, *Tribes and Castes*, 37.
14. Lisam, *Encyclopedia of Manipur*, 577.
15. Kosygin, *Wetlands of North East India*, 169.
16. Hatzaw, *Christianity in Manipur*, 10.
17. Hatzaw, 11.
18. Hatzaw, 11; cf. Akhui, *Short Account*, 40.

the supreme-being differed, they were united in their belief that it is he who created and sustained them.[19]

At the beginning of the eighteenth century, during the reign of "Maharaja Gharib Niwaz, the Vaishnava missionary, Shantidas Atnikary (Goswami) came to Manipur and converted the king to Hinduism."[20] The king then patronised Hinduism and declared it as the state religion, and offenders were persecuted.[21] However, the earlier indigenous religion, defended by Khongnangthaba along with his supporters, still exists today. It is generally accepted that the existence of the "temples of Thangjing at Moirang and Sanamahi at Imphal" today indicates the co-existence of the two strands of Meitei religious practices.[22]

3.3 Arrival of Christianity in Manipur

Christianity began to make inroads after William Pettigrew, a young and dynamic British national, arrived in Imphal on 6 February 1894[23] to begin his "school" ministry. He succeeded in "impressing the Acting Political Agent,"[24] A. Porteous, in Manipur[25] while his superior the Political Agent, Major Maxwell, was on a furlough.[26] As the door opened, Pettigrew envisioned that God's call for his life was "to preach the Gospel" to the Meiteis;[27] however, the "Hinduised Meiteis" felt that it was a conspiracy to impose the "government's religion."[28] When Major Maxwell returned, although he was greatly impressed with Pettigrew's work in the valley, to avoid antagonising

---

19. Hatzaw, 11.
20. Hatzaw, 10.
21. Roy, *History of Manipur*, 38; Foreign Department, *Secret Proceedings*.
22. Hatzaw, *Christianity in Manipur*, 39.
23. T. Luikham puts the date as 6 January of the same year; Luikham, *Short History*, 10.
24. Downs, *Mighty Works*, 75–76; Zeliang, *History of Manipur*, 21. Another missionary, Watkin Roberts from Wales, arrived at Senvon/Senvawn, in the Southern part of Manipur's Churachandpur district in 1910. Dena, *Christian Mission and Colonialism*, 49. Christian mission and preaching movements under other denominations or churches will not be within the purview of this research work, as the thesis title delimits its scope.
25. Dena, 32–33.
26. Hatzaw, *Christianity in Manipur*, 50; see also Dena, *Christian Mission and Colonialism*, 33.
27. Dena, 33.
28. Foreign Department, *Secret Proceedings*; Dena, *Christian Mission and Colonialism*, 33.

the goodwill of the "orthodox Hindu Manipuris," Pettigrew was asked to cease his missionary work in Imphal as "some objections had been raised concerning his preaching."[29] Probably the conversion of a Meitei man, Porom Singh,[30] and a woman named Kaboklei from the royal family caused a furore.[31] The contents of what he preached in Imphal are not known, but his preaching must have challenged the status quo of the religious doctrines of the Hindu Manipuris. Here is how he expressed the order from the government to leave Imphal valley for the hills:

> To accept one of the conditions was the ultimatum sent to us from Shillong a year and a half later. Say, "Yes" to proposal of leaving the valley alone and establishing mission headquarters among the headhunting Naga tribe called the Tangkhul Naga . . . say "No" and leave the State for good.[32]

Thus, Pettigrew shifted his base and began his missionary work among the hill tribesmen of Manipur. Although he surveyed and initially considered Senvon village (now in Churachandpur district) and Mao gate area (now in Senapati district) for his ministry base, he finally decided upon Ukhrul as his official ministry base in Manipur.[33] We will discuss William Pettigrew's mission agency, missionary work, and preaching in a later section, but here, we will give a brief overview of the Christian missionary and preaching work in India's North East to set a broader context.

3.4. The Early Preaching Movements in North East India (CBCNEI)

Years before Pettigrew came to Manipur, the American Baptist Mission (ABM) had begun their work in Assam. Apart from the missionaries of ABM, who first preached and brought the gospel to India's North East, it is recorded that some of the earliest indigenous preachers were Omed and Ramkhe, the first converts from the Garo Hills, the fruit of the Assam mission under Miles

---

29. Downs, *Mighty Works*, 76; Dena, *Christian Mission and Colonialism*, 33.
30. Parratt, *Wounded Land*, 62.
31. Parratt, 72; Vaiphei, *Advent of Christian Mission*, 69.
32. Quoted in Solo, "Captain the Rev. William Pettigrew," 64.
33. Hatzaw, *Christianity in Manipur*, 50–51.

Bronson.³⁴ Although "there was little to celebrate" during the 1861 Silver Jubilee commemoration of the missionaries' activities in India's North East, by the time of the Golden Jubilee in 1886, the work had progressed much, especially in the "Garo Hills area and Upper Assam."³⁵ Downs states that perhaps "the Nagas had not been quick to respond to Christian teaching" because "there were no dedicated, able members of their own tribes comparable to Omed and Ramkhe to preach among them." As such, apart from the missionaries, the pioneering preachers among the Nagas "were outsiders, unfamiliar with their language and thought"³⁶ and "systematic work" began only in the 1870s.³⁷ By 1871, with the encouragement of E. W. Clark, the first Assamese preacher to visit a Naga village (Haimong) was Godhula Babu, also known as Rufus Brown.³⁸ For the "next three years Godhula lived" in the village and "cared for the small congregation and preached in nearby villages."³⁹

Around that time, the mission work among the Angami Nagas began with C. D. King and his wife, starting at Kohima in 1878. King and his wife opened a school to educate the people, and Henry Goldsmith, "a consecrated young missionary" from Sibsagar in Assam, joined the ministry. They served together till 1886.⁴⁰ The ministry did not bear much fruit, if judged from external results. The mission work there was not easy, perhaps "no tribe or community in North East India was more resistant to the preaching of the gospel."⁴¹ ABM's work in India's North East later came to be known as the Assam Baptist Convention (ABC) and later as the Council of Baptist Churches in North East India (CBCNEI). It was after 1886 that the Christian preaching movement turned towards Manipur.⁴²

---

34. Downs, *Mighty Works*, 50–52, 62.
35. Downs, 55.
36. Downs, 62.
37. Downs, 63.
38. Downs, 64–65.
39. Downs, 65.
40. Downs, 68.
41. Downs, 68–69.
42. Downs, 72.

3.5 Christian Mission and Preaching in Manipur through the American Mission Society (AMS)

3.5.1 William Pettigrew's Mission Work and the Formation of Manipur Baptist Convention (MBC)

Pettigrew was sent to India by "a private society, the Arthington Aboriginese Mission" (AAM) in 1890.[43] Although he was originally a member of the Church of England, it is reported that due to his disagreement with the practice of infant baptism,[44] he approached the Baptist Missionary Society (BMS) missionary R. Wright Hay and received believer's baptism in India. Later when AAM decided to abandon the Manipur mission field, "the Assam Mission records . . . indicate that the Missionary Union 'took over' the Manipur field from the Arthington Mission – as if by mutual agreement – on 1 February, 1896,"[45] and Pettigrew was ordained and commissioned as a missionary of ABM to Ukhrul, Manipur, from Sibsagar Church, Assam.[46]

As discussed above, upon disapproval of Pettigrew's preaching work in the valley of Manipur, Major Maxwell encouraged him to locate his ministry to the hills, and Pettigrew arrived in Ukhrul with his wife in 1896.

Pettigrew wrote:

> The Manipuri Hindus of the valley was [sic] the first missionary objective, but objection being raised by the British authorities on account of their administering the State at that time on behalf of the young Rajah, then a minor, led the way in the providence of God for the opening of mission work among these mountains surrounding the valley.[47]

Pettigrew surveyed various places to establish his mission centre and finally decided upon Phungyo, where "the state Government gave him a plot

---

43. Downs, 75.

44. T. Luikham opines that perhaps it was because the AAM only recruited missionaries for one term of three years which was why Pettigrew must have approached the BMS. T. Luikham, *Short History*, 10. Another narrative is that Pettigrew wanted to marry Miss Goreham, which he finally did, but as the AAM did not recruit married couple missionaries, he contacted the BMS; Downs, *Mighty Works*, 78.

45. Downs, 78.

46. Downs, 79. For ABMU Conference Committee report and recommendation, see *The AM of the ABMU*, 5.

47. Pettigrew, "My Twenty-Five Years," i.

of land," and where he built the first "Christian village" in Manipur.[48] On their first preaching ministry, Pettigrew writes that during the initial months after their arrival they spent their time learning the native language and by the end of the rains in the summer of 1897, "it is hoped there will be sufficient known to enable us to go and preach the gospel to the villages around. We hoped to do so this cold season."[49] In 1898, the year of the Diamond Jubilee of the reign of Queen Victoria, Pettigrew organised a one-day event for the children of the school and later in the evening in the presence of "Raicho, the most influential chief in the village" and "four other minor chiefs of the village," he organised a gathering where the people "crowded (the) school to see the magic lantern and to hear the story of Jesus." Pettigrew recorded, "The Jubilee day thus ended with the preaching of the gospel, and we trust the seed sown that evening will bring forth fruit."[50]

One of the most important decisions Pettigrew took to spread the gospel was through education, by opening schools for the native people. He started a school in Ukhrul and "opened and supervised" many schools in "various parts of the state" in the capacity of "Honorary Inspector of Schools for the entire state," a title conferred by the Government of Manipur. In the early years, due to "official and secular activities" and the construction of the new mission bungalow, "he [Pettigrew] could hardly give himself to preaching,"[51] so he distributed the Bible as "literature" to the students. He firmly "believed that this work though time consuming was a valuable preparation for the time when preaching could be done openly."[52] For him, the "chief objective in giving education to the tribesmen was to propagate Christianity."[53] On the curriculum and social contexts of the schools, Pettigrew wrote:

---

48. Downs, *Mighty Works*, 78.

49. Pettigrew, "Beginning of Ukhrul Station," 526.; see also Zeliang, "Beginning of Ukhrul Station," 5–6.

50. Pettigrew, "Jubilee in Manipur," 25; see also "Jubilee in Manipur (1898)," 7–8; Klein, "Queen Victoria's Diamond Jubilee."

51. Dena, *Christian Mission and Colonialism*, 36. Contra, Zeliang says that although Pettigrew was busy, he continued to engage in "studying language, translation of Scripture into Manipuri, development of Tangkhul literature, preaching and disbursing of medicine to the sick"; Zeliang, *History of Manipur*, 26–27.

52. Downs, *Mighty Works*, 79.

53. Luikham, *Short History*, 30–31; see also Kashung, "Impact of Christianity," 128.

> A First and Second Primer were composed during 1897 and 1898 . . . the copies are now in the hands of the scholars. For them a Third and Fourth Primer, containing the Life of Jesus Christ have been composed . . . Also a Catechism is nearly ready, which is intended for the boys to study on every Lord's Day . . . No objection is made to Christian truth being taught (in the hills) . . . The books they study aim to inculcate Christian truth.[54]

However, in the valley, "Christianity propagated in any form is forbidden, with the exception of being allowed to distribute the Gospels" for the schools as their curriculum permits. Pettigrew writes:

> The last proofs of the *Acts of the Apostles* in Manipuri have just been returned to the printer and next year will see this word of truth finding its way into the homes of the Manipuris (people in the valley). God grant that these silent messages will find entrance into hearts prepared by the Holy Spirit.[55]

It is clear that "Pettigrew believed that education could illuminate the individual mind, which in turn would arouse conviction in the truth of the Gospel."[56] In the capacity of an inspector of schools,[57] "Pettigrew visited the hitherto unvisited hill areas of Manipur" and "the contacts made at this time proved useful in opening the way for Christianity in various parts of Manipur."[58]

By 1901, there were twelve boys regularly attending the school in Ukhrul and all of them "confessed Christ and were baptised."[59] Nettie Purssell Mason, during the seventy-five year celebration of ABM work in Assam (North East India) in 1911, said that in Manipur, the missionaries and evangelists made their maiden trip touring the villages in February 1907 and repeated the trip for the next two years until "almost every village has heard the Gospel message

---

54. Pettigrew, "Manipur Mission," 54–55; compare "Beginning of Ukhrul Station (1897), 13, 17.
55. Pettigrew, 54–55; see also "Beginning of Ukhrul Station (1897)," 12–13.
56. Kashung, "Impact of Christianity," 128.
57. For more information about Pettigrew's school ministry, see Zeliang, *History of Manipur*, 29–30.
58. Kashung, "Impact of Christianity," 138.
59. Downs, *Mighty Works*, 80.

and the name of Jesus is known by the whole tribe."[60] The number of converts increased, and by 1907, the first Baptist church in Manipur had "seventy members."[61] However, as there was no qualitative spiritual growth marked by Christian discipleship, the converts retained with their traditional and cultural practices. From among the twelve original students, seven students remained faithful. They were: Hollei, Leishisan, M. K. Shimray, T. Luikham, Kuishon, Machonthei, and A. Poromsingh.[62] It is said that the other five students along with many other Christians could not keep up with the Christian disciplinary guidelines Pettigrew framed. These restrained Tangkhul believers from participating in traditional and cultural festivals opposed to Christian beliefs and doctrines, including *Kathi Kasam*, a ceremony involving spirit worship in relation to bidding farewell to the soul of the dead.[63]

Mingthing clarifies that the real resistance to Pettigrew's work and teaching in Ukhrul was not theological but based on "social, cultural, and political grounds."[64] The people had no systematised written religious system or doctrine, therefore, "there was no need for theological reasoning. No debate or argument took place. There was nothing far to be sought to convince them."[65] It is perceivable that tribal people's resistance would be more on social and communitarian aspects, to protect tribal solidarity, as his teaching would bring division in the community and even in the family between those who believed and followed his teaching and those who opposed him. Tribal people believe that their strength lies in belonging to a community.[66]

During the next two decades, the mission efforts were "directed towards the peoples inhabiting the hills areas . . . Kukis, Zeliangrong Nagas, and the Mao Nagas," apart from the Tangkhuls.[67] It was during the years 1917 to 1928

---

60. Also see, Mason, "'These Seventy-five Years," 50; see also "Ukhrul Field Report for 1911," 34.

61. Zeliang contradicts Downs's figure, and reasons that going by Pettigrew's own report in January 1907, the figure is 29; Zeliang, *History of Manipur*, 29; see also *The AM of the ABMU: Report*, 1907, 91; *The AM of the ABMU: Report*, 1910, 74–75.

62. Downs, *Mighty Works*, 80; see also Sangma, *History of American Baptist Mission*, 276.

63. Sangma, 276.

64. Cf. 3.6.

65. Mingthing, "Role of Preaching," 83.

66. K. Thanzauva, *Theology of Community*, 136.

67. Downs, *Mighty Works*, 156.

that all[68] the churches under ABM in Manipur came to be known as "Manipur Christian Association" (MCA), which was later christened "Manipur Baptist Convention" (MBC), under which the founding members were the North East, Sadar, and North West[69] associations. Though progress had been slow in Manipur field during the "first twenty years of Christian work, good foundations had been laid for rapid growth" in the years to come.[70]

3.5.2 Preaching, Persecution, and Church Growth in Manipur

In 1910–1911, a great door for preaching ministry opened when the Manipur State authority appointed Pettigrew as the superintendent for a census among the hill tribal people, a project never carried out previously. It is said that Pettigrew recruited his students and teachers from Ukhrul School for the task and they visited the neighbouring tribes and villages, performing their responsibilities satisfactorily. During this official tour, they made inroads in spreading the gospel wherever they went. And after the census, it is said that many village chiefs invited Pettigrew to come and set up schools in their villages.[71] Pettigrew reported that the Kuki villages also requested the missionaries "to come over and help us." Consequently, he arranged for them to have a hymnbook in their own language.[72]

By 1917, another missionary couple, Dr. and Mrs. Crozier, were transferred to Manipur from Tura (now in Meghalaya), and joined the Pettigrews in their mission work. In 1920, the government gave another opportunity for the missionaries and the Christians to visit more villages and tribes for the next census. By the end of 1921, church growth was evident due to "vigorous evangelistic works" as Kuki church membership reached 525 with "four established Christian villages" and "four entire Tangkhul villages embraced

---

68. By 1909, the chief of Senvon village, Kamkholen Singson, invited missionary Watkin Roberts to his village and so the Welsh mission at Aijal (Aizawl) began its Christian mission work in the southern part of Manipur; Downs, *Mighty Works*, 166.

69. Downs, 158.

70. Downs, 81.

71. "ABFMS 1912: Ninety-Eight Annual Report," 72. Compare Dena, *Christian Mission and Colonialism*, 37; see also Zeliang, *History of Manipur*, 31.

72. Pettigrew, "Manipur," 23–24.

Christianity." By 1921, there were around three thousand converts in the state.[73]

Soon, a wave of spiritual renewal occurred. Some argue that this phase of spiritual renewal resulted from the revival that spread to Manipur from the corridors of "the southern part of the state from the Mizo Hills in 1922."[74] However, there are others who disagree with this and believe that preaching and extensive soul winning work had begun at least two years prior to it, and that the Manipur revival was just one factor among many others in church growth.[75] The revival movement brought spiritual renewal and enhanced evangelistic work to the extent that the number of the churches increased to twenty-four under ABM.[76] Narrating the positive outcome of this movement, Pettigrew said that "many false Christians (were) exposed, many backsliders restored, and many new converts" came into the fold.[77] However, the counter narrative is that this period marked the era of mass conversion without proper teaching on the basic tenets of Christian faith.[78] Another negative issue of the revival movement was that people "became more ecstatic and emotional . . . Strange teachings began to be given based on dreams and visions. The teaching of an imminent Second Coming led many people to go into jungles to prepare themselves for it." The missionaries were alarmed at this and Crozier, who was supportive of this movement in 1923, later in 1926 called it the "spasm of 1923" and of the devil, who was mocking "imitations of the work of the Holy Spirit."[79]

Concerning persecution, it was reported that Christian mission and evangelism flourished although there was active persecution (during the 1920s and 1930s)[80] during the years following the revival until after Pettigrew left the Manipur field in 1933.[81]

---

73. Pettigrew, *Annual Report Manipur*, 1921, 1–3. See also Zeliang, *History of Manipur*, 39.
74. Downs, *Mighty Works*, 161.
75. Downs, 163.
76. Downs, 161.
77. Pettigrew, *Evangelistic Report from Manipur*, 1.
78. Downs, *Mighty Works*, 163.
79. As quoted in Downs, 162.
80. Kashung, "Impact of Christianity," 137.
81. Downs, *Mighty Works*, 165.

As for preaching and the spread of Christianity in Manipur, beginning from Ukhrul in the early days, "the gospel was initially taught in school and those converted into Christianity spread the gospel in their own village and neighbouring village till all the Tangkhuls converted into Christianity."[82] Although some government officials were aware and allowed gospel preaching among the tribals in the hills, there were some government officials who were antagonised by this activity. Therefore, as detailed below, in some cases prohibitive laws were passed.

For instance, a certain sub-divisional officer (SDO),[83] L. L. Peter, in Manipur, passed several orders. Kashung records this in her thesis: "1. Preaching Christianity is restricted (vide order no. 123/Uk/P/2/12/1924), 2. Exchanging letters regarding Christianity is restricted (vide order no. 14-dated 14/11/24) and 3. Open preaching/ evangelistic work is restricted (vide order no. 106Ukh/P/7/11/24)." In this way, he discouraged many and even punished the offenders.[84] Even the church in Tamenglong constructed by the early Christians was destroyed by SDO William Shaw on following the complaints of the other villagers around 1929.[85]

In 1923, when twenty families embraced Christ from the village of Kaikao, Tamenglong, they were ostracised by the village elders, along with the SDO, who also did not approve of their personal religious choice and "ordered the Christians to leave the village within a week, forfeiting any property that they could not carry with them." However, with the intervention of Pettigrew, the government gave the new converts a new location nearby (Sempang) for settlement.[86]

Although in March 1928, through the Governor's order, many of the restricted areas in the hills were opened so that preaching and education work could be freely done,[87] persecution continued in the mission field,[88] especially

---

82. Kashung, "Impact of Christianity," 133–134.

83. A sub-divisional officer (SDO) works as the official in charge of a sub-division in a district in India; Kumar, "What Are the Role and Functions."

84. Kashung, "Impact of Christianity," 144.

85. Vaiphei, *Advent*, 71.

86. Zeliang, *History of Manipur*, 40–41; Downs, *Mighty Works*, 175.

87. Crozier, *Educational Report from Manipur*, 1.

88. Downs, *Mighty Works*, 164–65, 181.

the Mao region which was still closed.[89] Nevertheless, many people continued to embrace Christianity. The Pettigrews and Croziers were joined by several schoolteachers in preaching the gospel to non-Christians.[90] In 1931, Pettigrew reported the following evangelistic and educational data:[91]

Evangelistic	Organised churches		44	Native Contribution
	Branch churches		49	Rs. 6,439.00
	Pastors		49	
	Evangelists		20	
	Church members		4715	
	Baptisms		508	
Educational	Day schools		39	Native Contribution
	Night schools		13	Rs. 3,169.00
	Teachers		53	
	Students	Boys: 517	708	
		Girls: 191		
	Native Contribution			Rs. 9,608.00
	Government Grant in Aid			Rs. 1,420.00
	Grand Total			Rs. 11,028.00

In the years following the Croziers' resignation from ABM to join the Baptist Mid-Mission (BMM) in 1932,[92] and the Pettigrews leaving Manipur in 1933, the Baptist church continued to grow. Here is statistical evidence of Christian growth in Manipur:[93]

---

89. Zeliang, *History of Manipur*, 41.
90. Hatzaw, *Christianity in Manipur*, 58.
91. Pettigrew, *Evangelistic, Educational and Literature Report*, 2, 4. (Grand total has been added.)
92. Downs, *Mighty Works*, 171–72.
93. Arokianathan, *Tangkhul Folk Literature*; "Population of Manipur"; "Manipur Religion Census 2011"; "Population by Religious Communities"; Shimray, "Naga Population Scenario"; Singh, "Religious Landscape in Manipur"; Kashung, "Impact of Christianity," 134; Joshi, *Manipur*, 1; Pettigrew, *Evangelistic, Educational and Literature Report*, 2, 4.

Year	Total Population of Manipur	Christians (inclusive of all denominations)	
		Population	Percentage of Total Population
1931	445,606	10,401	-
1951	-	-	11.84
1961	780,037	152,043	19.49
1971	1,072,753	297,243	26.03
1981	1,420,953	421,702	29.68
1991	1,837,149	626,669	34.11
2001	2,293,896	737,578	34.04
2011	2,855,794	-	41.29

With the decline of persecution of the converts in 1936, the ministry of preaching no longer faced obstruction. While ABM supported eight workers, the native church supported 186 workers.[94] The increased number of workers in the field brought about more church growth and this evidence was seen during the ABM centenary celebration in Assam in 1936 where "Manipur had 101 churches with 6,316 baptized members."[95]

It is reported that Baptist Christian preaching among the Meiteis began in a more focused way, and that by the late 1990s, there were "132 evangelists . . . working among the Meiteis."[96] Christian mission in this context was understood as the "proclamation of the Gospel . . . proclamation of the Kingdom" and "to disciple people."[97]

3.6 Effect of Christian Preaching in Manipur: The First Half of the Twentieth Century

It is believed that the method of preaching in the early days was more like crying and appealing to non-Christians to repent. Apart from striking up conversations with individuals in any village they went to, the early preachers

---

94. Werelius, "Evangelistic Report," 40.
95. Werelius, "Kangpokpi," 43.
96. "Manipur Baptist Convention, Annual Report 2000–2001," 17; see also Hatzaw, *Christianity in Manipur*, 54.
97. Hatzaw, 54.

also met the village councils and appealed to them to quit drinking local rice beer and cease performing spirit sacrifices as they were sinful acts. The village councils often gave heed to their proclamation and responded promptly on whether they would accept or reject the message.[98]

One of the earliest educated preachers among the first-generation Christians included Ruichumhao from Somdal village, Ukhrul district, who gave up all the entitlements offered by the Manipur government and the chance for a better life after he returned from France, having served in the Labour Corps.[99] This young man's pastoral heart came to the fore at the battlefield in France, leading soldiers to "prayer and worship." Kashung wrote:

> Every morning at 4.30 a.m. he would go to a quiet place in the forest and pray for the labourers, soldiers, the wounded, the dying, and for the quick end of the War. Some of the 164 Tangkhul labourers became Christians after returning from the War. This is without ignoring the role of Ruichumhao's preaching and teaching to them.[100]

Instead of basking in the limelight of prominence and luxury, Ruichumhao chose the role of mission and "spreading the gospel" to various Tangkhul villages. His responsibility included serving as "the Superintendent Pastor cum Evangelist of the western region of Ukhrul area." This young preacher suffered from tuberculosis in 1931 and was advised to rest. It is said that the passionate pastor however did not heed the advice as "his passion for evangelism overshadowed his concern for his own health" and that "his burden for his people could no longer confine him to his bed. Trusting in God's grace he decided to risk his life by taking the gospel to all the Tangkhul villages." His life was cut short at thirty-seven years of age, but not before making a deep impression for the gospel among his people.[101] Ruichumhao preached passionately on the second coming of Christ which convicted many to the faith, because they imagined the nearness of the event by his appeal and urgency.[102]

---

98. Mingthing, "Role of Preaching," 69; see also Ringkahao, *Note Book*, 33.
99. Kashung, "Impact," 163.
100. Kashung, 163–64.
101. Kashung, 164.
102. As quoted by Y. L. Mingthing from R. V. Ringkahao's notebook (16), in his thesis, "Role of Preaching," 68.

He also strongly preached on the need for redemption from sin to receive salvation, by abandoning all the "pagan practices of drinking, giving sacrifice to the spirits and observance of the spirit worships."[103] He also preached on the issues of "life after death" from the book of Revelation.[104]

Another prominent convert, who also served in the Labour Corps in France was Kanrei Shaiza. On his return, he chose to preach the gospel, as he also taught in the Ukhrul Mission School. Later, he served as "the Head Evangelist of Northern Circle" among the Tangkhuls. Coming "with an aim of preaching the gospel to the students, he took up his passion of teaching and laboured at Govt. Upper Primary School, at the same time serving as the Hon. Pastor of Phungyo Baptist Church from 1937–39."[105]

The other important leader and preacher was Vashumnao Phanitphang from Talui village in Ukhrul district, who became the first indigenous leader of the Baptist church when the foreign missionaries were asked to leave Manipur.[106] Prior to this, his passion for preaching the gospel spurred him to take over as the "Superintendent Pastor, Manipur North East Western Sector in 1935,"[107] and he eventually became the leading preacher and leader of the entire Baptist family in Manipur. Phanitphang was the "first theological graduate in Manipur," having received a diploma in theological studies from Welsh Mission Theological College in Cherrapunji (now in Meghalaya), from 1932 to 1934, and later completing his BTh in 1951 from Serampore College, Calcutta (now Kolkata). He served the Baptist family in Manipur for fifteen years from 1960 to 1976. After his BTh, as the "only graduate theologian, he had to go far beyond his village to preach to the unreached areas" of Manipur.[108]

For her PhD thesis, Kashung also interviewed several second-generation Christians who remembered Pettigrew and other pioneer Christians' preaching and teaching. She has also mentioned some important personalities who preached the gospel and carried the flame of the gospel forward along with the foreign missionaries in Manipur. A brief discussion is given below.

---

103. Mingthing, "Role of Preaching," 68.
104. Mingthing, 69.
105. Kashung, "Impact," 165.
106. Kashung, 166–67.
107. Kashung, 166–67.
108. Kashung, 167.

In an interview, a ninety-three-year-old man, Rumthao, expressed the following to Kashung. During his student days at Ukhrul Mission School (UMS), the preaching and teaching of the missionaries on the universality of sin (based on Rom 3:23–24), convicted him and made him realise his sinfulness, although for many years he had considered himself a righteous person. Rumthao stated:

> In spite of hearing God's word regularly, I could not understand why I needed repentance. I thought that I was a good boy because I obeyed and respected my parents and elders. I neither stole nor lied. But when I meditated on Romans 3:23–24, I acknowledged my sin and could no longer cover up my iniquity. Thus, I confessed my transgression to the Lord who forgave the guilt of my sin. I then became the child of the Lord.[109]

Another convert, a ninety-eight-year-old man, Ruivanao, narrated that his parents accepted Christianity because of the exemplary lifestyle and preaching of Pettigrew on forgiveness. He recounted:

> My parents got converted after they perceived that William Pettigrew came to Ukhrul out of love. They were amazed when William Pettigrew forgave those people who tried to kill him and instead did everything that was good for them. He lived an examplary life. They were also taught to love one another – even to love their enemy. My parents said that he repeatedly preached to them from the book of Matthew 6:14–15 which says, "For if you forgive men when they sin against you, your heavenly Father will also forgive you. But if you do not forgive men their sins, your Father will not forgive your sins."[110]

Another ninety-five-year-old convert Ningatei also confessed that the earliest gospel message he heard preached was concerning the power of the Christian God. He recollected that some people in his village were

---

109. Kashung, 149.

110. Kashung, 152; Mingthing also agrees that the most important factor for the softening of people's heart was Pettigrew's "personal presence, his interest in them, his sincerity, humility, and concern for them"; Mingthing, "Role of Preaching," 83.

not willing to convert into [sic] Christianity though they were convinced to some extent that the Christian God is a powerful, a merciful God that would answer their prayer. Their fear of conversion was the worry they had over the need to discontinue practicing their traditional cultural practices like erecting poles, stone monuments etc. in the courtyard. I had to prove to make them understand that the Christian God is more powerful. Consequently, I removed the poles and monuments from their courtyard. When they learned that no harm falls on me, they converted into [sic] Christianity.[111]

A one-hundred-year-old woman Ngalashingai also recounted her mother's intensive labour of brewing *zam-khor* (rice beer) – from rice seed in the fields to harvesting and gathering in the granary, to sunning it and dehusking it, to the "long process of washing, soaking, and fermentation." Mrs. Ngalashingai shared how her mother experienced an indescribable joy when her brother, Phanitphang (the preacher discussed earlier), opened the Scripture and taught her that in the gospel there is "assurance and hope of salvation through Christ our Lord," and so this truth liberated her from an oppressive old system workload,[112] as rice beer was required for performing animistic rituals. Being set free from this oppressive structure, Ngalashingai's parents then began to invest in her and her sibling's education.[113] Thus, gospel preaching not only brought about spiritual freedom and alleviated social oppression, especially towards women, but it also became the catalyst for educational pursuit.

A few notable indigenous converts who carried the gospel to their fellow tribesmen or other tribes in Manipur may be mentioned. R. Luichumhao was active among the Tangkhuls,[114] Ngulhao Thomsong among the Kukis and Anals,[115] Pakho Sitlhou among the Rongmei Nagas,[116] Tongkam Singsit and Letjavum Sitlhou among the Burmese Kukis,[117] Namrijinpou and Jinlakpou

---

111. Kashung, "Impact," 153.
112. Kashung, 171.
113. Kashung, "Impact," 171–72.
114. Downs, *Mighty Works*, 164.
115. Downs, 167–170; Vaiphei, *Advent*, 63; Kabui, *Anal: A Transborder Tribe*, 27.
116. Downs, 170.
117. Downs, 170–71.

among the Rongmei Nagas in the western hills,[118] Helkhup among the Zeliangrong,[119] and Yirei of Somdal, Ngashanphung of Ukhrul[120] and O. Kathipri among the Maos.[121] It is said that Helkhup, along with Teba Kilong, Longkhobel, and Jamkithang who were converted during their student days at UMS, spread the gospel through preaching among the Kuki-Chin people, and they consequently became a large people group to accept Christianity in Manipur.[122]

Although several of the indigenous pioneering preachers were allowed to preach and sing in the villages they went to, there were some like Namrijinpou[123] who were denied entry into the village to preach.[124] It is said that the village elders allegedly tried to stone him to death, but he escaped and "defying order, he stood outside the village singing, preaching and reading from the Bible. In this way he was able to inspire two youngmen [sic] Hurong and Ngandiang and baptised them. Later, they were driven out from their village."[125]

On the method of preaching, Mingthing states that the early preachers

> had little knowledge of the historic role of preaching in the life of the church, or theological and textual explanation or any special forms of preaching. They used no notes. Even the most highly educated persons like Ruichumhao Shimray and others were not seen using notes. The Bible was their only source while preaching.[126]

The main themes preached by the preachers that helped people abandon paganism for Christianity were the second coming, life after death, and sin and salvation; and in later years, they preached on revival as a follow-up

---

118. Downs, 174–75; Vaiphei, *Advent*, 68.
119. Downs, 175.
120. Kashung, "Impact," 140.
121. Downs, *Mighty Works*, 182. Other preachers in Mao were Kholi Puni, Hepuni Ashikho, and Kholi Adaho, then came Koisu Kaikho and Mihru (Mikri) Loha; Vaiphei, *Advent*, 77.
122. Haokip, "Spread of Christianity," 45–46.
123. Also called Namrijinang. See, Haokip, "Spread of Christianity," 72.
124. Downs, *Mighty Works*, 176.
125. Haokip, "Spread of Christianity," 72; Downs, 176; Vaiphei, *Advent*, 71.
126. Mingthing, "Role of Preaching," 70.

theme.[127] However, it was observed that "the preachers tended to combine them often not knowing clear distinction between them. The definition was more a matter of emphasis."[128]

Christianity primarily gave the people "assurance and hope of salvation," liberating them from some of the oppressive cultural practices including *hau*, a ritualistic practice that wasted the resources of "time, labour and money."[129] It is believed that people's desire for the theme of sin and forgiveness in Christian doctrine was because the forgiveness that comes from Jesus Christ is free of cost, as according to ancient paganism, forgiveness could be attained only by killing either "a cow, a buffalo, a pig, a dog, a cat or at least a fowl" according to the gravity of their transgression.[130]

Mingthing is right in his evaluation of the preaching ministry of the missionaries and the early preaching when he concluded:

> While many church leaders in other parts of the world would feel that the gospel presented to the Tangkhul Nagas by Pettigrew and the early preachers was a limited one and neglected many important aspects of the Christian faith, it did succeed in converting a whole people and in establishing a strong and vital church amongst them. Through what the apostle called "the foolishness of preaching" they were saved and brought into a living relationship with God and one another in the Church.[131]

3.7 Health of the Baptist Church and Preaching in Manipur: The Second Half of the Twentieth Century

In this section, we will begin by tracking the tenure of the Executive Secretary (later known as General Secretary) of MBC, observing the emphasis of their ministry during their time in office. The advantage of this framework is that it is chronological and will shed light on the preaching ministry under MBC as well. We will analyse them from a homiletical standpoint. We will then engage

---

127. Mingthing, 72.
128. Mingthing, 87.
129. Kashung, "Impact," 169.
130. Mingthing, "Role of Preaching," 81.
131. Mingthing, 87.

with Mingthing's research on the role of preaching and church development in the Baptist churches in Manipur and analyse his works.

3.7.1 The Ministry Focus of MBC Leadership in Different Eras of Its History

The second half of the twentieth century in the ministry of MBC is an era of leadership transition from foreign missionaries to indigenous leadership and preachers. In 1951, it was recorded that there were 456 Baptist churches and a total of 26,747 baptised members, of which 2,461 members were baptised that year alone.[132] After India gained independence in 1947, the missionaries began to focus on primarily training the indigenous leaders and preachers keeping in mind the future health of the church in case they were asked to leave Manipur. And so in 1952, MBC opened a Vernacular Bible School in Kangpokpi.[133] In 1953, a five-week-long training program was conducted for the pastors and evangelists, and also a five-day Vacation Bible School was conducted, spreading to over thirty-five villages and attracting around 500 participants.[134] The Vernacular Bible School in Kangpokpi was later upgraded to Manipur Theological College (MTC).[135] In 1954, when the last Baptist missionary to Manipur, John S. Anderson, left Manipur, he wrote:

> The Church in Manipur will progress and God's purposes will be accomplished. He who has begun a good work in them will perfect it unto the day of Jesus Christ . . . Quite naturally . . . the ministry of Christ in Manipur by all means shall continue to be in our interest and prayers for a long time to come, even though we shall no longer have opportunity to be a part of that ministry. May God grant to our beloved brethren there the wisdom and the power to carry on.[136]

---

132. Moyon, "Manipur State Convention," 70.
133. Curry, "Kangpokpi," 47.
134. Anderson, "Manipur State-Kangpokpi," 42–43.
135. Later in 1953, it was called "Manipur Central Bible School" (MCBS) then upgraded to "Manipur Bible Institute" in 1967, and in 1984 it was further upgraded to "Manipur Theological College" as it exists today. Zeliang, *History of Manipur*, 113–16.
136. Anderson, "Manipur Annual Report, 1954," 66–67.

After the American missionaries left in 1954, Phanitphang took up the first leadership as Chairman of MBC[137] and this was one of his memorable statements:

> As is known to all, we have the total elimination of missionaries from the whole field since November last (1954). But we are not despaired, for we feel the invisible Master is always with us. The absence of missionaries here has done one good thing. As there is none to look up to for guidance, the nationals here are beginning to feel more responsible for and concerned in the work.[138]

The first national Executive Secretary of MBC was Rev. Seikholet Singson and he faithfully carried out both a preaching and administrative ministry during his five-year term (1955–1960). During his tenure, as many associations focused on administration, he "laid most of the foundations for MBC ministry."[139] Then, Phanitphang succeeded him and served the Convention for fifteen years. As a preacher he accelerated the evangelistic ministry, but because of the volatile Naga political situation, it "greatly retarded the general evangelistic work of MBC particularly in the Naga areas," as they had been declared a "disturbed area."[140] However, the churches continued to flourish. By 1963, there were thirteen associations, with eight hundred churches and around forty thousand baptised members.[141] The main method of evangelism during the mid-1960s was preaching to mass gatherings, accompanied by singing teams.[142] By 1969, it was observed that MBC[143] divided the associations along tribal and lingual lines and not necessarily to propagate the gospel. Moreover, it is said that instead of focusing on preaching and evangelistic works, many churches during this period also focused on building their own associations. In response to this situation, Phanitphang said, "the real needs are personnel with evangelistic zeal and for the due spiritual feeding of the

---

137. Zeliang, *History of Manipur*, 55.
138. Phanitphang, "Field Report – Manipur – 1954," 64.
139. Zeliang, *History of Manipur*, 56–57.
140. Zeliang, 57.
141. Phanitphang, "Manipur Baptist Convention Report," 71.
142. Phanitphang, "Manipur Field Report," 55.
143. Not necessarily the General Secretary but perhaps the Executive Council or the Annual Assembly.

sheep," that, "in reality our annual soul harvest" is more worth than the numerical size of the Associations which are "so scanty in real spiritual emphasis" and that the focus should be "winning those wallowing in the mire of sin."[144]

Under Phanitphang's leadership, the MBC celebrated its 75th year of the arrival of the gospel in Manipur in 1971. In 1976, he retired from MBC leadership. When the next national Executive Secretary, Rev. Ramkhun Pamei took over the leadership in 1976, there were fourteen associations, 921 churches, and 61,482 baptised members.[145] The last few years of the 1970s were remarkable for the harvest of souls as a

> revival movement swept across . . . some parts of Manipur particularly among the Zeliangrong churches. Many nominal Christians were revived and many non-Christians were converted. For instance, at Changdai village, sixty families were converted within a week and 190 people were baptised on one day. The movement continued to ZBA churches and it also spread to the Poumai Naga churches thereby bringing rich harvest of souls. Seeing the need of greater emphasis on evangelism, in 1979, MBC launched a mission movement called, "MBC Evangelistic Movement" . . . Rev. Ningwon Woleng was appointed as full-time secretary of MBC Evangelistic Movement in June 1980.[146]

After Rev. Pamei retired in 1990, Rev. Kaikho Hokey led MBC as the next Regional Secretary[147] until 2000.[148] The historical period during the leadership of Rev. Hokey in MBC was one of the darkest moments in MBC history due to the ethnic conflict between the Nagas and the Kukis in 1992, and the Kuki-Paite conflict and Meitei-Naga conflict in 1997. During this period, the main theme of preaching was peace and reconciliation. Under Hokey's leadership, the MBC peace committee was formed. It visited all the districts and conducted combined Christian worship, preaching the gospel of peace

---

144. Phanitphang, "Report of Manipur Baptist Convention – 1969," 76.

145. Pamei, "Manipur Baptist Convention Report," 73–74.

146. Zeliang, *History of Manipur*, 62; see also Ramkhun Pamei, "Report on Manipur Baptist Convention 1978," 72.

147. Nomenclature changed from Executive Secretary to Regional Secretary in 1990. MBC: *Minutes of the 110th EC*, 1; MBC: *Minutes of the 11th AA*, 3.

148. Zeliang, *History of Manipur*, 65.

and challenging people to work for peace. The committee members also visited refugee camps, villages that had been burned, and injured persons in the hospitals, and prayed with them and proclaimed the message of forgiveness and peace.[149]

The conflict period lasted for several years. Through God's grace, several Christian organisations from around the globe intervened to bring the warring groups together. During this period, the MBC leadership team worked hard and their labour bore the fruit of reconciliation and "a better relationship" between Kukis and the Nagas. Bridging this divide, they celebrated the MBC Centenary together along with other associations and churches at Imphal from 5–8 December 1996.[150]

The other conflicts lasted for almost a decade before normalcy returned.[151] For his outstanding reconciliation work both in the pulpit and in society, Rev. Hokey was awarded the title "The Man of Great Faith" when he left the office in 2001.[152]

Rev. Vumthang Sitlhou succeeded Rev. Hokey as the new General Secretary in 2001. His ministry also prioritised building mutual trust, especially between the Kukis and the Nagas. Because he comes from a mixed family where his father is a Kuki and his mother a Rongmei Naga, Sitlhou came into leadership at the right time, during MBC's ministry of reconciliation. He pursued peace, reconciliation, and confidence-building during his tenure. In 2003, during the MBC 22nd Annual Assembly in Tungjoy, the theme was "Let Us Rebuild" (Neh 2:10) and participants resolved "to maintain unity, fraternity, and integrity of the Convention and to fulfil the purpose for which it was formed (viz. faith, witness, and service), as well as to stand together as one body against evil forces such as communalism, tribalism, nepotism, and religious fanaticism."[153] During the 23rd MBC Annual Assembly, the convention recognised the need to expand its concern and embrace the focus on ecological care and physical well-being, apart from spiritual wholeness. Under the theme, "Healing of the Land," the following sub-themes were

---

149. Zeliang, 66; see also Hokey, "General Secretary Report," 1. It is not clear when the nomenclature changed from Regional Secretary to General Secretary.

150. Hokey, "General Secretary Report," 3–6; see also Zeliang, *History of Manipur*, 66–67.

151. Zeliang, 68.

152. *MBC: Minutes of the 19th AA*, 2.

153. *Report of the Resolution Committee of the 22nd MBC Annual Assembly*, 1.

endorsed: "(1) To heal our land from destruction and ecological imbalances; (2) To heal our physical sickness; and (3) To heal our spiritual life."[154] It was also under Rev. Sitlhou that MBC celebrated the MBC National Leadership Golden Jubilee in 2005.[155] According to MBC statistics of 2005, there were 28 associations, 1,358 local churches, and 176,094 baptised members.[156] Without much elaboration, it is here noted that in 2019 when MBC celebrated the 125th year of Christianity (Baptist denomination) in Manipur under the leadership of Wungnaoting Konghar (incumbent General Secretary), there were "29 Associations, 1407 local churches, and Fellowships with 206,257 baptized members."[157]

3.7.2 Eras of the MBC Leadership: An Analysis from a Homiletical Point of View

The continuance of the ministry of preaching in the churches even after the missionaries left is almost a foregone conclusion although there is no documentation to support it, as the nature of church history and Christian tradition suggests that reading of the Scripture or preaching is a part of Christian worship on the Lord's day (Sunday). But here we will engage with the homiletical theology and themes of the preaching ministry during each era of MBC history under various leaders.

First, during the era of the leadership of Rev. Seikholet Singson, we do not have much evidence of a rejuvenated preaching ministry other than the perpetuation of one that had existed in the past. However, we are informed that during his tenure, there were several associations decentralising into smaller groups. We are also told that he was actively involved in laying the foundation of MBC ministry. This could be seen from two angles, first, that he was strengthening the base of the central MBC ministry as indigenous leadership took over from the foreign missionaries or, second, that he was laying the foundation stones of various associations by visiting them and helping them to stand on their own after coming out of a bigger group or association. Whichever angle it might have been, we are aware that he must have been

---

154. Sitlhou, "Annual Report of the General Secretary," 3.
155. Zeliang, *History of Manipur*, 71.
156. Zeliang, 145.
157. Konghar, "Word of Welcome and Introduction," 10.

involved in strengthening both the micro and macro levels of leadership and church administration. Although we do not have much written about MBC's preaching ministry during this time, we could take a cue from Phanitphang's address in 1955 that the emphasis in preaching must be focused on leadership and responsibility, apart from the traditional evangelistic preaching which continued in every era.

Second, during the leadership of Phanitphang, we are told that active evangelistic activity carried on in other areas, although the Naga areas were restricted in evangelism and missionary activity. The growth of the church suggests that the preaching movement persisted in the convention. The evidence is found in Phanitphang's plea that the real worth from an eternal perspective was neither the size of the associations nor the numerical aspect of the church growth, but winning people who were lost in sin back into the kingdom of God. His rebuke of the church leaders for decentralising the associations on tribal lines and not on progressing the gospel's march, is evidence of his firm evangelical homiletical theology. The mass evangelistic preaching events accompanied by singing ministry only confirms this claim. Although he was apparently not focused on numbers, when he gave the leadership rein to the next Executive Secretary, around one hundred churches and twenty thousand members had been added into the convention. This figure does not mean that he was the only man who did all the preaching and conversion, but we could argue that under his evangelical conviction and evangelistic outlook, the pastors, preachers, and churches continued to labour with his vision. Not much can be derived about the theology of preaching during this time except that which is available for us, that is, to win souls and restore those lost in the mire of sin, and to feed the people with the word of God to deepen the spirituality of the members.

Third, Rev. Ramkhun Pamei took over the reins of MBC leadership when the second revival moment (the first being the one in 1922–1923) swept across some regions of Manipur, most importantly, the corridors of Zeliangrong and Poumai villages in the later 1970s. It is reported that to channel the wave and its impact on society and the churches, MBC strategically launched the "Evangelistic Movement" in 1980. Homiletically speaking, although there is no evidence of the form and content of preaching during this period, we could presume it was focused on soul winning, because the impact was evident in the multiple conversions happening in these two tribal areas. In the Poumai region, especially the villages of Liyai, Oinam Hill, and Saranamai (the village which celebrated the 50th year of the arrival of the gospel in 2018),[158] the revival movement was empowered by evangelistic preaching and mass singing around the villages.[159]

Fourth, when Rev. Hokey was chosen to be the new leader of the Convention, nobody knew, including himself, that his ministry would be one of peace and reconciliation between the conflicting people groups in the churches and society of Manipur. The homiletical theme during this period seems to be self-evident because of the turmoil and conflict situation the churches and society were in. It can be assumed that the churches must have preached the gospel of peace and reconciliation although there are no manuscripts or other documentation of the sermons. The impact of the sermons and ministry of peace was evident because the warring groups of people decided to set aside their differences and tragedies and come together to commemorate and celebrate the centenary celebration of the arrival of Christianity (with William Pettigrew) in Manipur. Such a display of forgiveness and reconciliation was a huge achievement in the history of Christianity in Manipur and preaching certainly must have had an impact in this transformation. As a renowned preacher himself, Hokey steadied the ship of the church during this tumultuous storm, although the dangerous tide of enmity did not subside immediately.

Although the years beyond 2000 do not fall within the purview of this section, it is important to mention this era to gauge the direction of the Convention's and the churches' homiletical theology and focus. Rev. Sitlhou, the sixth leader of the MBC, took over from Rev. Hokey in 2001. Although the warring groups came together and celebrated the gospel centenary in 1996, the undercurrents of suspicion and disgruntlement continued to run deep. The homiletical focus during the era of Rev. Sitlhou's ministry continued, as with his predecessor, on peace and reconciliation. Perhaps the theme for the MBC 22nd Annual Assembly, "Let Us Rebuild," suggests that much work still

---

158. The researcher went as a Golden Jubilee speaker during the celebration on 20 December 2018 on the theme "Saved by Grace."

159. Several villages in Poumai region experienced the wave of revival. Apart from evangelistic sermons in the churches, the church members walked around the villages, singing and "chasing the devil out of the village" (in conversation with Rev. R. L. Tennyson, 15 December 2018).

needed to be done to bring about communal harmony and holistic healing. Moreover, the resolution of the Assembly to intentionally fight for peace and unity possibly was the result of several years of labour both in the pulpit and outside the church by the pastors, preachers, and people striving for peace in the land. Another homiletical turn in this era was the focus of the pulpit on holistic transformation – ecological concern and physical healing, apart from spiritual vitality. It is yet to be explored what direction the homiletical theology has taken over the years since the MBC leadership of Rev. Sitlhou.[160]

3.7.3 The Role of Preaching for Church Growth: Y. L. Mingthing

In this section, we will engage with Mingthing's[161] work on the Christian preaching movement in Manipur and church growth during the second half of the twentieth century. As we have elaborately engaged with his observations, findings, and recommendations in the literature review,[162] we will not repeat them here, except for some cases that need more emphasis. We will then analyse them.

First, the preaching ministry continued to flourish in the years following the departure of the foreign missionaries; however, the growth of the church was relatively slow. Some ascribe this to the dearth of theologically trained pastors and poor economic conditions of the local churches.[163]

Second, although there was an emphasis on pulpit ministry, the books of the Bible and diverse biblical themes and doctrines were not adequately covered.[164] It is said that almost half of the pastors in the second half of the twentieth century "never preached on the Old Testament," and that their interpretation and exegesis were very poor and on many occasions they

---

160. Here we are speaking of the era of Rev. Dr. Wungnaoting Konghar, the incumbent General Secretary of MBC who took leadership in 2011. *MBC Quasquicentenary Celebration Souvenir*, 13.

161. Zeliang records that Mr. Mingthing was sent by Tangkhul Naga Baptist Convention (TNBC) around 1955 to be a missionary among the valley Meitei people and "through his hard work thirty-two souls were brought to Christ at Nepet Meitei village"; Zeliang, *History of Manipur*, 56.

162. Cf. 2.2.3.2.

163. Cf. 2.2.3.2.

164. Cf. 2.2.3.2.

prooftexted Bible Scriptures to preach what they wanted to say.[165] This created a deep divide between what was actually said and what was actually needed by the people,[166] concerning the complex life situations of the congregations, as they needed more concrete answers to cope with their stress and life's dilemmas.[167] Moreover, with higher education came critical thinking and the listeners were more analytical of the sermons.[168]

Third, the revival movement and preaching clearly impacted church growth. The number of converts multiplied in various parts of Manipur en masse.[169] However, their scriptural interpretation was flawed as it pitched the human body against the spiritual soul. The tone of preaching leaned heavily towards emotional blackmail. Their doctrines remained biased and one-dimensional, if not heretical.[170]

3.7.4 An Analysis of Y. L. Mingthing's Voice on the Role of Preaching for Church Growth

First, an analysis of Mingthing's finding that a lack of trained pastors was slowing down the growth of the church – while it is true that a theologically trained pastor can interpret the Scripture and preach more knowledgably, following the principles of homiletics, it would be improper to conclude that lack of trained pastors and preachers slowed down church growth. If we look at church history, especially of the MBC, we could argue that the church continued to multiply during the early 1920s when the word of God was passionately taught to the people, although there were no trained preachers, except the missionaries.[171] However, it must be acknowledged that not engaging a theologically trained pastor in the church due to financial burdens and instead, preferring a lay pastor and preacher who had to spend his time in the fields, would have minimised his impact, humanly speaking.

---

165. Mingthing, "Role of Preaching" 102–3.
166. Mingthing, 112.
167. Cf. 2.2.3.2.
168. Mingthing, "Role of Preaching," 112–13.
169. Zeliang, *History of Manipur*, 62; see also Pamei, "Report on Manipur Baptist Convention 1978," 72.
170. Mingthing, "Role of Preaching," 118–19.
171. Downs, *Mighty Works*, 163.

Second, Mingthing's evaluation is valid: the quality and focus of preaching in the Baptist churches should encompass the entire Bible and be gospel-centric and relevant to its listeners to avoid losing relevance for the young people who are exposed to higher education and modernity in terms of economy, politics, and society. Whether or not that had been fulfilled is unknown, as we do not know of any other study done on this subject. But we can argue that with the increase of more theologically trained pastors, the gap must have decreased.[172]

Third, analysing the approach the revival preachers took during the early Christian era, perhaps because of their unique historical situation, of emotional preaching and rebuking could have been one way to stir a sense of urgency on people in order to break down the walls of paganism and centuries of spiritual bondage. However, as Christians mature, the preaching of the church should include more of life's issues and needs. They cannot be just confined to the spiritual matter leaving out the physical realm anymore. The revival movements and their preaching have not totally disappeared from the churches. We see such traits of theology and preaching today in a different form called the prayer warriors and prayer centres which only focus on the spiritual aspect of human existence. This one-dimensional preaching is also not absent in the Baptist churches of Manipur even today.

Fourth, one could possibly argue that the widespread nominalism in Manipur[173] is mainly because during the era of mass conversion, church growth, and revival movements, there was a lack of proper preaching and teaching of the basic tenets of Christian doctrine and beliefs.[174]

One can argue that the result of a past Christianity poorly based on the word of God is being harvested today in the overdependence on prayer

---

172. This statement is more of a hypothesis. But the current research work will help in the investigation of the unknown situation of the quality of preaching in our churches, especially among the Baptist churches in Imphal. As for the evidence of theologically trained people within MBC, see appendix 4.

173. Mandryk, *Operation World*, 433.

174. Cf. 2.4.1.5.

warriors[175] to orchestrate believers' lives.[176] The situation is similar with Christians in the neighbouring state of Nagaland. As we discussed in the literature review,[177] Pongen considers this culture of Christians running "to these well-paid 'seer' and prayer centers for quick answers" during "sickness, decision making, (and) general guidance" as an aspect of nominalism.[178] Pongen laments that Christians are almost committing the act of idolatry because "they consider these prayer warriors as god for their family."[179] If one observes carefully, we can see a cyclical pattern – a poor foundation in the Word[180] leading to nominalism, and nominalism leading to dependence on the prayer warriors, which is again a non-dependence on the word of God. One only wonders if poor preaching in the church has led to the mushrooming of prayer centres in the region.

A word of caution could be added here, that holistic gospel preaching was not totally absent from the pulpits of the Baptist churches in the second part of the twentieth century. The rise of theological graduates and students from the Bible colleges has increased the resources of the church in terms of trained pastors and preaching. Even though not all theological graduates become good expositors of the Scripture, some of them do become good pastors and preachers. While it is perceptible that there is room for improvement in the preaching ministry of the Baptist churches in Imphal, we can say that there is an ever-growing appreciation of faithful exposition of the Scripture in the churches.

---

175. The need for prayer goes without saying; however, if its emphasis undermines the authority of the Scripture, there is a problem. How can one even pray correctly without knowing the truth and knowledge of God's word?

176. Dr. E. W. Clark, the first missionary to Nagaland, recorded, "Christianity was going to the *Arasentzur* (soothsayer). Whenever there was sickness, a soothsayer was employed to get a revelation from a deity"; Clark, *Naga Mission*, 5.

177. Cf. 2.4.1.4.

178. Pongen, "Nominalism," 39.

179. Pongen, 39.

180. An overemphasis on the matters of the soul at the expense of ignoring the issues of the body.

3.8 Conclusion

While the first half of the twentieth century mostly focused on the work of the missionaries, we have seen that the second half of the century marked the beginning of indigenous leadership in the church ministry of the MBC. We have also seen that during each tenure of the MBC General Secretary, the homiletical focus of the ministry was probably defined by the contexts of the society at large, although it is assumed that evangelistic preaching focusing on rebirth and salvation persisted in all generations, given the growth of membership in the church record.[181] Further, we have discussed what Mingthing thought about the health of the church, it's preaching ministry, the plight of the pastors and preachers in the Baptist churches under the MBC, and their need for training to enhance their homiletical skills and performance. It remains to be seen, in the succeeding chapters that focus on empirical research, if what Mingthing observed forty years ago is still true today.

---

181. The role of mass conversion also cannot be ruled out.

CHAPTER 4

Description of the Data

4.1 Introduction

In the research methods section, we clarified the employment of "an eclectic and multi-method approach."[1] In this chapter, we look at the first of the four steps, the "descriptive-empirical task" which engages with the data. This chapter aims to describe the data as received through the empirical surveys, interviews, and questionnaires, without interpretation. As the data proved far richer and less amenable to neat analysis according to my original questions, I have chosen to report it more fully and in a different way. For example, the data gave a picture of diverse issues related to the situation of the Imphal Baptist churches from 2000 to 2015, which stretched beyond preaching's impact on spiritual vitality and nominalism, as the main research question suggests.[2] However, at the end of the chapter, an observation will be made to connect the data to the research questions.

In the empirical survey, I interviewed twenty-five participants, including five individuals who took the pilot survey. The remaining twenty participants constitute the fifteen churches under investigation. The twenty participants include twelve pastors from twelve churches and eight members from eight different churches, covering all fifteen churches. All participants will be

---

1. Cf. 1.15.
2. The primary research question is "What do people perceive to be the effects of preaching on the spiritual life of the members of the Baptist churches of Imphal 2000–2015?"

identified with a pseudonym and as either as a pastor, a lay member, a lay leader, or a church/association/convention leader.

Initially about thirty questionnaires were sent out for the pilot survey under these headings: Practical Questions; Experiential-Reflective Questions; and Theological-Reflective Questions. After evaluating the fifteen questionnaires which were returned, the questionnaire was restructured and around 170 of them were distributed to the various members of the fifteen churches.[3] The questionnaire was restructured under four headings: Introductory and Practical Questions; Preaching and Spiritual Vitality; Preaching and Spiritual Nominalism; Preaching and Spiritual Impact. Seventy questionnaires were returned, some through hard copy and some electronically. Further, so the identity of the participants would remain anonymous, the interview participants were given a pseudonym, while the questionnaire participants are identified with participant 1 (P1) or participant 2 (P2), both in the main text and the footnotes.[4]

As for the structure and outline of this chapter, the data from the interviews will be its chief architect and the data from the questionnaires will then dialogically engage, either supplementing the findings of the interviews or contrasting the opinions and voices of the interviewees as conversation partners. Moreover, as the questionnaires come under the open-ended format of the qualitative research method, we will not focus on the quantification, numerical opinion polls, and percentages of the findings, but rather focus on the themes and expressed views on the various issues asked about.

As the research period ranges from 2000 to 2015, the researcher specifically asked the participants to keep these years in mind as they answered the questions. In cases where the participants reflected on their spirituality and the church before 2000 or after 2015, for comparison and discussion, these will be spelled out clearly. However, neatly categorising human experiences during a specific period has been difficult, as human spiritual experiences or emotions sometimes overlap into the previous or succeeding years. However, a sincere effort has been made to represent the general mood of spirituality of

---

3. See Appendix 2 for the questionnaire.

4. Once an interview participant (source) has been footnoted, it will not be repeated. As their names are all different and there will be no room for confusion, the names in the text will suffice. However, the questionnaire participants will be footnoted if they have not been already identified as P1 or P2 in the text.

the period. Before the data is described, it will be appropriate to understand how the entire data was arrived at. Below, we will briefly discuss coding and analysis of the data.

4.2. Data Coding and Analysis

This research used a computer-assisted qualitative data analysis (CAQDAS), the "NVivo 12 Plus" software which helped in coding, categorising, and analysing the data into themes. There are eighty-three items (codes)[5] in total, out of which there are six[6] superordinate themes[7] (or meta-themes),[8] which then have twenty-three[9] sub-ordinate themes.[10] Although CAQDAS was helpful in providing the tools to structure and thematise the entire data, it did not and "cannot help with decisions about the coding of textual materials or about the interpretation of findings."[11] After coding and analysis had been done in NVivo, the data was retrieved from the software to the text of the dissertation manually by the researcher,[12] following the "theory-generating structure"[13] and it had been reported "analytically" and "interpretatively."[14] A brief discussion of the process is mentioned below.

The first step was coding, aimed at "breaking down the data into smaller chunks and then later combining these chunks into a higher level of meaning."[15] This involves "generating an index of terms" to assist in the interpretation

---

5. As recorded in the project, "PhD Thesis_Johnson Raih.nvp – NVivo 12 Plus."

6. Church Members' Understanding of the Word of God; Spiritual Vitality; Nominalism; Preaching; Reading of the Scripture Inspired by Preaching; General Challenges to the Spirituality of the Members in Baptist Churches of Imphal.

7. Saldana, *Coding Manual*, 250.

8. Saldana, 179.

9. Cf. Dissertation content outlines.

10. Saldana, *Coding Manual*, 178, 205, 250.

11. Bryman, *Social Research*, 591; Weitzman and Miles, "Choosing Software," 1–5.

12. Bryman, 591.

13. It is a reporting style that eventually could lead to inductive theorisation. The other two are "Narrative Structure" and "Chronological Structure"; Langdridge and Johnson, *Introduction*, 572.

14. Saldana, *Fundamentals*, 148, 153. The other styles are "writing descriptively and realistically," "writing confessionally," "writing impressionistically," "writing literarily," "writing critically" and "writing collaboratively"; Saldana, 147–59.

15. Langdridge and Hagger-Johnson, *Introduction to Research*, 514; Saldana, *Fundamentals*, 95.

and theorisation of the data.[16] A code could be just "a word or a short phrase" that sums up the essence of the data.[17] In the next step, we identified relationships in the codes.[18] At some point of looking at these codes, they were linked and represented by more "general theoretical ideas in relation to the codes and data" under a common category.[19] To be "inventive and imaginative," this research initially had many codes so that this researcher would not "lose contact with" his own "data and the perspectives and interpretations of those being studied."[20] To make sure that the codes were relevant to what the people faced and experienced, they were guided by "the research questions and the research literature."[21] The same is true with the theme as "it must be relevant with the investigation's research question or research focus."[22] We will discuss this in a later section.

This research used both "in vivo coding" (using the participant's actual language to coin the code) and "process coding" (codes framed by the researcher)[23] and followed both the systems of "descriptive coding," which "assign labels to data to summarise in word or phrase – most often as a noun – the basic topic of a passage of qualitative data"[24] and "value coding system" which "identifies the values, attitudes, and beliefs representing his or her perspective or worldview."[25] In coding, we also constructed categories and clustered "the most seemingly alike things into the most seemingly appropriate groups."[26] Elaborating the process in NVivo terminology, after having the main "parent nodes," the researcher also observed and further categorised the other related and linking ideas as "child nodes" under the parent nodes[27]

---

16. Bryman, *Social Research*, 577.
17. Saldana, *Coding Manual*, 5.
18. Bryman, *Social Research*, 577.
19. Bryman, 577.
20. Bryman, 577.
21. Bryman, 577.
22. Bryman, 580.
23. Saldana, *Fundamentals*, 96–99.
24. Saldana, *Coding Manual*, 262, 104; It is argued that "descriptive coding is one of the most basic coding techniques and useful for all sorts of data and all coding experiences"; University of Glasgow, "Coding Qualitative Data for Categories and Themes."
25. Saldana, *Fundamentals*, 268, 105. For other ways of coding see Saldana, *Coding Manual*, 261–68.
26. Saldana, 91.
27. The terminology used in the NVivo data analysis.

by perceiving "interaction" on "how one or more categories might influence and affect the others."[28]

Coding and analysis are invariably interrelated. Data analysis aims to "reveal to others through fresh insights what we've observed and discovered about the human condition."[29] It is argued that there is no uniform way of analysing a datum, as it could be from the "factual," "conceptual," "interpretive," or "descriptive" aspects or towards "an emergent constructed" theory.[30] But in the data analysis, the primary focus is to discern the patterns of the data.[31] This research analysed the data from the descriptive and interpretive aspects, towards an emergent theory. Further, the researcher also analysed the data thematically by summarising the "manifest (apparent) and latent (underlying) meanings of data" through "superordinate and subordinate outline formats as an analytic tactic."[32]

It is generally understood that "a theme develops out of the codes via the categories"[33] and some therefore believe that it "transcends any one code and is built up out of groups of codes."[34] It must be acknowledged that thematic analysis has no clear "specific series of procedure,"[35] except that the data had to be read over and over again to see if there is an emergent and linking idea coming out.[36]

For example, as this researcher read through the interview transcripts, he came across various opinions on what makes a good sermon as assumed and experienced by the people. As such, all these different voices and ideas had been coded differently and then later brought under the subordinate theme "Characteristics of a Good Sermon," and then this subordinate theme along with other subordinate themes like "Characteristics of a Bad Sermon" and "Impact of Preaching," which also followed the same procedure of coding, were brought under the superordinate or meta-theme of "Preaching."

---

28. Saldana, *Fundamentals*, 92.
29. Saldana, 89.
30. Saldana, 90.
31. Saldana, 91.
32. Saldana, 108; Auerbach and Silverstein, *Qualitative Data*, 69, 136.
33. University of Glasgow, "Coding Qualitative Data."
34. Bryman, *Social Research*, 578.
35. Bryman, 581.
36. Bryman, 579–80.

Likewise, all the superordinate themes in the descriptive chapter were analysed; first, coding individual ideas, then clustering these linking ideas under a subordinate theme, and then bringing them under a superordinate theme, and in doing so, it was either a descriptive theme or an interpretive theme.[37]

Further, it is claimed that data analysis is an "elusive process in qualitative research" where each context is case specific and so each must be dealt with, with one's "unique analytic signature." So, in the final analysis, it is a "learning-by-doing process."[38] Moreover, the researcher employed the data triangulation process, to clarify and authenticate some of the information from the participants during the data analysis period. This exercise helped in the confirmation and validation of the data recorded.[39]

4.3. Description of the Data

Below, the data have been described thematically. The themes that emerged from the data have been randomly arranged and not necessarily in order of priority and importance, as the data from the field was rich; however, almost all the themes are related to the research questions.

4.3.1 Church Members' Understanding of the Word of God

4.3.1.1 Church Members' Understanding of the Word of God between 2000 and 2015

When Pastor Tomba was asked if his church members had a good understanding of the Scripture when he joined the church in 1999, he answered, "They did not know, they were still weak."[40] Pastor Matthew, who joined the pastoral ministry in 2015 answered the same question saying, "No (he laughed). Yes, that is one weak point!" He pointed out that his deacons and senior Christians are hardworking and responsible members of the church but "in terms of our Christian beliefs and doctrines, I find that they are still

---

37. It was interpretive in that the participants' interpretation and ideas were used as themes and not the researcher's interpretation, because the researcher's interpretation will happen only during the moment when he "steps out of the trees to look at the woods" in the next interpretation chapter.

38. Saldana, *Fundamentals*, 137–38.

39. For example, the researcher clarified with Hudson his ideas of "comfortably numb" (cf. 4.3.3.2.1) and "popular culture" (cf. 5.6.5.1).

40. Pastor Tomba, interview by author, "N Baptist church," Imphal, 22 December 2018.

very weak."[41] Pastor Samuel also felt the same about the members when he joined the church in 2015.[42] Pastor Mark, who has served in his church for almost two decades, thought that around 50 percent of his church members may not understand many things about the Scripture in the same way that they understand mathematics in a class; 2x2=4. He conceded, "I cannot say that they have understood everything I have taught them in the church."[43] Pastor Nathan who joined the pastoral ministry in 2013 agreed that most of the members have a weak understanding, although there are some who may be slightly better than others. Whenever he visits the members' homes, recognising the impoverishment of the Scripture in the homes, he encourages the family to read the Scripture together for their "spiritual guidance and protection from temptations." One must move beyond just hearing the preaching on Sundays for their spiritual growth.[44] He gently imposes this phrase, "A chapter a day keeps Satan away," for God's word is food for their soul. P2 cautiously answered,

> Only if it (the knowledge of God's word in a person) could be measured! But it must be mentioned – understanding God's word is a task for a lifetime and all the members of the church need support and prayer to find their path in it from time to time. And yes, I see fair understanding of God's word in our church, regardless of the quantity and amount in their lives and behaviour.

For Pastor Gideon, who pioneered and has nurtured the church since the 1980s, the problem is the "gap between actual teaching and actual receiving, and this gap is much. The gap is that members do not comply and accept what has been taught."[45] P25 substantiated this claim that the gap between their knowledge and life application is "shallow, not deeply rooted. Although there may be some genuine Christians, I find that most of the church-goers are compromising Christians."

---

41. Pastor Matthew, interview by author, "D Baptist church," Imphal, 11 October 2018.
42. Pastor Samuel, interview by author, "I Baptist church," Imphal, 10 October 2018.
43. Pastor Mark, interview by author, "L Baptist church," Imphal, 12 December 2018.
44. Pastor Nathan, interview by author, "H Baptist church," Imphal, 10 October 2018; P16 believes the same.
45. Pastor Gideon, interview by author, "M Baptist church," Imphal, 11 December 2018.

Abraham, a church leader, thinks that his church members were "inadequately aware of the word of God."[46] Twenty-one participants observed the same condition in their local church.[47] Abraham elaborated, "Even theological graduates like us cannot say that we know the Scripture, we must study the Scripture. It is not knowing word for word, but our knowledge of the Scripture is so limited." Hudson, a lay member, argued that it is time the church goes back to the basic doctrines of the Bible, as his church members also do not have a sufficient understanding, nor do they take knowing the word of God as a serious affair.[48]

4.3.1.2 Reasons for the Members' Poor Understanding of the Word of God

4.3.1.2.1 Word of God Not Taken Seriously by the People

Pastor Peter observed that on Sunday, "There is great enthusiasm among the people – the members come in their best clothes, the churches are packed – but in terms of spirituality, not many people take the word of God seriously. Herein lies the issue of not growing and maturing,"[49] because although "many people attend the church, only a few understand the Bible."[50] Pastor Oliver lamented that some people just come and attend church "to show their new clothes or shoes, take some selfies and pictures and post on Facebook, and go back" with no change.[51]

Pastor Peter reasoned that many preachers do not preach evangelically: "There is too much dry preaching, me and others included, so there is a serious decline of spirituality in this city also." Micah, a lay member, admitted that the previous pastor in his church took the word of God more seriously than the new pastor. He contrasted that the new pastor "keeps himself busy

---

46. Abraham, interview by author, "O Baptist church," Imphal, 10 October 2018.

47. P7; P9; P10; P13; P14; P18; P25; P20; P24; P25; P27; P29; P36; P42; P47; P41; P44; P45; P52; P60 and P63. *Contra*, two participants (P12 and P51) thought their church members have an adequate knowledge of the Scripture, but they are unable to translate their knowledge into action.

48. Hudson, interview by author, "A Baptist church," Imphal, 10 October 2018; Harry, a lay person, also expressed absolute lack of knowledge among the members. Harry, interview by author, "J Baptist church," Imphal, 11 December 2018.

49. Pastor Peter, interview by author, "B Baptist church," Imphal, 13 October 2018.

50. P68.

51. Pastor Oliver, interview by author, "K Baptist church," Imphal, 12 December 2018; P7 agreed.

cracking jokes, entertaining, and making people laugh, so the people get used to such an environment."[52] Abraham thinks that once the people laugh and enjoy the entertainment, the pastor is consciously or unconsciously influenced by the crowd's response. However, he thinks that some serious listeners may feel dejected in their spirit and even question if the preacher is serious about his assignment.

4.3.1.2.2 Pastors' Poor Understanding of the Word of God

When the question was asked if the pastors are teaching the word of God well to the members, this is how Pastor Peter replied,

> The pastors and leaders like me who lead the church, do not know our Bible,[53] and so we cannot teach other people. Since we do not teach them, how can they know? Many pastors are not theologically trained, the churches are pastored by lay people in this part of our world. There are government retired officers who serve as pastors or pastors-in-charge, because we cannot pay our pastors their salary.[54]

Kenneth, a prominent leader of the Convention also feels the same. He said,

> Honestly speaking, there is dissatisfaction. It may not be appropriate to put all the pastors together, but I doubt if all the pastors give primary importance to the study and preaching of the Word for the spiritual nourishment of the people. Pastors are all gifted in different ways – some are gifted in counselling, home visitation, development, and mission. But the primary calling of a pastor is to preach the gospel.[55]

Comparing pastors before and after the year 2000, Kenneth asserted,

> This generation of pastors should not be like the older generation of pastors who go for hunting and fishing even on Saturdays

---

52. Micah, interview by author, "C Baptist church," Imphal, 13 October 2018; P62 affirmed that her church pastor also preaches just to entertain.
53. Abraham felt the same.
54. Pastor Oliver agreed.
55. Kenneth, interview by author, "A Baptist church," Imphal, 12 December 2018; Bijoy, a lay member, thought the same. Bijoy, interview by author, "G Baptist church," Imphal, 11 December 2018.

and then go to preach on Sunday by reading a Bible text. I am not sure of the authenticity of the story but there is a saying that an unprepared pastor, one Sunday morning, carelessly picked up an algebra book which looked like the Bible, but when he reached the church, he realised that it was not the Bible. Such was the level of our seriousness towards preaching then, and we should transcend their standard today (laughter).

Harry claimed that because his pastor gives "bad and improper teaching, there is no improvement in the children and youth; the young people are not attracted to the standard of preaching in the church." Kamal, a former pastor revealed that, "whenever we pastors meet, we ask each other about the health of our churches; the answer is unanimous and overwhelmingly sad – our churches are spiritually dying. We need help, our pastors need help."[56] He reasoned that our churches that *are* pastored by theological graduates still do not feed the "lambs and sheep of Jesus" properly with the word of God; rather, they preach political and social matters. Therefore, skipping church happens.[57] Hudson also declared, "I have gone to various churches expecting to hear something different, but it is a disappointment – they are lame sermons." He supposes that today many members no longer go to church expecting to hear God's word; rather, they go because some event is happening there every alternate Sunday.

4.3.1.2.3 Disappointment in the Preaching Ministry of the Pastors

When asked if preaching the word of God had been the same or different before and after 2015, the responses were almost the same – "not too different." Hudson felt that for several years, even before 2015, there had been a longing to know who the preacher would be the next Sunday although the pastor was at home and not travelling. He expressed, "I want to know secretly, ah . . . (sound of deep anguish and frustration), if I feel that way, I think a lot of people must be feeling the same thing too."

On his experience of listening to sermons, Harry said,

---

56. Kamal, interview by author, "I Baptist church," Imphal, 16 December 2018; cf. Mr. Truth Episode 1, *Dreamz Unlimited*.

57. Hudson felt the same; Kamal's argument here is that good preaching happens not necessarily because of having a theologically trained pastor, but because a pastor loves the word of God.

I feel dissatisfaction. I experienced discouragement more.[58] Our church survives through rotational preaching. So, when one person preaches, he tries to project his own achievement and goodness. That's why I feel more discouragement than encouragement. I just listen to them with complete dejection because I know that a sermon without kernel or substance is coming.

That is why he said that there is absolutely no expectation whenever he goes to the church every Sunday. He mourned,

As a Christian I have to go to church on Sunday. I go primarily to worship God and also pray for the family and children. But not with the expectation of listening to God's word. There is no hope for a change and improvement in our church. But when we have some visiting preachers, there is an expectation and thirst to listen to them.[59]

4.3.1.2.4 Pastors' Poor Prayer Life

Pastor Peter is saddened that pastors have not been prayerful people. He thinks that they have been weak in this area. Although they have been praying for others, "we have not been praying much for our own selves, as I also reflect on my own life. So, preaching with prayer and preaching without prayer are different." Pastor Matthew also feels that "along with sermon preparation and preaching, we need to engage in a spiritual battle; to be on our knees. Unless we pray for our sermons, people's lives will not be impacted by our preaching, because it is a spiritual battle."

4.3.1.2.5 Some Older Pastors Cling on to Their Position Despite Their Inability to Feed Others with God's Word

Abraham shared from experience that unfortunately today, we have pastors who do not mind being insulted, so long as they can hold on to their position. He claimed that because of this attitude, "many well-trained candidates from the Bible colleges go away – unfortunately they do not work in our midst." Kamal added that as

---

58. Bijoy also shared the same disappointment.
59. Bijoy echoed the same dejection and hope.

many older pastors are vernacularly trained, they cannot read the commentaries and magazines in English even if they are being provided, except for the Manipuri resources. Even these Manipuri resources, if provided, may not be enthusiastically utilised because the pastors do not value them, they no longer have the habit of reading, and they have become lazy. They want to only narrate stories. Moreover, the situation is worsened, because the older pastors no longer preach systematically and keep preaching old sermons dangling with confusion, so people feel really discouraged.[60]

4.3.1.2.6 Spiritual Blindness or Ignorance Despite Hearing the Word of God

Pastor Patrick[61] shared his disappointment that there are some people in his church, such as a highly educated and cunning Christian couple, who he thinks will never change from their crooked behaviour of backbiting and evil gossip, despite regularly hearing the word of God in the church for decades. He ruminated that

> if we reflect upon the lives of Jesus and Stephen, the people who killed them knew very well what they were doing and killed them. But they prayed to God saying they do not know what they are doing. So, I am now thinking that this Christian couple really do not know God. They are still spiritually blind, otherwise they will not be sharp tongued, criticising people purposefully and hurting people's sentiments.[62]

On the other hand, Pastor Luther thinks that people who refuse to change know the truth but continue to live the wrong life knowingly; he sees this as a trait of nominalism.[63]

---

60. P55 argued that preaching the same topic over and over is dangerous.
61. Pastor Patrick has pastored his church from 2010.
62. Patrick, interview by author, "G Baptist church," Imphal, 11 October 2018.
63. Luther, interview by author, "F Baptist church," Imphal, 11 October 2018.

4.3.1.3 Reasons for Attending Church Despite Not Being Fed with the Word of God

Bijoy reasoned that as people from other religions go to the temple or mosque, many Christians feel they must go to church. It is to fulfil a ritual. Moreover, some people go just for entertainment. They are not bothered even if there is no feeding of the word in the church. However, he feels that there could be a small group of people who genuinely want to worship God. They keep coming back to the church to worship God, hoping against hope to hear God's word, although they continue to be disappointed.

4.3.1.4 The Danger and Consequence of Not Knowing the Word of God Properly

One participant expressed, "If you don't know the word of God and what it says on the issues related to life, then you will be victimised."[64] This is because not knowing God's word can lead to wrong judgments based on one's own limited knowledge[65] as "the world and temptations always target us in a subtle way or contextualise it in the name of 'humanism.'"[66]

As a tree cannot withstand a storm unless it is properly rooted, such a person can be vulnerable[67] and become "half-baked," "overconfident," and have "a confusing lifestyle."[68] Therefore, teaching the word of God properly and knowing it properly is crucial so that believers do not get "stuck in between the worldly and spiritual life" not knowing how to "differentiate between the two."[69] But if the word of God dwells in a believer, such a person will stand differently – like light against darkness[70] and firm in one's faith – because "God's word which is living will set us apart for Christ."[71] An overwhelming majority of the questionnaire participants agreed that not knowing the word

---

64. P8.
65. P11.
66. P36; P25 agreed that he also personally struggles with this.
67. P37.
68. P49.
69. P12; P47 and P48 endorsed the same.
70. P15.
71. P16.

of God properly can jeopardise one's spiritual life towards compromise and nominalism.[72]

There was a contradictory voice which disagreed. One participant argued that it is not the limited teaching and knowledge but "our misunderstanding and misinterpretation that can lead us to dichotomise our lives."[73] However, we could caution that one could misunderstand and misinterpret *because* of one's limited knowledge of the Word.

4.3.1.5 Church Members' Understanding of the Word of God after 2015

When Pastor Matthew was asked whether there was any sign of the members' improvement in scriptural knowledge since 2015, he answered:

> I cannot say how keen they are, but one thing that I . . . I am afraid if I will be blowing my own trumpet. But from my little observation, I think there is some realisation among the church members. I am not saying that the previous pastor is not good, he is a strong prayerful man, all his knees are like the camel's knee. Yet in terms of preaching or teaching . . . I don't know what to say . . . but I see people, at least some of them, who are realising the value of knowing the word of God and what the Bible is about.

He said that they have begun Bible study, focused on the basics of the Bible: "Next year our plan is to read through the Bible by giving certificates."

Pastor Samuel also shared that the regular reading of the word of God in the church has begun to enhance scriptural knowledge, thereby encouraging deeper spirituality:

> We are reading the Scripture in the church beginning from Genesis, one chapter each Sunday. We have reached Numbers. Bible reading has made them grow in understanding the Christian faith. Even in preaching, I began textual[74] preaching

---

72. P7–9; P11–12; P17–21; P24–25; P27–29; P31–38; P41–43; P45; P47–49; P51–54; P60; P62–64; P66.

73. P28.

74. He is referring to expository preaching.

after I came to the church in 2015. Now I believe that they are getting something more concrete.

4.3.2 Spiritual Vitality

In this section, we will explore the characteristics of a person with spiritual vitality, the relationship between preaching and spiritual vitality, and the types of preaching that will enhance spiritual vitality.

4.3.2.1 Characteristics of a Person with Spiritual Vitality

Pastor Nathan claimed that a Christian with spiritual vitality is voluntarily active and involved in the church's work: social work, mission work, and others. He reasoned that "something is growing in their hearts."[75] Pastor Gideon supported this claim and asserted that as James writes, a spiritual person must "demonstrate with his life the beliefs he has in his heart, enlightened by the word of God. Without action, I do not trust a person who people think is spiritual." Bijoy affirmed that "change in behaviour" and a "life that shines in the midst of the unbelievers" is a sure sign of spirituality.[76] He added that for parents, it could be the desire to share with family members the spiritual truths they have heard in church. Ultimately, a thirst for God's word[77] and the desire for a personal quiet time indicate something special.[78] Pastor Mark thinks that a person who kneels and prays with tears and gives like the proverbial widow in the gospel shows signs of spiritual vitality. Then he contrasted that a person who attends the church regularly and gives his tithe may not necessarily be a spiritual person; what matters is the heart of sacrifice. Pastor Sunil stated that such a person loves fellowshipping with believers.[79] Abraham thinks such a person is "someone who walks the straight path of life, one who does not harm others, and one who, after seeing wrong deeds in other people, would correct them in an encouraging way."[80] However, he said

---

75. Pastor Mark also shared the same view.
76. P7; P11; P19; P20; P24; P32; P34; P36; P39; P44; P45; P50; P51; P56; P57; P62 and P68 endorsed this view.
77. P8; P27; P29; P30; P31; P38; P61 supported this view.
78. Bijoy agreed.
79. Pastor Sunil, interview by author, "A Baptist church," Imphal, 10 October 2018; P16; P17; P28; P37; P47; P49; P52; P58 and P65 also talks about "desire for worship and fellowship."
80. P10; P22; P40 and P53 supported this view.

that as mortal human beings, "I have not met a person who is totally perfect without any weakness. There is no uniformity to it, so it is difficult to say."

Moreover, an important aspect is that such a person is marked by a new birth through the power of the Holy Spirit,[81] one who has faith[82] and one who not only cares for matters of the spiritual realm but cares for the environment – the flora and fauna.[83] One participant summed up well that, because of the transformation through the gospel, "his heart is filled with gratitude and kindness, he speaks with carefulness, and his countenance is clear and light."[84]

Further, Harry believes that a pastor with spiritual vitality draws people to himself: "As he preaches with the Holy Spirit, people are drawn towards him and his sermon. There is silence in the pews. The Holy Spirit's presence brings connection. Even the uninterested and restless listeners can be moved to listen to the sermon."

4.3.2.2 Relationship between Preaching and Spiritual Vitality

Pastor Nathan argued that preaching and spiritual vitality are related, in fact, "indispensably related."[85] He reasoned that "God's word through preaching is food for people's spirituality, and if there is no feeding through preaching, where else can they get the feeding?" One participant affirmed that as "good food nourishes and gives us good health, bad food spoils and affects our health. Therefore, bad preaching incubates spiritual lethargy just like bad food spoils our health."[86]

Pastor Nathan testified that his preaching based on God's word is paying dividends; that there is a continuing "need of the word of God for the people to be spiritually vibrant." Hudson cautioned, "When we talk of this generation, I think preaching short sermons are the key to be effective for all the young people, say, a maximum of fifteen minutes." Pastor Gideon revealed that when a preacher preaches with a prayerful heart and the anointing of the Holy Spirit, there is deep satisfaction. He confessed, "Only when my spirit and

---

81. P18; P56; P59 and P60 considered this an essential hallmark.
82. P43 and P66.
83. P26.
84. P50; P67 endorses this view.
85. Pastor Matthew also felt the same. He went to the extent of saying not any preaching but expository preaching.
86. P34.

knowledge merge with God's Spirit when I preach, will people listen silently, accept it, and be strengthened. But to get to this situation is not easy. It is hard to bring people to this stage." Pastor Matthew elaborated that

> without strong biblical preaching, there will be no spiritual growth and vitality. We don't know what we believe in, why we believe in what we believe in and so, we are just floating Christians,[87] we are not going deep. But with a good preaching – systematic exposition and doctrinal preaching – our faith can be vitalised. Preaching can only transform our church.

Pastor Tomba reasoned that the spiritual life of the members is definitely in the hands of the pastors and that "it is through preaching that Christianity comes to life." Pastor Luther claimed that pastors transfer that which has impacted them through the word to the people, thereby bringing conviction and change. Pastor Patrick asserted that a pastor's ministry, especially his preaching, holds the key for the church's spiritual health, even though there are several departments in a church.

However, five participants expressed their disagreement with the view that preaching lifts up their spiritual life.[88] Six participants claimed that they do receive spiritual fulfilment sometimes.[89] Three participants revealed that spiritual uplifting through preaching depends on the preacher concerned.[90] On the other hand, a large number – forty-four participants – were positive that preaching lifts their spiritual life on a consistent basis.[91]

4.3.2.3 Types of Preaching for Spiritual Vitality

Systematic exposition is the key for Bijoy, even if a preacher chooses to preach a topical sermon occasionally. Pastor Patrick said that because the members have heard disjointed bits and pieces of the biblical stories and doctrines, they

---

87. P30 agreed that bad preaching gives birth to floating Christians who are nominal in their commitment.
88. P3; P7; P10; P61 and P63.
89. P9; P15; P25; P26; P49; P52.
90. P11, P29; P32.
91. P1-2; P4-5; P17-24; P27; P28, P30; P31; P34; P36-41; P43-45; P47-48; P50-51; P53-60; P62; P64-68.

think that they have sufficient knowledge, but when the pastor systematically teaches them in detail, they realise their own ignorance:

> If I preach a topical sermon, it will seem as if I am targeting someone; but if it comes systematically through exposition, for example, if I teach this Sunday on "addiction" and the next on "husband-wife relationship," they will accept that it is an outcome of the sequential[92] treatment of the text.

Pastor Luther argued, "only using expository or topical or textual methods may not be enough to grow the church. There is a need for a comprehensive and holistic contribution. As individuals are all different, their needs are all different; their spiritual maturity levels are all different." He shared his struggle because "there will be new seekers visiting the church every now and then; their visit is random – some come again after one year or two years or even five years. As the congregation is a mixed group, so preaching becomes very difficult, in choosing the diet pattern of the listeners."

Moreover, from a practical point of view, Pastor Patrick expressed that exposition is needed so that believers will know their own doctrines and statement of faith in the face of criticisms from other denominations.[93] Moreover, the consequence of a church without expositional preaching[94] is that young people will randomly choose their life partners from other religious groups and denominations without knowing the cost of such decisions. A participant expressed that "expository type of preaching, focusing on the deep meaning of the text can bring spiritual vitality." Moreover, "one may be a believer of Jesus Christ, but he or she may have backslidden or weakened in spiritual life as human beings are weak. Such a person needs the exposition of the word of God and preaching in order to be strengthened spiritually."[95] Seventeen participants believed that exposition is the best way to bring spiritual vitality in a person.[96]

---

92. Pastor Patrick uses the term "expository preaching" and "sequential preaching" interchangeably.

93. Seventh Day Adventist or the Roman Catholics or the Laymen (a sect).

94. Pastor Patrick narrated that his predecessor lulled the entire church to sleep without any systematic teaching of the word for several years.

95. P50; P2.

96. P11; P16; P18; P23; P25; P27; P30; P43; P44; P45; P47; P50; P52 and P63.

On the other hand, there are others who argued that testimonial preaching is a better option. One participant asserted, "Testimonial preaching from a person who had experienced" God's work in his life can bring spiritual vitality.[97] Altogether, nine participants endorsed this method.[98] A few participants believed that exposition and testimonial sermons could go well together.[99]

4.3.3 Nominalism

In the literature review, we discussed the various characteristics, descriptions, and definitions of nominalism in the global platform through the Lausanne movement and regionally in India's North East. We also came up with a working definition of it for this research.[100] However, here, we will not be imposing the working definition; rather, we will be observing what the people said about it as they see and experience it in their diverse contexts.

4.3.3.1 Awareness of Nominalism in the Church

Bijoy thinks that around "70 to 80 percent of the members in my church would be nominal Christians."[101] Pastor Oliver spoke of "white shirt"[102] nominal Christians who come to church to show off and to seek appreciation and attention.[103] Pastor Mark remarked, "In my church also, out of fifty to sixty church members, half of them will fall under this category," especially the young believers.[104] Pastor Gideon confirmed that this is a big issue "prevalent in our church and in my tribal association." He revealed that today, many people ask,

> "How can I get money, through any means?" So, trying to get what is not his is nominalism. People try to build houses near the roads to get compensation from the government, also for

---

97. P7.
98. P7; P37; P39; P6; P53; P57; P58; P60 and P66.
99. P23; P27 and P52.
100. Cf. 2.5.
101. Harry and Pastor Samuel agreed that there are many nominal Christians in their churches.
102. Pastor Sunil also commented that the worshippers are mostly well dressed.
103. Pastor Matthew agreed.
104. *Contra*, Pastor Luther believes that immaturity is not nominalism. He contrasted ignorance and wilful acts of disobedience.

money, people want to project themselves as the owner of a land although they are not. Then, during parliament and state legislative assembly elections, many people sell their votes for money.

He is also critical of theologically trained pastors and workers because he finds them spiritually lethargic.

Kenneth identified the infection of nominal Christians in his church as a grave issue. He argued that although the hill churches claim to be 90 percent Christians, "we tribals carry this disease to the cities, including Imphal. We don't understand why we are Christians."[105] Forty-nine participants confirmed the presence of nominal Christians in their churches and acknowledge its looming threat.[106]

4.3.3.2 Description of a Nominal Christian

The characteristics of a nominal Christian emerging from the context of the study will be examined here.[107] Some of them are not new; however, they will be mentioned to reiterate the discussion in the literature review. On the other hand, some of them are new. These new characteristics will be analysed in the next chapter.

4.3.3.2.1 Comfortably Numb

Hudson concludes that there are people who love to come to church because the entire programme looks like a secular event and "maybe, they think that they are not in the church." Arguing from an opposite perspective, Hudson says, "nominal Christians do not necessarily leave the church; they love the church and keep coming back to it because the church service does not look like a church but a secular event as there is no biblical teaching, and the sermons sound like speeches in a secular event." So, many people "feel awesome" and don't care about the need for biblical truths for their lives. They have become "comfortably numb,"[108] because they were not taught and challenged in their faith for a long time.

---

105. Pastor Sunil agreed this is happening.
106. P7–9; P11; P13; P15–31; P33–40; P43–47; P49–56; P58–68. *Contra*, there were some participants who thought otherwise – P4; P10; P42; P57.
107. We discuss here what we earlier said we would. Cf. 2.5.
108. A phrase Hudson said he took from the band "Pink Floyd."

4.3.3.2.2 Self-Made Man Attitude

Hudson views a Christian who says, "I am successful because I tried" as a nominal Christian, because the picture of God's supremacy and blessing in his life does not exist. Some participants in the questionnaire survey agreed that nominalism could be highlighted in a person who is proud and selfish.[109]

4.3.3.2.3 Ritualistic Christian

Pastor Samuel considers a Christian who fulfils all the external requirements of a Christian life but is hollow inside without actual authentic application as a ritualistic Christian.[110] However, he argues that such a person has a gaping hole in his actual life. Such a person considers Sunday as holy; he fasts every first Sunday of the month, but all these he does ritualistically. Twenty-two participants responded that a nominal Christian is one who is focused on just the externals.[111]

4.3.3.2.4 Lazy Christian

Pastor Samuel claimed that a lazy person, whether it is in terms of church attendance, reading the Bible, praying, or church work, is a nominal Christian. However, he thinks that such people will be offended if they are not addressed as Christian. Six participants thought that a nominal Christian does not read the Bible, perhaps because of the same syndrome.[112]

4.3.3.2.5 Self-Projection through Smooth Talk

According to Harry, a nominal Christian is one who loves to project self with one's smooth talk. He said, "We are smooth talkers; as if we can talk our way into heaven without deeds." He thinks that smooth self-projection talk is an indication of being a nominal Christian.

4.3.3.2.6 Indifferent and Confused Christians

Kenneth critically described a nominal Christian as one who is being careless with his food and drink habits (intoxicants), his church membership may be in one church, but he goes everywhere and anywhere, and is not bothered about the Christian life and its belief system. Such a person is not sure of the

---

109. P35 and P46.
110. Hudson endorsed the same.
111. P7–11; P15–17; P19; P21; P24; P25; P27; P28; P30; P40; P44; P56; P58; P62; P3; P66.
112. P9; P10; P17; P39; P44; P49; P51.

assurance of salvation.[113] Kamal reiterates that such people are confused and simply follow others without any clear personal conviction.

4.3.3.2.7 No Prominence of Christ in One's Talk

Pastor Tomba thinks that one prominent mark of a nominal Christian is the lack of prominence of Christ in one's conversations and the inability to say, "if it is the Lord's will." He claimed that such people cannot think of Christ as being in control of their life; rather they prefer to say, "'I don't know, we Christians also (he laughs),' we don't know what Christians are doing now-a-days, and become clueless about Christ's reign in one's life and become disappointed, if not despondent, being a Christian."

4.3.3.2.8 Dichotomising One's Life between Sacred and Secular

Nominal Christians dichotomise their lives. Their lives inside the church and outside the church are different; "they live two lives"[114] and have "two faces." Although they wilfully commit various kinds of sin, they act like sheep inside the church. This kind of people may be violent but talk about love and forgiveness in the community.[115] Pastor Oliver asserted that true spirituality is best displayed during the seasons of want, need, and a plethora of temptations, and not in the church nor during promotion or on salary day. Pastor Samuel shared that a contractor in his church said,

> it is not possible to glean everything clean in terms of living our lives in the society. We cannot give the exact one-tenth tithe, as every government job and contract needs money; abiding by the straight line of the Bible is not possible, rather we need the imagery of a curved line, not a straight line.[116]

Pastor Matthew argued that tribal religion and indigenous culture never separated the sacred and secular, and so he wonders where this dichotomisation has come from. He grieved that this dichotomy could have happened because they are not informed by the word of God, and the non-believers were able to notice a life of nominalism. Abraham thought that many people

---

113. Pastor Gideon thinks on the same line.
114. Bijoy.
115. Pastor Oliver.
116. Pastor Matthew shared a similar experience as faced by Pastor Samuel.

have the attitude that "God is not in the market, he is only in the temple," and Christians have bought this argument to direct their lives from the world. Pastor Tomba agreed that this is a reality in his church – that some secular leaders observe Sunday with respect but trample on their ethics and spirituality on other days. He added that there is also another wrong conjecture: "If I pay my regular tithe, I have access to heaven; even if I marry two wives; steal or rob from others; even if I siphon off the funds of the government, it is not a problem, I have access into heaven."

On the gap of the members' knowledge of the Bible, Pastor Tomba confessed that it could have been because the pastors have not taught their members well[117] on the sacredness of every weekday, and that Sunday is set aside for corporate worship.[118] Pastor Luther revealed an interesting factual picture of how nominal Christians behave:

> Last time, my father's friend told me that if you want to go to Moreh[119] and buy anything, go on Sunday. Why Sunday? Because you don't get looted on Sunday by various Christian armed groups,[120] because all the looters go to church on Sunday (after saying that he laughs loudly) for worship and so you don't get looted on Sunday.

Supporting the reality of this phenomenon, a participant claimed that "dichotomisation is the lifestyle of today's world. Christianity has become a phenomenon for social attachment only."[121] Therefore, some consider a nominal Christian as a "fake, acting Christian without faith and fear of God."[122] Ten participants asserted that a nominal Christian is one whose moral and ethical standard is low as the person does not hesitate to switch colours on Sunday and the other days.[123]

---

117. Bijoy echoed the same explanation.
118. Kenneth asserted the same argument.
119. A thriving business town situated in the international border of Myanmar. Moreh is an important eastern corridor from where all the goods from China and other South East Asian countries come to India.
120. They are not the Indian government military groups, but local insurgents.
121. P7.
122. P54.
123. P8; P10; P34; P35; P42; P44–46; P52; P63.

4.3.3.2.9 Occasion Related Christians

Pastor Sunil declared, "They are namesake Christians; no membership, no tithe and they attend the church only on special occasions like Christmas, Good Friday, Easter Sunday, Cultural Sunday, and Environment Sunday, especially on days when there are feasts." A participant supported this view that there are "namesake Christians, Sunday Christians, festival or occasion Christians."[124] Further, it was argued that namesake Christians are without any personal commitment and received no teaching from their parents.[125]

4.3.3.2.10 Compromised Christians

Pastor Mark felt that many new believers can become nominal Christians by reverting to their old religion, and he sees this prevalent among the Nepalis, Kabuis, and Meiteis. For the Meiteis, he said that the mighty current of compromise comes from the neighbourhood. For example, some younger believers will be told by their non-believing aunties, "You go to church later, but let us first join the *Usop*."[126] Then the church members will later confess to pastor, "I went to eat the *Usop* in the Mandir because my aunty told me to do so." Pastor Mark is convinced that this arises because of compromise. He calculated, "I believe this compromise will be with at least 50 percent of my church members, and this is one gateway to nominalism." Pastor Sunil argued that these people have "no inner compulsion from within, no obligation, they go wherever the wind blows; there is no demarcation." Pastor Luther talked about the role of the influence of non-believing friends in the office in terms of the practice of bribery and corruption. He remarked that

> because of mixing with non-Christians, we are unable to maintain purity. When the tribal Christians come to Imphal, they have light, but their light gets dimmer with time. If there is bright light, it will dispel the darkness, but the valley's religious influence is too strong that they are unable to fight against such influence and force.[127]

---

124. P42.

125. P55; P56.

126. It is a ritual anniversary meal before the Hindu deity in the mandir after the demise of a person in the family.

127. Pastor Nathan and Hudson believe that there are members who dichotomise in their churches.

4.3.3.2.11 Self-Righteous and Ascetic Christians

Pastor Oliver shared that there are some people on the extreme end of the spectrum – the ascetic Christians. These people by God's grace know the word of God, but "they are too one laned and do not want to mingle with other people." They prefer to meditate and worship God at home and avoid Christian fellowship. These people wrongly interpret Jesus's conversation with the Samaritan woman and claim, "We can worship alone because the Samaritan woman also, while talking with the Lord, was told that believers can worship the Lord on any mountain, provided it is done in truth and Spirit." He argued that this is another form of nominalism.

4.3.3.2.12 No Hunger for the Word of God

Pastor Matthew thinks that not thirsting for the word of God is a symptom of being a nominal Christian. If there is "no hunger for the word of God" during weekdays and if "there is no passion to study the word of God," something is wrong. Not wanting to know one's own Scripture but desiring to know that of other religions is one sort of nominalism. However, there was another voice that explained it differently: "When a new believer comes to faith, his cup is still a quarter full, so we cannot brand him as a nominal Christian because he has just come in yesterday. It is because he does not yet know."[128]

4.3.3.2.13 Secular Worldview

Hudson expressed that there are Christians who agree with whatever the world agrees. They do not mind following other peoples' worldview to survive in a corrupted society like Manipur's. Moreover, such people may be interested to come to the church for the entertainment quotient, because they are not controlled by any authority. Such people "come to the church because some church sermons are filled with secular ideas and entertain the congregation like a secular programme." One participant asserted that such a person views "religion as a social construct" and this is an "ungodly influential wave from the secular worldview."[129]

---

128. Pastor Luther.
129. P43; P44.

4.3.3.2.14 Floating and Drifting Christians

Giving a pictorial description, pastor Matthew believes that "a floating Christian is a nominal Christian." In his language it is translated as, "just floating and drifting to anywhere the wind blows. We don't know what is inside, we don't know where we are going. We don't know how far we have gone away. We are just floating aimlessly."

4.3.3.2.15 Unteachable and Easily Offended

Pastor Patrick observed that there are some groups of people who get easily offended when he teaches the word of God and asks his members to abide by it. He revealed, "When I try to straighten the wrong in them, their egos felt threatened." He reasoned that nominal Christians are proud because a true Christian should be willing to own up to their mistakes and be open to correction. Another voice affirmed that the various forms of "pride – not allowing others to correct one, not willing to change or say sorry and accept one's mistake, and not willing to forgive other people without condition" are signs of being a nominal Christian.[130]

4.3.3.2.16 A Life without Integrity

Micah, an unskilled worker, thinks that a nominal Christian has inconsistency between his speech and life. Such people would preach that there should not be any "segregation between *achao apik* (the big and the small) because we are all children of God, but when it comes to eating and drinking together (he laughs), these preachers want to be treated above others." He revealed that these leaders would remark that those "who work in the low and menial job should not eat and drink with the big people (presidents, secretaries, preachers and pastors). Pastor Luther considered a life without integrity, a life that is inconsistent between words and deeds, as a trait of nominalism. "These people," he said, "attend the church, but there is no commitment. They do not have the scriptural authority guiding and controlling their actions." He explained, "They will have a tag of a Christian, but they will not wear that brand as shown in the tag."

---

130. P3.

4.3.3.2.17 Superficial or Not a Born-Again Christian

Pastor Moses feels that there are people who think that nominal Christians are those who are caught in the trappings of superficiality. They come to church with "very good dress and they look out for technological powerpoint presentations during the sermon, but they have not been touched by Jesus." These people ask the pastor to visit the family for prayers and to dedicate new purchases – house or vehicle – but they do so, following the rituals of other religions.[131] He argued that

> a person who is bitten by the snake knows the *mahu* (poison) and impact of the snake's bite; conversely, a person who has been touched by God will know very well the touch of God. People who have not experienced the touch of God, although they are highly qualified in the secular field or education, will not understand what healing, God's grace and love, is in their life.

One participant claimed, "A nominal Christian is a traditional Christian, one who has not repented of sin and responded to the forgiveness of Jesus Christ and put faith in him as one's personal Saviour and Lord."[132] Thirteen participants from the questionnaire considered a traditional or superficial Christian who is not born-again as a nominal Christian.[133] Another participant declared that such a person knows only how "to teach others, not self; looking for handsome monetary help; groupism; backbiting; not accepting suggestions and correction; dirty food habit and immoral character."[134]

4.3.3.3 Reasons for the Incubation of Nominalism in the Church
4.3.3.3.1 No Teaching of the Word of God in the Churches

Kamal argued that malnutrition because of the famine of the word of God in the pulpits of the churches has led many church members to their spiritual doom and death. Real satisfaction is not gained because of the preacher's oratory skill but when "God's word is opened and served to the people." He elucidated that

---

131. Pastor Moses, interview by the author, "E Baptist church Imphal," 13 October 2018.
132. P32.
133. P18; P26; P29; P31; P32; P34; P37; P38; P40; P43; P50; P56; P59.
134. P44.

even a person whose eyes are not opened to see the value of prayer and spiritual truths, if taught properly, will follow good teaching. Many times, the sermons are all unconnected and full of husk, people's mind begin to wander here and there. After the church [service], the sermon is easily forgotten.[135]

Pastor Oliver affirmed that many preachers do not delve deep enough into the word, and so end up preaching superficial sermons without focusing on the personal and spiritual life of the members. He reflects that people tend to listen to social gospel sermons, but these sermons do not change lives.[136] A person argued, "When the word of God is interpreted according to one's own convenience, stretchable like a rubber belt, we cannot stand against the world system. It is because we have become respecters of men and politicised our pulpit."[137] Kumar firmly believes that "transformation and impact in the lives of the people is in the hands of the pastor."[138]

Pastor Patrick argued, "there are people who accept bribes in my congregation (laughing)." He mentioned a disconcerting accusation of the Meitei Hindus against the Christians that "the Meitei Hindu could be negotiated to do a work in the office with a betel nut, but the tribal Christians cannot be negotiated with until they are paid their satisfied bribery amount from the client." He thinks that this has happened because the previous pastor had failed to teach the word of God.

Four participants argued that a pastor's lack of knowledge of God's word[139] and want of good preaching is an indisputable reason for nominalism to slide into the church[140] because insufficient knowledge of God's word prevents a person from making the right decisions in life's varying circumstances.[141]

4.3.3.3.2 No Reading of the Scripture at Home

Pastor Nathan thought that his church members lack the knowledge of God's word because they do not make it a habit to read it both individually and

---

135. Kenneth agreed that this situation exists.
136. Hudson argued many pastors feed "junk food" in the church.
137. P1.
138. Kumar, interview by the author, "E Baptist church Imphal," 13 October 2018.
139. P15; P16; P29; P49.
140. P21; P47; P48; P49; P58; P61; P62; P63.
141. P67.

corporately as a family. He claimed, "I think nominalism also occurs because people do not read the Scripture." He continued, "forget about studying the Bible, even holding the Bible and coming to the church has decreased over the years."[142] One participant substantiated this argument: "While there is an inadequate spiritual feeding in the church, the members are interested in gossiping and there is lack of Bible reading and spending time in prayers."[143] Another participant remarked, "the home should be the first church" for a child, and children "whose parents exercise discipline in reading the Scripture grow in their Christian life."[144]

4.3.3.3.3 No Implementation of One's Knowledge and Lack of Spiritual Discipline

Although Pastor Oliver agreed that knowing God's word is essential for spiritual growth, he perceived that nominalism also grows "not because we do not know the word of God;"[145] "we may know where Jesus was born," but "Jesus had never been born in their lives. The word has not impacted their lives."[146] Some participants believed that this problem is closely connected with the weak exercise of spiritual discipline because although they know the necessity of prayer, fasting, and other spiritual disciplines, people do not do it.[147]

4.3.3.3.4 Too Many Worship Services and Fellowships

With sarcasm, Pastor Oliver stated that perhaps one reason why nominalism has slipped into our lives is because "We attend too many church services, we are too spiritual, that's why . . . (he laughs)."[148] He feels that this makes his members "lazy and dull during our corporate worship." Unlike in the metropolitan cities, where his own tribal people worship once a week, he remarked,

> we have services on Wednesday (mission focus), Thursday (men's department), Friday (women's department), Saturday (youth department), Sunday morning (all the church members),

---

142. It is not because people have Bibles in their Smartphones.
143. P52.
144. P8.
145. Pastor Oliver.
146. Bijoy; Pastor Gideon gave the same reason.
147. P31; P48; P52.
148. *Contra*, P24 argued that lack of fellowship could be a reason for nominalism's growth in the church.

Sunday noon (Sunday school), Sunday evening (main service). Only two evenings are left free, I think these departmental fellowships are making the church very heavy. During the departmental service, people are bored (he demonstrates by scratching his head and looking here and there, because they do not want to hear a sermon that is boring). People wait for the preacher to say, "let me end my sermon." They mostly come because the church has set a rule for attendance and also for their conscience's sake. I believe this is also one of the reasons why we are becoming nominal Christians.

He critiqued his own church system by remarking that a living church need not be wrapped up in functions and programmes. Another person credited institutionalisation of Christianity as a reason for spiritual degradation.[149]

4.3.3.3.5 The Influence of the Technological World

Pastor Gideon expressed that the abuse of technology can bring in nominalism in the homes as the "degree of enjoyment and entertainment has increased." Pastor Patrick expressed a similar opinion that "technology has wounded believers" as many elders also have become "addicted to watching movies on their laptops late into the night, which affects their Christian discipline and spirituality." Some participants confirmed this allegation.[150] Another participant vividly expressed that it is because of "over exposure to [the] internet where what we see and hear are not practically applicable, which in turn lead many youths astray from what a real Christian should be."[151]

4.3.3.3.6 No Cell Group or Small Group of the Church

Hudson recollected that during his younger days, the church systematically organised cell groups and small groups on the basis of locality. This really encouraged spiritual activity between Sundays. This movement also strengthened family devotions. But he lamented that during the past decade or so, this trend has dissipated, and that it is "rare to see family singing and having family devotion. This could be one of the reasons for falling into nominalism."

---

149. P26.
150. P36; P38; P40 and P59.
151. P40.

4.3.3.3.7 Misinterpretation of the Word of God

Hudson suspected that there are some members of the church who swallow everything the pastor preaches without any critical filtering. He lamented that these people do not know the road they are taking, and they are walking like zombies. Pastor Samuel affirmed that if "the wrong doctrine is taught, they will take the bad teaching as right and go back home," which will lead to spiritual confusion and nominalism.[152] Kenneth remarked that some Baptists even think that good works before faith in Christ will assure them of their salvation, because of misinterpretation of the Scripture.[153] There are voices that caution that misinterpretation gives birth to confusion in a believer's spiritual life.[154] Other participants warned that misinterpretation also discourages the believers' church attendance.[155] Further, some participants warned that misinterpretation and bad preaching can lead to a different denomination or sect, pointing to the fatality of such a possibility.[156]

4.3.3.3.8 Religio-Cultural Influence

Pastor Moses maintained that blind allegiance to one's cultural influence is a definite gateway for the entrance of nominalism. Many people think that if "we do not revive our cultural practices abandoned after the arrival of missionaries, we do not have any identity." For example, according to his cultural tradition, they have a festival called *Lamlei* – path-cleaning festival. Literally, this is related to cleansing the water source of the village. He stated:

> Our ancient parents believe in the existence of aquatic spirits or deity and they believe in cleansing the water way. In a way we need to cleanse it annually because we need water for our survival. But the people want to commemorate it with drinks (wine and alcohol) that the Christians have stopped practicing, and thus try to pull the Christians back.

Moreover, some regular members of the church believe in *maiba* (sorcerer or shaman), and some Christians who have been baptised, want to deliberately

---

152. See also P52–54; P59.
153. P32 and P53 affirmed that there are wrong teachings that endorse the same.
154. P17; P47.
155. P19; P31; P38–40; P60; P66.
156. P37; P56.

learn the trade today, technically and not just orally, like the olden times. Kumar lamented, "These Christians verbally believe in God, but instead of sieving and filtering the cultural practices through the Scripture, they have put culture above the authority of the Scripture."

Pastor Oliver shared that when a couple wants to get married, they approach the church, and the pastor solemnises their wedding under the authority of the Bible and gives them a certificate. But when there is marital discord, not amounting to adultery, and the couple wants to divorce, they do not approach the church but settle the separation between their two families by slaughtering some animals. This is where cultural tradition takes precedence over the Bible and our lives are directed by culture.[157]

Pastor Tomba was critical of his church members and people of his community by saying that perhaps his tribesmen are the people most resistant to repent and change from their ancestral cultural captivity. He said that there are some Christians who have been trapped in the "syncretistic religion called *Tingkao Ragwang* where around 75% of their teachings are taken from the Bible and 25% from the Hindu and animistic culture." Another issue is the *Gaan-Ngai* festival where Christians tend to become like non-Christians. During this festival, people "carry out the traditional ritual of drinking rice beer – *Yupan Thaba* (ovation – to pour out the rice beer), and chant, addressing the deity of the four corners of the village for protection. The deities are *Kaipi, Kaiba,* and *Bambau.*" He argued that we Christians can commemorate the *Gaan-Ngai* festival led by the pastor and worship Jesus as the protector of our land without other religious trappings.

Among another tribal group, Pastor Tomba observed that "Nominalism comes through the festival of *Meira Houchongba* where tribal Christians mix with the Meitei religious tradition, by worshiping the Meitei deity for the act of commemorating coronation, to install the king." He narrated that "The Rongmei people will come and sacrifice two or three roosters by beheading them, then the Tangkhul people will come with their traditional attires and sing the cultural songs. After this, the Meitei people will worship the *Sanamahi* deity (*Umanglai, Lainingthao,* and *Nongdaleiren Pakhangba*). So,

---

157. *Contra,* in the case of Pastor Gideon, he said that as his church is situated in the midst of animists and pagans, there is an unspoken competition between them, so there is a minimal chance his members will fall aside and compromise on their testimonies.

there is complete mess and mix." He was surprised to learn that during that occasion, "Many Christians dance with all the non-Christians so that they may promote secularism." "In the name of secularism," said the pastor, they "try to wriggle out and refuse to accept their mistake." However, he thinks that the festival can be rebaptised and conducted under scriptural authority.

Abraham shared that his church members also experience a great pull from culture. The debate on cultural influence is ongoing; however, if the people think "culture is bigger than God, then they are wrong." In the name of culture, "we do *lengkhawm* (dancing in group as we sing). Since people cannot drink alcohol inside the church, many people want to do *lengkhawm* outside the church and then drink. The abuse of culture helps in the spreading of nominalism."

For Kamal, the influence of culture for his tribe is particularly evident during the time of sickness. Even after becoming Christians, "we observe many of our ancestors' rites during the time of sickness. We label certain sicknesses as the evil spirit's attack." For example, if a person has a stomach ache we say that perhaps *rume* (evil eye) had cast his eye on him. We forget that prayers healed the sick, the lame, the blind, and others in the Bible. Sometimes, "the deacon board is invited to come and pray, and in front of the deacon board they slaughter a chicken and pull out its innards; they look at the liver for some signs and do several things with the dead chicken." Many Christians are neck deep in this practice and think that such a practice is in alignment with Christian tradition.

4.3.3.3.9 Generational Gap and Ministerial Insensitivity

Bijoy thought that the generational gap could be one of the factors that make church services unattractive. As the world around them is changing, the young people do want to see some change, but when that is not seen, the young people tend to drift away. Further, many people come to the church burdened in their hearts. If the church leadership is insensitive to the members' needs, spiritual disillusionment could set in.[158]

---

158. P25.

4.3.3.3.10 Immodest Fashion Statement

Kumar claimed that in his church, youths come with "transparent and immodest dress, especially in summer." He remarked that they may look beautiful, but they create a "gross environment in the church" as people gathered in the church are fallen people, not angels. He asserted, "I believe that blindly following immodest fashion design is a part of nominalism, because a truly born-again and vibrant Christian will not be insensitive enough to put on such clothes and tempt people by what they wear."

4.3.3.3.11 Mass Conversion and Its Ramification

Pastor Oliver thought that many Christians in his church became Christians because of mass conversion. Pastor Peter observed that as "the flood water brings wood and stones; the people also just flow along with the current." So, he "feels as though if the leader stops believing in Jesus, they will all stop believing in Jesus too." Only a few are genuine about the matter of their faith. He then remarked that mass conversion with a lack of proper teaching is a fatal combination.

4.3.3.3.12 Lack of Prophetic and Evangelistic Sermons vis-à-vis the Presence of Entertainment Value

Bijoy observed that if one looks at the churches and the crusades taking place in the city, there is an increase in entertainment value and a decrease or nonexistence of prophetic and evangelical preaching and teaching. Hudson talked about the presence of "pop culture" which people want to follow blindly, especially the youth. He claimed that the church does not talk about doctrinal truths but "speaks in a way that fits the congregational taste, and which the congregation wants to hear . . . they don't want to confront the listeners with the word of God; nominalism is creeping in." Talking of the danger of this trend, he said, "This kind of mindless imitation can snowball and wreak havoc in the lives of other smaller churches who look up to the bigger churches in the city as role models."

Harry declared, "we need more leaders and pastors who are stubborn, in a good way, stubborn to the word of God, whose no is no and yes is yes. We need that for a change, because many pastors comply with what the members are requesting."

4.3.3.3.13 Not Recognising the Identity of Jesus and Loving Him Enough

Pastor Tomba argued that many people do not love Jesus enough. There is a tendency to equate Jesus to ourselves, so we do not want to live under the authority of Jesus. The ramification is that one's reverence for Christ will decrease and if that happens, "everything will become acceptable, as we are not under his authority." Further, he argued that we "fail to fully understand the supremacy of Christ in our lives." There are people who pursue a political kingdom over the kingdom of God. This belief can infect and plague our conviction.

Pastor Patrick stated that a woman in his church is controlled by an evil spirit because she refuses to forgive people. He remarked that a person who has been born-again would not behave the way she does. He felt, "the evil one is only whispering criticism into her ears."[159] He shared that all his teaching and encouragement for years to forgive people fell on deaf ears, as she retaliated that she would not forgive intentionally. The pastor also felt personally attacked by her. He declared that this is a different kind of nominal Christian in his church; a life not impacted by the word of God, and one who has not accepted Jesus into her heart with a clear conviction.

4.3.3.3.14 Only Preaching and No Teaching in the Church

Pastor Peter strongly believed that preaching poorly could be one factor for the breeding of nominalism in the church, but the main factor for him was because, "we have failed much in our teaching and Christian education and have overemphasised on preaching. If I only preach and not teach in the church, even my own children, who are from a pastor's family, will not be able to understand God's word."

Even for Kumar, "a believers' life is not complete without teaching. Preaching is not enough to mature a Christian life as I observed this for so many years; discipleship is really important." He went on:

> To address nominalism, we must build up disciples. Teaching goes deeper, where preaching is unable to go. Preaching can make a person convicted and conscious of God, but teaching will help a person understand the will and ways of God. Preaching

---

159. P2 also talked of the evil spirit's work in breeding nominalism in a person.

alone will not ripen the fruit – every believer must become a disciple, then he will become ripe. And a disciple must reach out for more disciples like the networking methodology of various beauty products.

4.3.3.3.15 Compromised Nature of the Content of Church Worship

Bijoy observed that our churches are absorbing the pattern of the worldly and secular programmes into our worship pattern, and we "uncritically copy and paste them."[160] The Baptist church's principle of the autonomy of the local church allows a local church the freedom to choose the nature of the church service order. Pastor Sunil expressed that many items like choreography, songs, and other special items are necessary because they help "stimulate the interest of the members, especially the young people." He said, "We invite singers to present at least two songs from different places by paying them. This is important because it creates an opportune moment to speak something of importance, and people are willing to listen" following such a presentation.

However, there were contrasting opinions. Hudson, a member of the same local church, expressed that the whole church service looks like a carefully planned out social gathering. He expressed repulsion about the activity of welcoming special guests with garlands, citations, frames, and flowers. He said that the church prepares all these during the week because they know that some particular people are coming for the Sunday morning service. The whole service is extended because of many "unnecessary special numbers and choreographies." Then he remarked, "For the families who come with children, they are already restless by the time sermon begins, other people are also just itching to go home; they just want to finish the service without listening to the preaching." Here, Hudson unambiguously critiqued the casual approach and lamented that "only when people's concentration time is up, the preacher begins to preach."[161]

4.3.3.3.16 The Responsibility of Pastors and Church Leaders

There were voices that linked the rise of nominalism in the churches to the pastors' own spirituality. Harry claimed that the problem of nominalism "is

---

160. P27 called this the influence of globalisation and pop culture.
161. Bijoy agreed that this situation is a matter of deep concern.

more with the leaders and pastors. They are worse. To retain their position as a deacon or the pastor, they exaggerate their own goodness. The lay people do not reach their level of nominalism." He also revealed that he himself is a nominal church leader. Similarly, Pastor Peter thought that because of the dry spiritual life of the pastors, "there are many dry preaching, me and others included, so there is a serious decline of spirituality in this city also."[162] Some participants agreed that pastoral responsibility and integrity is non-negotiable.[163]

4.3.3.3.17 Bad Exemplary Lifestyle from Graduates of Bible College

Pastor Gideon appreciated the contribution of the theological graduates in the church ministry but recalled that many testimonies had been destructive. He remarked, "Some of our theologians unexpectedly join politics and are unable to exhibit the worth and value of a child of God. Their deeds have negative impact on the people." Many also tarnish the mission workers' image by their dangerous choice of taking up contract work, playing petty politics, and exhibiting wrong lifestyle choices.

4.3.3.3.18 Not Knowing How to Take the Members to the Next Level

Pastor Luther argued that many pastors do not know how to take the spiritual life of the members to the next level. He claimed that many churches

> experience the same spirituality for several years after having received their salvation and the Holy Spirit, and the pastors do not know what to do next to take the believers to the next spiritual level. They preach the same sermon and theme continuously; they seem vibrant, but after this, what? The preachers and pastors must look into this matter. If this continues, there may come a stage of nominalism.[164]

4.3.3.3.19 Improper Use of the Pulpit

Pastor Nathan admitted, "Pulpits have been abused and politicised. Many have used it as a public information dissemination centre for public organisations

---

162. Pastor Oliver emphasised the same condition concerning the pastor's life of integrity in the family.
163. P60; P63; P66.
164. Pastor Oliver echoed this argument.

and the government. This is rampant, preaching is overshadowed." Pastor Oliver expressed that he had warned people who take the pulpit in his church not to scold people from there. He claimed that there are some church elders who have the habit of bluntly pointing out the mistakes of people wherever they get to the pulpit, in the guise of telling the truth, which oftentimes is not the truth at all. He remarked that "although pigs love to eat potato and some other delicious food, they run away, if the food is thrown at them." So, "although it is the Bible, sermon, and spiritual food, if we do not try to win the hearts of the people with love but instead with our power and authority, that will not make the church very healthy. People will stop coming to the church."

4.3.3.4 Ways to Address Nominalism
4.3.3.4.1 Love the Word of God and Preach the Biblical Gospel

Pastor Patrick advised, "Whatever preaching style it may be, try your best to make others understand the word of God." He admitted that he had faced many people asking him, "How can I be born again? I do not know how to be born again." He continued, saying that

> if we do not teach them from the Bible on how and what it means to be born-again, as this is a spiritual matter, if we do not give them spiritual food, teaching, and guidance, what can we give? We must give them *machen oiba chinjak* (solid food), not only soup and vegetables, but meat, and that also a good piece. I do not know how to make people laugh. Just to make people laugh and entertain them is not good enough. So, solid food that contains protein and vitamin is the word of God.

Pastor Sunil affirmed:

> We must study the text better. We mostly share testimonial and topical sermons. But we need to prepare and feed the word of God better. Sometimes I am torn apart, as I don't have time to study because of all the church ministries. Morning and evening, I am heavily engaged and my schedule is tight. I do not have time even for my family, my children.

When asked what preaching the biblical gospel means, Pastor Nathan understood it as basing one's preaching purely on the word of God, although other elements cannot be totally ignored in a thirty to forty-minute sermon. Patrick declareed that biblical gospel preaching must be based on the basic tenets of the Christian faith. He narrated that some people were offended and responded negatively because many of them felt that the message was too basic for them and that they have graduated from spiritual kindergarten. However, Patrick argued that they responded like that because they were born into a Christian family, but needed to hear the gospel to come out of nominalism.

Hudson observed that in his church, the pastor does not preach either legalistic sermons or gospel sermons. It is only once in a while, when a guest speaker comes, that the speaker preaches on grace and the gospel. He asserted that there is a need to go back to the doctrines of "creation, sin, and re-creation in Christ," appealing to the people "like the mobile sim card company does, by giving us repeated calls to announce their offers. This persistence is needed to address nominalism." One participant argued, "I consider understanding the word of God thoroughly to be imperative, as we all know God's word is our spiritual food, and if we are not well fed then we will starve spiritually, which will eventually lead to becoming spiritually stagnant and nominal."[165] But if we are fed well, "God's word can protect the believers from exhaustion; as watering the plants can rejuvenate them, God's word can strengthen the Christian life."[166] Moreover, a person who fully understands[167] the word of God will not remain "spiritually stagnant and nominal but become zealous and passionate for lost souls."[168] A participant stated that camps are necessary to impart systematic teaching to the believers.[169]

4.3.3.4.2 Preach with Love

Pastor Sunil cautioned that a pastor must not practise favouritism. He disclosed that in the past, there was favouritism in his church. He said that people can be distanced if he practises favouritism, and his sermon will be valueless as it will fall on deaf ears. He argued that a good relationship and a

---

165. P27.
166. P8.
167. *Contra*, P53 warned that "sufficient understanding of God's word without faith is dangerous."
168. P52.
169. P67.

life of moral integrity are essential because, "even if my voice is angelic and my biblical sermon is theological," if the relationship between the pastor and believers is not good, the door will be closed.[170] Kamal affirmed that the pastor must be a *kungvado* person (to draw and attract the people).

Pastor Gideon said that love must be the primary motivating factor for a pastor's preaching ministry. He shared how a beloved member's backslidden life and eventual demise before coming back to Christ, greatly affected his heart, and that was how his own health challenges began.

Harry firmly asserted, "even if you know or you don't know the word of God, if you have love, you will be able to win souls and activate people spiritually." He went on, "as Jesus loves and calls us, if the pastors also call us with love, winning people will be done effectively. Without love, you cannot do anything." He explained, "Even a small child who is still breastfed by the mother knows the language of love; how can we not know whether someone is preaching to us with love or without love? In our church our pastor only loves the good people, not the sinners."

4.3.3.4.3 Prayer and Spirit-Controlled Preaching

Pastor Oliver asserted that preaching that addresses nominalism cannot be through the certificate received from any brand of university, theological association, college, or denomination. Preaching that impacts should first be undergirded by the Holy Spirit; however, it does not mean that one must ignore theological depth. He dismissed the type of preaching which has no clear focus but simply states "as the Spirit leads." Further, he talked of prayer and strongly believes that prayer, along with wrestling with deep theology in studying of the word, is another important pillar for effective preaching. Moreover, he agreed that a good homiletical skill in terms of body language, dress, and presentation is required. However, he warned that without prayer and scriptural depth, the sermon will fizzle out.

4.3.3.4.4 Preaching to the Believers' Context

Kumar believed that the exposition of the word of God must be brought into the believers' context for application. Pastor Oliver said that the application of preaching should not be generic and focused on the larger issues of the

---

170. *Contra*, Harry stated that his church pastors only favour good people, not sinners.

nation and society, but rather should meet the needs of the individuals; such as a mother who has a nursing baby or an employee who goes to the office amidst various temptations waiting to pounce on him.

Bijoy argued that in his church there are seekers, members who have just received baptism, and Christians who had been Christians for fifty or more years; their life situation, the battles of life and the needs of the people coming to the church are diverse. In this context, he said that preachers have a big responsibility, to make sure that every member of the congregation receives the attention of the preacher, and an application appropriate for their life situations during the preaching.[171]

4.3.3.4.5 The Pastor's Life of Integrity

Many felt that pastors must scrutinise their personal lives so that their sermons will be impactful. Bijoy analysed that "many of the members do not care about the word of God. They don't care about what you are preaching, but they care about how you live. If you live right, they will begin to accept what you speak." Abraham suspected that "preachers tend to have a dichotomy between their preaching and their lives." Harry argued that a preacher's living faith demonstrated by a life of integrity comes before preaching. Micah animatedly expressed, "We observe the life of the preacher and his preaching. When his life is consistent with his preaching, it touches our lives. We then want to take his sermons into our lives. But if his life does not measure up to his sermons, we do not feel like taking in his sermon."[172]

4.3.4 Preaching

4.3.4.1 Characteristics of a Good Sermon
4.3.4.1.1 A Sermon Marked by Personal Encounter with Christ

Pastor Peter admitted that "encountering Christ personally and preaching" is different from preaching "without knowing God personally." He confessed that he had preached hundreds of sermons for a long time without having met Jesus Christ. He argued, "If I have never experienced something, I cannot speak about that something with authority." A participant asserted that a good sermon is one which has a "personal testimony and biblical application,

---

171. Kamal also talked about need-based application in preaching.
172. Kumar also mentioned a preacher's "Christly character." Pastor Sunil agreed that this is a valid argument.

which is to the point."[173] Moreover, another voice claimed that sharing one's own experience and testimony and speaking about Christ alone makes a good sermon.[174] This is so because tentative preaching without conviction and personal experience is disastrous.[175]

4.3.4.1.2 Scriptural Authority

On the authority of a sermon, Pastor Luther argued, "Illustrations are needed for lay people, the intellectuals need other things; as listeners are diverse, we need to plan accordingly. But yes, in terms of authority, it is the word of God." Kenneth claimed, "Church is a place for worship and not a place to entertain people or to be entertained; a preacher must focus on how one can satisfy the people's spiritual thirst." He lamented that many of our pastors are one dimensional; they just read something and then tell some stories without making the Bible prominent in the sermon. Kenneth advised that without focusing on what people want to hear and what the preacher wants to speak, a preacher must preach God's word for God's people according to their need for repentance to happen – "let the word of God speak!"

Another voice expressed, "A good sermon is one rooted in the text; it should not be interpreted according to one's ideology or assumption."[176] A participant also argued that "a good sermon is one that is scripturally faithful and addresses the spiritual and contextual needs of the congregation."[177]

4.3.4.1.3 Addressing Individual Hearts

Kamal claimed that the listeners must be made to feel that the sermon is addressed to them individually. Pastor Oliver declared, "Pulpit ministry is individual focused; we speak to the mass, but we focus on the individuals and home visits." He then said, "A good sermon is one that touches the heart of the people, whether it is an expository sermon, textual sermon, or other types of sermons." He declared, "Even if I preach for the whole world, if somebody is not changed, there is no use."

Pastor Mark believed that a good sermon is one which is preached with illustrations and emotions, like Jesus did, and one which moves the people

---

173. P24.
174. P39.
175. P29; P50.
176. P29.
177. P33; P27.

to tears.[178] Similarly, Bijoy affirmed that a good sermon is defined by whether it "challenges and motivates you, one that wakes you up." A participant asserted, "A sermon which talks of personal struggles can be considered as a good sermon."[179] Moreover, another participant thought that a good sermon happens when "the right person preaches the word of God to the right people in the right time by the power of the Holy Spirit."[180]

4.3.4.1.4 Talking about the Good News of Jesus Christ

Harry observed that there are preachers who preach with an intention to make people laugh. Although it is nice to laugh and be entertained, "there is no meaning in returning from church laughing without hearing the good news of Jesus Christ." But when we go back with the thought, "this is true of what Jesus said" and if it evokes the response, "yes," such is a good sermon. Pastor Patrick also shared that Christ must be preached at all cost.[181]

4.3.4.1.5 Holy Spirit's Anointing and Skilful Preparation

Abraham was convinced that a good sermon is one that is anointed and powered by the Holy Spirit. Kenneth was critical of the Baptist's cliché, "as the Spirit leads," when it comes to sermon preparation. He critiqued, "Some people may say, 'as the Spirit leads,' but they end up speaking whatever they want to speak." Before saying "as the Spirit leads," a preacher must be well prepared and ready with a weekly, monthly, or annual plan to feed the congregation with the word of God. Then he said, "in the midst of that preparation, we need to be aware that it is God's word, not our words, and we must seek the guidance and inspiration of God, asking, what does God want to speak to my people or what does God want me to speak?" A participant argued that a good sermon is given birth through "the Holy Spirit's inspiration" and prayer.[182] Four participants believed that a good sermon must operate under the power of the Holy Spirit.[183]

---

178. Pastor Gideon talked of the application aspect too.
179. P27.
180. P34.
181. Pastor Peter also talked of putting Jesus first; P39.
182. P3; P65.
183. P1; P3; P34 and P65.

4.3.4.2 Characteristics of a Bad Sermon

As human experience and taste are subjective, opinions on this question are no different. As the interviews did not cover this aspect well, the responses from the questionnaire will be used to discuss the issue here.[184] P1 represents the first group who argued that a sermon that is "lengthy,[185] non-biblical and not to the point," is boring and brings dissatisfaction. P6 expressed the view of the second category that a sermon that reads "too many verses" disappoints. P8 echoed the opinion of the third group that a sermon "from the OT without any relevance to the modern day" is disappointing.[186] The fourth group claimed that unprepared[187] and directionless[188] sermons that are not aligned with the chosen topic [189] are boring. P15 expressed the fifth view that a sermon that is not based on Scripture but merely talks about the socio-cultural and political situation of the people is disappointing.[190] P20 represented the sixth opinion that mere exposition alone is boring, on the other hand, "too many unnecessary illustrations, examples," and jokes dishearten people.[191] P34 argued for the seventh group that misinterpretation of the Scripture is fatal.[192] P53 spoke for the eighth category and reflected that sermons that are hypocritical and praise the self,[193] while targeting to hurt someone[194] by criticising and backbiting others,[195] and reprimanding others, is counterproductive.[196] P10 represented the ninth group that narrational preaching is boring because the preacher often takes too long to get to the point.[197]

---

184. Although it was mentioned earlier that the content of the interviews will shape the primary outline of the chapter. The issue on "the characteristics of bad preaching" is an exception as it will be covered under the responses from the questionnaires.
185. See also P10, P21, P26, P39 and P51 who expressed the same.
186. See also P28; P36; P57; P58 and P59 who talked of the same thing.
187. P11 and P45 supported this view.
188. P32 supported this view.
189. P26 and P56 supported this view.
190. P29; P6 and P66 shared the same view.
191. P20; P27 also affirmed this view.
192. P34.
193. P37; P40; P45 and P62 held with the same view.
194. P38.
195. P39.
196. P42.
197. P18; P43; P51; P54; P63 and P64 endorsed the same view.

4.3.4.3 Can Prayer and Bible Study Replace Preaching?

Luther disagreed with this hypothetical question and argued that if preaching is left out then we "we will leave out a big part of God's work in our lives. Preaching is a major part of our spiritual growth." Further, he claimed that we may read our Bibles at home but when "an anointed servant of God who has thoroughly prepared the sermon expounds the Scripture, there will be a vast difference between his exposition and mere superficial skimming of the text." He asserted that the impact of the word of God on the listeners will be deeper because, first, they will be listening to a preacher who has personally engaged with the message of the text, particularly if he has prayed and surrendered to the anointing of the Holy Spirit; second, the preacher would have engaged the text with commentaries and other resources; and third, such a preacher would have received some revelation from God for his people based on the text, which may not be the case in an individual's casual reading.[198]

4.3.4.4 Impact of Preaching

4.3.4.4.1 Positive Impact of Good Preaching

Listening to a sermon is "to listen to God's word and not of any other. It is the medicine for the soul, it always gives hope and happiness in one's life,"[199] and it "builds faith in God."[200] The response of the participants was overwhelmingly positive on their perception of the impact of preaching in their lives. Fifty-three of them agreed that listening to preaching on a regular basis makes them feel energised, stimulated, and secure.[201] However, there are some of them who either confessed that they do not feel positively impacted or that they feel encouraged only sometimes,[202] because preachers criticise others[203] or beat around the bush in the pulpit.[204] Below are some discussions on the positive impact of preaching.

---

198. Bijoy, Hudson, Abraham, Moses, and Micah all spoke of the irreplaceability of the preaching ministry.

199. P8.

200. P9.

201. P1–2; P4–5; P7–12; P14; P16; P18–34; P36; P37; P39–41; P43–46; P49–59; P60; P63; P64; P66–68. *Contra*, P42 thought that the question on whether one is positively affected by preaching is "an inappropriate question."

202. P35; P38; P47–49; P52; P61–62.

203. P24; P52; P53; P62.

204. P29.

4.3.4.4.1.1 Church numerical growth

Pastor Gideon shared that his church began as a small church. But because of God's grace and his preaching ministry, he saw the increase from less than ten to over one hundred households within a span of a little more than two decades. Today he claims that his church supports three missionaries and six evangelists. The number of members continues to increase and Pastor Gideon says, "this is a signal that the people are being blessed by the worship service." Pastor Sunil supported this point of discussion and said, "Yes, I see. There are many who want to come to the church, their participation, their tithing, all these have increased."[205]

4.3.4.4.1.2 Conflict and mistrust vis-à-vis peace and reconciliation between ethnic groups in the society

The ethnic groups that constitute MBC are diverse and numerous. Pastor Oliver expressed concern about the vulnerability of youths who can be easily misled because of ethnic chauvinism. The fragility of this social fabric is precisely what Pastor Tomba also talked about as he reminisced on his early years of church ministry. He said that when he joined the church, which he pastored last, in the late 1990s, society was experiencing a communal conflict between two groups of people. He recalled:

> When I joined the ministry in 1999, one group of people was totally absent from the church, except for a family. All the leaders belonging to one tribal group left the church. No one chased the other away, but the resentment feeling was too strong. My preaching during that period of time was focused on "forgiveness and love." I preached, "no one can skip love. We cannot leave out love. We initially may think that we have won over our enemy, but then love will chase after you, but if you do not respond, you will face your own destruction."

Pastor Tomba shared that during his initial years as a pastor in the early 2000s, his ministry focus was "to involve the leadership of various tribes – Kuki, Naga, and Meitei churches" under one umbrella again. He recalled that during those years, he preached twice a month and "tried my best to persuade several leaders belonging to other tribes which left the church to come and preach,

---

205. Pastor Matthew also felt the same.

and they did on the theme of 'love and forgiveness' because it is the core issue and teaching of Christianity, and without it Christianity is nowhere." By the end of 2000, he claimed, "I noticed that many of those who had left the church came back. From then on, I began preaching – that if we are Christians there should never be discrimination on the basis of caste, colour, tribe, and status."

4.3.4.4.1.3 Love from the congregation towards the pastor

Pastor Luther thought that the love received from the congregation is a sign of the positive impact of preaching. He shared that over the twenty years of his preaching ministry in the current church, he had seen various people come and go in the church, and anyone who had come to the church had shown love to him. In other churches pastors keep changing, but in his church, the members wanted him to continue. He felt that this love shown to him is an indication of the impact of his preaching.

4.3.4.4.1.4 Members' loyalty to the church

Pastor Luther argued that one way of looking at the positive impact of preaching is to observe the loyalty of the church members and their desire not to leave the church. He said, "I have heard of people who say that they have been to other churches, but they do not want to leave this church because of the preaching they receive from this church." Pastor Luther talked of a member, a professor from a medical college, saying, "because of coming to this church, my spirituality has grown." Moreover, he said that there is a professor from Manipur University who concludes, "after coming here I do not want to go anywhere else for worship now."

4.3.4.4.1.5 Personal experience of seeing people change

Pastor Mark talked of the listeners' change of heart and life's priorities as a result of listening to his preaching. He revealed that one of the deacons in his church was once a strong devotee of the snake deity, and his father is a religious writer of the *Pakhangba* Meitei religious group. This man came to change his priorities from snake deity worship to putting his trust in Jesus Christ as his Saviour and Lord after Pastor Mark's ministry of preaching and counselling. Pastor Mark also shared that he sowed the seed of the gospel to another renowned social scientist.[206]

---

206. He did not mention his name; Hudson also saw his friends change through good preaching.

Pastor Tomba attested this truth in his own preaching ministry:

> I had no idea that a young, confused man was listening to my sermon attentively, he came even to the point of wanting to take his own life, he kept listening to it regularly for three months, but later, by God's grace he went to Shillong, studied well there, and got a job now. One day he brought his father and met me. He told me, "God used you as a means to change me, otherwise I would have been somewhere else." I did not know him but because of his feedback I got this information."

Then, Pastor Tomba narrated another miraculous incident through his Christmas sermon broadcast in the All India Radio Imphal (AIR). He said that an underground faction leader had been on the run because members of the other factions were seeking his life. With nowhere else to run, the man decided to end his life on Christmas night after having a good meal with his family. After dinner, and before the time scheduled (7:00 p.m.) to end his life, he decided to turn on his radio at around 5:20 p.m. It was during that window of opportunity that he heard the sermon on "Peace." He heard:

> You will never find peace although you run from one corner of the world to another, because peace is centred around one person – Jesus Christ. If you find Jesus Christ and lean on him, peace will come to you because the things of the earth will gradually grow dimmer. By giving your life to Jesus, you will receive salvation and the power of love, the power to love your enemies, as I have also experienced this myself.

This message transformed his life situation and "later after several years I got the opportunity to meet him in person, and he revealed this story to me." Then he said that this was the work of God.

Pastor Patrick stated that some fifteen years ago, the church which he currently pastors was pastored by a man who faithfully taught the members about salvation and being born again. He said that the impact of the preaching ministry of that pastor could be seen in the people's change of heart and spiritual lives even today, although there had been a tenure gap between him and the previous pastor's tenure. Pastor Patrick narrated how through the ministry of his former pastor, he heard that two engineers in his church who were captives to drugs, alcohol, and gambling changed their lives.

Similarly, there were some members belonging to the Roman Catholic church who became born-again Christians because of Pastor Patrick's preaching ministry. Another family confessed, "Oja (equivalent to sir), because of your preaching, we have stopped taking bribes from the office." He claimed that there was another couple who often fought. He stated that the "wife was a little more on the cunning side. She fought with her husband and her neighbourhood." By the grace of God, through preaching, they have given their lives to God and the woman especially no longer became a nuisance in the neighbourhood. Now their neighbour remarks that she has become like a lamb. Pastor Patrick described another couple working in two different government offices who were deeply infatuated with money, and took a lot of bribes. But now they confessed, "We used that money to raise our children and because of the influence of that money we have been fighting and fighting endlessly. But now, we have left everything." Now this couple is never absent during the dawn prayer time if they are in town.

Pastor Oliver recounted that once, a gentleman who studied in Delhi came back home with drug abuse, and he had since then been on the streets. He was not even a member of the church. This gentleman one day came and met the pastor and testified that his sermon changed his life, and he is now pursuing theological studies.

However, according to Bijoy, "for the past twenty to thirty years, I do not see much change. Maybe before that, there might have been change during the time of the missionaries and the pioneer missionaries, but now I think it is not so much anymore."

4.3.4.4.1.6 Personal experience of change because of good preaching

There were several participants who declared that sermons had changed their lives.[207] One of them said that sermons were the reason for his born-again experience.[208] Another said, "I was once a haughty, selfish, and hot-tempered person. But after continuous listening to the word of God and fellowship with God, now my family is at peace, I love them more, I recognise others as God's children."[209] Several others also revealed that they have refrained from using

---

207. *Contra*, P52; P62 declared that there is hardly any change in his life as a consequence of listening to the word of God.
208. P8; P34.
209. P50; P60; P64.

foul language and ceased their bad behaviour, unbecoming of a Christian[210] and "the harshness that is within them has changed."[211] Others expressed that they were able to make "right judgements" in various life circumstances;[212] increased refinement in their speech and moral life;[213] quitting of many bad habits;[214] developed and improved their leadership skills;[215] "more polite to strangers; respect to elders; love and caring to family and friends; more active in the church activities";[216] sparked a desire to become a prayer warrior;[217] became more mindful of the way they live and relate to friends;[218] know more about God, his work, the purpose of life;[219] seek to please him more;[220] and avoid temptation.[221]

Pastor Nathan shared his experience of being a member of another church before he became a pastor of the current church. He said that the pastor then always preached something substantial in every sermon. He recalled, "Every time I go to church, I get a lesson for my life. As a senior pastor he takes his preaching very seriously. There is evidence of people's growth in his preaching. He mostly preached topical sermons."

Micah also testified that,

> because of preaching I have experienced coming back home and reading the Scripture. This has brought so much joy in my life. Moreover, when I hear sermons that touch my life, I come back and try to straighten up and follow exactly what the preacher has taught me. Some people are touched by songs; they weep and come to repentance through listening to songs. For me, it is because of preaching. I do not know anything. Through

---

210. P41; P44; P46; P55; P56.
211. P9; P66.
212. P10; P30.
213. P16.
214. P23; P28.
215. P24.
216. P31; P54.
217. P32.
218. P36.
219. P39.
220. P58; P59.
221. P46.

preaching, I learn what it is to be a father, ways of parenting, and how to give guidance to my children.

4.3.4.4.1.7 A continual thirst and craving for preaching

Pastors Patrick and Oliver connected the members' thirst to hear their preaching as one of the symbols of the positive impact of preaching. Pastor Patrick argued that there are some people in his church who love his systematic biblical exposition. He had received compliments from them saying, "I've heard something which I have never heard in the past and I look forward to what you're going to teach in the next preaching."[222] Moreover, he remarked that an elder spoke in the church one day that he had begun to enjoy coming to church because "our pastor preaches the word of God comprehensively. I do not want to miss any Sunday now to avoid a gap in my understanding. This, for me, comes as a great encouragement."

Pastor Oliver also shared that in his church there are some government employees, especially police personnel, who get transferred to other nearby towns. Some of these policemen have revealed to him that they come and spend their weekends in Imphal because they do not want to miss his Sunday sermons. This made him think that "maybe some of our sermons are used by God to touch people's lives."

4.3.4.4.2 Negative Impact of Bad Preaching

As much as good sermons are talked about by the members after they leave the church, the same is also true about bad sermons and preachers who really disappointed them. Sometimes people complain that they could have stayed home and done something more constructive instead of attending church, because the sermon had been very discouraging.[223] Other times, as Pastor Samuel narrated, members evaluate the bad preaching of the pastors and preachers in the roadside tea hotels as they have their tea and snacks, which is a public platform. Below are some of the discussions on the consequences of bad preaching.

---

222. Pastor Gideon shared a similar experience.
223. Bijoy.

4.3.4.4.2.1 Increase of nominal Christians

Pastor Oliver concluded, "there are lots of nominal Christians in the churches because preaching is not affecting their lives."[224] Pastor Mark answered that in the context of bad preaching, "I am 100 percent sure that nominalism will be there. I can see nominalism with my eyes, not only in my church but in other places too. I have observed preachers scolding and teaching without love, having an ego about themselves."[225] Harry asked, "the preachers who come up to rebuke people, how good are they? (he laughs sarcastically). Sometimes they do that for show and to get a leadership position[226] by impressing people that they know the problems of the church, and that they can fix them." This kind of preaching, he remarked, "will not bear spiritual fruit." A participant argued, "desire for leadership and power, popularity and worldly personal benefits" can subvert spiritual vitality and bring in nominalism.[227]

On the issue of preaching that majors on entertainment, Pastor Tomba argued that as he does not serve himself, his family, or anyone but Christ, the question of entertaining the listeners does not arise. But Bijoy confirmed that the pastors do not preach what the listeners need but what listeners want to hear. They need spiritual food but unfortunately, many pastors feed them with feel-good sermons that scratch the surface only. We preach too many sermons that tickle without substance. This is happening in many churches and therefore they contribute to backsliding or nominal Christians.

Pastor Luther observed that in some churches, he saw evangelists being made pastors, and so the sermons of those pastors were only about "soul winning – repent, accept Jesus." There was no in-depth study. As the pastors repeat the same sermon Sunday after Sunday, people get bored because there is no sermon that takes them to the next level. This leads to members' spiritual lethargy. Several voices also associate boredom with bad preaching and consequently a malnourished spirituality.[228]

---

224. Pastor Samuel agreed that bad preaching can bring nominalism.

225. Fifty-five participants in the questionnaire survey agreed that bad preaching will promote spiritual lethargy and nominalism.

226. P37 and P54 also opined that leadership tussles in the church are dangerous.

227. P54.

228. P41; P45–56; P58–60. *Contra*, there are others who think that bad preaching does not exist and if it does exist, it is not related to spiritual lethargy; P36; P43–44; P62.

Hudson recollected, "In the past, say some two decades ago, preaching was like fire, some of the old folks preached solid sermons. And so, a lot of older generations prospered and did well in life, but starting from a batch older than me, nominalism has set in."

4.3.4.4.2.2 Decline in believers' spiritual vitality
Kamal observed that instead of hearing that preaching has transformed these people, villages, localities, or communities, he hears that because of bad preaching or no preaching, "many churches are dying and decaying. I see the negative more." He clarified that older pastors are good people because they know the Scripture and have a strong prayer life but because of old age, they have become lazy, unable to keep up with the times and a changing world. Referring to the congregation, he argues, "Although the listeners in the pews are illiterate or semi-illiterate, they are wise, mentally alert, and discerning, they can easily identify if the sermon is worth their attention." Therefore, he concluded, "there is no improvement in the spiritual health of the church and the people," and instead there is decline.

Several participants thought that preaching that is irrelevant to the context of the listeners tears down their spiritual enthusiasm and vitality.[229] One participant declared, "Feeding the lamb or sheep with the right food is very important; if the word of God is not preached correctly, then there will be no growth of the church."[230] Some of the sermons which are not biblical will hurt the sentiments of the people, especially those who know the Bible better than the pastors do.[231]

4.3.4.4.2.3 Absence of prophetic preaching and the increase of confusion
Abraham was of the opinion that in the absence of prophetic preaching, there will be confusion. He claimed that some of our pastors "preach only the things people want to hear; they do not confront, although they see the problem of corruption in the lives of the members." He thinks that this is perhaps because "they do not want to lose their jobs." Moreover, in the name of maintaining a good relationship, they do not want to embitter others by speaking the truth. He believes that if the wrongs are not confronted, the members will

---

229. P27; P28; P33; P48.
230. P51.
231. P19; P29; P47.

be confused about Christian values and ethos. Abraham wondered if this kind of scenario exists because "the pastors do not have the conviction deep in their hearts that God's word has to be taught and preached to the people."

Bijoy agreed, "We are not confronting the members with their sins. I have not seen any pastor confronting their members on corruption and injustice. Jesus himself spoke against injustice; he spoke the truth. We don't preach what they really need to hear but what they want to hear." Pastor Peter expressed that there are pastors "who want to please people and not God, so many of our ministries are failing, mine included."

However, Pastor Tomba had a different story to share. During the early 2000s, when the ethnic conflict was at its height in Manipur, Pastor Tomba had to choose whether he should avoid delicate and sensitive topics or be the prophetic voice in society through his pulpit ministry. He chose the latter, a challenging task for him. He revealed, "I began a sermon series on the topic, 'Messages people don't want to hear.' It was to confront the sinful hearts of the people." Through this series, he challenged them to look at their physical realities through spiritual eyes. With his strong-worded appeal, he reminded them that Jesus also pleaded with sinners, including us, to leave their lives of sin. He feared backlash from the major tribes who were in conflict, but to his surprise, the same tribesmen were the ones who encouraged him to be bold and they "stood up for me and my ministry" during those trying years. Pastor Tomba's story highlights a different narrative, that despite a growing hesitance and decline in prophetic preaching, there are exceptions.

4.3.4.4.2.4 Short-term impact

Abraham reflected that he could see some change in his church because of preaching. But he qualified that the preachers in his church dichotomise between God and the Holy Spirit. These preachers blackmail the people by using the phrase, "The Holy Spirit tells me that if you do not do this or that, then you will be punished." This kind of preaching "frightens people, thinking God will do punitive actions against them," consequently, we can see tremendous change impacting their behaviour and lifestyle. But because this response is not out of love for the Lord, they quickly pick up their old lives again as soon as the emotion of fear departs. This kind of preaching does not impact people for long as it is like going to a *maiba*.

Further, a participant argued that bad preaching makes demands only on the congregation; for example, the pastor keeps asking the members to give their tithes and resources for the church.[232] Abraham argued that although there is a short impact, and it is a right thing to give to God and the local church, one can feel burdened and not joyful in giving in the long run. Though the giving may have taken place, the impact of the message is not long lasting.

4.3.4.4.2.5 *Disappointment with the pastor and the church*

Although there are some churches where the congregations compliment the pastor for his exposition of the word, there are also a few churches where the listeners feel betrayed and disappointed. Hudson claimed, "When I don't receive spiritual food from the church, church becomes boring and going to church becomes tiring because I know that I will be sitting there for three hours straight without actually receiving anything." He added that he is even more upset with the church leadership when he sees some members of the congregation walking like dead men, absorbing everything without filtering. Harry also shared the same disgust. He pointed out that there is much preaching going on in his church without any profit. He reflected, "My excitement before the church service turns into dejection after hearing the preaching from our pastor. With disappointment I go back home, without getting any profit, but loss on my part for having attended the church." He added that because there is no theological graduate to take the pulpit, "someone will take the pulpit and read just a Scripture passage then speak about the city or college or office or high school or friends, we laugh in response and go back home."

Further, using the metaphor of the Naga traditional village king giving his royal announcement at the *Tabu* (a specially elevated stone stage) to describe the pastor mounting up the pulpit to preach, Harry asserted that the preacher must revere the pulpit. As the king announces with authority, purpose, and dignity, the preacher should not be irreverent in the pulpit by joking and not speaking from the word of God. He added that one must discern what subjects to preach. If preaching is done with the power and presence of the Holy Spirit, "people who do not have faith and those of us who are crooked before God will repent. But as the pastor stands and preaches 'dry sermons,' no one wants to eat from his word (he laughs uncontrollably)."

---

232. P46.

Furthermore, he recollected that the pastor creates animosity in the pulpit by targeting individuals. He admits that

> when I know that the preacher is targeting me, I do not want to listen to God's word, we dislike it; the word of God becomes repulsive to us. Although we cannot preach, people are able to decode the direction of the sermon. When sermons are without any kernel and coloured by the preacher's prejudice, even the facts in the Bible seem to become repulsive. The preacher can even usher in Satan into our hearts by making us angry. My faith gets destroyed and I leave the church.

Harry remarked that one of his sons said, "Whenever I go to our church, I come back home without having any peace in my heart." Some agree that spiritual stagnation and lethargy can happen when we criticise and put others down from the pulpit.[233] Micah also shared that there are times when the "pastor preaches from his lips and not from his heart with conviction. And so, when I hear such sermons without kernel, I feel disappointed." Some participants say that they come to church out of obligation[234] and do not look forward to the subsequent church services because of their disappointment with the preaching of the pastor.[235]

4.3.4.4.2.6 Polarisation between spiritual healing and scientific medicine

Pastor Matthew claimed that bad theology in the pulpit is not only disastrous for the soul but for the physical body also. He told about a member from a different church who was discouraged by several pastors from going to the hospital, but was encouraged instead to visit a Christian healing centre, a place where many went and died. Some people, even with sports injuries, were taken to the prayer centres and local healers instead of going to the hospital and getting help from medical practitioners and sports physiotherapists. He remarked that bad theology posits medical science against theology. He recalled the death of a young lady who left behind her three kids because of this bad theology although they come from a well-to-do family. Pastor Matthew

---

233. P8.

234. P10.

235. P51. *Contra*, a majority of the participants disagreed and claimed that they look forward to the church service. P7–9; P12–22; P24–28; P30–50; P53–64; P66.

remarked, "We should never pit one against the other, they both have a place. God has given medical doctors for our healing purpose."

4.3.4.4.2.7 Careless and irresponsible life of young people today

Bijoy detected a decline in the moral life of the young people, and he credited this moral slump to the absence of sermons that address moral and ethical issues young people face in the world. Consequently, young people are "just living with and eloping with all kinds of non-believers." He remarked, "We don't preach about marriage, abortion, and premarital sex. We leave them for seminars and workshops. But where will they learn and be warned?" Moreover, he claimed that if "doctrines on the holiness of God are taught properly, it will prepare them, but we don't preach them."

4.3.4.4.2.8 Members switching from one church to another

Abraham made an analogical argument:

> As tribal people come down to Imphal from the hills, they get down from the buses and try to find a good hotel to have their lunch; likewise, the Christians are searching for a good place to hear sermons in Imphal. They will tell each other, "we have eaten in this hotel earlier, but it was not tasty, so let us look out for a different one." The church members are today asking who is going to preach this Sunday, although they know that the pastor is in station. They also want to know beforehand on what topic the preacher is going to preach. Even in our local church, there are people who confess that "if our local pastor is preaching, we don't want to come to the church, because we know that he will do his usual antics again." Therefore, we need to train our pastors on how to preach well.

Pastor Nathan agreed, "I have heard members of other churches coming to share that our pastor does not preach the word of God faithfully. The situation in the city is that believers will go to the church that gives the best preaching, whether it is my church or others." He continued, "There are eight churches belonging to my tribe here in the city. Members move around searching for good preaching; it is important to them." Kenneth also reiterated that people are on a constant lookout to switch their church according to the satisfaction they receive from the preaching of the word of God.

4.3.4.4.2.9 Preference for implication over application because of lack of love by the preacher

Harry said that his pastor does not preach his sermon out of love for the congregation, but to take certain people to task, and this experience is very hurtful. Then he said that there may be some positive things in what the pastor said in the church, but he does not want to accept it and say, "This thought or truth applies to me," but rather, "This thought is true as a principle."

4.3.4.5 Recommendations for Preaching to Be More Impactful

4.3.4.5.1 Need for Pastoral Training

Pastor Patrick claimed that the pastor's role in building up the community of believers is very crucial. He said, "The growth of our Baptist churches is in the hands of the pastor. If the pastors cannot shape or build the church, then it collapses. We need good pastoral training."

4.3.4.5.2 Preachers Need to Cultivate Humility

Pastor Luther remarked that if a preacher is arrogant, people will not accept his sermon, "even before the delivery, people will switch off their minds. Preachers need humility and our attitude should be correct. In a way it is like promoting a commodity, so we need to have the right attitude."

4.3.4.5.3 Preaching Goes beyond Pulpit Ministry

Pastor Oliver declared that preaching is not limited to the pulpit, but includes home visits, because in the privacy of the home, he is able to share God's word, and visitation also encourages members to come back to the church to listen to the sermons. Pastor Mark suggested the same. He said, "Preaching is not only in the pulpit, it must be everywhere. For example, when I ride my bike with a friend, I talk to him about God's beautiful creation. Then, I quickly present the gospel. This is preaching, everywhere it can be preaching."

Pastor Tomba agreed that preaching should move beyond the church pulpit. He shared that in his church, there are members who cannot attend church regularly, because the government job they hold requires them to come to office even on Sundays sometimes. So, Pastor Tomba visits the absentee members' homes and preaches to them there. This helps the members not to be disconnected with the upcoming sermon in the church, as the sermons are often in series.

Out of his own experience, Micah shared that preaching the word of God should not be limited to the pulpit, because the members' spiritual lives face many threats on weekdays, and if the pastor can visit them and encourage them it strengthens their faith. He also shared that this will make many who are still on the fringe come to the presence of Christ. He revealed, "Preaching can convert people, but I have seen people who have been converted leaving their faith just like that. My advice is, don't leave a person after preaching, visit them to find out if they are doing well." He continued, "When all five of us in the family were sick, and none was able to serve water to each other, somebody came and visited us, she helped us, read Scripture, and prayed with us. It was a fertile time to receive the word of God."[236]

4.3.4.5.4 Deacons' Role in Pastor's Preaching

Preaching is primarily the responsibility of the pastor, but there are people who argue that deacons are also equally responsible for the quality of the pastor's preaching on Sunday worship services, because they must work together in the planning of what they would like their church members to learn (weekly, monthly, and annually). An active and discerning deacon board will elevate the quality of the pastor's sermon.[237] Kenneth argued that people are not only discouraged by poor preaching of the pastor but also by the poor selection of deacons in the church, because the deacons' role is crucial in giving guidance and advice to the pastor. Pastor Matthew also appealed the same to his deacons to give him constructive criticism. He told his deacons, "We need to go together – you must check on me; if you don't, I can be just preaching indiscriminately according to my wish. Only that way, we can guide one another. I am accountable to you, at the same time, you are accountable to me."

4.3.4.6 Impact of Preaching on the Society

Harry was negative about whether there was any visible impact on society due to preaching. Some participants also made the following admission: "Some individuals have changed but society has not changed much as a whole";[238]

---

236. Pastor Luther endorsed the same.
237. Hudson.
238. P41.

"In Manipur, I don't see Christians avoiding corruption";[239] "No, I do not see any impact as nominalism has increased. Listening to preaching does not have much effect in the society, as many people attend church as a duty."[240]

However, the claim of a positive impact of preaching on society far outweighs those who perceive that there is little or no impact. Almost all of the participants agreed that there is some visible positive impact. Some of their admissions are mentioned here: there is visible change in believers' "character and morality in their social interaction";[241] "there is love and kindness to each other in the society";[242] "eagerness to serve and help each other";[243] "I see some people standing their ground and not compromising and some people giving their possessions to the needy";[244] "reconciliation in the society;" "living in unity";[245] "some people's financial management and relationships with their neighbours and society have improved";[246] "there is consciousness for environmental care";[247] "less violence, less importance given to personal and one's tribe interest";[248] "Christians do not want to go back to their old traditions, festivals, and politics";[249] "I see great contribution in education, health care, welfare, and protection of children and family";[250] "Christians abstain from a variety of anti-social elements; and there is a visible difference between Christian lives and non-Christian lives."[251]

Although there is a remarkable positive impact, there are also some underlying currents of negativity from the society. Pastor Mark testified that through his preaching and counselling ministry, several drug and alcohol addicts have been liberated and therefore people in the neighbourhood would recommend families who have such problems to go to Pastor Mark to be

---

239. P45.
240. P60.
241. P13–14; P1–5.
242. P15; P16–18; P46; P53–54; P59; P68.
243. P19.
244. P23; P27; P47.
245. P29; P50.
246. P34.
247. P38.
248. P39.
249. P44.
250. P55.
251. P2; P63.

healed and liberated. He said that it is ironic because, "although people[252] know that what I am doing is good for people, and they appreciate it secretly, still many people want to pull me down, they betray me." He revealed that

> there are around 20 to 25 percent of people in the neighbourhood who like and support my work, but around 75 percent of them superficially greet me: "Hey reverend, how are you? You're doing a good job." But behind me they will say, "What is he doing? He is worshipping a *Hao*[253] god." I have seen and heard it personally.

Pastor Mark also mentioned that through his preaching ministry in the state jail, he has seen several Meitei police officers tone down their rude and inhuman behaviour in their interpersonal relationship with the inmates. He claimed that many of the police officers "have received Jesus, but they are unwilling to publicly demonstrate their acceptance of Jesus for the sake of the larger Meitei Hindu society."

Pastor Luther also declared that he has seen the impact of his preaching ministry in the society. He concluded that,

> since the society is non-believing, although the outcome is positive, the reaction to the impact is somewhat negative because they don't like Christianity. They like the transformation happening in the individual person or life, but after that transformation, that's it; they do not want anything to do with Christianity. So, we have this among the valley people. But among the tribals, people will really appreciate it and society will accept it. But in Imphal valley, it is different.

Further, he revealed that there have been several Brahmins, especially women, who regularly kept visiting his church from a particular locality in Imphal. They visit the church but want to keep a low profile in order to avoid social stigma.

In contrast, Pastor Tomba narrated the consequence and impact of his sermon on the Meitei Hindu families of the two different brides during two

---

252. The non-Christians in his neighbourhood.
253. Derogatory word referring to tribal people.

different wedding ceremonies, who came and attended the ceremony, which they had staunchly opposed in the beginning.

In the first wedding sermon, the pastor presented a gospel message. Pastor Tomba reflected,

> I think the sermon during the wedding deeply engaged and impacted the parents. The parents came to me and said, "Son, we have been really satisfied. We Meitei act as if we are the one, but soon everybody will come to faith and believe in Jesus Christ." This was how the parents gave me their feedback. "We also will eventually come in," they said. I do not really know, if they have become believers now, as I have left the earlier church and now am serving in another church in a different locality.

About the second wedding ceremony and his sermon, Pastor Tomba narrated,

> So many Hindu Meiteis came for the wedding ceremony. I presented a gospel message clearly demarcating the boundaries and beliefs of Christian faith; what trusting in Jesus is like; if we want our state, Manipur to be filled with love,[254] we must trust in Jesus; so, I took the opportunity and shared these things. I thought they will be angry with me for having said what I have said. After the wedding ceremony, when we were having our refreshments, the parents and elders of the girl came and told me this, "Son, we could not hold back our tears, as it was so good, ahhhh, if it is like that, why can't we become Christian? Please continue to spread this good news. People (Meiteis) will eventually, little by little, begin to worship Jesus Christ." So, they called me aside and told me this. So, what I am saying is that there is impact.

Pastor Tomba further remarked, "In Imphal valley we may not feel and know, but there certainly is impact. Slowly and slowly, without the knowledge of the Christians, the Meiteis have been coming to the Lord continuously, in diverse ways. So, we need pastors with integrity."

---

254. A theme that echoes well with the people as the state has been torn apart by ethnic violence for decades.

Pastor Oliver cited one valuable incident in his ministry: "Whether it is through the preaching of God's word or God's Spirit working in the heart of a senior police officer, we see a positive impact in his life." When the church leaders visited him for fundraising towards a pastor's housing construction, he made the following confession. The policer officer said to the pastor that, earlier for the church building construction, he donated a huge amount, "but it was not my money." But he said that the Lord "spoke and chastised me," and so he decided to stop walking on the road of corruption and donated Rs. 10,000 only towards the construction project out of his own salary.

Pastor Patrick shared the story of a family who were making waves in the society due to their changed behaviour. Earlier the couple were

> a thorn in the flesh to live and mingle with in society, but now they have become harmless, humble, and patient. Previously they were like ferocious hens – biting and scratching others – but now they have become very different. Like this, there are one or two other families whose lives have become different. This is because of the word of God.

4.3.4.7 Themes and Goals in Preaching

A participant expressed, "Preaching always had a central role in the life and work of the church. The focus or goal of the sermon is to develop Christlike convictions (thinking); Christlike character (feeling), and Christlike conduct (acting)."[255] With regard to the themes, Pastor Nathan likes to feed the congregation from the epistles. At other times, he preaches topical sermons. Pastor Samuel claimed that he has a holistic aim. Pastor Oliver focuses on the practical life of a believer so that "people will be able to recognise their role in Christian life and the ongoing process of sanctification." Pastor Mark preaches more from the New Testament, although he does not ignore the Old Testament. He claimed, "I believe that with the coming of Jesus, the New Testament is important." For Pastor Gideon, he preaches seriously on the triune God: the Father, the Son, and the Holy Spirit. His other priority is "salvation and the assurance of salvation; that even if I die, I will rise up again. I tell the congregation that there should be no confusion on this. Otherwise,

---

255. P55.

there is no use of being a Christian."[256] Eighteen participants also pointed to salvation as the main theme preached in the church.[257]

Pastor Tomba shared, "My ministry focuses on these four words: reconciliation, repentance, resurgence, and reaching out with the gospel." Twenty-four participants declared that the main themes in their churches are love, unity, and togetherness.[258] Pastor Tomba asserted, "Without mincing words, when I get the opportunity to preach in other churches, I confront people against non-repentance, unforgiving spirits, broken homes and conflicts; instead of appealing, I tended to go towards chastisement and rebuke." In his present church where he joined a little less than ten years ago, he operates differently because he says that the context is different.

Bijoy said that having a theme is good for the church because it keeps the pastor and the preachers focused. But he argued that the flip side is, when the focus is only on one aspect, the members' spiritual hunger and needs are not met because "People do need some other spiritual food for their growth other than the particular theme of the year (for example, missions)."

As far as Micah's church is concerned, as the pastor is not theologically trained, he focuses more on family growth than biblical matters. Pastor Patrick argued that he knows the importance of the epistles, especially the Pauline epistles, and the Old Testament, but he teaches his church the teachings of Jesus as the main diet for their spiritual lives.

Pastor Sunil said that he does not have any theme or goal but preaches "according to the seasons of the year and situation of the society. If there is a need for giving, peace, or love," he elaborates on the theme of giving. He revealed that before he came to this church, "The annual income was around ten to eleven lakhs, but the income leapfrogged to around 1 crore, twenty lakhs annually. The impact on giving is evident."

Sharing a different opinion, there were a significant number of members from various churches, including Hudson who thought that many church leaders and pastors do not have a weekly, monthly, or annual goal or theme in mind to feed the people. The people come to church and get their emotional

---

256. Pastor Luke also shared that salvation is the theme that keeps coming up in the church annual assembly.

257. P2; P12; P13; P14; P20; P24; P26; P29; P32; P40; P41; P42; P49; P55–59.

258. P9; P10; P11; P14; P18; P26; P28; P30; P31; P35; P38; P39–41; P43; P45–48; P59; P60; P62; P64; P66.

high and go back without getting anything. Harry confessed, "We don't have any focus. One verse is being read and then they speak whatever they want to speak." One participant argued that her pastor preaches "without any goal; without proper knowledge of the Bible, and using God's word to propagate the hearer's view alone."[259]

As a church leader, Kenneth observed that many churches do not have a vision, theme, or goal, although "every church ought to have a yearly plan for preaching." Others felt that the pastors generally teach some doctrines and relate them to spirituality.[260] Kenneth felt that a pastor must tell himself, "during my time in this church, with other responsibilities, I want to achieve this spiritual dimension in the lives of the members." He lamented that unfortunately, the pulpit is indiscriminately given to anybody who requests it, and so we hear confusing sermons without any theological validity and proper interpretation.

4.3.4.8 *Types of Sermons Preached in the Baptist Churches*

According to the questionnaire survey, the seventy participants ticked the following kinds of sermon structures preached in their pulpits:[261] Narration or storytelling approach–19; Expository approach–22; Testimonial approach–25; Topical–54; Textual–3; and Others–4. When Pastor Nathan looked around at the churches of Imphal, he observed, "I see more dissemination of current affairs, no serious emphasis on the Scripture." As for his sermons, he claimed, "mine is more of topical preaching,[262] not textual. But my main focus is to bring spiritual growth to the people." He added that because he has a big congregation, he prefers to identify with and speak to the various needs of his members.

Pastor Samuel observed that in Imphal churches, pastors mostly preach expository sermons. However, he follows the "textual method, the one closer

---

259. P63.
260. P18; P30; P33; P36; P39; P43–47; P52; P56–59; P64.
261. Here, the style of preaching (topical, expository, etc.) is discussed as understood by the participants, not according to a scholar's definition. In the succeeding chapters, a more elaborate discussion will occur.
262. Kenneth also observes that this is the more common approach in the city.

to the Bible study."[263] He stated that the older generation prefers the topical method with stories, but he focuses on "reading the text, and consulting the commentaries" for his sermons. As his congregation is comprised of highly educated people, he thinks that this is a better method that will not bore them. For Pastor Mark, "the personal evangelism,[264] and conversational style of preaching to two or three people works best, and as my ministry is among the people who are not yet Christians,[265] I need to hear their story first." According to Hudson, the text-based sermon is almost a famine in the churches he has visited. For Pastor Gideon, he preaches sermons moved by the Holy Spirit; technically, his approach leans towards the text-based sermon.

Bijoy remarked that exposition and doctrines of the Bible are avoided and kept aside for Bible camps. Pastors prefer topical sermons because they opt for an easy way out. Although he preaches expository sermons, Pastor Matthew remarked that the more common approach in the city churches is topical sermons. For Pastor Moses, his sermon is shaped according to the existential realities of the people: social disharmony, celebration and festival, and others. Pastor Luther makes some distinction between churches where tribal people congregate for worship and churches where valley people worship. He argued that

> the tribal communities have become Christian ahead of the valley Meitei people; their Christian background is firmer, many members have gone for theological training, and so preaching can be done in depth. But the story of the valley churches is different – they are relatively new, the preaching will be lacking in depth.

Then he continued that as he looks around, he sees mostly topical sermons. He remarked that teaching is for those who already have growth, whereas the gospel is for the seekers and new believers. So, "the method of preaching is defined by the context." He then added, "As far as possible, I try to avoid topical sermons. I try to deliver textual sermons."

---

263. Some see no distinction between expository preaching and textual preaching, while others distinguish between the two. For more, see Matthewson, "What Makes Textual," 412–417.

264. P30; P32 and P50 confirm that their church focuses on the theme of evangelism.

265. They comprise mostly rickshaw drivers, carpenters, drivers, and other manual workers.

Pastor Patrick claimed, "I employ topical sermons on special occasions. But I use the Bible, book by book, chapter by chapter or portion by portion. I want to let the people hear what the Bible teaches, not what I prefer." Pastor Sunil confirmed that he uses topical sermons although there has been a shift towards expository sermons lately. But he remarked, "There are people who do not want to hear such preaching. Many people prefer to listen to sermons that bring laughter and that entertain them, but such sermons are difficult to be written down, because we can't find substance to note them down."

4.3.5 Reading of the Scripture Inspired by Preaching

There are a few pastors who think that their members have begun reading the Scripture because of their initiatives. Pastor Luther observed a change in his congregation's Scripture reading pattern after he encouraged them through his personal testimony to read the whole Bible once in a year. He shared, "During the house fellowship, when I give them opportunity to share, I can see evidence of their reading the Scripture. That they read and understand the Scripture. That there is effort and progress."[266] Forty-five participants in the questionnaire survey were positive that Bible reading has increased because of the ministry of the pastor through preaching and corporate reading in the church. However, their reasons and situations are all mostly different and are nuanced differently.[267]

On the other hand, people like Hudson think that it is his pastor's preaching which made him read the Bible "once or twice, but it's getting very rare nowadays." Three participants felt the same discouragement.[268] Abraham sighed and remarked evasively that there are times when a lay preacher encourages him to read the Bible. He then said that when a theologically trained pastor prays over his sermon, that sermon makes him want to read the Scripture. Bijoy claimed that he has his own personal quiet time when he reads the Scripture, so there is no question of the pastor inspiring or discouraging him to read the Scripture. Like Bijoy, four participants believed that the desire to read the Scripture should not be influenced by preaching.[269]

---

266. Pastor Luther.
267. P1–2; P4–5; P9–15; P17–26; P28; P30–32; P37–42; P44–47; P49–50; P53; P60; P62; P64–67.
268. PP7; P36; P43.
269. P8; P29; P61; P63.

Then Bijoy remarked that he does come back home to read the Scripture after church, but that is not because he is inspired but to check out if the interpretation of the scriptural text by the preacher was actually right or wrong.[270] While three voices expressed tentativeness,[271] one participant revealed that life's struggles and problems compel her to read the Scripture.[272]

4.3.6 General Challenges to the Spirituality of the Members in Baptist Churches of Imphal

The participants in the interviews engaged with several issues, going beyond the narrow focus of preaching and spirituality. Here, we will report the wider comments made by them.

4.3.6.1 Pastor Overburdened by Numerous Ministries of the Church

The responsibilities of a pastoral ministry are diverse. Pastor Oliver complained that due to the enormity of responsibilities, "sometimes we don't get enough sleep; sometimes I even forget my own name (laughs)."[273] Pastor Sunil also revealed the nature of his work and the division of his time (see figure 8). He confessed, "My work is overloaded, I am exhausted, I am burnt out to be honest. We need more pastors in this church not just one."

Pastor Oliver claimed that he had visited over 460 families during his time in the church for almost a decade, and it had not been easy. The frequency of his visitation depended on the need of the members and their invitation, and not because of favouring one over the other. Moreover, he shared that hospital visits were crucial. He said, "If you visit them during their time of need, they fondly remember you, and if you miss that opportunity, they still remember you for that" (he laughs).

However, Bijoy was wary of the argument that multiple responsibilities of a pastor undermine the priority of preaching ministry. He asserted that the pastor is called to preach, and one must refer to the "Great Commission again and see what Jesus says. Jesus did not talk about other activities, Jesus simply talked about preaching and teaching the word of God and that whoever

---

270. P67 also reads to cross-check what was preached.
271. P16; P27; P48.
272. P34.
273. Here he humorously exaggerated and laughed at himself, because of the nature of his work and schedule.

believes should be baptised. That should be the priority of the pastor." Then he lamented that our pastors have too many activities and we try to overshadow the ministry of preaching, which is wrong. Preaching must be the number one priority in the church.[274]

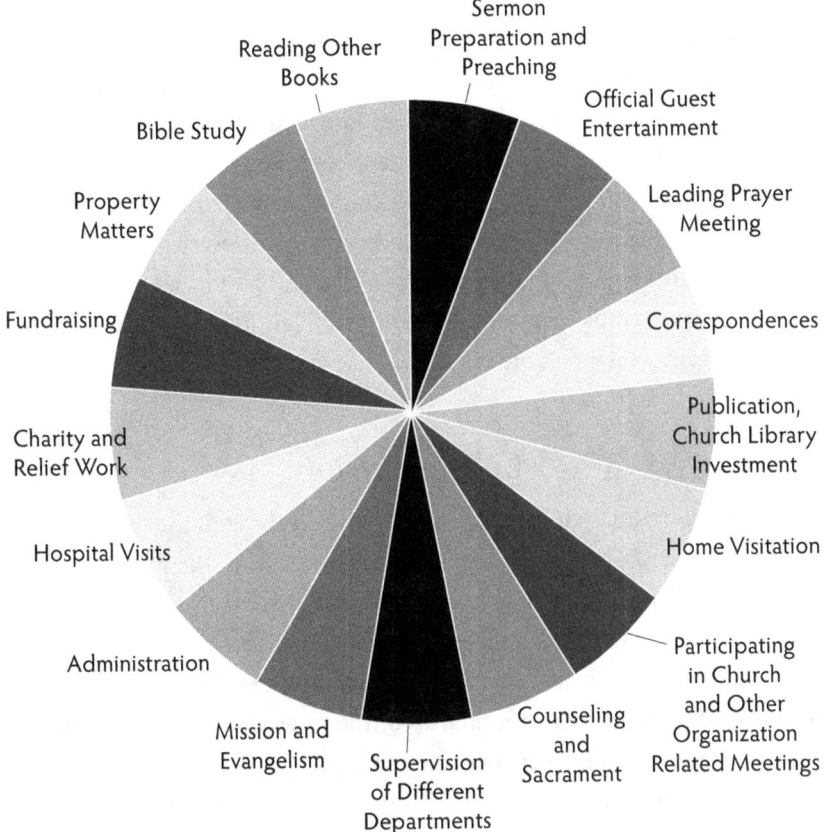

Figure 8: Holistic Ministry of Pastor (for descriptive purpose only)

---

274. Abraham also agreed that a pastor's primary task is preaching and teaching the word of God.

4.3.7 Observation of the Data and Connection with the Research Questions

The empirical survey was primarily shaped by the main research question.[275] The secondary questions also assisted during the data collection. The concern of the main research question was dealt with in the following sections: the data on the relationship between preaching and spiritual vitality;[276] the types of preaching for spirituality;[277] and the positive impact of good preaching[278] addressed the positive aspects, and the other aspect was addressed by the negative impact of bad preaching[279] and the various issues surrounding preaching and nominalism.[280] All the secondary questions have been addressed under the broad headings of church members' understanding of the word of God;[281] spiritual vitality;[282] nominalism and preaching (its positive and negative impact);[283] the impact of preaching on society.[284] However, this does not mean that the other data that do not come under these headings are less important. They helped by shedding more light on the questions under investigation.

4.4 Conclusion

In this chapter, the findings of the data gathered through the twenty semi-structured interviews and seventy questionnaires from the fifteen selected Baptist churches in Imphal have been described, as received from the participants, without interpretation by the author (interpretation will be done in the next chapter). The data from the field survey yielded much information and extended beyond the boundaries of the research questions. However, they have been included here because the complete data emerging from the research determine the outcome of the research, as required by the phenomenological approach adopted in this research study.

---

275. Cf. 1.8.
276. Cf. 4.2.2 and 4.2.2.2.
277. Cf. 4.2.2 and 4.2.2.3.
278. Cf. 4.2.4; 4.2.4.1; 4.2.4.4.1.
279. Cf. 4.2.4; 4.2.4.4; 4.2.4.4.2.
280. Cf. 4.2.3.
281. Cf. 4.2.1.
282. Cf. 4.2.2.
283. Cf. 4.2.3; 4.2.4.4.1; 4.2.4.4.1.1 to 4.2.4.4.1.7.
284. Cf. 4.2.4.6.

CHAPTER 5

Interpretation of the Data

5.1 Introduction

In the previous chapter, we described the data emerging from the empirical research. Here, the research questions[1] will guide the interpretation of the data and the literature review will be referred to, to identify the gaps of knowledge discovered during the empirical research so that an appropriate evaluation and interpretation may be constructed. It must be mentioned here that some of the participants' own experiential interpretations have been covered in the previous chapter since some of their experiences were simultaneously interpreted by them, as they described their own experiences. As this research follows an eclectic design,[2] in this chapter, we move to the second stage (the Interpretive Task) of Osmer's Practical Theology model. This model allows the researcher to step out of the trees to look at the woods and interpret why the participants think the way they do regarding the role of preaching in people's spiritual lives.

5.2 The Task of Interpretation

If qualitative analysis of data would be "systematically categorising participant's statements into a hierarchy of themes that are then presented as 'findings' of the study," interpretation of the data steps into the picture when "links

---

1. Cf. 1.8.1 and 1.8.2.
2. Cf. 1.15.

are made between the 'findings' of the study and the relevant literature and theories in the field."³

It is argued that there is no single rule or procedure in interpreting a data. However, the task begins by gathering all the data together, where,

> the themes and connections should be used to explain findings. A good place to start is to develop a list of the key points or important findings one discovers as a result of sorting and categorising the data. Further, the research questions of the study should be revisited and recalled. This can be followed by trying to situate the findings in the theoretical framework selected for the study. Interpretation therefore basically involves attempting to put one's data into perspective.⁴

By nature, "interpretation is an act of imagination and logic."⁵ It must be understood that the same findings can be interpreted by different people differently by asking different questions as to "what is important and what is worth paying attention to as well as what can be known about and through the text (data)."⁶

On whether the interpretative task should be the prerogative of the participants alone or if the researcher could come up with an alternative narrative, it is recommended that there should be

> levels of interpretation in qualitative study. This ranges from empathetic descriptive level where meaning is found out from the point of the participant to a critical humanistic level, wherein an alternative narrative is built by the researcher by drawing from pre-existing theoretical perspectives. Such an exercise results in a deeper understanding of the phenomena."⁷

Thus, this researcher will employ an "alternative narrative" to interpret the findings by consulting with the "pre-existing theoretical perspectives"⁸ from

---

3. Willig, *Qualitative Interpretation*, 17–18; cf. Pathshala, "Interpretation."
4. Pathshala, "Interpretation," at 19:14.
5. Peshkin, "Nature of Interpretation," 8.
6. Willig, *Qualitative Interpretation*, 10.
7. Pathshala, "Interpretation," at 20:20.
8. Pathshala, at 20:20.

the literature review, theories of arts and science,[9] and logical induction and inferences. Moreover, as a Practical Theology discipline, the study will engage with some particular situations theologically.[10] Osmer reasons, "The interpretive task is based on an attitude of openness to the world. It depends on a thinking faith willing to learn from the intellectual resources of contemporary culture"[11] which is "a challenge of cross-disciplinary dialogue."[12]

It is argued that with different interpretations, even those derived from the same findings, "the final destination remains unique for each enquirer, known only when – and if – arrived at."[13] Ultimately, "interpretation means attaching significance to what was found, making sense of the findings, offering explanations, drawing conclusions, extrapolating lessons, making inferences, considering meanings, and otherwise imposing order."[14]

On assuring validity to the act of data interpretation, it is argued that "the key lies in realising that no interpretation is 'the interpretation' and alternative explanations would always exist. Therefore, as a researcher, you should always try to search for other possible explanations for the same data."[15] There are two helpful principles to guide the interpretation towards its validation. First, "it should be dependable or authentic," which means that "if two researchers would assess the same process using the same set of evidence, they should arrive at the same or similar conclusions." Second, "it should be credible," which signifies that "the researcher should provide so much evidence that his or her conclusion and inferences" are so believable that "any independent audit of the entire research can be done if needed."[16]

---

9. Osmer, *Practical Theology*, 83.
10. Swinton and Mowat, *Practical Theology*, xv; Osmer, *Practical Theology*, 100.
11. Osmer, 93.
12. Osmer, 100.
13. Patton, *Qualitative Research*, 432.
14. Patton, 480.
15. Pathshala, "Interpretation," at 24:56.
16. Pathshala, "Interpretation," at 25:40.

5.3 Theories and Literature Review vis-à-vis the Interpretative Task

The interpretative task should evaluate every theory according to "a communicative model of rationality" which has three aspects – argumentation, perspectivalism, and fallibility.[17] First, it is argumentative because people try to rationalise and provide "reasons to others in support of their assertions,"[18] as scholars do so for peers to review their position.[19] No argument is complete in itself, so the dialectical and dialogical discussion must go on. Second, on the issue of perspectivalism, each of the theories "makes its case from a particular point of view."[20] Therefore, there is a need for multiple theories to address various dimensions of a problem because "the explanatory scope of a theory is limited by its disciplinary perspective" and "a theory is good for some purposes but not for others."[21] Thus, the employment of multidisciplinary theories, forms of thinking, and dialogue help in interpreting "complex, multilayered systems, and problems that are multidimensional."[22] Finally, theories require "epistemic humility" because all "theories in a communicative model of rationality are viewed as fallible."[23]

There may be other ways to get the interpretive task done, but a widely accepted way which we will follow is to inductively arrive at the theories from the data collected,[24] as described in the descriptive chapter. Moreover, at this stage, the researcher will relate the data "to what is already known" in the literature review and make "links to other ideas and disciplines not envisaged at the outset" so as "to enrich the presentation of the research."[25] Keeping in mind the literature review, the researcher will aim to identify anything that leaps out "as either confirming or contradicting what has emerged" from the "data analysis." Here, the goal is to answer the question, "What does your data

---

17. Osmer, *Practical Theology*, 100–103.
18. Osmer, 102.
19. Brown, *Rationality*, 74–76, 86–87.
20. Osmer, *Practical Theology*, 102–3.
21. Osmer, 119.
22. Osmer, 119.
23. Osmer, 102–3.
24. Bryman, *Social Research*, 404.
25. Cameron, *Studying*, 40–41.

add to what had gone before?"²⁶ The research questions help in defining and delimiting the scope of our engagement in this chapter.²⁷

5.4 Interpreting the Impact of Preaching in the Church

There are two opposing voices arguing for their respective case on the impact of preaching on the spiritual lives of the church members – one claiming a visible positive impact while the other is convinced of a negative impact. Below is a discussion of these two conflicting interpretations. Proverbially speaking, this is our "stepping back to look at the woods" moment, to interpret why these two voices make their respective claims.

5.4.1 Interpreting the Positive Impact of Good Preaching

The first voice claims preaching has a visible positive impact. The following evidence supports this argument: church numerical growth; conflict and mistrust replaced by peace and reconciliation between ethnic groups in the society; love from the congregation towards the pastor; members' loyalty to the local church; personal experience of seeing people change; personal experience of change because of good preaching; and a continual thirst and craving for preaching.[28] Below is a discussion of the evidence they put forward.

Can a congregation's numerical growth be related to the effectiveness of the preaching ministry? Yes, good preaching does motivate people to attend church, for when the word of God is properly opened, people can experience a new lease of life and their commitment to church attendance can drastically improve. This is true in the case of many church members who have expressed to their pastors their unwillingness to miss any sermons, because then they would have missed a link in a series.[29] This is true even for some government officers who are posted in a different district who come home for weekends primarily to listen to the preaching of the pastor.[30]

---

26. Cameron and Duce, *Researching*, 106–7.
27. Cf. 1.8.1 and 1.8.2.
28. Cf. 4.3.4.4.1.
29. Cf. 4.3.4.4.1.7.

30. Although this is good, we could argue that this indicates an unhealthy pastor-dependent relationship.

On the other hand, one cannot take the numerical increase at its face value[31] and uncritically conclude that it is because of good preaching, for good attendance is also possible because preachers do not confront people with their sins and do not make them uncomfortable. It is in this context that a participant argues that nominal Christians flood to the church because they get what they want and do not have to feel awkward or uncomfortable because of the preaching in the pulpit, as they do not have to lose face in the presence of those who know their nominal lifestyles.[32] The findings show that some churches regularly have attractive programmes like singing, choreography, dancing, and several other items sometimes resembling any secular event.[33] It does not mean that such items are bad in themselves but it is observed that these items were made more prominent than the exposition of the word. So, some participants argue that the high entertainment value in some churches makes the service not look like a church worship service.[34] Therefore, it would be preferable to claim that although church numerical growth could be a legitimate barometer to judge the quality and good effect of preaching on people, the finding suggests that the entertainment quotient is also a major reason for a church's numerical growth. Therefore, this argument remains inconclusive.

The participants described reconciliatory and restorative preaching based on the gospel of Christ as the reason for peace and reconciliation, after a string of ethnic conflicts ravaged the harmonious fabric of the society in Manipur.[35] We could argue that based on the information elaborated by the participants and the reality of the prevailing socio-political situation during the conflict, nothing could have restored peace, hope, and trust in society other than the gospel of Christ, where faithful preaching had been one of the tools for its propagation. As some participants experienced, good gospel preaching

---

31. *Contra*, Adams argues that, "Whether our preaching is effective is determined not by the number of persons who attend it, nor the number of professions of faith, but by the faithfulness of preachers to the message that we are called to preach"; Adams, "Theology," 33.

32. Cf. 4.3.3.2.1.

33. Cf. 4.3.3.3.15.

34. Cf. 4.3.1.2.1; 4.3.1.3; 4.3.3.2.13. D. Martyn Lloyd-Jones was grieved by the multiplication of entertainment activities in the church thereby reducing the time for the ministry of the Word; Lloyd-Jones, *Preaching and Preachers*, 24.

35. Cf. 4.3.4.4.1.2.

brought reconciliation in the lives of the people and the churches during the era of ethnic conflict in Imphal.

Another question at hand is, can we interpret love from the congregation towards the pastor[36] as a legitimate impact of good preaching? We can argue that this is a valid claim because no matter how good a pastor is towards his church members in terms of personal relationship, if his preaching is mediocre and brings dissatisfaction to the members, a cordial relationship may not last. If a member genuinely seeks for spiritual feeding, he may raise his voice of discontent about the pastor's preaching, although as a person, the pastor may be a good man. However, there can be a different narrative too. Like the argument in the previous point, a church member who is not serious about his spiritual life can love the pastor because of the entertainment the church service provides and for a sermon devoid of teeth; however, this kind of love would be questionable. There could still be a further narrative to this argument. Although a pastor's preaching may be crucial for some, for some other members, his people-relating skill and member care aspect of his ministry may become the reason of their endearment for the pastor. Therefore, based on these arguments, it remains questionable if love from the congregation can be claimed as a legitimate impact of good preaching.

Another argument is that members' loyalty to the local church[37] can be regarded as a positive impact of preaching. The proponents of this claim believe that it could be because of their preaching that people prefer to stay on in a particular church. This is a plausible argument based on the findings that people move from one church to others, as they would change restaurants to eat, based on their satisfaction with the pastor's preaching.[38] So, if they find a church that meets their spiritual thirst in terms of preaching, they seldom move away from it. While validating this claim as reasonable, there is a difficulty in accepting it without a clarification. A person can become a loyal member of the church for many reasons: if the Sunday school is strong and the children are taught well; if the church belongs to a monolingual ethnic group and a person feels more comfortable worshipping there; if the church is convenient in terms of distance and worship schedule; if the church gives a

---

36. Cf. 4.3.4.4.1.3.
37. Cf. 4.3.4.4.1.4.
38. Cf. 4.3.4.4.2.8.

member opportunities for leadership and the privilege of preaching occasionally; if a person is positively patronising the church by giving his resources for its growth; if a person agrees with the mission and evangelism policy of the church; if a person has a voice and authority in the leadership or deacon board; and several others. Therefore, this argument is also inconclusive because it is not necessarily only for preaching that a person remains loyal to a church, although the possibility of it cannot be ruled out.

Another claim of evidence of the positive impact of preaching is that some pastors have seen change in the lives of people through their preaching.[39] This is a very subjective experience and therefore a third person cannot argue for or against it, because, unless the same experience is being repeated and experienced by other people as in a laboratory, one cannot postulate a counterargument or make a judgement. However, we could make a cautionary statement from a theological point of view. God's Spirit only can bring change, not through human wisdom in preaching, as Paul wrote to the church in Corinth.[40] While some of the pastors acknowledged that it is through "God's grace" or because of "the Lord's doing" this change is seen in people, some did not mention it; perhaps they overlooked the obvious or expected the researcher to understand it although it was not verbalised. But the danger remains, for ultimately, change in the spiritual realm is "not by might nor by power but by my (God's) Spirit."[41]

Furthermore, can one determine a positive impact of preaching because a person experiences change in his life because of preaching?[42] Like the argument made above, this is also a subjective experience which cannot be repeated in a laboratory. Personal experiences must either be taken at face value or rejected (although it is measurable to some extent, as seen in their changed lives). Before rejecting the argument by saying that personal experience without witnesses or external evidence is implausible, it will be good to answer the following questions: How does the Holy Spirit of God work? Does God operate in the same way in encountering various people? What does history, both biblical and secular, say in terms of God revealing himself

---

39. Cf. 4.3.4.4.1.5.
40. 1 Cor 2:4–5, 10; cf. Litfin, *Paul's Theology*, 230, 340.
41. Zech 4:6.
42. Cf. 4.3.4.4.1.6.

to people? What are the contemporary stories around the world of how God encounters people? Based on how the legal system works, this argument may not carry much weight as there may be none to stand as a witness to this claim. Nevertheless, from the standpoint of theology and Scripture, this interpretation can be validated because God works above and beyond the confines of our categories and limitations. However, personal transformation stories are not a common phenomenon discovered from the research data during the research period, although isolated experiences were reported by the participants. On the contrary, there were voices which argued that for the past several decades, they have not noticed any visible change in people's lives due to preaching, except during the missionaries' era.[43] Therefore, although the personal experience of change through the preaching event cannot be ruled out, the number of people expressing such an experience is minimal. Consequently, the argument remains inconclusive.

Further, some argue that a continual thirst and craving for preaching[44] can be interpreted as a positive impact of preaching. As argued earlier, it is true that there have been some church members who did not want to miss any sermon of the pastors. A thirst to listen to the preaching, and not tiring of it, is indeed a positive sign. However, there were also findings that church members kept coming back to the church again and again, craving and thirsting for the word of God despite their disappointments, hoping every passing Sunday that the pastor would deliver a good sermon, unlike the previous Sundays.[45] Therefore, this interpretation also remains inconclusive.

5.4.2 Interpreting the Negative Impact of Bad Preaching

The second voice talks about the impact of bad preaching, ranging from the internal issues of the decline of spirituality and subsequent increase of nominalism to serious external issues like: the absence of prophetic preaching and the increase of confusion; short-term impact; disappointment with the pastor and the church; polarisation between spiritual healing and scientific medicine; the careless and irresponsible life of young people today; members

---

43. Cf. 4.3.4.4.2.1.
44. Cf. 4.3.4.4.1.7.
45. Cf. 4.3.1.3.

switching from one church to another; and a preference for implication over application because of lack of love by the preacher.[46]

This second voice speaks against the idea that preaching had affected spiritual vitality during the research period. Many from this camp argue that change seen through preaching is minimal, although they believe in the theory that preaching must affect both spiritual vitality and social change.[47] Some in this group argue that if any change had happened, it had happened in the bygone years, before the dawn of the twenty-first century, and not since.[48] According to them, the above evidence is the basis for interpreting the impact of preaching as more negative than positive. Why do they think so? Below is a discussion on the negative impact of preaching from the researcher's perspective.

Some participants argue that change in the lives of individual church members, both in terms of personal spiritual life and social responsibility, does not happen because there is no primacy of the word of God in the pulpit.[49] Some even link the cause to the absence of expository preaching in the Baptist churches,[50] and the lack of reading the word of God in the homes of members.[51] Some even claim that the misinterpretation of the word is causing serious havoc to the spiritual lives of the people.[52]

Consequently then, it is appropriate to ask if the exposition of the word of God and a personal knowledge of God's word are indispensable for a spiritual life to be vital and vibrant. Several participants believed that the knowledge of the word of God can protect them from temptation and sin in their professional as well as personal lives.[53] We could refer to scriptural theology[54] and agree that God's word causes a person to spiritually flourish, keeps one pure, and protects a person because it teaches them the ways of God and corrects them from going astray. So, according to this theological position,

---

46. Cf. 4.3.4.4.2.
47. Cf. 2.2.1.5.
48. Cf. 4.3.4.4.2.1.
49. Cf. 4.3.4.4.2.1.
50. Cf. 4.3.2.2.
51. Cf. 4.3.3.3.2.
52. Cf. 4.3.3.3.7.
53. Cf. 4.3.1.4.
54. For example, Pss 1; 19:7–14; 119; 2 Tim 3:14–17.

the absence of regular feeding on God's word leads to a weakening of one's spiritual life. Peter Adam, arguing for the power of the word of God, claims that it must guide to "true Christian spirituality. Its common neglect results in confusion about spirituality." Moreover, "the Bible gives us God's point of view on every area of our lives, and is the means God uses to speak to us." Further, if one neglects the "Bible as a spiritual resource, we will easily slip into confusion, error, imbalance, idolatry, lack of spiritual discernment, and be seduced away from the worship of Christ."[55] In this context we can argue that, in the absence of the word of God in the form of prophetic preaching, we can be demoted from spiritual vitality to spiritual lethargy, even nominalism.

While the argument on the supreme adequacy of the Scripture stands, there are voices from among the participants who argued that knowing the word of God without a living faith and integrity[56] will do no good. We can agree with this argument since Satan also knew the word of God[57] and knew that Jesus was the Son of God,[58] but did not believe the Bible nor place his faith in God. Consequently, a person may have received the word of God through preaching but could still be without faith in Jesus Christ. In a similar vein, the writer of Hebrews in 4:2 argues that the preached word of God (or the good news of the gospel of Christ) can bring no impact and change in a person's life if the message is not received with faith. We found in the empirical survey that some Bible school graduates[59] have caused more harm than good to the faith of other church members because of the discrepancy between their personal lives and their theological degrees. They might know or possibly could have studied the Scripture thoroughly, but in the absence of the synchronisation of head knowledge with the devotion of the heart and authentic action with their hands and feet, the knowledge of the word of God in the head remains useless. They need to be people of integrity where all three aspects – head, heart, hands and feet – display the virtue of the trinitarian undivided oneness.

However, the argument suggesting that having a "living faith" is as important as the knowledge of the word of God cannot be uncritically accepted. This

---

55. Adam, *Hearing God's Words*, 19–20.
56. Cf. 4.3.3.4.5.
57. Ps 91:11–12.
58. Mark 1:24; 3:11.
59. Cf. 4.3.3.3.17.

is because "faith comes from hearing, and hearing by the word of Christ."[60] Moreover, a person is saved by grace "through faith," and this faith is a "gift from God."[61] Although we believe that we need faith to please God,[62] the word of God brings forth faith in a person, as the material world came to existence because of God's word, and that faith is a gift from God, not something generated by human beings.[63]

The inductive logical conclusion concerning the argument between the priority of the knowledge of the word of God versus having a living faith boils down to the following contention: human beings' knowledge of the word of God and the ontological priority of the word of God are two different things. Knowing concerns an epistemological shift from not knowing to knowing by human beings as a consequence of hearing the word of God within the constraint of time, whereas the ontological priority of the word of God is a necessary reality not conditioned by the sequence of time. Therefore, the ontological word of God comes ahead of one's living faith, which is brought forth to life by the word of God itself.

Now concerning the knowledge of the word of God, according to this discussion, there can be two types of people. The first group are those who accumulate knowledge of the word of God as mere impersonal information, but there is no visible change in their lives although they know the word of God. It is to this category we can include Satan and his knowledge of the Scripture. However, the second group are those whose knowledge of the word of God has brought forth a living faith in their lives, because they have surrendered to the authority of the word in their lives. Thus we can argue that the authority of the word of God in a person's life or in a church's life is fundamental. Consequently, in the absence of the authoritative presence of the word of God in the preaching event, there will be confusion, nominalism, and spiritual degeneration both in the individual and congregational spiritual health.

---

60. Rom 10:17.
61. Eph 2:8–9.
62. Heb 11:6.

63. There is a debate on whether faith is a gift from God or whether it is through human effort. For a discussion on this, see Lopez, "Is Faith a Gift," 259–76; Adam, *Hearing God's Words*, 137–38.

5.5 Interpreting the Impact of Preaching on Society

As mentioned earlier, several participants doubt the positive impact of preaching on society; however, there are others who think and give evidence of a positive impact of preaching on society. It is true that overwhelming evidence may not be there; however, several participants claimed that there is a visible influence and impact on society, both by the believers in their social interaction and through a direct interaction of the gospel with non-Christians.[64]

Although there continues to be a general objection towards Christian beliefs by the Meitei Hindu people who form the majority in Imphal, there is evidence that the Meitei community is more and more open to the teachings of the Bible. Whether it is the Meitei Hindu mothers who are secretly coming to church with prayer requests and asking the pastors to befriend their sons, or those who recommend drug addicts and socially ostracised people to the ministry of the church, or the members of the Meitei Hindu families who came and experienced the Christian wedding of their daughters with Christian boys, the resistance against gospel preaching is softening.[65] In fact, we can assume that based on what Pastor Tomba said after the two weddings he solemnised, it is because of the gospel preaching that these non-Christians were moved to tears and confessed their openness and willingness to join the Christian community soon. These kinds of stories are rarely heard and most of the time go unnoticed. But small as they are in their sample size, they are valuable indicators of the growing acceptance and openness to the message of the gospel, which they once despised and looked at with suspicion.[66]

From the five homiletical-theological surveys discussed in the literature review,[67] we learned of the presence of the fifth category, where good preaching may cause spiritual renewal of individuals and social responsibility. Above, we saw that the Meitei Hindu people have been moved by the preaching of the gospel and have become more open to Christians; moreover, preaching had addressed several of their social ills. Here, it was not only the spiritual and theological impression made on them but also a visible change in the social stance and acceptance because traditionally and culturally, the Meitei people

---

64. Cf. 4.3.4.6.
65. Cf. 4.3.4.6.
66. Many of them still do. But there are more people who are opening up.
67. See Figure 7.

tend to look down on the Christian belief system. This could be because they either consider Christianity a foreign religion or a religion embraced by the *Haos*.[68]

5.6 An Engagement between Research Findings and Literature Review

The aim in this section is to link the findings as analysed in the descriptive chapter to the literature review and discuss the gaps that are discovered and the aspects that contribute to the epistemology of the effect of preaching on spiritual vitality or nominalism, and then make some inferences.

5.6.1 The Advantage of Qualitative Approach

In the literature review, we surveyed the research work of Newman and Wright[69] and determined that the findings of the effect of preaching on the participants' spirituality will better emerge if a qualitative rather than a quantitative method is employed, especially when asking experiential questions, for example, about "the effect of sermons on 'problems of your life.'" This current research method enabled the participants to freely express what they felt or experienced when they heard preaching in the churches. This approach enabled both the theologically trained and lay people to freely share their experiences, unlike the research work of Newman and Wright where the researchers confessed that their approach restricted the voice of the lay people as they did not know how to answer several questions. The face-to-face interviews and open-ended questionnaires gave participants more freedom to express their experiences. Although there was both negative and positive feedback on what preaching did to their spiritual lives and also on what they perceived to be the effect of preaching in the churches and in society, the advantage of this approach was that we could listen to the voices of the people, either in their expressing satisfaction and a sense of fulfilment or their disappointment and pain.

---

68. Derogatory term used to refer to the tribal peoples in Manipur by the Meitei people in general.

69. Cf. 2.2.3.1.

5.6.2 The Effect of Preaching: The Homiletical-Theological Survey

This section relates to the main research question concerning the effect of preaching on the spiritual life of the members.[70] In the homiletical-theological survey section of the literature review chapter, we discussed the theories of what preaching does. The five theories are: good preaching may have minimal effect on spiritual renewal; good preaching may cause good morality; good preaching may cause social transformation; good preaching may cause spiritual renewal (primarily) of individuals; and good preaching may cause spiritual renewal of individuals and social responsibility.[71]

According to the findings, no participant thought that preaching has no effect on the people. There was no sign that economic growth and prosperity is the reason for spiritual vitality, as one theory argued; however, there were some who considered behavioural and moral change as an important aspect of the effect of preaching. A few pastors considered this as a positive impact of their pulpit ministry.[72] Other participants also expressed that good preaching had impacted change in their behavioural and moral lives for good.[73] However, it remains unclear both for the pastors and the other participants if they rank moral and behavioural change higher than a person's spiritual life, including the issues of salvation, as none of them separately discussed these two issues. There were no advocates for the primary role of preaching being social change, without effecting spiritual change. Moreover, there is no visible evidence that the participants perceived that preaching's purpose is solely for salvific purposes without any Christian role in social responsibility.[74] The fifth theory is what the participants endorsed. Whether preaching of the pastors practically met the spiritual needs of the people or not, people expect preaching to address both the spiritual and practical issues of their everyday lives in society, including character, behaviour (testimony and ethics), and contribution to society.[75] In the research survey, several participants believed

---

70. Cf. 1.8.
71. Cf. 2.2.1; Figure 7.
72. Cf. 4.3.4.6.
73. Cf. 4.3.4.6.
74. The prayer warriors preach this kind of theology, but the pastors and members generally do not seem to subscribe to this. See Appendix 12.
75. See 4.3.4.4.1.6.

that preaching had positively affected both the spiritual and social aspects of the listeners.[76]

5.6.3 Preaching and Spiritual Vitality

The participants were aware of the relationship between preaching and spiritual vitality. Some of them compared this relationship to the food we eat and the health it brings to a person.[77] Although some disagreed that preaching brings about spiritual vitality or that it depends on the pastors who preach it, most of the listeners agreed on its positive impact. Several pastors also demonstrated a knowledge of the impact of their preaching on the people, especially one pastor who claimed that whenever he aligns his spirit with God's Spirit, he witnesses the work of God in the listeners' life.[78] Although there is no doubt that some bad preaching is happening in some Baptist churches of Imphal, in other churches, preaching is not simply going on as an element of the worship liturgy without significance. People are aware of its role in bringing spiritual vitality and are also aware of the situation in churches where it is neglected.

Moreover, as we surveyed Enosh Anguandia Adia Edre's thesis[79] in the literature review, the findings in the field reveal that the situation faced by Edre among the churches he researched is similar to that of the Baptist churches in Imphal. First, the congregation strongly believes that pastors' preaching is related to the spiritual vitality of the members. Like Edre's finding, the members of the Baptist churches in Imphal claim that many pastors do not preach the biblical gospel clearly. However, it was also found that in some churches, when the pastors preach the "biblical gospel," the congregation says that they are out of spiritual kindergarten and so preaching should move beyond the gospel.[80] This could only suggest a lack of the understanding of word of God and the congregation's ignorance. Second, similar to Edre's findings, there are some churches which do not have systematic and thematic preaching. It is inconclusive whether the pastors intentionally avoided some elements of the

---

76. This will be discussed later in more detail.
77. Cf. 4.3.2.2; 4.3.4.4.2.2; 4.3.4.4.2.5; 4.3.4.7; 4.3.3.3.1; 4.3.3.3.19; 4.3.3.4.1.
78. See 4.3.2.2.
79. Cf. 2.2.3.3.
80. Cf. 4.3.3.4.1.

gospel for "fear of losing adherents" as Edre argued, but in order to make the church service attractive and retain the listeners and also to pull in others who are on the outside, some churches give much emphasis to entertainment and feel-good factors while planning the church worship service.[81] Third, Edre argues that spiritual stagnation can be "traced back to failure in preaching this (the) biblical gospel of repentance and saving faith in Jesus."[82] Many participants argued similarly, implying this is true in the Baptist churches of Imphal as well. In fact, Kamal lamented that our churches (believers in the church) are "dying" spiritually because there is gospel starvation, as the pulpit is flooded with topics of politics, projects relating to building construction, vehicle purchases for the church, and other matters.[83]

5.6.4 Preaching and Nominalism

5.6.4.1 Evaluating the Findings vis-à-vis Some North East Churches

In the literature review, we pointed out Lawmkunga's observation about the decadence of Mizo spirituality in the context of a flourishing preaching ministry in the churches of Mizoram.[84] He did not mention the kind of preaching methods employed in the Mizo churches; however, the findings show that in the Baptist churches in Imphal, pastors and preachers employ more topical sermons.[85] (An evaluation on the methods of preaching is discussed later in a separate section.) Molem Ronrang claimed that because of the absence of a good preaching ministry in the churches of Arunachal Pradesh, people are disappointed and weak spiritually. Moreover, the people there have become dispassionate about the word of God.[86] In the churches of Meghalaya too, we find that nominalism has become a concern because biblical preaching is weak.[87] In Nagaland, Nuh lamented the depravity of the Naga society and

---

81. Cf. 4.3.1.2.1; 4.3.1.3; 4.3.3.2.13; 4.3.3.3.12.
82. Cf. 2.2.3.3.
83. Cf. 4.3.1.2.2. *Contra*, we can argue that a holistic gospel proclamation does not dichotomise physical and spiritual needs, because it includes both realities. However, Kamal is here expressing his exasperation on the extended famine of God's word for the souls of the members.
84. Cf. 2.4.1.2.
85. Cf. 4.3.4.8.
86. Cf. 2.4.1.3.
87. Cf. 2.4.1.3.

the slumber and irrelevance of the preaching ministry of the church.[88] Kevi Meru also linked nominalism to the mediocre preaching in the pulpits of Nagaland churches.[89] Pongen in his thesis mentions the link between "lack of sound biblical teaching" and nominalism in Nagaland.[90]

The findings suggest that in the Baptist churches of Imphal also, there is a perceivable link between poor preaching and spiritual lethargy, including nominalism.[91] The finding is not one-dimensional, and there are exceptions: there is faithful preaching in some Baptist churches,[92] and in others there is a slow shift towards appreciating and preaching expository sermons.[93] However, in a good number of other churches, there is an indication that members no longer trust their pastors' preaching nor enjoy their sermons.[94] There is a rift between what the pews expect and what the pulpit actually delivers.[95] It is unfortunate that what Mingthing discovered in his research is still true.[96] It is inconclusive if the same pulpit-pew chasm has continued from the time of Mingthing's research or if this is a different development. Thus there are a variety of situations prevalent in the Baptist churches of Imphal.

5.6.4.2 Evaluating the Findings vis-à-vis the Baptist Churches in Imphal

The research findings clearly reveal that nominalism is a real threat in the churches. It was also discovered that irrespective of people's awareness of the positive impact of preaching, they expect preaching to touch the spiritual as well as social dimensions of a person. The question remains why church members become or remain nominal Christians despite the right understanding of the theoretical framework that preaching must produce spiritual vitality

---

88. Cf. 2.4.1.4.
89. Cf. 2.4.1.4.
90. Cf. 2.4.1.4.
91. Cf. 4.3.4.4.2.1.
92. Mostly topical and testimonial preaching (in which the preacher shares much of his personal experiences). Cf. 4.3.3.4.1.
93. Cf. 4.3.4.8.
94. Cf. 4.3.4.4.2.5.
95. Ramesh Richard recalls how a church member in a prominent Asian city lamented, "My pastor does not feed sheep. He addresses giraffes!"; Richard, *Preparing Expository Sermons*, 16.
96. Cf. 2.2.3.2; 3.7.3.

and social change. In the descriptive chapter, we have discussed why church members think preaching had not positively impacted people's lives; whether it was because of the method of preaching, wrong placement of authority in preaching, or other reasons.[97] Below is a discussion coming out of these questions, linking nominalism to preaching.

In the literature review, it was found that unless the church's preaching among the Baptist churches in Manipur moves away from the missionary period style and themes to contemporary realities, issues, and needs of the people in the context of competing worldviews, our pulpits will one day become irrelevant.[98] The research finds that many pulpits have already become irrelevant for the listeners.[99] Many people, especially the younger generation and educated people who know the Scripture, continue to move out of the church, searching for better sermons and churches.[100]

In the literature review, we found there is a limited understanding of homiletics as to form and genre among the preachers and pastors in the Baptist churches in Manipur. Moreover, it was observed that the themes preached during that time were not systematic.[101] Unfortunately, not much has changed. What could be the reason for this? According to the evidence derived from the survey, it can be argued that many of the churches are pastored by lay pastors who are not able to interpret the Scripture properly, and in some cases, there are older pastors who are no longer passionate about hard work and reading additional resources and commentaries while preparing their sermons.[102] Moreover, many pastors prefer topical and testimonial sermons which focus on storytelling and illustrations and prefer to avoid expository and textual sermons that require more labour.[103] In fact, some pastors claim that expository preaching is distasteful for the listeners and that they cannot give sermon applications through such a method. Some of the pastors know that expository preaching is a good method, but they are unable to preach

---

97. Cf. 4.3.4.1.2.
98. Cf. 2.2.3.2.
99. Cf. 4.3.4.4.2.2. *Contra*, speaking from the perspective of some pastors, they have been conscious of the needs of the congregation in their preaching.
100. Cf. 4.3.4.4.2.8.
101. Cf. 2.2.3.2.
102. Cf. 4.3.4.4.2.2.
103. Cf. 4.3.4.8.

a good exposition.[104] We also found that some members think some pastors try to hide under the cover of multiple responsibilities and church projects.[105]

The argument that expository sermons are boring can be justified in cases where it has been confined to exegesis and has no connection to the world of the listeners. But sweeping statements against text-based sermons simply reveals how ill-informed people are in their understanding of such types of sermon. This could be because the pastors might have rarely seen good models or predecessors who preached text-based sermons that impressed them enough to adopt their approach.

It was also found that although some churches do have good gospel preaching, which Mingthing called "Christian preaching,"[106] there are some where misinterpretation of the Scripture happens and the members are appalled at the poor quality of preaching. As Lama poignantly depicted the church members' complaint of sermons that lack good interpretation,[107] the problem of misinterpretation remains nearly the same today. Several participants lament that their zeal to come to church receives a blow because of scriptural misinterpretation in the sermons. Some members confessed their concern that many people might have accepted the misinterpreted Scripture because they will not have the needed ability to filter the scriptural and theological fallacies.[108] This predicament points to the fact that although some of the pastors are theologically trained, their hermeneutical skill and scriptural soundness are found wanting, as Lama lamented.[109] The lack of capable pastors remains a big threat to the spiritual health in some churches. Perhaps, this has contributed to the growth of spiritual lethargy and nominalism and the downward spiral of members' interest in the church and its activities.

In some churches, members get offended if the biblical gospel about the birth, death, and resurrection of Jesus Christ is preached, because they argue

---

104. Cf. 4.3.4.8.
105. Cf. 4.3.6.3.
106. Cf. 2.2.3.2; 3.6.
107. Cf. 2.2.2.
108. Cf. 4.3.3.3.7.
109. Cf. 2.2.2.

that they have graduated from "spiritual kindergarten."[110] But what do we understand by biblical gospel?[111]

While Paul uses *euangelion* in Greek to mean gospel or the "good news,"[112] Bryan Chapell considers it the news of God fulfilling his "promise to send a Saviour to rescue broken people, restore creation's glory, and rule over all with compassion and justice . . . a good summary of the gospel is 'Christ Jesus came into the world to save sinners (1 Tim 1: 15).'" Daniel Meyer also elaborates that the gospel is

> the good news of Christ's life-giving victory over the sinful separation from God that disfigures human character, blinds people to truth and leaves them without reliable power to overcome the brokenness of creation, the darkness of death, and the limits of human love. This gospel is God's wonderful invitation to be saved from sin for a beautiful new life through him.[113]

Edre argues that the scope of the biblical gospel contains the following realities: "God's sovereignty, holiness, and righteous judgments"; "human rebellion against God"; "the atonement as the focal point"; and "repentance and faith as the response."[114] In the light of these thoughts, we can argue that the "biblical gospel" concerns the loving act of the sovereign and holy God, reconciling the broken relationship between him and human beings, brought about by sin, through the birth, sacrificial death, and resurrection of Jesus Christ, and restoring the ruined reality of interhuman and intrahuman relationships and creation[115] through the power of the Holy Spirit.

Perhaps people get offended when the pastor talks about the gospel because of their immaturity, ignorance, weak understanding of scriptural theology on what constitutes the biblical gospel, or their own spiritual pride, which is a form of nominalism. Or perhaps the pastors and preachers themselves do not know what the biblical gospel is and their inability to present a gospel

---

110. Cf. 4.3.3.4.1.
111. Cf. page 6 for a preliminary discussion.
112. Bromiley, "To Proclaim," 269–70. Cf. Dunn, *Jesus, Paul, and the Gospels*, 45.
113. Meyer, *Witness Essentials*, 36. Cf. Dunn, *Jesus, Paul, and the Gospels*, 45–46. There can be other definitions, but these two thoughts capture the essence of what the Bible says about why Jesus came into the world, and so they are sufficient for our purpose.
114. Edre, "Christian Nominalism," 178–91.
115. The scope of the work of the gospel includes the whole of creation (Col 1:19–20).

sermon by avoiding the trappings of stereotyped sermons again and again, as championed by the evangelists and missionaries – "repent from your sin and be saved."[116] Although the relevance of the gospel is timeless and no one can outgrow the need for the gospel, there are ways of presenting a gospel sermon from different texts of the Scripture without making it sound so didactic, monotonous, and repetitive.[117]

We also found in the literature review that the revival movement and its preaching undermined the role of biblical and holistic preaching;[118] nevertheless, it was a serious factor for Christian spiritual growth for many people in the past. It was found in the current research that the revival type of spirituality led by the prayer warriors does have an impact on society, but the impact does not last because they blackmail people to change so as to avoid accident or misfortune. When the emotional period of fear wanes, they go back to their old lives.[119] Moreover, the unholistic preaching of the prayer warriors has pitted medical treatment against faith and many have lost their lives because of wrong theology. Science (medical treatment) and faith should never have been kept in two different camps.[120] Based on what the participants have expressed, there is a very weak and shallow understanding of the word of God or scriptural theology in the churches.

A spiral effect seems to have emerged from these discussions – bad preaching, including sermons with scriptural misinterpretations, give birth to a weak understanding of the Scripture or a weak theology among the people, and a weak theology gives birth to spiritual lethargy and nominalism. Nominalism then leads people to low or indifferent expectations, as they would rather pursue entertainment in church worship. Uncritical listening or indifference and search for entertainment[121] then causes pastors to preach bad sermons again to tickle the itchy ears of the people.

---

116. Cf. 4.3.4.4.2.1.

117. Many participants revealed that most of the pastors and preachers have their favourite books, texts, and topics in the Bible. Cf. Keller, "Gospel-Shaped Life."

118. Mingthing; 2.2.3.2.

119. Cf. 4.3.4.4.2.4.

120. Cf. 4.3.4.4.2.6.

121. Haddon Robinson warns that preachers are not called "to entertain people," but to "proclaim the Word of God"; Robinson, "Dramatic Expository Preaching," 405.

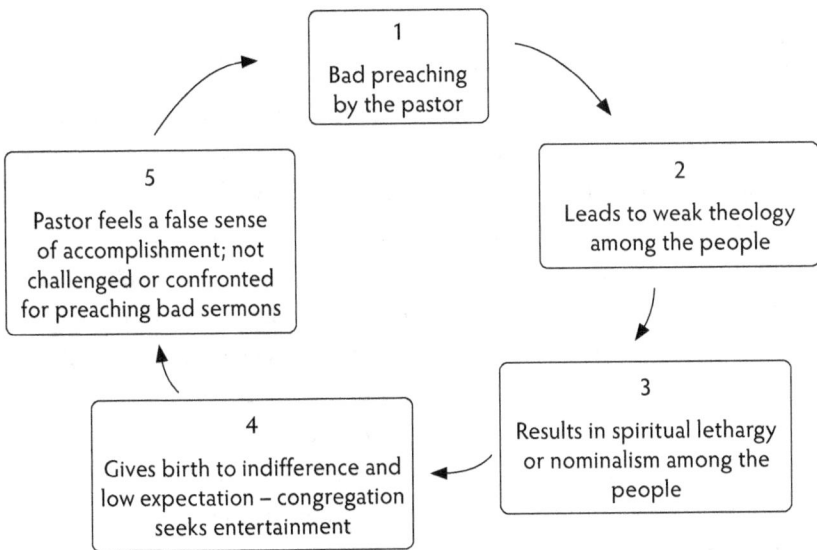

Figure 9: Sequence of Bad Preaching and Nominalism

When there is a bad sermon, for example, if the text of the Scripture is abused by not properly exegeting it or by misinterpreting it, then the word of God in the chosen text cannot strike "at the heart of nominal, easy-going Christianity as it did at the heart of Judaism," when the people of Israel refused to obey the word of God through the prophets.[122]

An analytical interpretation on why preaching possibly has a negative impact is given here. Preaching happens in a context and not in a vacuum, and the context is controlled by a structure. Below is an appraisal of the context and structure where preaching happens. Could it be that the preachers in the Imphal Baptist churches are not screened properly by the church leaders, deacons, and pastors? Should a preacher have his manuscript ready and be scrutinised by a pastoral team before each delivery? Could it be that the pastor is not made accountable to the church leadership in terms of his sermon preparation and delivery? Should the church decide for every speaker, including the pastor, on what theme, topic, or book to preach from? Could it be that the church does not have a policy to seek and appoint a theologically trained pastor who is a seminary graduate? Could it be that the church does not have a policy to send the pastor for in-job training seminars or workshops

---

122. Baldwin, *Haggai*, 218.

on preaching? Could it be that the church does not have a budget to buy books and resources for the church library, especially resources that will enrich the pastor's preaching? Could it be that the church leaders do not consider the pastoral candidate's preaching skill and pulpit experience as one of the primary qualifications for his appointment? Could it be that the church is not paying the pastor well and therefore the pastor has to seek additional income for his family?[123] Could it be that the church leaders are giving the pastor too many responsibilities and not helping him with administrative work?[124] Ramesh Richard rightly critiques church leaders and pastors for losing sight of their ministerial priority of preaching over "counselling ministries," "organizational leadership" and other social works, and laments that "preaching the Bible has become secondary in the hierarchy of ministry tasks."[125]

Unlike the bad sermon and its cycle, good preaching will, on the other hand, build strong biblical theology and the scriptural clarity of the congregation. A strong theology will result in spiritual vitality in the congregation. Spiritual vitality will give birth to warm but critical and high expectations. This will make the congregation want to grow in the word. Encouraged and challenged, the pastor has a clear assessment of the congregational needs and prepares his sermon faithfully. Figure 10 presents a possible alternative cycle of good preaching.

Coming back to the discussion on context and structure, it is possible that an absence of or loose structure can lead to no accountability, and preaching may become mediocre. However, again, if the system is too demanding, restrictive, and stifling, the preaching may become devoid of life and creativity, simply fulfilling the legalistic demand of the structural system. Therefore, a balanced context of preaching could be revisited and formulated, to vitalise preaching and congregational spirituality.

---

123. Cf. 2.2.2; 2.2.3.2.

124. See Figure 8.

125. Richard, *Preparing Expository Sermons*, 17. This is not to undermine the importance and necessity of other pastoral responsibilities, but the issue here is the need for pastors to prioritise the ministry of preaching.

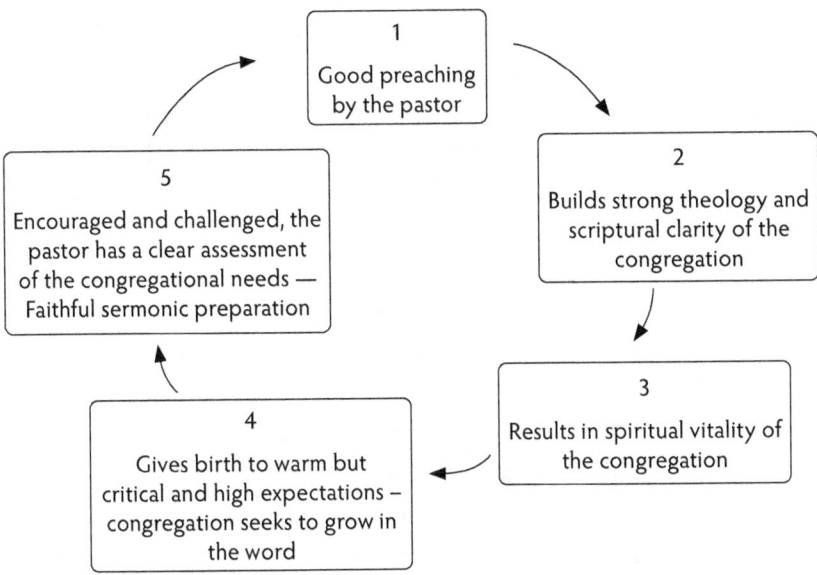

Figure 10: Sequence of Good Preaching and Spiritual Vitality

5.6.5 Nominalism: Description and Definition

5.6.5.1 *Nominalism Description*

Several aspects and characteristics of nominalism have been identified and included in the descriptive empirical chapter. Some of them were discussed at the Lausanne consultations, and will not be addressed in this chapter.[126] However, we will discuss some characteristics of nominalism which were not discovered or identified in the literature review and then interpret them. Then we will link all the discovered characteristics of nominalism to the role of preaching, on how preaching is related or not related to these characteristics of nominalism, and why people think so. Finally, we will integrate our findings on nominalism to the working definition of nominalism as one arising from the contextual situation of the Baptist churches in Imphal.

There is an awareness of the presence of nominalism in the Baptist churches of Imphal. Almost all the participants agree that nominalism is a great concern for the Baptist churches in Imphal as it is around the world. The participants described nominal Christians in the following ways: comfortably

---

126. Cf. 2.3.1.1; 2.3.1.2.

numb; self-made man attitude; lazy Christian; self-projection through smooth talk; indifferent and confused Christians; no prominence of Christ in one's talk; one who only comes on special occasions;[127] self-righteous and ascetic Christian; no hunger for the word of God; floating and drifting Christian; unteachable and easily offended Christian; a life without integrity; and superficial Christian.[128]

Some of these categories may not be directly related to preaching, but we can argue that many individuals could be in this spiritual condition because they do not know the word of God nor do they surrender to it. As Christians consider the word of God to be the compass of life, in the absence of it, people will head in whichever direction they think is the right one, only to sink deeper into the territory of confusion and destruction. Many of the participants claimed that proper exposition of the word is absent in many churches, although the presence of it in some churches should be acknowledged. Some participants further argued that it is not about the minimum frequency of the exposition, but the misinterpretation of the word, which is a grave concern. Misinterpretation of anything can be disastrous because what that text actually means will not be what is being communicated; in fact, it could be just the opposite of what the text wants to communicate. Out of several descriptions of nominalism mentioned above, we will interpret two of them below, engaging with some theories and literature.

A probable reason why many Christians are branded "comfortably numb" is the influence of popular culture.[129] Hudson observed that the members come to church because they receive entertainment; whether it is through preaching, singing or dance, just like what they would receive in secular functions and programmes.[130] He critiqued the churches for blindly copying what the secular world is doing, without any critical reflection and consideration. He interpreted this influence as that of popular culture. Popular culture has been interpreted as one seeking entertainment, in fact of being "highly entertaining." It is argued that they have to do so "to remain

---

127. Related to celebration or festival.
128. Cf. 4.3.3.2.
129. Cf. 4.3.3.2.1.
130. Cf. 4.3.3.2.13.

popular."[131] Popular culture is also considered "the common language" of our times[132] which has become "unstoppable as a form of expressive culture, challenging moral stodginess and aesthetic pretentiousness, while entertaining masses with its earthiness."[133] For example, Asha Kasbekar includes "film, video, music, television," and popular sports like cricket in the realms of popular culture.[134] Some assert that popular culture has become morally corrupt.[135] Shirley Fedorak agrees that "popular culture is often criticised for its commercial nature; its product appeal to the masses" and "conspicuous consumption."[136] However, with these allegations, Fedorak argues that, "despite numerous criticisms – over-commercialisation, marginalisation, skewed values, and elitist disdain – popular culture is an integral part of any culture."[137] It is argued that the danger of rejecting popular culture "by taking the moral high ground" will mean a rejection of its ardent followers and the trends of the time. Chris Rojek laments that many people simplistically consider "popular" equivalent to the idea "of the people," and naively consider pop "to mean the expression of what is practised or well favoured by the majority."[138] The debate on the scope of the definition will not be discussed here; suffice it here to say that the preaching of the churches could have been influenced by the popular culture and its philosophy, and consequently have numbed the members' spiritual lives.

A probable interpretation of why many Christians prefer to be "special occasion Christians" and remain absent on other Sundays of the year could be looked at through the lenses of the tribal and modern ways of life. K. Thanzauva argues, "Communitarianism is a concept and life principle of tribal community in which a homogeneous people live together sharing their joys and sorrows in mutual love and care."[139] It is true that the tribal way of life brings people together whether it is to care for the sick, to build a house,

---

131. Irwin, "Philosophy Engages," 12.
132. Irwin, 55.
133. Danesi, *Popular Culture*, 1–2.
134. Kasbekar, *Pop Culture*, 10.
135. Irwin, "Philosophy Engages," 52.
136. Fedorak, *Pop Culture*, 9.
137. Fedorak, 13.
138. Rojek, *Pop Music*, 41.
139. Thanzauva, *Theology*, 136.

labour in the fields or celebrate together by throwing feasts.[140] However, could it be that the tribal Christians, with the influence of the modern-day way of life, have consciously or unconsciously tilted towards individualism,[141] de-traditionalising an affiliation to the past,[142] and so have begun to avoid communitarian activities except during the occasion[143] of feasts and festivals, which they do attend to show their kinship with the community, and because it is a time to receive something? It could also be they are not ready to abide by the discipline of the church in their everyday life within the community of believers.

5.6.5.2 Nominalism Definition

Here we will integrate our findings of nominalism, arising from the contextual situation of the Baptist churches in Imphal, to the working definition of nominalism we have proposed in the literature review. As mentioned earlier, the working definition reads,

> A nominal Christian is one who is a Christian in name only and lacks the corresponding reality of a personal conviction associated with authentic Christian experience. It may either be defined as one whose relationship with God is characterised by stagnation after a genuine personal encounter and walk with God or a false optimism of salvation because of one's Christian heritage and ritualism.[144]

In the light of the findings, the revised definition might read as follows:

> A nominal Christian is one who is a Christian in name only and lacks the corresponding reality of a personal conviction associated with authentic Christian experience and biblical authority. Such a person may have one or more of the following traits – no hunger for God's word, superficial, full of oneself (unteachable, indifferent and easily offended), lazy, confused, without integrity,

---

140. Thanzauva, *Theology*, 143.
141. McClure, *Moving Beyond Individualism*, 89.
142. Musschenga, "Many Faces," 7.
143. Related to celebration or festival.
144. Cf. 2.5.

spiritually numb and floats without direction, but shows up during Christian occasions and celebrations. The person could also be a self-righteous ascetic Christian who refuses fellowship with other believers, influenced by a pharisaic practice. These could happen because their relationship with God is characterised by a weak theology or stagnation after a genuine personal encounter and walk with God, or a false optimism of salvation because of one's Christian heritage and ritualism.

5.7 Interpreting the Believers' Poor Understanding of the Word of God

The participants have expressed numerous reasons for the poor understanding of the word of God among the believers of the Baptist churches in Imphal. Some argued that misinterpretation of the Scripture is the main issue.[145] Others maintain that it is because the parents in the family do not teach and model a Bible-reading lifestyle to their children.[146] Some claim that the believers are not serious about their faith, so there is a gap between teaching and compliance.[147] Still others contend that most of the pastor's preaching is dry and without an evangelical thrust, lacking appeal, and a sense of urgency.[148] Further, there are some who reason that a pastor who has a poor knowledge of the word of God and one who does not demonstrate seriousness in teaching God's word cannot build a congregation who knows the word of God.[149] So, the arguments are manifold.

However, could it be that there is a deeper contextual learning issue at hand? Could it be that because the church members who are mostly tribal people[150] have a different way of learning, as they are more oral-oriented than written word or print-oriented, so they unable to learn the word of God as much as they should? We will pursue this perspective in our discussion here.

---

145. Cf. 4.3.3.3.7.
146. Cf. 4.3.1.1.
147. Cf. 4.3.1.1.
148. Cf. 4.3.1.2.1.
149. Cf. 4.3.1.2.2.

150. Although there are some churches where the church members are not tribals, most of the churches under the study belong to various tribal groups.

According to the tribal people's ancestral heritage, they are people with oral cultures.[151] Ancestral tribal knowledge, songs and dances, and the stories and wisdom anecdotes were passed down from one generation to another and preserved through narration and oral means for posterity and not through any written book or record. With the arrival of Western and modern education, the means to store and pass down knowledge has changed. But could it be that their primal oral culture subconsciously controls their psyche? This argument may not hold water because many of the tribal church members who are, for example, government officers, teachers, and students are highly literate and have already had exposure to reading and writing. In fact, many of them regularly read and write for their studies or for their professional work in the office. So, the argument that perhaps they are not inclined to the habit of reading is unlikely. Moreover, even if there are some rare cases of old people who are illiterate and are unable to read and write, there are audio Bibles and audio sermons circulating today, and they could get access to them through their families and friends, if not by themselves. Thanks to the digital revolution, the tribals can feel at home again because they can learn through oral and aural means. So that cannot be a legitimate excuse. Nevertheless, it is arguable that some people are indeed aural learners. However, the presence of numerous church members who still do not know the word of God properly despite all these facilities point to other more serious factors.

Could it simply be due to the human tendency to forgetfulness? Some can argue that one may not necessarily remember all the kinds of food one eats during a week or a month, but because of the food, one is alive and growing healthier. So one could ask if it is really necessary to know the items of food one has eaten every week, as long as it is making the person healthy? But the problem with the situation of the church members is that many of them neither know and remember the word of God nor do they grow or thrive spiritually. So the problem is not because of the human trait of forgetfulness but the lack of spiritual growth. There could still be other factors.

Could it then be due to the sheer negligence and indifference of the people influenced by the pagan culture and way of life of the majoritarian community in Imphal? Christians and non-Christians work together in offices, they live together in the same neighbourhood, and students attend the same

---

151. Nag, *India and North East*, 20; Snaitang, "Christianity and Change, 140.

educational institutes. Could it be, as Pastor Luther reflected, the light of the Christians gets dimmer because the culture and worldview of the non-Christians swallow the Christian convictions?[152] As a consequence, possibly, the church members do not rely on the word of God to give them direction and light for their path, but randomly follow the common and accepted way of life lived out by the ungodly society. Could it be that because of this many Christians have no qualms in practicing corruption and bribery? This argument has some probability, although it is not conclusive.

Apart from all the theoretical possibilities we have discussed, one could argue or support the presupposition that the peoples' inner thirst for the word of God has not been stirred by the preaching of the pastors, although there are some exceptions.[153] We could argue that primarily, the fire in the hearts of the people must be ignited by a sermon that is faithful to the text and relevant to the people. If such a type of sermon is periodically preached, then there will be a growing desire and thirst for God's word even on weekdays, to fill and touch their lives. Consequently, instead of having the habit of reading the Bible to check if it had been misinterpreted in the church, people will instead read the truth of God's words (exhortations, challenges, and promises of God) and commit their lives based on the Scripture they have heard in the sermon.

5.8 Goals and Themes in Preaching

Although some participants claimed that their churches do not have a theme or goals for the pulpit ministry, either short-term or long-term, some churches do have them, but they are diverse: life situations, salvation, reconciliation, repentance, resurgence, reaching out, love, peace, giving, unity, togetherness and an unforgiving spirit, broken homes, conflicts, the Trinity, parenting, and others. All these could be preached either from the Old Testament (OT) or New Testament (NT) texts. However, there seems to be a gravitational pull towards the NT as several of the pastors and preachers exposit these themes from its perspective and avoid the OT. Perhaps one pastor's statement that

---

152. Cf. 4.3.3.2.10.

153. *Contra*, Timothy Keller argues that preaching is not necessarily the only means to convert or change a person spiritually. He claims, "No church should expect that all the life transformation that comes from the Word of God . . . comes strictly through preaching"; Keller, *Preaching*, 5.

with the coming of Jesus Christ his teachings in the NT are considered more significant, sums up the bias of many church pulpits towards the NT,[154] although the OT is not completely ignored.

Why is the NT given preference over the OT? Is this one-dimensional preaching and listening creating a malnourished and imbalanced Christian community? Can there be a link between NT bias in preaching and nominalism? Below is a short discussion.

The NT was conceived in the womb of the OT. We cannot think of the existence of the NT as an independent entity without any heritage or foundation from the OT because "the normal path to a genuine understanding of the New Testament is by way of the Old."[155] Jesus declared that he did not come to abolish the law but to fulfil it.[156] Jesus's teaching was firmly grounded on the OT, except that he took its teaching to the next level. To say that Jesus's teaching is more important than the OT would be a contradiction, because Jesus built his theology, humanly speaking, from the OT. Some examples are: when he claimed that he was before Abraham;[157] his teaching about the greatest commandment;[158] the "I am" claims;[159] the Nazareth manifesto;[160] the true vine metaphor;[161] and many others. He was going back to the OT. Apart from what Jesus said, some other examples are the Pauline and Petrine epistles and the book of Hebrews which are filled with OT theology and metaphors.[162] Therefore, for a pastor to say that the NT is more important than the OT is an inappropriate statement. A preacher can preach the gospel and the epistles well only by going back to the OT. For instance, salvation, resurrection, and the birth of Jesus find their meaning and theological significance in the context of the story of Adam and Eve, and the OT messianic expectation. To

---

154. Cf. 4.3.4.7.
155. Brunner, "Significance," 249.
156. Matt 5:17.
157. John 8:48–59.
158. Matt 22:36–40.
159. Found in the Gospel of John.
160. Luke 4:16–21.
161. John 15.
162. For example, "our paschal lamb" (1 Cor 5:7); "with the unleavened bread of sincerity and truth" and "the old yeast, the yeast of malice and evil" (1 Cor 5:8); "once for all" (Heb 7: 27; 9:6–14, 23–28; 10:10, 14; cf. 1 Pet 3:18); "circumcision" (Rom 2: 28–29; 1 Cor 7:19; cf. Gal 5:6; 6:15); see Allen, *Theological Approach*, 88.

preach sermons on a regular basis without periodically going back to the OT would be to skim the surface without going into the text in depth.

Therefore, if the sermons are only scratching the surface of the NT, there is a great possibility that the congregations will never grow deep and firm in the word of God. Disjointed sermons without any correlation and connection to the larger themes and narratives of the entire biblical theology will not inform nor enlighten the minds and hearts of the congregation, nor can they persuade the people towards a committed and critically informed Christianity. Such sermons will produce a Christianity that is bound to be shallow and swept to the right and left by winds of doubt, wrong teachings, misinformed self-talk, and human tradition.

Moreover, an absence of balanced teaching of the covenantal law in the OT will pit law against grace, and legalism against antinomian philosophy. OT law must be preached not necessarily to bring Christians under its yoke, but to drive home the message of a loving God and his redemption,[163] and consequently human being's grateful response to live a life of obedience.[164] It will also teach a sense of ethical responsibility along with the gospel of freedom.[165] The gospel surely talks about believers' responsible living, and the OT has scores of narratives, prophecies, and oracles that teach God's people how to live a life as God's covenant partner. They are not cumbersome because teachings on laws must be interpreted and read in the light of the grace of God.[166] Therefore, the gospel teaching in the NT does not obliterate or nullify teaching on responsible living. Rather it confirms and takes the teaching to a higher level, once a person has received the grace and forgiveness of God. A church that does not teach its members the laws of God and God's high standard of righteousness that surpasses that of the pagan nations, and consequently that of the Pharisees, will indirectly signal to its members a weak

---

163. Love was at the centre of God's relationship with human beings. Loving God is the greatest commandment (Deut 6:5).

164. The Ten Commandments begin with the statement, "I am the Lord your God, who brought you out of the land of Egypt, out of the house of slavery" (Exod 20:2).

165. For example, the Corinthians needed to be taught that law and freedom were not adversaries. Paul, who propagates freedom in Christ, and Peter, who earlier in his ministry leans towards Jewish traditionalism, were not opposed to each other. Cf. Montague, *First Corinthians*, 78; Longman and Garland, *Proverbs–Isaiah*, 289ff; Stott, *Living Church*, 84ff.

166. Although we could argue that to do such a thing in one's sermon requires skill.

theology of cheap grace,[167] consequently harvesting an attitude of leniency and tolerance of sin.

Further, a congregation that does not hear preaching from the book of Psalms will not know how to relate to God in seasons of struggle, sorrow, and pain, and not only during joy and celebration. The book of Psalms is a great reservoir for believers to learn how to express their tears and align their emotions in the light of God's righteous character and it teaches us how God turns our seasons of "disorientation" to "new orientation."[168] This reflection comes in light of the experiences of several participants, that the sermons in some churches do not relate to their practical struggles in life.

The books of the prophets, both major and minor[169] can teach believers about God's standard of righteousness and the warning of God's impending judgement in the face of God's people's unrepentant lives. The ministry of the prophets spanned the pre-exilic, exilic, and post-exilic periods. If the pre-exilic period prophecies and oracles can warn believers about God's abhorrence of a life of sin (spiritual idolatry, spiritual adultery, spiritual lethargy, and God's jealousy over his people), the prophecies during the exilic period can teach believers about God's faithfulness, compassion, and hope beyond the ashes, and the post-exilic prophets can teach believers about the importance of spiritual renewal, warning against regression into spiritual lethargy, warning the pastors, mission workers, and theologians against a lackadaisical attitude towards the work of God[170] and emphasising a recommitment to the word of God.[171] As such, we can only imagine the quality of a congregation whose spiritual diet is deprived of the prophets.

A congregation that listens only to the NT and avoids the OT misses out on about 78 percent of the Bible.[172] Thus, there are several aspects from other

---

167. As criticized by Dietrich Bonhoeffer. It is a kind of grace that justifies "sin without the justification of the sinner," grace that does not require discipleship; Bonhoeffer, *Cost of Discipleship*, 43.

168. For more discussion on Psalms and spirituality, see Brueggemann, *Spirituality*.

169. Some prefer to avoid the term "minor" and argue that all the prophets are of the same value. But here we take the term "minor" purely as to the length of some books, not their value. See Chase, *Old Testament*, 6.

170. Malachi was vocal against the priests for their apathy towards their religious duties and obligations. We will elaborate on this later.

171. Ezra and Nehemiah are not among the minor prophets but they returned to Judah and brought back the tradition of reading the Scripture.

172. Kent, Kissling and Turner, "Introduction," 11.

OT genres and books that could minister to the contemporary congregation.[173] However, the purpose here is not to engage with all the possible themes and subjects that can be preached from the OT, but to serve as an argument in principle to demonstrate the malnutrition and impoverishment of a congregation without the OT texts preached to them and the possible consequence of spiritual lethargy.

5.9 Methods of Sermons Preached in the Baptist Churches

The findings suggest that the Baptist churches in Imphal employ various methods of sermons in their preaching. When the seventy questionnaire participants were asked to mark any one or more options of the methods (from the multiple methods provided) under the question "What types of sermon structures/methods (narration; expository; topical etc) were preached in the churches?" the following were the number of responses:[174] Narration or storytelling approach–19; Expository approach–22; Testimonial approach–25; Topical–54; Textual–3, and Others–4. The responses from the questionnaires suggest that there are diverse methods of preaching happening in the churches. Moreover, the twenty interview participants also generally agreed that there are different methods of preaching employed by pastors; however, if we look closely at the questionnaire figures, the weight tilts towards topical preaching. Further, the interview participants also indicated that although some of them preached expository sermons, the most common method in the pulpits of Baptist churches in Imphal is the topical method.[175]

5.10 An Analysis of the Methods of Sermons

Based on the figures of sermon structure discussed above, the purpose here is not to uncritically link topical preaching to the existence of nominalism in the church, because some of the pastors from the interview clearly disclosed

---

173. Read Kent et al., *Reclaiming*; Kaiser, *Preaching and Teaching*; Greidanus, *Preaching Christ*; Wright, *Sweeter than Honey*.

174. The questionnaire participants ticked multiple options of the types of preaching provided, and not just one. Cf. 4.3.4.8.

175. Cf. 4.3.4.8.

that they preached topical sermons to build the spirituality of the congregation.[176] Some even claimed that the topical method gives them a better grasp or handle to address the existential situations and problems in society.[177] Further, some of them justified that this method helps them to feed the seekers, the new believers, and mature believers according to their levels of need.[178] The justification provided by some of these pastors certainly has legitimacy.

Therefore, it will be inappropriate to connect the spiritual predicament of the members to the topical preaching method they regularly listen to without a critical evaluation. Instead of asking the question, "Why is there nominalism despite some pastors claiming that topical sermons were prepared to vitalise the spirituality of the church members?" a better question to begin with would be to ask, "How many pastors and preachers have the same spiritual goals as these pastors have, to preach topical sermons in order to bring about spiritual vitality in the church members?" According to the survey, there are not many. On the contrary, some of the congregation members and pastors confessed that there are many pastors who employed topical preaching to please the listeners by entertaining them, and to escape the hard work of personal study.[179] But what constitutes topical preaching? A brief discussion is made below to describe it.

It is argued that a topical sermon is one where one's "subject (topic) is based on a given Scripture text while the main points and the subpoints are *not* based on that text"[180] necessarily. It is said that even in cases when the subject or subpoints are based on the text, the contents of the sermons are mostly developed by asking "questions (who, what, where, why?), faceting (looking at a subject from various angles or perspectives), or formal reasoning (deduction or induction)."[181] Describing what a topical sermon usually looks like in the Indian pulpits,[182] Isaiah Gaddala states that, generally, once

---

176. Cf. 4.3.2.3; 4.3.4.7.
177. Cf. 4.3.4.8.
178. Cf. 4.3.2.3.
179. Cf. 4.3.1.2.1; 4.3.3.3.12; 4.3.4.8.
180. Hamilton, *Homiletical*, 25.
181. Hamilton, 25.
182. Clayton J. Schmit (Associate Professor of Preaching, Fuller Theological Seminary) in his foreword to Gaddala Isaiah's book, *Preach the Word*, claims, "At the present moment, Dr. Gaddala is the only remaining trained homiletician among the entire population of India." Schmit hopes that Gaddala's work will spur a growth in the preaching movement in India.

a preacher chooses the topic, the text tends to lose its influencing role. He states that, "most of the time, the context and the form of the text are not even alluded to. The biblical text simply becomes a pretext in the hands of the preachers for accomplishing their agenda."[183] Although a good topical sermon generally has depth, the method has been often critiqued for being shallow.[184] Before we move on to analyse expository preaching, let us first discuss some strengths and weaknesses of topical preaching.

Topical preaching certainly has strengths. First, a preacher can discuss an important topic at length. Second, the method trains a preacher to look at a subject from a wide spectrum and perspective. Third, it allows the preacher to preach the various facets of a subject within a short time. Fourth, "it ensures sermonic unity."[185] Fifth, for a lay preacher, it takes away the stress of intense sermonic preparation in terms of exegesis and the pressure of "staying faithful to the text." Sixth, "the topic can be developed freely according to the ability of the preacher," and preachers with advanced oratorical skill thrive in this method. Seventh, it is best suited when one needs to exposit doctrinal subjects and ethical issues.[186]

However, the topical preaching method also has several weaknesses. First, the greatest danger is the abuse of context. Preachers following this method are often alleged of prooftexting, taking texts "completely out of their contexts," and preach their sermons "as if they have no historical, literary or theological roots." Second, many preachers avoid in-depth study, as they can often impose their ideas and opinions onto the text, regardless of the boundaries set by it. Third, the complaint against this method is of being "biblically shallow," because a systematic and in-depth teaching of the Bible and theology is often absent.[187]

Then there are some pastors and members who claim that expository preaching must become the steady food of the church members, to bring

---

Perhaps he is right; I have not come across many resources on preaching from the Indian context.

183. Isaiah, *Preach the Word*, 90–91.

184. Hamilton, *Homiletical*, 25–26. For more discussion on topical preaching read Sunukjian, "Biblical Topical Sermon," 421–23; Warren, "Topical Preaching," 431–33.

185. Hamilton, *Homiletical*, 25.

186. Isaiah, *Preach the Word*, 91; Hamilton, *Homiletical*, 26.

187. Isaiah, 92.

about spiritual vitality, because it systematically exposes the word of God. Moreover, in this method, they claim that the word of God or the text of the sermon sets the agenda, the direction, the scope, and the application, not the mind of any human being.[188] Arguing for its need in the pulpits of the Indian churches, Isaiah says that the expository preaching method must be used

> because this is the need of the hour in our (Indian) churches. For too long, preachers have offered only fragments of biblical teaching; the time has come now to feed them with the "solid meat" of the Word. This can happen only when they are fed on the "solid diet" of the word of God.[189]

Further, some of the pastors who themselves preach topical sermons also endorse the need for prioritising expository preaching.[190] Nevertheless, we will be committing a homiletical fallacy to pit topical preaching against expository preaching because both have a place in Christian worship and homiletics if done properly. Moreover, good topical preaching is better than bad expository preaching. And ultimately, in the grand scheme of things, it is not the form but the content that matters.

However, we believe that in an academic discussion, there can be a healthy conversation on the advantages and disadvantages of both methods of preaching and an evaluation of what method would be more appropriate for the Baptist churches' context, taking into consideration the spiritual outcome of the people who have been listening to the sermons of the pastors for over a decade. If we observe some of the pastors who endorse an expository preaching method and have practiced it in their churches, these pastors joined the pastoral ministry during the ending years of the survey period (between 2014 and 2015),[191] although a few senior pastors did practice it for over a decade within the survey period.[192] These pastors who joined the ministry in the 2014 to 2015 period consider that their respective church members did not have an

---

188. Cf. 4.3.3.4.1; 4.3.4.8. Timothy Keller also argues "expository preaching should provide the main diet of preaching for a Christian community"; Keller, *Preaching*, 32. Keller then gives six arguments to support his claim. For further discussion see, Keller, 32–39.

189. Isaiah, *Preach the Word*, 101.

190. Cf. 4.3.4.8.

191. Cf. 4.3.1.1 (Pastors Matthew and Samuel).

192. Cf. 4.3.4.8.

adequate understanding of the word of God when they joined the ministry.[193] Some of the congregations were also critical of the topical preaching method and perceived a connection between it and spiritual lethargy and the lack of biblical knowledge of the people.[194] However, a contrary case exists that there are some pastors who made use of the topical preaching method and impacted the spiritual lives of their members and their biblical knowledge positively.[195] Therefore, we cannot argue that a certain type of preaching always brings spiritual lethargy and a lack of biblical knowledge. However, it is also true that not every pastor who used topical preaching bore significant spiritual results in the lives of the believers. We could argue that pulling off a topical sermon consistently for the spiritual health of the people depends on the individual pastor's charisma, knowledge of theology, homiletical ability, and oratory skill, because most of the pastors could not do so in the Baptist churches of Imphal. According to the findings, their sermons were more focused on pleasing the listeners, scratching the surface, and even misinterpretation. We can therefore argue that although topical preaching is as good as any other method of preaching, much of its accomplishment depends on the individual preachers and therefore in general, this method has been found wanting in the context of the Baptist churches in Imphal. Below, we analyse expository preaching.

Is the absence of expository preaching then the reason for the spiritual lethargy and nominalism of the congregations of the Baptist churches in Imphal? The answer is not a simple "yes" or "no"; it needs more discussion. All the pastors and the interview participants revealed the existence of nominal Christians in their churches, including those churches where the pastors claim that they follow the method of expository preaching.[196] So, expository preaching is not a ready-made automatic remedy to address spiritual lethargy in the churches, nor can nominalism be unfailingly neutralised by expository preaching. However, we argue that the pastors who employed expository preaching do provide some insight into the congregation's increasing knowledge and growth in the word of God. A few pastors claimed that expository

---

193. Cf. 4.3.1.1.
194. Cf. 4.3.2.3.
195. Cf. 4.3.2.3.
196. Cf. 4.3.1.2.6; 4.3.3.1. A majority of the questionnaire participants also claimed that nominalism is a real threat and issue in their churches.

preaching increasingly built up the congregation's passion for the word of God. A few of them asserted that systematic and sequential preaching of the texts and books builds up the interest of the members for the following Sunday's preaching, and therefore the members make an intentional effort not to miss the next church worship service.[197] One of the advantages of expository preaching is that the preacher is controlled by the text, and therefore he cannot jump from one Bible verse to another and become a biblical tourist, pitching a tent here and there without depth; rather, the preacher is compelled to unravel the word of God, not what the preacher thinks is good for the people. According to the findings, the participants have frequently expressed that most of the sermons in many churches have not been controlled by the text of the Scripture, but they had been tailored according to the appetite and taste of the listeners. Can one therefore perceive that in the presence of this kind of preaching, spiritual lethargy can germinate and grow? Further discussion on this method of preaching will continue in the normative chapter which follows.

5.11 Conclusion

The current chapter moved beyond the participants' perception and interpretation of their own experiences in relation to the impact of preaching in the Baptist churches of Imphal and the spiritual lives of the listeners in society, for more than one decade. The researcher has attempted to interpret the participants' perceived understanding of the impact of preaching on their spiritual lives. There are several other issues and themes that could be a part of this chapter; however, as the scope of this chapter has been steered by the research questions, the writer only engaged with issues directly related to the research questions.

---

197. Cf. 4.3.4.4.1.5; 4.2.4.4.1.7. A few participants felt that apart from expository preaching, nominalism could also be addressed through disciple-making, mentoring, church planting, and regular Bible study. See Appendix 3.

CHAPTER 6

Normative Task

6.1 Introduction

In the previous chapter, the interpretation of the research findings was guided by the question, "Why is this going on?"[1] In this chapter, the task is to be guided by another question, "What ought to be going on?"[2] or what is the best practice that could happen here? We will initially establish the existence and the problem of spiritual lethargy in the Scripture and see how they have been addressed homiletically. Then we will evaluate the role of charisma in topical preaching arising from the previous chapter and its alleged role even in the expository style of preaching. Then we will discuss the theological rationale and methodology of the expository style of preaching from two of the prominent proponents of this style of preaching, namely, John Stott and Timothy Keller. We will then evaluate the strengths and weaknesses of expository preaching and recommend it for the Baptist churches of Imphal to combat nominalism.

6.2 Spiritual Lethargy in the Bible and a Homiletical Response

Most evangelical Christians believe that the Bible is God's revealed word for humankind. It records the vertical relationship of God with human beings as

---

1. Osmer, *Practical Theology*, 4.
2. Osmer, 4; Cf. 1.14.3; 1.14.3.1.

well as the horizontal relationship with fellow human beings and with nature.[3] The transparency with which the Bible records[4] these relationships is to us quite shocking, because the "Bible unhesitatingly records the sin and weakness of the best of men,"[5] and it is not "afraid to tell the ugly stories . . . about murderers and harlots."[6] Here in this chapter, we are interested in engaging with the issue of spiritual lethargy,[7] and so a distinction and elaboration of the term will be helpful. Are sin and spiritual lethargy the same thing, or do they mean different things? Sin is primarily disobedience to and rebellion against the authority of God, his word, and his will in our lives,[8] because of which we fall short of his glory.[9] On the other hand, spiritual lethargy may not necessarily be an outright rebellion and wickedness against God, but rather an expression or one of the recurring outworkings of sin. It can be seen as being "lukewarm"; a regression of one's affection for God, and a degeneration of one's sensitivity to the word and things of God, as Jesus accused the church at Laodicea of being guilty.[10] When Paul writes to the church at Ephesus, "Awake, sleeper, and arise from the dead, and Christ will shine on you,"[11] Paul was addressing the believers, not people outside the community of faith. A. W. Tozer argues that here, in Ephesians 5:14, "death is a spiritual sleep or lethargy" of the believers. Many Christians unfortunately "get used to things" and "get sophisticated." He elaborates, "Spiritual sophistication lacks freshness and warmth; God is far away, and there is little communion and little joy in the Lord. To have a cold heart with little pity, little fire, little love, and little worship is spiritual lethargy."[12] Carl Haak argues that though

---

3. Kevin Vanhoozer talks of God's gift of language as a medium for communication between God and human beings, and human beings with fellow human beings and the world. Although his emphasis here is on language, nevertheless he agrees that there is a certain type of relationship between God and human beings through this communication. See, Vanhoozer, *Is There Meaning*; Vanhoozer, *Drama of Doctrine*, 177.

4. Hawkins, *From Legal*, 69–70.

5. Chafer and Walvoord, *Major Bible Themes*, 14.

6. Wright, *From Patriarchs*, xiv.

7. The issue of spirituality and spiritual lethargy was briefly discussed under 1.1.

8. Gen 3; 1 John 3:4–6.

9. Rom 3:23.

10. Rev 3:16.

11. Eph 5:14.

12. Tozer, *Dangers of a Shallow Faith*, 55. Trevor Feltham likens spiritual lethargy to "being a couch potato in your faith"; Feltham, *Deep Spiritual Thoughts*, 105. Cf. Nee, *Spiritual Man*, xxii.

we may have been born again and reconciled to God through Christ, because we live in this fallen world and due to our own carelessness, we may experience a downhill slide and "decline in our own soul – a painful process of spiritual disease, which may advance slowly, imperceptibly, silently, and unobserved." Then eventually our lives experience a lack of "holiness" and "joy" as there is no repulsion towards sin; instead "there is an actual playing with sin and a lukewarm attitude toward the church . . . the sin of spiritual lethargy."[13] Spiritual lethargy is therefore a state of being a diseased Christian, like an unhealthy plant, due to the presence of termites eating up the roots. This is because of a discrepancy between the word of God and its expression in one's life.[14]

So, when does spiritual lethargy raise its ugly head in the community of faith or in a believer? For some it happens in the days of prosperity, when all is going well. For others it takes root in the context of a tragedy or loss. Further still, for some it could happen when routine takes over one's spiritual life and enthusiasm. In this chapter, our concern is to engage with the concept of spiritual lethargy as a diverse and multi-dimensional concept and to observe it when it shows up its ugly head.

The Bible records the story of the fluctuating graph of Israel's spirituality and it's obedience to God. Spiritual inconsistency and lapse had been a recurring reality. In the history of Israel, we find various eras when the people of God became lukewarm and indifferent to the authority and lordship of God. For example, after the Israelites were delivered from centuries of Egyptian bondage by God through his mighty acts, instead of steadfastly clinging to him during the wilderness journey, they displayed diseased spirituality by grumbling against God,[15] and they slumped into idolatry by moulding a golden calf.[16] Their commitment to God faltered because of life's tribulations. Then, after the Israelites entered the promised land, and before the era of the kings in Israel, the spiritual condition of the people was described by the statement "everyone did what was right in his own eyes."[17] Their spirituality

---

13. Haak, "Spiritual Lethargy."
14. Cf. 1.1.
15. Exod 16.
16. Exod 32.
17. Judg 21:25.

lacked judgement and discernment as they failed to keep the covenants of Abraham and Moses, which God made with the nation, and his command before Israel's entry into the promised land to "be careful to do according to all the law which Moses My servant commanded you; do not turn from it to the right or to the left, so that you may have success wherever you go."[18]

The quest to completely engage with the theme of spiritual lethargy among God's people from the OT to the NT would be a colossal task. However, we do not intend to engage with all periods here, but rather take up one case study each from the OT (Malachi) and NT (Corinthian church) to study this theme. The findings of the research have established the existence and crippling presence of spiritual lethargy or nominalism in the Baptist churches of Imphal; the discussion will not be repeated here. Rather, the objective is to identify and discuss the presence of this problem in these two case studies, and then evaluate how spiritual lethargy was responded to homiletically: first, by the prophet Malachi and second, by Paul. These case studies suit our purpose because the prophet Malachi addressed the priests[19] and the people of Israel,[20] and Paul addressed the believers[21] in their spiritual lethargy; each then responded homiletically in their respective contexts. In this way, both groups of people in the Baptist churches in Imphal – pastors and laity – are covered in the study.

6.2.1 Spiritual Lethargy in the Old Testament: Malachi

6.2.1.1 Author and Date

Although the prophet who wrote the book of Malachi is generally known as Malachi, his exact name is unclear because in Hebrew, *malachi* simply means "messenger."[22] Recent scholarship talks of "two defensible positions"; first as "the proper name of the writer of the oracles" and second, as "a title or appellative" given to the unidentified compiler of the book.[23] Hill locates Malachi

---

18. Josh 1:7.

19. Contextually speaking, they are the pastors and preachers of the Baptist churches in Imphal today.

20. They can be compared to the church members in the Baptist churches of Imphal today.

21. The church members in the Baptist churches of Imphal today.

22. Smith, *Works on Prophets*, 323; Schuller, *Post-Exilic Prophets*, 58.

23. Hill, *Malachi*, 15; There are some who believe that Malachi is the surname of Ezra the Scribe, but there is no conclusive evidence. For more see Calvin, *Twelve Minor Prophets*, 459. This debate is beyond the scope of the study.

before Nehemiah, somewhere "between the rule of King Darius I (522–486 BCE) and the death of King Artaxerxes I (424 BCE)."[24] He further narrows it down to "a date of near 500 BCE" considering "Malachi's linguistic affinity to Haggai and Zechariah 1–8."[25] Elizabeth Achtemeier puts the beginning of Malachi's ministry "from about 460 BCE, during the Persian period of Israel's subjugation." During that time, "Jerusalem and its immediate surroundings form a little subprovince of the Persian Empire" and "the temple has been rebuilt for some forty-five years but is a rather mean dwelling compared to its former glory."[26]

Although we cannot be exact or specific, scholars agree on the general historical situation of the returnees which forms the context of Malachi. Below, we will consider the historical situation of the returnees along with their leaders from the exiles.

6.2.1.2 Historical Situation of the Postexilic Jews

Sheshbazzar, a "prominent member of the tribe of Judah,"[27] led the first wave of returnees from the Babylonian exile and helped the Jews to re-settle in their homeland.[28] Sheshbazzar also took up the leadership and began laying the ground work of rebuilding the temple which Zerubbabel later took over.[29] There are some who consider Sheshbazzar and Zerubbabel to be the same person.[30] However, Hill argues that they are different individuals and under the leadership of Zerubbabel, the second wave of Jews[31] returned to Jerusalem and the restoration work among the people continued[32] along with laying "the foundation of the temple of God."[33] The time of Ezra's return from the exile to

---

24. Hill, *Malachi*, 51. *Contra*, some date Malachi after Nehemiah; Baldwin, *Haggai*, 213. *Contra*, some date Malachi as a contemporary of Nehemiah and Ezra; Petersen, *Zechariah 9–14*, 5–6.
25. Hill, *Malachi*, 83; see also Baldwin, *Haggai*, 212, 16; Verhoef, *Books of Haggai and Malachi*, 180.
26. Achtemeier, *Preaching*, 126; Hag 2:3.
27. Hill, *Malachi*, 67.
28. Ezra 1:11.
29. Hill, *Malachi*, 66–71.
30. Hill, 69. Cf. Hussell, *Commentary*, 190.
31. Hill puts the second wave of returnees at "nearly 50,000 former Israelite captives"; Hill, *Malachi*, 69.
32. Ezra 2.
33. Ezra 3:10.

Jerusalem is not clear, although it is generally accepted that "Nehemiah came to Jerusalem in 445 BCE, the twentieth year of King Artaxerxes I."[34] Therefore, it is thought that "Ezra preceded Nehemiah by way of chronological order" although they remain contemporaries in regard to "religious and political activity in Jerusalem during the Persian period."[35]

As we have dated Malachi before Nehemiah, consequently, what information does this chronological location of Malachi reveal about the emotional, social, and economic situation of the postexilic Jewish community?[36] The Jewish people who returned from the exile did not come back rich, nor were they welcomed by the Jewish people in Jerusalem. There was also a disparity between the poor and the rich among the Jewish people who remained in Jerusalem when the exiles returned. Nehemiah records how he addressed the oppressors of the poor in Jerusalem and how he fed many poor labourers for twelve years from his own funds.[37] The people during the time of Malachi could not have been more economically well off than those during Nehemiah's time, because the people's economic struggle was only addressed by Nehemiah in the later years of his arrival in Jerusalem.[38]

As for the society during the prophet's ministry, it was a time when the people and the priests were indifferent and unconcerned about the ways of God.[39] During that time, "None of the wonderful messianic promises of former prophets have been fulfilled. Judah struggles for existence in the face of poverty, crop failure, inflation, and moral and religious indifference."[40] The suffering and plight of the people was in stark contrast to the prophecy of hope and comfort,[41] plan, prosperity, and future[42] as was given by the prophets of old. Moreover, there certainly was great disillusionment, because for once, they felt that the predictions of Haggai about "the treasures of the nations flowing in the Temple (2:7)," "Zechariah's vision of peace and prosperity

---

34. Hill, *Malachi*, 72; Cf. Neh 1:1; 2:1.
35. Hill, 72.
36. Hill, 73.
37. Neh 5.
38. Neh 5:1–13.
39. Schuller, *Post-Exilic*, 318.
40. Achtemeier, *Preaching*, 126.
41. Isa 40.
42. Jer 29:11; Ezek 36:26–30.

for Jerusalem (8:3–5)" and "Ezekiel's vision (chapters 40–48) of an Israelite Temple-state centered in Jerusalem had quickly faded" as "failed prophecies," and have become to them, a sign of God abandoning his people (cf. Mal 1:2).[43]

Some argue that the societal problems faced by the postexilic Jews were due to the worship of Baal.[44] However, Hill claims these problems were because of more practical reasons, due to the downward spiral of the local economy, and that marital union with the migrant residents in Israel, looking down on the poor and the have-nots, and pilfering tithes and offerings, are a clear indication of the collapse of the economic situation, faced by both the subjects and the authority of the day.[45] It is argued that one of the ways for poor postexilic Jews to climb up the ladder of economic prosperity and social acceptance was to "marry into the 'brokerages' of the resident aliens." It was believed that many Jewish marriages were influenced by the motive of economic stability, rather than a religious factor.[46]

From a religious point of view, it was a tragic scenario because the Israelites had just returned from exile; temple worship had begun, but the people's spiritual vision towards God had become blind. Malachi ministered in Israel during this era of spiritual lethargy.[47] As Malachi ministered to both the priests and common people, we will also engage with these two groups, especially with the priests, and then relate this to how the congregations in the Baptist churches in Imphal perceive their own pastors' and preachers' spirituality.

Israel's collapse in her vertical relationship with God, especially that of the priests, led to the downfall of relationships of the Israelites during the post-exilic period when Malachi prophesied, because not only were the common people indifferent to God, but the priests who were supposed to be the fountain of truth had become dry and parched spiritually. This is because the depth of one's relationship with God can impact one's relationship with other human beings.[48]

God was also against his people because they took wives from other nations who worshipped different gods, eventually breaking their allegiance to

---

43. Hill, *Malachi*, 76. Cf. Ezek 11:17–18.
44. Glazier-McDonald, *Malachi*, 85.
45. Hill, *Malachi*, 75. Cf. Clines, *Ezra*, 207; Petersen, *Zechariah 9–14*, 20.
46. Hill, *Malachi*, 75. Cf. Gottwald, *Hebrew Bible*, 432–34; Nogalski, *Redaction Process*, 198.
47. Schuller, *Post-Exilic*, 318.
48. Baldwin, *Haggai*, 217.

him.[49] The priests did not prohibit such marital union because they prioritised the praise of people, not God.[50] Further, in the society Malachi served, there was rampant breakdown of marriage and an increase of divorce, which God did not approve of.[51] It is plausible to think that if a person cannot revere God, that person will not cherish human relationships. Similarly, if a person does not hesitate to dishonour and break human relationships, it amounts to despising God.

Instead of preserving and teaching the knowledge of God as priests, they had "caused many to stumble" and had "corrupted the covenant of Levi."[52] Verhoef claims,

> Through these marriages, Judah has brought their Father and Creator into the "family" of pagan gods. Through this breach of faith Judah has committed idolatry! At the same time the mixed marriages were a desecration of the "sanctuary of God," a violation of Israel's spiritual existence as covenant people. Through these marriages the frontiers between covenant people and heathen, between church and world were obliterated.[53]

Malachi was critical of the priests because they had "turned aside from the way" (2:8) and had not stood upright by carrying out their task of warning the people about the road of destruction and national punishment. Verhoef agrees with Baldwin and argues, "mixed marriages" were toxic for their faith and national prosperity because it could easily open the door "for apostasy and idolatry"; this is a dreadful truth given that apostasy had led to Israel's exile.[54]

Led by the priests, the people had become apathetic to their horrific history of the exile.[55] We can agree with Peter Adam as he applies this to the contemporary church:

---

49. It is argued that this opposition is more on "religious grounds" and is not a "racial" issue. See Schuller, *Post-Exilic*, 217; Verhoef, *Books*, 265, 269–270. *Contra*, some would argue this from economic grounds; Hill, *Malachi*, 75.

50. Jones, *Haggai*, 121.

51. Mal 2:14–16; Verhoef, *Books*, 263.

52. Mal 2:7–8.

53. Verhoef, *Books*, 270. Cf. Exod 34:16; Deut 7:3; the reforms under Ezra, Ezra 9, 10; Neh 9:2, 10, 31; 13:1–3, 23–29.

54. Verhoef, *Books*, 272. Cf. 2 Kgs 21.

55. Exod 32:1–35; 2 Kgs 17:7–23; Ezek 16; Longman and Garland, *Proverbs-Isaiah*, 450.

They (the people of God) were in a state of mind that is very common for churches and Christians today; not brave enough to turn away from God, but not brave enough to love and serve him whole-heartedly. We imagine that we can live in a neutral zone, and avoid decisive action. But there is no neutral zone . . . If we are not dying to sin, then sin is growing in power. If we are not living in righteousness, then we are walking away from it. If we are not keeping in step with the Spirit, then we are walking to a different drumbeat, our own selfish desires. If the fruit of the Spirit is not increasing in our lives, the works of the flesh will be gaining in powers over us. . . . Here God's people had drifted into or embraced a settled, consistent, and shared attitude of distancing God.[56]

6.2.2 Malachi's Homiletical Response

6.2.2.1 *Malachi's Homiletical Structure*

On the language and style of Malachi, there are voices who argue whether "Malachi was composed as poetry or as a prose,"[57] but our concern here is not to engage in this debate but to pursue Malachi's homiletical engagement. Looking at the unique way Malachi was written, it is acceptable to say that the prophet's homiletical approach is a "dialectical style, or a question-and-answer method of preaching."[58] According to the NASB, there are a total of twenty-nine questions in Malachi: the Lord questions the people thirteen times;[59] the people ask God ten questions;[60] and the prophet addresses six questions to the people.[61] The "frequent use of quotations, rhetorical questions, and polemical argument gives it a distinctive character. It is often referred to as comprising a series of 'disputation speeches,' where charges are raised and

---

56. Adam, *Message of Malachi*, 39–40.
57. Merrill, *Haggai*, 330. For more discussion on Malachi's homiletical outline, see Kaiser, *Malachi*.
58. Miller, *Nahum–Malachi*, 352; Cf. Troxel, *Prophetic Literature*, 161.
59. Mal 1:2 (twice), 1:6 (twice), 1:8 (five times), 1:13 (once); 3:2 (twice); 3:8 (once).
60. Mal 1:2 (once), 1:6 (once), 1:7 (once), 2:14 (once), 2:17 (twice); 3:7 (once), 3:8 (once), 3:13 (once), 3:14 (once).
61. Mal 1:9 (twice), 2:10 (three times), 2:15 (once). Different versions will yield slightly different results.

evidence presented in a confrontational mood."[62] Malachi is slightly different from a traditional "disputation speech" where "a quotation from the people" is raised and then "a refutation by God or the prophet" is made, because here, "God's view is stated, an objection of the people is raised, then God proceeds to convince the listeners of the original point."[63] Similarly, Miller argues that the following will be seen in Malachi's homiletical pattern:

> 1) Statement of the truth, 2) objection in the form of a question, and 3) the prophet's substantiation of the truth. These rhetorical questions probably reflected Malachi's actual public debates with some of the priests and people.[64]

Moreover, on the structure of Malachi's homily, it is argued that "Malachi did not start with an outline. Instead he moved from topic to topic and occasionally went back and picked up an idea touched on earlier in the book."[65] The above discussions give a view on how Malachi's homily was structured; first, as a three level "disputation speech" and second, as an unstructured flexible outline.

Malachi's interrogative approach is also exclamatory in nature. Here is a prophet who is totally absorbed and overwhelmed by the message he receives from God as "he functions as the mouthpiece of the Lord of Hosts."[66] Having discussed the style and approach of Malachi's homily, below we will briefly discuss Malachi's theology of preaching and see if his preaching had any impact on the people.

6.2.2.2 Malachi's Theology of Preaching

Malachi allowed "God to speak for himself (of a total of 55 verses, 47 record the first-person address of Yahweh)."[67] Malachi constantly took the people

---

62. Taylor and Clendenen, *Haggai, Malachi*, 218. The term and idea of "disputation speech" is attributed to Gunkel. See Taylor and Clendenen, *Haggai, Malachi*, 218–19; cf. Graffy, *Prophet*, 2–23.

63. Graffy, *Prophet*, 16, 22. For more discussion see Murray, "Rhetoric of Disputation," 95–121.

64. Miller, *Nahum–Malachi*, 352.

65. Alden, "Malachi," 7.708. For more discussion on outline and structure, see Taylor and Clendenen, *Haggai, Malachi*, 228–29.

66. Wendland, *Prophetic*, 355.

67. Wendland, 355.

back to the mouth and word of God, and not to his own reasoning and argumentative skill, although the human element was always there in crafting the structure of the message. For example, God says: "I have loved you" (1:2); "A son honours his father, and a servant his master . . . where is my honour?" (1:6); "And now, O priests, this commandment is for you" (2:1); "And this second thing you do. You cover the LORD's altar with tears" (2:13); "Will man rob God? Yet you are robbing me!" (3:8); "But for you who fear my name, the sun of righteousness shall rise with healing in its wings" (4:2). Not every aspect of his theology of preaching will be covered here; nevertheless, some of them will be discussed.

6.2.2.2.1 Malachi's Homily Was Based on the Nature and Character of God

Malachi took the people back to the nature and character of God. He began by talking about how much God loved them (1:1). However, the people responded by asking how God had loved them, as they were bitter.[68] The proof God gave was the claim that out of his love, he chose Jacob (Israel) over Esau (1:3).[69] Malachi did not begin his preaching with the problem the people had, by accusing them from the start, but by gently reminding them of God's everlasting love, although they doubted and rejected it.[70]

Then Malachi reminded them of God's holiness, the otherness of God. He revealed more of God's character, that while God is loving and cherishes a relationship with human beings, his standard of holiness is non-negotiable (1:7–8). Also, God despises defiled food and diseased animals on his altars for sacrifice.[71] Because God is loving and holy, he hates a mocking response that is inimical to his love and holiness.

Malachi then confronted the people with God's sovereignty, his majestic identity, as King of the whole earth – the LORD Almighty[72] – not just a local deity, a god confined to a territory or geographical boundary like those

---

68. Achtemeier, *Nahum to Malachi*, 173.

69. Although this kind of disputational dialogue continues in the book, for our purpose, we will not follow the disputational narrative. Instead we will first dwell on the nature of God and then on the issues and questions of the people.

70. Cf. 4.3.3.4.2.

71. Cf. 4.3.3.3.7; Cf. 4.3.3.3.1.

72. NIV translates LORD of the "armies" (hosts) of heaven as LORD "Almighty"; Ham, *Minor Prophets*, 217–18.

of Israel's neighbours (1:1). Malachi refers to God as the LORD Almighty twenty-two times,[73] in the four chapters with fifty-five verses. Malachi then reminds the people that this transcendental God who is the transnational and transborder King is sovereign over time and space and all human plans and schemes (1:4–5, 11).

Having described God as transcendent and one who is to be feared and worshipped, he then introduced him as father and master, using anthropomorphic imagery (1:6). Here, the prophet concretised God's relationship with his people, as someone who could be related to and approached, and not just a grand abstract idea in the minds of the people.

Moreover, despite Israel's faithlessness, Malachi exulted in the faithfulness of God, because God upheld the covenant he made with Levi,[74] although the priests during his time did not hold up their end of the covenant (2:4–6). Notwithstanding an overwhelming wave of spiritual lethargy and wilful rebellion against God, Malachi needed to show the heart of God to the people: unlike their fickle-mindedness, God's decision and character does not change like shifting shadows (3:6). In the book of Malachi, we also see many actions performed by God.[75]

6.2.2.2.2 Malachi's Homily Addressed the Fallen Nature of Human Being's Character

After describing and grounding his homily on the nature and character of God, Malachi turned his face towards the priests and the people and confronted them. Thus, after establishing the doctrinal foundation, he stood on it and addressed the folly of their compromised and agnostic[76] worldview and made a scathing attack on their spiritual blindness and lethargy.

---

73. Mal 1:6, 8, 9, 10, 11, 13, 14; 2:2, 4, 7, 8, 12, 16; 3:1, 5, 7, 11, 12, 14, 17; 4:1, 3 (ESV); Malachi also has the distinction of containing 43.6 percent of the titls "LORD of hosts" from the entire Bible. ESV, *Global Study Bible*, 1306.

74. David L. Petersen claims that the covenant is identified with the Levites because they honoured God's name and helped the people avoid the path of destruction; Petersen, *Zechariah*, 191. *Contra*, Glazier-McDonald argues that it is because all the priests, including the Aaronids, trace their beginning to the Levitical order. See Glazier-McDonald, *Malachi*. Cf. Merrill, *Haggai*, 328.

75. In Malachi, God speaks, loves, rules, expects, reigns, judges, creates, observes, wearies, refines, purifies, listens, warns, destroys, curses, defends, invites, challenges, blesses, heals, protects, and provides.

76. They were agnostic in some sense because they asked God so many questions, the answers to which they did not know.

Malachi charged the Jewish men for taking foreign wives, women outside the commonwealth of the nation of Israel (2:11). He reprimanded them because such unions undermined the holiness of God and compromised their own spiritual sanctity as a people of God. Such unions diverted the attention and devotion of God's people towards foreign gods and goddesses. History is replete with such blundering examples from King Solomon and his marriage alliances (1 Kgs 3:1; 11:3) to King Ahab marrying Jezebel who served Baal (1 Kgs 16:1–32).[77]

Malachi then reproached the Jewish husbands for their faithlessness in the union of marriage, and for breaking the marriage covenant by divorcing the wives of their youth (2:14). This condemnation stemmed out of the contrast of God's faithfulness and love against human beings' treacherous disloyalty. The prophet warned them that God was taking up the case, on behalf of the wives as a witness (2:14) and admonished the husbands that their sacrifices, offerings, and tears would come to nothing (2:13). God was the chief prosecutor against them, because when they abandoned the wives of their youth, they offended God himself. Here again, Malachi based his homily on the character of God's faithfulness, holiness, and justice.

Malachi also warned the "sorcerers, adulterers, and perjurers . . . those who defraud labourers of their wages, who oppress the widows and the fatherless, and deprive the foreigners" of "justice" (3:5) that, he himself would testify against them. Malachi is here intensifying the argument that, when God who is the final authority, judge, and arbiter of justice becomes the witness of the case himself (3:5), there is no escape for the wicked. Therefore, the appeal to return to God so that God may return to them was the most reasonable thing to do. Here again, Malachi based his homily on God being the loving father, a just master, the faithful God, and a holy King.

Then Malachi charged the people of God with robbing God by refraining from giving their tithes and offerings. God challenged the people with a providential outburst of his blessings, which would be far beyond what they could handle, if they would be faithful enough to bring tithes and offerings into his house (3:8–9). Here, Malachi built his homily on the theology of the sovereignty of God, because, as God created the earth and everything in it

---

77. There are other stories, but suffice here to mention these two as examples for our purpose.

out of nothing, God could surely open the "floodgates of heaven and pour out so much blessing" on his people (3:10).

Furthermore, Malachi, who "belongs to a pious remnant of his people, who are overborne and perhaps oppressed by the majority,"[78] claimed that there was a remnant of a faithful people who still revered God, a stark contrast to the spiritually lethargic majority population during that time in Judah. Malachi instructed the people on God's righteous judgement – that God would spare those who fear and honour his name like a benevolent father does (3:16–18). Achtemeier argues,

> God has never left himself without witnesses, according to the biblical history. Within a faithless, indifferent, rebellious Judah in the time of Malachi, there is an obedient little group who recognise the divine Kingship, not merely as a theory . . . but as the power in which they live their lives . . .[79]

Malachi gave encouragement that for the righteous who revere God's name, "the sun of righteousness will rise with healing in its wings" and they "will skip about like calves from the stall" (4:2). But God's judgement would catch up with the wicked, although they seemed to be escaping the radar of God's punishment for a while. Malachi described the fate of the wicked in fiery imagery (4:1). In this section, Malachi once again rooted his homily in the holiness and justice of the God who keeps his promise.

Finally, Malachi exhorted the people to heed the law God had given through Moses at Mt. Horeb (4:4). Perhaps some of the people had forgotten the law, some might have become indifferent to its requirements and teaching, while some might have considered it irrelevant and obsolete in the new social context of mixed marriages. Further still, some might have had a faint regard for it, but did not see a need to strictly adhere to it, as most of the population and especially the priests did not abide by its regulations anymore. Whatever the situation and context of the people and society, God through Malachi appealed to his people to live their lives under the authority of Scripture.

---

78. Smith, *Works*, 325. Cf. Mal 3:16ff.

79. Achtemeier, *Nahum*, 193. Based on this claim, it can be argued that in God's sovereignty and will, he might be preserving a group of people faithful to him in the Baptist churches of Imphal, although many members may be nominal Christians. This must come as an encouragement for the churches.

6.2.2.2.3 Malachi's Homily Confronted the Priests for Their Lackadaisical Attitude

Malachi was keen that Israel kept the covenant their ancestors had made with God[80] by maintaining a vibrant relationship, because sin could eventually jeopardise and destroy their covenantal relationship again.[81] However, beginning with the priests, they "corrupted" and "profaned" this covenant, and demonstrated their "apathetic" attitude towards God.[82] They offered to him contemptible food[83] and sacrificed diseased animals, which not only dishonoured God but showed their contempt for God's standard of holiness.[84] Malachi attacked the priests because instead of being the source of truth, they had become a fountain of lies and deceit. He rebuked them:

> "For the lips of a priest should preserve knowledge, and men should seek instruction from his mouth; for he is the messenger of the LORD of hosts. But as for you, you have turned aside from the way; you have caused many to stumble by the instruction; you have corrupted the covenant of Levi," says the LORD of hosts. (Mal 2:7-8)

The prophet condemned them and pronounced this "stinging indictment on their careless, haphazard, and profane service to the living God,"[85] because they had become co-conspirators and were found guilty in not rebuking the vices of the people but speaking and doing just what the people liked to listen to.[86] When those who had been called to serve God fail to live up to the holy demands of God, we can argue that the fabric of society will begin to corrupt, because there is no one to teach the people.[87]

Although it is argued that church members are today drifting away from God as in the days of Malachi, it was contended by some church members and pastors that some pastors are more spiritually lethargic and nominal than

---

80. Cf. 2 Kgs 23:3.
81. Baldwin, *Haggai*, 216.
82. Baldwin, 216; Mal 1:13, 14; 2:8, 10; 3:8.
83. Mal 1:12.
84. Mal 1:7-8, 13-14; Jones, *Haggai*, 121; Verhoef, *Books*, 208-17.
85. Kaiser, *Malachi*, 31.
86. Jones, *Haggai*, 121; Cf. 4.3.4.4.2.3.
87. Achtemeier, *Nahum-Malachi*, 178.

the church members themselves.[88] Many pastors and members are grieved at the way some of the Baptist pastors in Imphal lead the church and preach to the people. Instead of being the guardian of the word of God where their "lips ... preserve knowledge" and they feed those who "seek instruction"[89] and even those who do not, by faithfully expounding his word book after book systematically as to the correct way to live and worship God, many pastors have been accused of scriptural misinterpretation, either deliberately or non-deliberately. Some educated and mature church members expressed the fear that many of the church members might have been led astray, because they would have absorbed and swallowed all the misinterpretation done from the pulpit without any filtering.[90] We can contend that a bad sermon that is preached by misinterpreting the text is like sacrificing a diseased animal at the altar of the temple of God.

Several of the pastors and preachers have also been accused of prioritising entertainment in the church and neglecting the proper feeding of the word of God.[91] It is claimed that many pastors are found wanting in the realm of prophetic preaching, because many of the church members claimed that their pastors do not talk about sin and church discipline, rather they prefer tickling the ears of the listeners, for fear that they may displease some influential leaders in the church who are capable of either extending their ministry in the church or ending it.[92] The evidence before us can make us conclude that the situation of the Baptist churches in Imphal is in some ways similar to that of Malachi's ministerial context.

6.2.2.3 Malachi's Homiletical Methods of Preaching

Having discussed the theological aspect of Malachi's preaching, now we turn toward his homiletical methods of preaching as an expository preaching model and a prophetic preaching approach respectively.

---

88. Cf. 4.3.1.2. *Contra*, many are convinced of the positive impact of good preaching. Cf. 4.3.4.4.1.
89. Mal 2:7.
90. Cf. 4.3.3.3.7.
91. Cf. 4.3.3.3.12.
92. Cf. 4.3.4.4.2.1; Cf. 4.3.4.4.2.3.

6.2.2.3.1 Malachi's Homily as an Expository Preaching Model

A brief discussion on the advantages of expository preaching and what it constitutes was undertaken earlier[93] and more will follow later under "The theology and method of expository preaching."[94] In this section, we will discuss how Malachi possibly employed an expository style of preaching based on what we deliberated on earlier and hopefully, the later section will clarify and vindicate our present argument.

Malachi began his address by talking to the people about who God is – his nature and being. All his subsequent addresses, whether comparisons, contrasts, or rebukes, were deduced from this one truth – the truth about who God is and what God spoke. The structure or form of the homily is interrogative in nature, but its homiletical spine is firmly based on the theology of the character of God as we have discussed earlier in the preceding two sections. Smith argues that whether addressing the wicked or the devout Israelites, Malachi addressed them based on God's character.[95]

We also observed that his homily on the issues of the people was delimited by what he introduced to the people about God. We can argue that whatever issues he wanted to bring up later in the conversation with the people, they had been firmly laid on the foundation of the character of God. Further, as mentioned earlier, out of "a total of 55 verses, 47 record the first-person address of Yahweh."[96] Malachi structured his homily in this way because he wanted God's word to be prominent as he dealt with the issues of peoples' sins and spiritual lethargy. Analysing his homily as a sermon, his unique interrogative style wove together the text of the sermon (the spoken word and the being of God), the worldviews of the people (2:17; 3:15), the issues of individual members (3:5),[97] pictorial illustrations (4:1), and a persuasion for change as an application (3:7). Furthermore, the prophet ended his homily with an appeal to abide by the law (word of God) as was given to Moses.

Technically speaking, many would argue that Malachi's homily cannot be considered expository preaching because he did not take a unit of thought

---

93. Cf. 5.10.

94. Cf. 6.4.

95. Smith, *Works*, 330.

96. Wendland, *Prophetic*, 355. Only the following eight verses do not have a first-person address of Yahweh: 1:1; 2:11, 12; 3:2, 3, 4, 16; 4:1.

97. Issues of the foreign wives, divorce, injustice, and others.

from an inspired text of a Torah or Pentateuch or some other texts from the Scripture and expound it, but rather that his preaching was prophetic[98] in its disposition.

In Malachi's homiletical engagement, it can be argued that he considered the word coming from the mouth of God as the revealed word of God, and therefore one with supreme authority. That revealed and spoken word of God would eventually be written, preserved, and canonised, and become the Scripture as it is understood today. Elucidating this, Adam is convinced that "*God has spoken*," and that "His words remain powerful, and that without this historic revelation of God in words there can be no ministry of the Word. The basis for any true human speaking for God is that God is a speaking God."[99]

Although Malachi did not refer to a written word of God or a text of Scripture as recorded in the past in his homiletical engagement, if he had based his preaching on the revealed word of God, then that revealed word of God, whether in its oral form or later in its written form, remains the same in its essence and authority because they originate from the same source – the mind, heart, and being of God. Further, Karl Barth argues for the "three forms of the Word of God as revealed, written, and preached."[100] According to him, "if 'written' and 'preached' denote the twofold concrete relation in which the Word of God is spoken to us, revelation denotes the Word of God itself in the act of its being spoken in time."[101] Influenced by the threefold aspects of the word of God as espoused by Barth, Paul S. Chung argues, "The revealed Word of God as the *ratio veritatis* precedes and grounds the written Word of God and the proclaimed Word of God."[102]

Arguing from this perspective, although Malachi did not refer to a written text of the Scripture as expository preaching is expected to do, we could claim that as long as Malachi grounded his homily on the revealed word of God, then the question of whether it is oral or written in nature does not arise, for its authority remains the same. We can therefore argue that Malachi's homily fulfils the criteria of being considered expository preaching as it is

---

98. The idea of prophetic preaching will also be discussed below.
99. Adam, *Speaking God's Words*, 15 (emphasis original).
100. Barth, *Church Dogmatics*, 7.
101. Karl Barth, *Church Dogmatics*, 116.
102. Chung, *Karl Barth*, 282.

based on the authoritative word of God. Hence, as Malachi did, the pastors in the Baptist churches in Imphal could employ this preaching method for their situation, which is somewhat similar to Malachi's context. We now turn towards Malachi's homily as an act of prophetic preaching and discuss how it will be suitable for the Baptist churches in Imphal.

6.2.2.3.2 The Prophetic Preaching Approach of Malachi

Before delving into the prophetic preaching approach of Malachi, it will be helpful to set the context and define what we mean by "prophetic" as well as what we do not mean. The ministry of a prophet (prophecy or prophesying) can be understood as "foretelling" about the future[103] or "forthtelling" of God's word to the people in relation to some issue in society.[104] Here, in this research, we will refer to prophecy as "forthtelling" of God's word.

Distinguishing forthtelling from preaching a sermon, Hale and Thorson argue that although there are some similarities, the difference is that "biblical prophecies were directly inspired by the Holy Spirit" and that the OT prophets declared that "their messages were the very 'word of the Lord.'"[105] It is true that although preaching a sermon is theologically grounded on Scripture, and dependant on the empowerment of the Holy Spirit for its impact, forthtelling (prophesying) and sermonising are different in some ways. First, God's prophets prophesied with the statement, "Thus says the Lord," whereas the preachers cannot claim that authority, because their roles in history are different. Second, "the prophets are not preaching 'eternal truths.' They are announcing reactions of Yahweh to specific situations in Israel."[106] Whereas in preaching, God's eternal truths are not restricted to a particular context, rather his eternal truths are applicable to various specific situations of human realities.

However, they do have similarities. Neither forthtelling nor preaching talk of a futuristic issue (although they warn of the consequences of disobedience), but they bring God's word to the people[107] by confronting and pleading with them to change their ways, and by teaching and guiding them to obey,

---

103. Chapman, *Rightly Dividing*, 43.
104. Hale and Thorson, *Applied Old Testament*, 80; Adams, *Revelation*, xi.
105. Hale and Thorson, 80; Jer 1:4; Hos 1:1; Joel 1:1.
106. Achtemeier, *Old Testament*, 139.
107. Johnson, *Glory*, 118.

follow, and glorify God in their lives. Second, both forthtelling and preaching demand urgency of obedience and action.

While comparing forthtelling with preaching, some claim that mere preaching is not forthtelling, rather "prophetic preaching is forthtelling."[108] Hughes Oliphant Old sub-categorises preaching into more narrow and nuanced branches, where prophetic preaching is one of them.[109] Delimiting the use of the term "prophetic preaching" here does not mean confining it to "social-justice preaching," "liberation preaching," or "public-issues preaching" as some conceive them to be.[110] However, as mentioned above, it would generally mean confronting and pleading with God's people.[111] Below, we will discuss Malachi's preaching as prophetic and the contradistinction of prophetic preaching and what it is not.

Michael Quicke distinguishes prophetic preaching from non-prophetic preaching by using two pictorial phrases, "full-blooded preaching" and "thin-blooded preaching" respectively, accusing the latter of ruining the churches.[112] He lists ten characteristics of thin-blooded preaching: "individualistic"; "aimed at head or heart but rarely both together"; "spineless theology"; "generic application";[113] "avoids conflict";[114] "low compliance";[115] "absence of process issues"; "solo role"; "cowardice"; and "missionally defective."[116] Moreover, he indicts it as one that is "anesthetizing rather than energizing."[117] It is true that preaching defined by these characteristics would have a minimal positive impact; rather, it could be counterproductive to believers' spirituality.

---

108. Loritts, "Grace-full Prophetic Preaching," 42.

109. Old's categories are: expository preaching; evangelistic preaching; catechetical preaching; festal preaching and prophetic preaching. Old, *Reading and Preaching*, 8.

110. González and González, *Liberation Preaching, passim*; Tisdale, *Prophetic Preaching*, 5–6.

111. J. Philip Wogaman argues that any type of preaching that "speaks for God" is prophetic preaching; Wogaman, *Speaking the Truth*. *Contra*, this is too broad an argument, and so we will not subscribe to this category. For a more detailed study on prophetic preaching, see Tisdale, *Prophetic Preaching*; Chan, Ortberg, Keller et al., *Prophetic Preaching*.

112. Quicke, *360-Degree Leadership*, 17.

113. Quicke, 37.

114. Quicke, 37.

115. Quicke, 38.

116. Quicke, 35–39.

117. Quicke, 70.

On the other hand, Quicke contrasts "full-blooded preaching" as one transcending from merely teaching how to receive one's salvation to teaching believers how to live a purposeful and distinctive life for God.[118] He further argues that God can only transform his church when a preacher, after hearing and personally internalising God's word, speaks to the members through the power of God's Spirit.[119] Thus, prophetic preaching must challenge members to move out from the prison of their old habits, assumptions, and worldviews to the new and abundant life offered by Jesus Christ himself.[120] Quicke explains,

> God-empowered, full-blooded preaching always brings people into *corporate* visions and dimensions of community. It is *holistic*, avoiding extremes of both cerebral and emotional preaching. It has *theological* spine, expressing the power of God – Father, Son, and Holy Spirit. It is *specific*, grounded in a particular congregation's transformation, not some generic fit-all program. It is *real*-facing conflict, healthily aware of the consequences of God's counterstory, and calling for commitment. It reinforces the *process* of transformation as people learn to do God's word together, and it is *courageous* because the preacher is first exposed to God's challenge and then dares to tell out what it means. It is also *missional*, challenging people to be and live as missionary communities.[121]

In the light of what we have discussed above, let us analyse Malachi's homily to God's people by taking up three examples. First, in 1:6–9, 14, God stringently reprimanded the people through Malachi for their lack of reverence for his name by using anthropomorphic relational imageries of "son and father" and "master and slave" respectively. In this section, he also rebuked the priests for their detestable and abominable acts of offering blemished sacrifices at the altar of God, thus defiling it. After the rebuke, he appealed to them, "But now will you not entreat God's favor, that He may be gracious to us?" (1:9). Although it was "full-blooded preaching," shaking the very

---

118. Quicke, 52.
119. Quicke, 18.
120. Quicke, 66.
121. Quicke, 60 (emphasis original).

foundation of the people's lethargic situation, Malachi's rebuke was not aimed at making the people and the priests feel terrible and abandoning them there. Rather, his aim was fuelled by a desire to revive their devotion and affection towards God; thus he pleaded with them to come back to him.

Second, in 2:1–9, Malachi reproached the priests for their insolence and false sense of entitlement for having the privilege of blessing the people. In the most vivid imagery, God confronted the priests by warning, "I will spread refuse on your faces, the refuse of your feasts" (2:3). Here God condemned the priests for their apathy to God's holy standard and for misusing their positions as priests. After the condemnation, Malachi again reminded them of God's prior relationship with Levi saying, "My covenant with him was one of life and peace" (2:5). God desired that the priests return to that holy relationship as he reminded them of how Levi walked with God "in peace and uprightness, and he turned many back from iniquity" (2:6). Malachi then appealed that like Levi's uprightness, "the lips of a priest should preserve knowledge, and men should seek instruction from his mouth; for he is the messenger of the LORD of hosts" (2:7).

Third, in 3:8–12, God confronted the people about their lackadaisical attitude while giving their tithes and offerings. He admonished them as robbers of God's temple. He pronounced everyone guilty, "and cursed with a curse" (3:9). Again, it did not end with an accusation; rather, he extended his invitation, asking the people to bring tithes and food into his temple, so that "the windows of heaven" will "pour out . . . a blessing until it overflows" (3:10). In all these, God's purpose was to confront and build up his people and restore them.

The above examples clearly depict the prophetic nature of Malachi's homily, which contained confrontation against the people's sins and entreated them to repent from their wickedness and spiritual lethargy, so that God might bless his people again. Here we see a courageous and selfless preacher without any sense of self-preservation but with the sole aim of defending the honour and truth of God's word. Here is a preacher whose only goal was to convict the people of their wrongdoings and lead them to repentance.

Jensen also affirms that faithful preaching is not conforming the message from the word of God to the expectation of the church nor is it "domesticated to the fads and fashions of society or to church traditions." The role of the word of God is clear: it must "keep challenging, rebuking, penetrating, dividing, judging, correcting, training in righteousness and teaching God's people."[122] He is convinced that our message must make comfortable people uncomfortable because the word of God is fire.[123] Below, we will evaluate this section and recommend it for the Baptist churches in Imphal.

6.2.2.3.3 Evaluation and Recommendation of Malachi's Homiletical Method for the Baptist Churches in Imphal

Many of the members in the Baptist churches in Imphal have expressed their disappointment over the absence of prophetic preaching in many of their churches. Some of them have also expressed that instead of being the guardian of God's word, many of the pastors have become entertainers who tickle the ears of the listeners.[124] Looking at the prophetic approach of the preaching of Malachi as discussed above, we can argue that the Baptist churches in Imphal will benefit from this approach because here, the preacher is concerned about achieving only one thing: repentance of the people by speaking the truth in love. We could therefore claim that in terms of sermonic construction, idea development, and basing one's homily in the word of God, it can be expository in nature, whereas in terms of engaging with the people, tackling the issues of the society, and a passionate desire to persuade[125] the listeners, we can endorse a prophetic preaching approach for the Baptist churches in Imphal.

The book of Malachi ends without revealing whether his homily bore any fruit, as the next book in the Bible is Matthew, the first New Testament book, written perhaps four hundred years later.[126] So there is no biblical evidence[127] to support the claim – positive or negative[128] – on the impact the sermon

---

122. Jensen, "Preaching," 144.

123. Jensen, 144.

124. Cf. 4.3.4.4.2.1; 4.3.4.4.2.3.

125. This does not mean that the expository preaching model is devoid of passion and engagement with the issues of the people and its application, but that in a prophetic preaching model, it could become more evident and intense.

126. Kaiser, *The Christian*, 56.

127. Although there is no biblical evidence, it is argued that Malachi's preaching produced "a general reformation in the minds and manners" of various people lost in the mire of spiritual stagnancy. Amald, *Critical Commentary*, 238. *Contra*, it is argued that historically speaking, there were no more reliable sources after "Nehemiah (BC 434) . . . we gather little or nothing of historical relation"; Cotton, "Introduction," xvii; deSilva, *Introducing the Apocrypha*, n.p.

128. D. W. Ekstrand argues that during the four hundred years, the people of God went through "spiritual declension"; Ekstrand, "Intertestamental Period."

made in terms of style or content, except for eternity to reveal its impact on what went unnoticed to the human eye.

6.2.3 Spiritual Lethargy in the New Testament: 1 Corinthians

6.2.3.1 Occasion and Purpose of Writing

During his second missionary journey, Paul established the church at Corinth[129] around AD 50.[130] He taught the gospel of Christ and lived there for over eighteen months[131] and left probably in the spring of AD 52.[132] It is argued that he wrote the epistle of 1 Corinthians around AD 55, after receiving the devastating news of the lethargic spiritual life of the Corinthian church.[133] He is said to have written other epistles,[134] but the present second epistle to the church at Corinth is the only other epistle that has been found. Here, among other teachings, Paul defends his apostleship around AD 56 or 57, about two years after writing the first epistle.[135] But our concern in this section is to discuss the spiritual problems of the Corinthian church raised by Paul in his first epistle, after he heard a report from Chloe's household and through their earlier correspondences about several crippling sins that had infested the church.[136] Paul was grieved because even after several years the Christians were still unsure of their beliefs and even "tried to domesticate theology to make it a servant of their lust"[137] and disunity. He writes the letter to address the problems the believers were facing.

6.2.3.2 The Debate on the Root of the Corinthian Church Problem

The problems in the Corinthians church used to be explained in terms of Gnosticism,[138] but in recent times that view has given way to a discussion of

---

129. Acts 18.
130. Stevens, *2 Corinthians*, 5.
131. Acts 18:11.
132. Carson, *Model of Christian Maturity*, 17–18.
133. Stevens, *2 Corinthians*, 6. *Contra*, there are other voices who claim it was written around 56 AD; Barentsen, *Emerging Leadership*, 171.
134. 1 Cor 5:9.
135. Barnett, *Message of 2 Corinthians*, 15.
136. 1 Cor 1:11; Best, *Second Corinthians*, 1.
137. Carson, *Model of Christian Maturity*, 173.
138. Pearson, *Pneumatikos-Psychikos*; Horsley, "Pneumatikos-Psychikos, 269–88.

the "Greco-Roman setting of Corinthian Christianity."[139] Another suggestion is that the members of the Corinthian church lived their lives as they did because they were influenced by a concept called "over realised eschatology."[140] According to scholars like C. K. Barrett, Nils Dahl, F. F. Bruce and others who held this view, the Corinthians were "stressing the 'already' of salvation to the detriment of the 'not yet.'"[141] This discussion was further accelerated when Anthony C. Thiselton published his article on the issue in 1978 in response to the critique given by Earle Ellis and others that if there is any hint of a realised eschatology, it is confined to just 1 Corinthians 4:8 and chapter 15.[142] After analysing all the chapters of 1 Corinthians, Thiselton concludes,

> We have now seen that in every single section from the beginning of the epistle to 14:40, there occurs evidence of *both* a realized eschatology *and* an enthusiastic theology of the Spirit on the part of the Corinthians. That these phenomena are usually related can hardly be doubted. The criticism made by Earle Ellis and others to the effect that arguments about an over-realised eschatology depend on 4:8 and 1 Cor. 15 cannot be sustained.[143]

However, in recent scholarship, there are views[144] which disagree with crediting the problem in the Corinthian church to doctrinal matters and give more emphasis to the influence of the Greco-Roman socio-cultural context.[145] N. T. Wright argues,

> The Corinthians were attempting to produce a mixture of Christianity and paganism; their "puffed up" posturing came not from believing that a Jewish-style eschatology had already brought them to God's final future, but from putting together

---

139. Adams and Horrell, "Gnosis in Corinth," 119. (An extract is reproduced in Adams and Horrell, *Christianity at Corinth*, 119–28.)

140. Kreitzer, *Jesus and God*, 250; cf. Harrison, *Incessant Theology*, 207.

141. Adams and Horrell, "Realised Eschatology," 107. See also: Barrett, "Place of Eschatology," 302–5; Dahl, "Do Not Wonder," 322–36; and Bruce, "Paul on Immortality," 457–72.

142. Ellis, *Prophecy and Hermeneutics*, 78–79; and Thiselton, "Realised Eschatology," 510–26.

143. Thiselton, 523.

144. Barclay, "Thessalonica and Corinth," 49–74; Litfin, *St. Paul's Theology*; Martin, *Corinthian Body*.

145. Adams and Horrell, "Realised Eschatology," 108.

their beliefs about themselves as Christians with ideas from pagan philosophy.[146]

Further, Bruce W. Winter believes that Thiselton's argument does not stand up to scrutiny and thinks that a social analysis could be a better framework for understanding the issue.[147] Over the years, Thiselton became more open to the idea of the Greco-Roman influence and revised his previous argument on realised eschatology in 2000 so that, along with realised eschatology, he believed that the church at Corinth struggled with a syncretistic secular worldview imported from the culture.[148] Thiselton also makes a corrective argument and critiques the Corinthian's triumphalist attitude in the following way:

> The well-known lifeboat analogy is well worn but still suggestive. Someone may have been saved (past) decisively from a sinking ship; but as the lifeboat brings him or her through choppy, uncomfortable seas (present), the final safe landing on the solid shores lies still ahead (future). Celebration comes then. The "strong" mistakenly act as if they have already "arrived" (4:8), and look down on the apostles and on others who seem still to struggle in blooded conflict and danger (4:9–13).[149]

Further, he agrees that there had been a considerable "impact of the culture of Corinth upon the developing faith of newly converted believers."[150] It is also argued that the challenge of the Corinthian church was that they were "uncritically perpetuating the norms and values of the pagan culture around them."[151] So Paul appealed to the Corinthian church for "the conversion of the imagination" "in order to form a Christian identity within a pluralistic world" and to stop living the way the people in the Greco-Roman society lived.[152] Similarly, some assert that "the problems Paul addresses in 1 Corinthians

---

146. Wright, *Resurrection*, 279.
147. Winter, *After Paul Left*, 25.
148. Thiselton, *First Epistle to the Corinthians*, 40.
149. Thiselton, 99.
150. Thiselton, xviii.
151. Hayes, *First Corinthians*, 71.
152. Hayes, 11.

reflect the infiltration of Corinthian social values into the church."[153] Thus, "Corinthian problems are not to be attributed to their faulty theology or premature eschatology so much as to their conformity to the norms and values of pagan culture" and "inflated self-understanding of pagan philosophy."[154]

Below we will list and discuss the problems and issues faced by the Corinthian church members, as recorded in Paul's first epistle to the church, and compare them with the kinds of spiritual problems and spiritual lethargy the believers in the Baptist churches of Imphal have themselves experienced. Then we will see Paul's homiletical response to the problems.

6.2.3.3 The Problems in the Church of Corinth

Paul lists several issues faced by the Corinthian church and addresses them. His letters "provide important data for the study of the social and theological issues of early Christian teachings under the influence of the Roman Empire."[155] Paul brings up the issue of factionalism and disunity (1:10 – 4:21); immorality (5:1 – 6:20); disputes among the believers (6:1–11); marital and sexual issues (7:1–40); questions of social status (7:21–24); food offered to idols (8:1–11); hairstyle and head covering (11:2–16); issues related to the Lord's supper (11:17–34); spiritual gifts (chs. 12–14); and the resurrection (15:1–58). Only two of these issues will be covered in the discussion – those which are more relevant to the context of the study.

6.2.3.3.1 Factionalism and Disunity

Paul was troubled to hear that the body of Christ at Corinth was infected by differences of opinion, where each claimed allegiance to either Paul, Peter, Apollos, or Christ.[156] Traditionally, this difference of opinions had been understood as "factions"; one stemming out of the difference of worldviews between Jewish and Gentile Christians, who followed Peter and Paul respectively, a position made popular by F. C. Baur's thesis in 1831.[157] However, later

---

153. Ciampa and Rosner, *First Letter*, 4; cf. Winter, *After Paul Left*, 27–28; Terry, *Discourse Analysis*, 13.
154. Ciampa and Rosner, *First Letter*, 180.
155. Coutsoumpos, *Paul, Corinth*, 12.
156. 1 Cor 1:12–13; 3:4–6; Thiselton elaborately discusses their conflict from the doctrinal and theological point of view; Thiselton, *First Epistle to the Corinthians*, 122–32.
157. Baur, "Die Christuspartei," 61–206. This thesis is also found in Baur, *Paul, the Apostle*, 268–320; Goulder, *Paul*, 1–16.

scholarship argued that Baur misunderstood the issue, and that it was not an issue of "factions" but "disunity" and "bickerings" between the believers.[158] The purpose here is not to debate for or against either of these views, but to discuss the spiritual problem of the church arising out of their difference of opinions. We could use both the terms "faction" and "disunity" (and the weight of the arguments that support both these views) because they serve our purpose well, as they represent a deeper spiritual symptom of lethargy. However, we will use the term "faction" and its corresponding argument because of its relevance to the context of the study on the Baptist churches in Imphal.

The Corinthian church suffered from a lack of theological consensus in terms of worldview and the doctrinal position they wanted to adopt, in the context of the overwhelmingly Greco-Roman social structure they lived in. Their differences manifested when they pitted one leader against another, just as secular society functions – to serve and justify their own agenda.[159] Whenever there is groupism and faction in a local body of Christ there is much tragedy, because the spiritual vitality of the believers is drained away, and the work and fruit of the Spirit is resisted. Consequently, the believers fail to live as light for the world to see, as the gospel teaches.

Although there is no factionalism among church leaders based on biblical doctrines and religious worldview in the Baptist churches in Imphal, they do have the issue of factionalism and conflict based on ethnicity and political history. Pastor Tomba clarified that one of the positive impacts of his preaching was to have seen healing and reconciliation between the various conflicting groups despite a deep emotional chasm of mistrust and division caused by ethnic factions over the years.[160] Apparently, there has been a peaceful atmosphere in the state for some years, during much of the second half of the research period, but as the mistrust between various ethnic groups runs deep, factional conflicts based on political issues flare up from time to time which threaten the unity among the MBC churches even today.

---

158. Munck, "Church without Factions," 135. Winter, *Philo and Paul*, 10–11, 147, 185 and others; Welborn, "On the Discord," 85–111.

159. 1 Cor 1:12.

160. Cf. 4.3.4.4.1.2.

6.2.3.3.2 Foods Offered to Idols

Paul was concerned over another serious issue in the church of Corinth – eating food offered and sacrificed to idols – so he addressed the church on two matters arising out of it. First, Paul rebuked those members in the church who claimed to have superior knowledge[161] about foods offered to idols and yet were not being sensitive to other believers who had a weaker conscience.[162] Paul agreed that food offered to idols counted for nothing because "there is no God but one" (8:4), although there may be many "gods" and "lords" that pagans worshipped (8:5). But Paul rebuked the believers for being puffed up with their knowledge and for not displaying the love of Christ to the weaker believers for whom Christ also died (1:1, 3, 11). Second, Paul argued that as one partakes in the body and blood of Christ when they break bread, and as Israelites participated in the altar when they ate the sacrificed food (10:16–18), similarly a Corinthian believer participated in pagan sacrifice when they ate and drank the foods offered to idols, because the food had been offered to the "demons" (10:20). Paul warned, "You cannot drink the cup of the Lord and the cup of demons. You cannot partake of the table of the Lord and the table of the demons" at the same time (10:21).

The teaching of Paul concerning food offered to idols in Corinth has been discussed from sociological and theological viewpoints by several scholars. Sociologically speaking, the church at Corinth, like the diverse populace of its city, had a cosmopolitan flavour with a mixed congregation of Gentiles and Jewish believers.[163] Theissen claims, "The majority of the members, who come from the lower classes, stand in contrast to a few influential members who come from the upper classes. The internal stratification is not accidental but the result of structural causes."[164] Defending his case for a three-tier social structure in the Corinthian church, he asserts, "At first glance such a passage [1 Cor 1: 26–29] would seem to confirm the romantic idea of a proletarian Christian community, a religious movement of the lower classes." However,

---

161. Cf. Collins, *First Corinthians*, 309–11.

162. 1 Cor 8:9–13; Horsley argues that the term "weak," concerns Gentile believers. Horsley, *1 Corinthians*, 115. *Contra*, Thiselton refers to it from the angle of "low socioeconomic status"; Thiselton, *First Epistle to the Corinthians*, 609. However, either of the arguments cannot be generalised and our purpose here is simply to focus on the matter of knowledge and love related to food. Cf. Theissen, *Social Setting*.

163. 1 Cor 8:1, 4; Collins, *First Corinthians*, 384.

164. Theissen, *Social Setting*, 69.

drawing closer he finds more categories along with the rich, noble, and the privileged citizens;[165] it was comprised also of "poor, slaves, and of the lower classes."[166] It is argued that the affluent and the rich in the Corinthian church were also influential in society and they ate meat during social occasions "as a way of maintaining and improving social status." It is perceived that these affluent people "regarded their poorer brothers and sisters as 'weak' and immature for displaying such scruples; since an idol did not really exist."[167] Moreover, it is argued that if these socially affluent Christians do not participate in such social eating, the prospect of their "social advancement" and improvement in their economic field would fail miserably.[168] "Those deeply enmeshed in the social networks of Christian life at a higher level would certainly have a lot to lose if they adopted too sectarian a mentality."[169]

From a theological viewpoint, Ciampa and Rosner discuss Paul's argument that the insensitive act of the "knowledgeable" Christians eating food offered to idols amounts to emboldening the weaker Christians to violate their own consciences. They claim that "Paul has already explained that the so-called edification leads not to greater Christian maturity, as the 'knowing' supposed, but to an idolatrous spiritual breakdown."[170]

As we have argued above, along with negative theological ramifications, the heart of the problem in the Corinthian church was the sociocultural pressure coming from the pagan religious-cultural society. However, the believers themselves may not have understood or may not have been aware of the powerful effect they had on the believers' worldview, because as Horsley rightly claims, many of the believers had not experienced genuine conversion and so they were still unable to confess, as Paul said, that "there is no God but one" (8:4).[171]

To be influenced and dictated to by the pagan environment, and not having the ability to care for the spiritual welfare of the spiritually weaker fellow believers, is not only insensitivity but a sign of spiritual immaturity and

---

165. Theissen, 99. Cf. Horsley, *1 Corinthians*, 42.
166. Johnson, *1 Corinthians*, 24.
167. Wilson, *Warning-Assurance*, 80.
168. Wilson, 80.
169. Barclay, "Thessalonica and Corinth," 193.
170. Ciampa and Rosner, *First Letter*, 392.
171. Horsley, "Gnosis," 124–25.

indifference. We can link this weakness to their spiritual apathy or lethargy because spiritually vibrant or genuinely converted Christians will always look out for their fellow believers at the cost of their own lives, like Paul their father in the faith[172] and Jesus Christ who demonstrated this truth on the cross.

The cultural and religious influence on the believers of the Baptist churches in Imphal does not pertain to food offered to idols, like the Corinthian church; however, the research survey found an unbroken link of paganism and religio-cultural influence and bondage on the people on several fronts.[173] Although we live two millennia later than the Corinthian church, the problem and challenge of the church is similar, if not the same. Below we will discuss how Paul addressed the issues homiletically and determine if there had been any visible impact.

6.2.3.4 Paul's Theological Response

In this section, the aim is to discuss how Paul in his homiletical theology engaged with the two issues raised above. First, Paul took them back to the gospel of Christ; in fact, the entire epistle is built on the foundation of the gospel. Paul began his epistle not by chastising the Corinthians, but by reminding them of their identity in Christ, to whom they belong, and therefore how they should behave. With all their blemishes, Paul still addressed them as "the church of God which is at Corinth, to those who have been sanctified in Christ Jesus, saints by calling" (1 Cor 1:2). Here, Paul reminded the Corinthians of their esteemed status in Christ despite their overwhelming failures, which he would eventually address. In this address we also see his attitude that the Corinthians were worthy of respect in Christ.

After this, he introduced the cross and crucifixion where he dealt with factionalism and division in the church, by rhetorically asking the question, "Has Christ been divided? Paul was not crucified for you, was he?" (1:13). Then, he clarified their confusion by revealing the commission he received from Christ; as one sent "to preach the gospel" with the power of "the cross of Christ" (1:17 – 2:5). Paul then asserted that neither he, Paul, who planted the seed of faith among the Corinthians, nor Apollos who watered the gospel of

---

172. 1 Cor 8:13.

173. For a detailed discussion on how culture and paganism influence our churches, see 4.3.3.3.8.

Christ by teaching the gospel of Christ to the Corinthians after Paul left the city was anything, because ultimately, "God was causing the growth" (3:6). Further, he added that although he "laid a foundation" for the believers, the foundation is Jesus Christ himself (3:11). Thus, Paul in his homily confronted the Corinthian believers on the issue of factionalism and division based on the centrality of the gospel.

Second, Paul began his engagement with the Corinthians on the issue of food offered to idols, by quoting the phrase they most probably used, "all of us possess knowledge" (8:1 ESV), then turned it on its head by saying that only those who love God are "known by God" (8:3 ESV). Paul connected the idea of the Corinthians' supposed knowledge, to the very act of loving God and consequently God knowing the believers. Paul subjugated the boastful self-centred and self-serving knowledge of the Corinthians by making it subservient to the idea of being known by God. He brought the Corinthians back to the right beginning, the primacy of the knowledge of God and the supremacy of the love for God and fellow believers. Paul then built up his argument and declared that there is no god except God the Father and only one Lord, Jesus Christ (8:5–6). Further, Paul linked the idea of being one with whose table one participates; either the Lord's or the demon's (10:21). He then climaxed the argument by exhorting the believers to "do all to the glory of God" (10:31).

In all these arguments, Paul did not employ other methodologies or philosophies but a simple theological and logical correlation by establishing every argument on the gospel and glory of Christ. Paul's method of engagement with the problems of the church through the gospel of Christ is an exemplary model for the Baptist churches in Imphal to follow. One of the main complaints among the believers is that some pastors do not preach the gospel by making its message relevant to the problems people are facing in their everyday businesses of life.[174] Paul demonstrated how the everyday problem of the Corinthians could be engaged with by applying the gospel truth. The specifics of the contexts of the Corinthian church and the Baptist churches of Imphal may be different, but the underlying spiritual issue, and its remedy, are the same.

---

174. Cf. 2.2.3.2; 2.4.1.5.

It is argued that although Paul's first epistle contained a wealth of doctrinal and ethical teachings beneficial to the church of God at Corinth, the letter had minimal impact, if not a total lack of positive response, because it is believed that soon after receiving the letter "conditions within the church there [at Corinth] deteriorated."[175] It is also claimed that other letters subsequent to the first one had to be written (although 2 Corinthians is the only other one found) because there were more issues to be dealt with; for example, the authority of Paul's apostleship.[176] Although the impact of Paul's homily on the believers remains questionable because of brewing troubles within the church, we can argue that his theology of preaching – an emphasis on the cross of Christ which is the foundation of the gospel – will be a good model to adopt for the Baptist churches in Imphal. This method takes the believers back to the basic foundation of their faith, Jesus Christ himself, for all matters of faith and conduct. And now we turn to Paul's homiletical method.

6.2.3.5 Paul's Expository Homiletical Method

Before we start analysing Paul's homiletical method in First Corinthians, it will benefit us to set the stage by looking at it from an educational approach, by outlining the book briefly and then selecting one of the sub-points for a more elaborate discussion on Paul's homiletical method. In 1:4–9, Paul encouraged the believers;[177] in 1:10 – 4:21, he spent his time appealing and explaining; in 5:1–12, he corrected them for knowing certain things but being unappreciative, and so, he revealed their basic assumptions. For example, he repeatedly asked them, "Do you not know?";[178] in 7:1 to perhaps chapter 14, he began to answer their queries by saying, "Now for the matters you wrote about . . .";[179] in 15:1, he rekindled their memory; in 15:12–34, he asked them questions; in 15:35–58, he engaged in debate and refuted some objections; and finally in 16:1–24, he talked about the need of the church, his itinerary,

---

175. Harris, *Second Epistle*, 58.
176. Best, *Second Corinthians*, 1–3; Hafemann, *Paul's Message*, 63.
177. Also, in 1 Cor 11:2, Paul encouraged them for their act of remembering him.
178. 1 Cor 3:16; 5:6; 6:2, 3, 9, 15, 16, 19; 9:13, 24.
179. Paul also used other phrases like "I do not want you to be ignorant" (instruction) and "I don't want you to be uninformed" (information) to answer their questions in 10:1 and 12:1 respectively (NIV); as he answered their questions, he also talked about how he passed down the tradition to them. Cf. 1 Cor 11:23; 15:3.

gave some more instructions and sent his greetings. From the above sub-points, we will focus on the unit of thought in 1:17 to 2:5, which falls under the "appealing and explaining" section (1:10 – 4:21). We will contend that Paul's homily to the Corinthian church as evidenced in these verses is expository[180] in nature.

First, Paul began by taking them to the OT texts which many of them (at least the Jewish Christians) knew. In 1:19, Paul quoted from Isaiah 29:14.[181] Then again in 1:20, he quoted from Isaiah 19:12 and 44:25. He frequently based his homily on the written Scripture of the OT, where he distinguished and asserted the supremacy of God's wisdom over that of the mortals.[182] Further, on the issue of "content and context," in 1:17 – 2:5, it is argued that Paul's quotation of the OT texts here is not a prooftext, but situated in "the midst of some Oracles of Woe" for Isaiah, and "in the midst of some Oracles of Judgement" for Jeremiah, where human wisdom was rebuked and deposed by God.[183]

God revealed his mind to the people by speaking through the prophets. This revealed message of God was later written down and canonised and Paul was faithful to the written text.

Second, Paul's homily was engaged with the worldviews of the society of his listeners. In 1:22–23, we see him interacting with that society. He talked of the Jewish religious presuppositions and expectations in prioritising "signs," and then he talked of the cultural and societal worldview of the Greeks which emphasised "wisdom." He was not only basing his homily on the OT texts, but was also actively engaging with the sociocultural and religious realities of the people which, according to Timothy Keller, is relating with the people's "baseline cultural narrative."[184]

Third, Paul's homily as discussed above, culminates in the gospel of Christ.[185] In 1:23–25, he twisted and unmasked the assumptions of the Jews and the Greeks by shifting the focus towards the cross and crucifixion. Thus, what had been presumed as weak and foolish once, became the redeeming

---

180. More discussion on expository preaching is found under 6.4, 6.5, and 6.8.
181. Cf. Jer 8:9; 9:23–24; Job 5:12–13; Isa 40:13.
182. Cf. Perkins, *First Corinthians*, 49.
183. Windsor, "What Is Preaching?", 2–3.
184. Keller, *Preaching*, 19, 103.
185. Cf. 6.2.3.4.

factor for the people because for Paul, "the foolishness of God is wiser than men, and the weakness of God is stronger than men" (1:25).

Fourth, Paul not only engaged with the cultural narratives of the time, but also delved deeper by relating to the personal lives of the people and their existential situation. In 1:26, he brought up the issue of the people's societal and economic makeup – most of them were not privileged people, but poorer members of the church.[186] He spoke to them in their situation. Then, in 1:27–31, he encouraged them as people of worth because of what Jesus Christ had done.

Fifth, in 2:1–5, Paul testified how as a preacher, he carried the message of the gospel to the people. He did not go to them in the power of his wisdom and persuasive skill but through the power of the Spirit. Here, he demonstrated what the posture of a God-dependent preacher should be – "in fear and trembling" (2:3) – and how God used that posture for God's Spirit to exercise his power. This issue is not necessarily limited to those preachers belonging to the school of expository preaching, but also has an important message for preachers belonging to other methods, as carriers of the message.

In summary, Paul based his homily on the written word of God, the OT texts; it culminated in the gospel of Christ; it moved out from the chamber of textual exegesis to the streets of the listeners, engaging with and speaking their worldviews. Not only that, he went further and related his sermon to the listeners' individual situation; even further, we discovered what a preacher's posture should be for God's Spirit to work in people's lives. Thus, we can argue from this unit of thought that Paul's first epistle to the Corinthian church contains a model of an expository sermon.[187]

6.3 The Role of Charisma in Topical and Expository Preaching: An Evaluation

Here we pick up the issue of charisma in topical preaching as discussed in the previous chapter.[188] As every individual is created differently, every preacher

---

186. Wilson, *Warning-Assurance*, 80.

187. As we have not engaged with all the chapters of 1 Corinthians in our discussion, it would be more appropriate to use the word "contain."

188. Cf. 5.10.

is also unique in their choice of sermon preparation and presentation; for example, in their use of a topical or expository method. If "preaching is the bringing of truth through personality,"[189] as Phillip Brooks rightly argues, then much depends on an individual preacher's personality, irrespective of the school of preaching method they belong to. As discussed earlier, some pastors in the Baptist churches in Imphal are better preachers than others, although they followed the same topical method of preaching. It had been argued earlier that the individual pastor's capability (knowledge of theology, homiletical ability, and skill)[190] and charisma[191] separated the preachers who could see spiritual growth and vitality among the members against those whose preaching was critiqued by the members as shallow and unhelpful, although they employed the same topical method. So, although this method proved useful for some of the preachers with higher capability and charisma, it could not be seen as a good method for every pastor who employed it.[192] Hence, we can argue that the "make or break" issue in topical preaching boils down to the capability and charisma of the preacher, and not the topical method itself. Our finding suggests that most preachers are not capable in many ways, and do not have charisma. So, if topical preaching's accomplishment largely depends on individual gifting and ability, there are more questions asked than answers found for the Baptist churches in Imphal.

This takes us to the next question: What then is the role of capability and charisma in the field of expository preaching? As discussed earlier, the issue of capability and charisma is a subjective matter in relation to expository preachers, because not all expositors have either capability or charisma. We can suggest that capability and charisma are as valuable to expository preaching, if not more, than to topical preaching. But what difference does it make when capability and charisma are absent in either of the methods? It is conceivable that in the case of expository preaching, even when there is an

---

189. Brooks, *Lecture on Preaching*, 5.

190. It was found during the research that not all the pastors and preachers have the required knowledge and skill of preaching, because many churches employed lay pastors and not theologically trained ones, to cut salary costs.

191. Cf. 5.10.

192. It can be argued that although "charisma" is a gifting unique to a person, one which may or may not be developed with time, "capability" is something which preachers can develop with the right exposure to good resources and the exercise of self-discipline. So, a preacher cannot just say that he or she is not capable enough and refuse to grow as a preacher.

absence of advanced capability and charisma, it has the advantage of a framework where the given text controls and helps navigate and shape the entire outline of the sermon; it also hedges the preacher from jumping to other texts for "hitchhiking," but rather to remain faithful to the chosen text. Although advanced capability and charisma are an asset, even in their absence, if the steps of expository sermon preparation are properly followed, the text can be opened and related to the needs of the people even by a lay pastor.

6.4 The Theology and Method of Expository Preaching

So far, we have analysed the problem of spiritual lethargy in the Bible by discussing one example from the OT (Malachi) and one from the NT (1 Corinthians). We have also evaluated how the prophet Malachi and the apostle Paul dealt homiletically with the problems in their respective contexts. Then, we have engaged with the issue of charisma, its importance and significance in both topical and expository preaching. Below, we will examine the theology and method of expository preaching.

If we look at the history of preaching, we find the names of many great expositors whom we could engage with here. The names include Jonathan Edwards, Charles Simeon, Charles Haddon Spurgeon, D. Martyn Lloyd-Jones, W. A. Criswell, Haddon Robinson, John Stott, Timothy Keller, and others. However, we will engage with only two of them – John Stott and Timothy Keller.

Stott and Keller were chosen because they are homileticians both in theory and practice. Both have written books on preaching.[193] Both of them served in the pastorate as preachers for several years. Moreover, both seriously endorsed an engagement with the world of the listeners in their methodology. While Stott describes it as "double listening,"[194] Keller refers to it as engaging with the "baseline cultural narrative"[195] of the listeners. Further, Stott's[196] and

---

193. We will engage with their books below.
194. Stott, *Contemporary Christian*, 110.
195. Keller, *Preaching*, 19, 103.
196. Stott's life and work have become a subject of academic interest and research for at least ten universities around the globe; Cameron, "John Stott: Preacher and Writer."

Keller's[197] ideas about preaching are the subject of contemporary discussions in both the academic and church setting. Although other homiletical theologians and practitioners may also fit these descriptions, we have chosen them because they best serve our purpose.

6.4.1 John Stott

6.4.1.1 *Stott's Theology of Preaching*

A theology of preaching can be understood as one that defines and justifies what preaching is and what it does when questions arise from Scripture and theology.[198] John Stott argues for his theology of preaching as follows:

> In a world which seems either unwilling or unable to listen, how can we be persuaded to go on preaching and learn to do so effectively? The essential secret is not mastering certain techniques but being mastered by certain convictions. In other words, theology is more important than methodology.[199]

Stott believes that "to preach is to open up the inspired text with such faithfulness and sensitivity that God's voice is heard and God's people obey him."[200] On preaching as a divine event, Stott declares that the "locus of authority" in preaching "resides only in God . . . and not at all in us who quote them [the Scriptures] today."[201] He also affirms that the origin of every sermon which the preacher preaches is from God and not from anywhere else. He argues that "in the ideal sermon it is the Word itself which speaks, or rather God in and through His Word."[202] On the other hand, Stott is clear about the importance of the human role in preaching, which is after all a human event as well:

> Here, then, is the biblical case for biblical exposition.[203] It consists of two fundamental convictions, namely that God has given

---

197. Two PhD theses on Keller's works are listed here: S. P. Hill, "Jesus Christ and Him Crucified"; Galdamez, "Worldview Preaching in the Church."
198. Ritschl, *Theology of Proclamation*, 7.
199. Stott, *Between Two Worlds*, 92.
200. Stott, *Contemporary Christian*, 208.
201. Stott, *Between Two Worlds*, 58.
202. Stott, *Preacher's Portrait*, 30.
203. Stott prefers the term "biblical exposition" to expository preaching, although he uses expository preaching as well; Stott, *Contemporary Christian*, 211–12.

us in Scripture a text which is both inspired (having a divine origin and authority) and to some degree closed (difficult to understand). Therefore, in addition to the text, he gives the church teachers to open up the text, explaining it and applying it to people's lives.[204]

Further, elaborating on the human dimension in preaching, Stott brings up the issue of a preacher's experience with God that will empower his preaching. He says, "by 'experience,' I do not mean experience of the preaching ministry or experience of life in general, necessary as these are to the preacher. I mean rather a personal experience of Jesus Christ Himself. This is the first and indispensable mark of the Christian witness (preacher)."[205]

On the importance of context in preaching, Stott talks about bridge-building between the world of the text and the world of the listeners. Stott advises that a preacher must, before preaching, "seek to enter into the other person's world of thoughts and feelings" so that he may rightfully "contextualise the gospel." For this to happen, Stott says that "double listening" is vital. He then states that preaching stands

> between the Word and the world, with the consequent obligation to listen to both. We listen to the Word in order to discover ever more of the riches of Christ. And we listen to the world in order to discern which of Christ's riches are needed most and how to present them in their best light.[206]

So, a preacher's responsibility is to let this ancient truth touch contemporary lives.[207] On the role of the Holy Spirit, Stott says that a preacher must cultivate the "humility of dependence"[208] and argues that ineffectiveness in preaching happens due to pride.[209] This is so because human preachers are "finite, fallen, frail, and fallible creatures" and that the "words we speak in human weakness the Holy Spirit carries home by his power to the mind, heart,

---

204. Stott, 211–12.
205. Stott, *Preacher's Portrait*, 70–71.
206. Stott, *Contemporary Christian*, 110–11.
207. Stott, *Between Two Worlds*, 138.
208. Stott, 328.
209. Stott, 329–30.

conscience, and the will of the hearers."[210] It is not in the power of the human preacher to bring to life and transform the "spiritually and morally blind, deaf, dumb, lame, and even dead or imprisoned by Satan ... Only Jesus Christ through his Spirit can ... wake up the conscience, enlighten the mind, fire the heart, move the will, give life to the dead, and rescue slaves from Satan."[211]

6.4.1.2 Stott's Method of Expository Preaching

Stott claims that expository preaching cannot be stereotyped as "a verse-by-verse explanation of a lengthy passage of the Scripture," rather it points to "the content of the sermon (biblical truth)." He clarifies,

> The expositor pries open what appears to be closed, makes plain what is obscure, unravels what is knotted, and unfolds what is tightly packed. . . . Whether it is long or short, our responsibility as expositors is to open it up in such a way that it speaks its message clearly, plainly, accurately, relevantly, without addition, subtraction or falsification. In expository preaching, the biblical text is neither a conventional introduction to a sermon on a largely different theme, nor a convenient peg on which to hang a ragbag of miscellaneous thoughts, but a master which dictates and controls what is said.[212]

Stott lists six steps to be followed in preparing an expository preaching: "1) Choose your text. 2) Meditate on it. 3) Isolate the dominant thought. 4) Arrange your material to serve the dominant thought. 5) Add the introduction and conclusion. 6) Write down and pray over your message."[213] On the methodology of Stott's preaching, Daniel L. Dockery writes, "The text controls the structure and theme of the sermon. The text provides the authority and impetus for the sermon. Stott undoubtedly believes in the centrality of the Scripture in preaching."[214]

---

210. Stott, 334.

211. Stott and Scharf, *Challenge of Preaching*, 98.

212. Stott, *Between Two Worlds*, 126. To see more on the "value of systematic exposition" see 315–20 of the same book; for further discussions on expository preaching see, Chapell, *Christ-Centered Preaching*, 57; Keller, *Preaching*, 32; Lamb, *Dynamics of Biblical Preaching*, 16; Bromiley, *Preface to Homiletic*, 14; Old, *Reading*, 11.

213. Stott, *Between Two Worlds*, 164–99.

214. Dockery, "Theology of Scripture," 180–81.

Stott sets out four advantages of following an expository preaching method. First, "exposition sets us limits," the boundary we must not traverse. Second, "exposition demands integrity," helping us to focus on "the plain, natural, obvious meaning of each text." Third, "exposition identifies the pitfalls" which every preacher must avoid – "forgetfulness and disloyalty" to the chosen text. Fourth, "exposition gives us confidence to preach" as we are convinced that whatever we preach is from God's word not ours.[215]

Shedding light on Stott's own preaching methodology, Greg R. Scharf comments that his preaching is "faithful to Scripture, clear, and relevant."[216] Moreover, "John Stott's own life in the Word of God and his prayerful desire to be shaped and transformed by it was the soil where his sermons grew."[217]

6.4.2 Timothy Keller

6.4.2.1 Keller's Theology of Preaching

Timothy Keller says that preaching is "engaging with the authoritative text" and "not your opinion."[218] He argues that when a preacher preaches the Scripture, he is speaking "the very words of God,"[219] that preaching biblically involves making "clear the meaning of the text in its context – both in its historical time and within the whole of Scripture."[220] Further, he declares,

> Expository preaching grounds the message in the text so that all the sermon's points are in the text, and it majors in the text's major ideas. It aligns the interpretation of the text with the doctrinal truths of the rest of the Bible. And it always situates the passage within the Bible's narrative, showing how Christ is the final fulfillment of the text's theme.[221]

On the role of the Holy Spirit, Keller says, "The sermon's differing impact on individuals is due to the work of God's Spirit,"[222] that the "difference

---

215. Stott, *Between Two Worlds*, 126–33. For more on the advantages of expository preaching, see Richard, *Preparing Expository Sermons*, 17–18.
216. Scharf, "John Stott," 350.
217. Scharf, 348.
218. Keller, *Preaching*, 20.
219. 1 Pet 4: 11.
220. Keller, *Preaching*, 20.
221. Keller, 32.
222. Keller, 10.

between good preaching and great preaching lies mainly in the work of the Holy Spirit in the heart of his listeners as well as the preacher."[223] Keller says this is so because the Holy Spirit ultimately holds the key to all the secrets of "God's wise plans."[224]

Keller's theology of preaching also concerns engagement with the "baseline cultural narrative" of the listeners:

> In the course of expounding a biblical text, the Christian preacher should compare and contrast the Scripture's message with the foundational beliefs of the culture, which are usually invisible to people inside it, in order to help people understand themselves more fully. If done rightly it can lead people to say to themselves, *Oh, so that's why I tend to think and feel that way.* This can be one of the most liberating and catalytic steps in a person's journey to faith in Christ.[225]

Further, Keller argues, "To reach people, gospel preachers must challenge the culture's story at points of confrontation and finally retell the culture's story, as it were, revealing how its deepest aspirations for good can be fulfilled only in Christ."[226]

For Keller, the goal of every sermon is to point people to Christ. He contends, "Remember that biblical accuracy and Christo-centricity are the same thing to Paul. You can't properly preach any text – putting it into its rightful place in the whole Bible – unless you show how its themes find their fulfilment in the person of Christ." Furthermore, he claims that "unless we preach Jesus rather than a set of 'morals of the story' or timeless principles or good advice, people will never truly understand, love, or obey the Word of God."[227] Thus for Keller, two things are prominent: "As we preach, we are to serve and love the truth of God's Word and also to serve and love the people before us. We serve the Word by preaching the text clearly and preaching the gospel every time. We reach the people by preaching to the culture and to the heart."[228]

---

223. Keller, 11.
224. Keller, 11.
225. Keller, 19–20.
226. Keller, 20.
227. Keller, 22.
228. Keller, 23.

Keller is convinced that a preacher must preach the gospel every time. He argues, "To preach the gospel every time is to preach Christ every time, from every passage. Only if we preach Christ every time can we show how the whole Bible fits together." Arguing that Christ must be preached even from the OT texts, Keller refers to Luke 24:44 where Jesus himself "blamed the confusion of the disciples on their inability to see that the Old Testament is all about him and his salvation"[229] for "the Bible is in the end a single, great story that comes to a climax in Jesus Christ."[230]

On how to avoid legalism and antinomianism at the same time in preaching, Keller advises,

> It is crucial in our preaching that we do not simply tell people all the ways they must be moral and good without relating such exhortation to the gospel. Nor should we simply tell them over and over that they can be saved only by free grace without showing how salvation changes our lives.[231]

6.4.2.2 Keller's Method of Expository Preaching

On the human dimension and effort in expository preaching, Keller recommends that the following steps be followed in a sermon preparation.

> Understanding the biblical text, distilling a clear outline and theme, developing a persuasive argument, enriching it with

---

229. Keller, 57.

230. Keller, 58; C. H. Spurgeon also endorses this argument by narrating a story of a Welsh minister speaking to a young man, where the senior minister said, ". . . and so from every text in Scripture, there is a road to the metropolis of the Scripture, that is Christ." An Abstract from Sermon 242, "Christ Precious to Believers." From the archive of Charles Spurgeon's sermons, Mid-Western Baptist Theological Seminary. See, https://archive.spurgeon.org/sermons/0242.php, accessed July 14, 2021; cf. Keller, *Preaching*, 67–68. This researcher perceives that sometimes it may be genuinely difficult, but one must keep trying, using the following principles: "1. What aspects of the character of God does this passage reveal, and how does Christ exemplify this? 2. What aspects of the identity of humanity does the passage reveal, and how does Christ fulfil this? 3. What aspects of the promises of God does the passage reveal, and how does Christ complete this? 4. What aspects of the need of humanity does the passage reveal, and how does Christ meet this?"; Chester and Honeysett, *Gospel-Centred Preaching*, 76; cf. Millar and Campbell, *Saving Eutychus*, 77–99. *Contra*, some people claim that to preach Christ every time from every passage of the Scripture is a highly contentious issue. For instance, it reduces the trinitarian theology to Christology. Other evangelicals believe Scripture can only be rightly expounded if a wider perspective is adopted; Gibson and Kim, *Homiletics and Hermeneutics*, passim.

231. Keller, *Preaching*, 51; cf. Gibson and Kim, *Homiletics and Hermeneutics*, 117–54.

poignant illustrations, metaphors, and practical examples, incisively analysing heart motives and cultural assumptions, making specific application to real life – all of this takes extensive labor.[232]

On the practical aspect of writing an expository sermon, Keller recommends the following steps.

1. Discern the *goal* of the text by itemizing all the things that it says and looking for the main idea that all the other ideas support.[233]
2. Choose a main *theme* for the sermon that presents the central idea of the text and ministers to your specific listeners.[234]
3. Develop an *outline* around the sermon theme that fits the passage, with each point raising insights from the text itself, and has movement towards a climax.
4. *Flesh out* each point with arguments, illustrations, examples, images, other supportive Bible texts, and most important, practical application.[235]

On the advantages of following expository preaching, Keller makes the following arguments. First, it will reveal one's rootedness and commitment to the biblical truth for doctrinal and practical issues through one's sermons.[236] Second, it will increase people's trust in the sermon by seeing its authority coming from God and the Scripture.[237] Third, it allows God to decide what he wants the community of God to be. Fourth, it sets "the agenda for the preacher" to focus on the given text and address the corresponding issues related to it.[238] Fifth, it will educate the listeners in the method of their personal Bible study by systematically structuring their pattern of thinking when they face a Bible passage.[239] Sixth, it will assist a preacher in gaining a

---

232. Keller, 10–11.

233. For more, see Robinson, *Biblical Preaching*, 21; cf. Robinson, "Dramatic Expository Preaching," 406.

234. Cf. Willhite and Gibson, *Big Idea*.

235. Keller, *Preaching*, 214 (italics original).

236. Keller, 32–33.

237. Keller, 36.

238. Keller, 37.

239. Keller, 38.

higher ground to have a piercing perspective so as to view any biblical theme emerging from a sermon holistically.[240]

Although we could analyse Stott and Keller's theology and methodology of expository preaching here independently, without linking them with the critiques made against this preaching method, it will serve our purpose better if we analyse them later, after hearing what the critics have to say on this preaching method.

6.5 Critique against Expository Preaching

6.5.1 Critique against Expository Preaching by the Proponents of the New Homiletic (NH)

It must be acknowledged that expository preaching, also known as traditional preaching, is not without any counter viewpoints. We hear critiques from proponents of the NH and from others who may not necessarily belong to this school. The NH is an umbrella term which comprises various sub-branches. To have a better understanding of the NH and what its proponents have to say, it will help to observe a contrast made by Scott M. Gibson between traditional preaching and the NH.

> The New Homiletic refers to a revolution in homiletics that began in the 1950s. It indicates a departure from the old homiletic that is characterized by point form, mechanical notions of structure, vertical notion of authority, use of the Bible in propositional ways, deductive sermons, stories used as illustrations of points already made, objective ideas of truth, religious experience as universal, and sermons that stressed faith as information. By contrast the NH emphasizes organic form, narrative plot, horizontal notions of authority, recovery of the Bible for the pulpit, inductive sermons, stories making their own points in their own ways, contextual understandings of truth, dynamic and tensive notions of language, and sermons as transformational experience.[241]

---

240. Keller, 38.
241. Wilson, "New Homiletic," 398–99; cf. Gibson, "Critique of the New Homiletic," 478. For a more detailed discussion on New Homiletic, see Appendix 1; cf. Lowry, *Sermon*;

Below are some critiques from this school. Some of these points may have a close affinity with each other, but they have been separately categorised as they do have subtle differences. First, they argue that a sermon's main task must not be to ascertain the meaning of the text but to focus on the experience of the people as a result of the preaching event,[242] because of what preaching does.[243] Thus, this school prioritises the contemporary authentic human experience ahead of finding out what the word of God said to the original audience. Consequently, their critique against expository preaching is that it gives preference to the written text over people's experience.[244]

Second, the expository preaching method tends to be more of a monologue and leans towards dictating what the people should do.[245] On the other hand, the NH recommends that the listeners should participate in a sermon as "co-creators of the sermonic experience,"[246] deriving their own conclusions as in a dialogue, although they remain silent during a preaching event.[247]

Third, expository preaching is critiqued for fearing to engage with human culture, thus locking itself up to biblical history and stories of antiquity, without much relevance for the present times.[248]

Fourth, Eugene Lowry argues that expository sermons suffer from a lack of smooth "transition" from one point to another. Instead of focusing on this problem, he claims that expository preachers are more interested in arranging subpoints under the larger points.[249] He argues that to address this problem, the method of sermonic preparation has to change from thinking of the sermon as something one constructs with disjointed pieces, to the

---

Randolph, *Renewal of Preaching*; Craddock, *As One without Authority*; Buttrick, *Homiletics*; Buttrick, "On Doing Homiletics"; Lowry, *Homiletical Plot*.

242. Gibson, "Critique of the New Homiletic," 477.

243. Gibson, 477; cf. Randolph, *Renewal of Preaching*, 19.

244. Randolph, 1; *contra*, good expository preaching would not neglect the experience and existential situation of the people. But they are not entirely wrong, because bad expository preaching ignores human experience and just disseminates information.

245. This critique includes topical sermons too, because the NH sees itself as belonging to one camp and the other camp comprises those who follow the deductive preaching method.

246. This is how Gibson describes Craddock of thinking about a listener's role; Gibson, "Critique of the New Homiletic," 478.

247. Randolph, *Renewal of Preaching*, 14; Craddock, *As One without Authority*, 114.

248. Buttrick, *Homiletics*, 18.

249. Lowry, *Homiletical*, 7; cf. Jones, *Principles and Practices*, 87–102.

idea of developing it like a "rose blossoming," like a "living organic matter."[250] Speaking about the challenge of transition, Craddock argues that the expository approach is challenging because it is like a hiking trip where the preacher has to take the listeners up several hills, after each one is ascended. Instead, he argues for a smooth linear movement for the entire journey.[251]

Fifth, an expository sermon is critiqued because it prioritises logic and the flow of ideas because for Lowry, a sermon is "an event-in-time."[252]

Sixth, Lowry believes that a sermon should be seen as a plot awaiting resolution, unlike an expository sermon which is seen as a predictable body of ideas. He believes that a preacher must be imagined as a good storyteller, who takes the listeners through various twists and turns during the sermonic experience but finally brings them to a climactic end.[253]

Seventh, expository preaching is accused by Buttrick of reciting "churchly faith" and employing old-fashioned language in the preaching event. He recommends that the language of preaching must be one which the people themselves speak.[254] The emphasis on the correlation between the pulpit-and-pew language is also endorsed by several other homileticians.[255]

6.5.2 Critique against Expository Preaching by Some Evangelicals

Calvin Miller argues that many people in the evangelical churches were tired of the predictable method of expository sermon preparation and delivery. However, many declined to air their grievances and disappointment with the pastors and church leaders because they were unwilling to be "branded as a liberal."[256] Moreover, according to Jerry Vines and Jim Shaddix, many accuse

---

250. Lowry, *Homiletical*, 8; Grady Davis also talks of the imagery of a branch of a tree that thrusts out because of a life force within it; Davis, *Design for Preaching*, 15.

251. Craddock, *As One without Authority,* 56.

252. Lowry, *Homiletical*, 8; cf. Randolph, *Renewal of Preaching*, 19.

253. Lowry, *Homiletical*, 12.

254. Buttrick, "On Doing Homiletics," 18, 88–104; cf. Thiselton, "New Hermeneutics," 78.

255. Ebeling, *Word and Faith*, 318; Craddock, *As One without Authority,* 42; Gibson, "Critique of the New Homiletic," 476. For further discussion on the term, "language-event" see Fuchs, *Studies of Historical Jesus*, 196; for Ebeling's "word-event" see Ebeling, *Theology and Proclamation*, 28–29.

256. Miller, *Preaching*, 20.

expository preaching of "dullness,"[257] "irrelevancy," "monotony," "spiritlessness," "formlessness" and "detail overload."[258] They concede that people do "dislike *poor* expository preaching," though not expository preaching in itself.[259]

6.5.3 Challenges of Expository Preaching in Terms of Its Homiletical Method in Comparison to Topical Preaching Method[260]

Apart from the critiques mentioned above, there are other challenges pertaining to the choice of the expository preaching method. The first challenge is the restriction of the scope of the sermon[261] this method brings to the table. Unlike a topical sermon[262] where a preacher could move around the entire landscape of the Scripture, both in the OT and NT, and build the sermon outline, an expository sermon is restricted to the particular text, passage, oracle, story, or thought unit, which a preacher has chosen to preach from.[263] An expository preacher can definitely go back to the OT and forward to the NT passages as this process gives a much wider vista and strengthens the biblical theology and the eschatological aspect of the chosen sermon text.

The second challenge pertains to the demands of time and "hard work."[264] One could argue that all sermon preparation needs time and hard work, which is true. However, in topical sermon preparation, a preacher could depend on a concordance and choose the scriptural verses linking to the chosen theme or title of a sermon. But expository preaching is different because in this

---

257. Vines and Shaddix, *Power*, 55; Charles agrees that many consider expository preaching "boring"; Charles, *On Pastoring*, n.p.

258. Vines and Shaddix, *Power*, 55–58.

259. Vines and Shaddix, 53.

260. Refer to notes on pages 207–208 on the strengths and weaknesses of topical preaching.

261. *Contra*, some may consider it an advantage because it helps them in their focus. D. A. Carson argues, "it (expository preaching) is the method least likely to stray from the Scripture"; Carson, "Teaching the Whole Bible," 127.

262. Cf. Allen, *Preaching the Topical Sermon*.

263. Carson, "Teaching," 404; Robinson, "Dramatic," 406; Mathewson, "Verse-By-Verse," 408.

264. Etter, *Preacher and His Sermon*, 302; Fullerton, Orrick, and Payne, *Encountering God*, 73.

approach, the preacher must labour hard to bring out the meaning of the text,[265] to make it the message of God for the people through a particular sermon.

The third challenge is when an entire book is chosen to be preached in a series of expository sermons, a preacher does not have the choice and luxury to skip any difficult passage.[266] However, in a topical sermon, it would be easier for a preacher to choose other scriptural portions in case of hitting such a roadblock.

The fourth challenge is for a preacher who likes to use some favourite stories or illustrations in the sermons now and then, because in an expository series setting, as every scriptural text or portion is different, the preacher must labour hard to find relevant illustrations and cannot depend on favourite illustrations. This is primarily because the "philosophy" of the expository method is that you "bend your thoughts to the text," and do not "bend the text to your thought."[267]

The fifth challenge is that the preparation method, by following a regular set of steps and procedures, can sometimes become mechanical and monotonous. A preacher who prefers to freely choose the sermon preparation method without following a procedure will find it hard because expository sermon preparation invariably follows a set pattern.[268] However, these seemingly dull, monotonous, and repetitive steps can lead a preacher to liberation if one begins to master the procedure of sermon preparation. Moreover, if we are genuinely following the shape of the text, we will be using different sermon shapes and not always stick to the three-point sermon structure.

---

265. Here a preacher does several studies like exegesis and word study. This does not mean the topical method does not follow these processes, but that in the expository method, it could be more intense and routinely intentional.

266. *Contra*, there are some who claim that this method "enables the preacher to expound systematically the whole counsel of God." Some argue that expository preaching "forces the preacher to handle the tough questions"; Carson, "Teaching the Whole Bible," 404; however, there are others who claim that one need not preach a whole book of the Scripture verse by verse but can find a way to cover the book section by section or by unit of thought, following the framework of the materials as organised in the Scripture. Cf. Mathewson, "Verse-by-Verse," 407–11; Wilkerson, "Trends in Sermon," 443–46.

267. Robinson, "Dramatic," 405; *contra*, this exercise of searching for new illustrations on the other hand can become an advantage if the preacher takes it positively, as it can infuse creativity and life in the sermons, and trigger interest and anticipation on the part of the listeners.

268. Cf. Stott and Keller's method of preaching, 6.4.1.2 and 6.4.2.2.

The sixth challenge is that bad expository preaching runs the risk of being termed boring because it could end up just "retelling history about better times when God was alive and well . . . orthodox but removed from life."[269] If a preacher refuses to come out of the exegesis chamber and go into the streets where people live, and address the real-life issues they face and "applies the meaning to the listeners' lives,"[270] the sermon will suffocate in its chamber. Thus, it also runs the risk of being called too "cerebral and less moving,"[271] "too doctrinal, and 'over their head'" by the listeners.[272]

The seventh challenge is that this method of preaching will make it difficult to deliver doctrinal and festal sermons. As doctrinal teachings cannot be confined to a particular text, the preacher may have to go to different texts and take the help of the topical method to holistically address a particular doctrine.[273] Moreover, during Christian festivals or occasions, expository preaching (especially when a series is going on), cannot meet the need of the church because during such a time in the Christian calendar, the preacher will need to switch to topical preaching.[274]

6.6 Rebuttal against the Criticisms of the New Homiletic on Expository Preaching

Gibson gives a systematic response to the criticisms levelled against the expository method of preaching by the advocates of the NH. Although his argument will act as a lens, other voices will be incorporated, and finally we will evaluate the whole discussion.

---

269. Robinson, *Biblical*, 20; *contra*, Robinson argues that if for example, one understands the spirit in which Paul wrote to the Galatians, "It will not be a pedantic plodding through the text, sentence after sentence as though there were no great issues at stake"; Robinson, "Dramatic," 406.

270. Mathewson, "Verse-By-Verse," 408.

271. Robinson, "Dramatic," 406.

272. Fullerton, Orrick, and Payne, *Encountering God*, 19; *contra*, if expository preaching is done well, then it has the advantage of "preaching so wide a range of religious thought . . ."; *Home Missionary*, 278.

273. For a discussion on how expository preaching and topical sermons cannot be exclusive in themselves but are interrelated see Keller, *Preaching*, 31; cf. Warren, "Can Topical Preaching," 418–20; Sunukjian, "Biblical Topical Sermon," 421–23; Warren, "Topical Preaching," 431–33.

274. *Contra*, some could argue that a careful planning of a series can to some extent mitigate this problem, which is true to a great extent.

First, concerning the relationship between text and the interpreter, Gibson observes that in the NH, the interpreter comes with certain presuppositions and so, "The text is not considered to be the object with the interpreter as the subject. Instead, the interpreter is himself or herself the object of interpretation. The text then is spoken into and creates the community of faith." In this school of thought he remarks that the "centre of authority" is not in the text but in its relationship with those who listen to it and who have been influenced by a certain context.[275] There is no fixed position in regard to the place of scriptural authority. For example, Buttrick observes, "We must not say that preaching from Scripture is requisite for sermons to be the Word of God."[276]

Second, because the place of authority is not in the Scripture, another presupposition of this school of thought is the indirect promotion of the "superiority of the self." Craddock argues, "It is, therefore, pointless to speak of the gospel as Truth in and of itself; the gospel is *Truth for us*."[277] Consequently, it is perceivable that the NH critiques expository preaching for undermining the role of the human factor in textual interpretation.

Third, the NH school argues that in expository preaching, the preacher derives the sermon's meaning and application for the people, but in the NH, the preacher and listener co-create experience to bring meaning and application.[278]

There are some from within the NH itself who are critical of the movement. Buttrick observes, "The movement came and went with startling dispatch. Probably the fatal flaw was a lurking assumption – namely, that the gospel addresses human beings in their existential self-awareness."[279] Another homiletician also comments, "The real question comes: Is the Word-event really happening? What appeared to be a most promising homiletical theory has not produced, in spite of all the scholarly care that has gone into its formulation, a significant new movement in preaching."[280] Gibson echoes the same pessimism: "The values of the NH will remain important, but whether

---

275. Gibson, "Critique of the New Homiletic," 478.
276. Gibson, 478; cf. Buttrick, *Homiletics*, 458; Troeger, *Imaging*, 122.
277. Craddock, *As One without Authority*, 71; cf. Woodfin, "Theology of Preaching," 408–19.
278. Gibson, "Critique of the New Homiletic," 479.
279. Buttrick, "On Doing Homiletics," 101.
280. Skoglund, "Towards New Homiletic," 57.

it can offer anything new or assist the theological purposes of preaching is now questioned."[281]

On this researcher's evaluation of the NH and its claims, along with Gibson, it is possible to say that there are several advantages that the NH brings. For example, I agree with Gibson that induction is a good method for stories and narratives in the Bible to be preached. Further, it must be acknowledged that the NH draws our attention back to the importance of human experience and the use of language in engaging human imagination. Moreover, it must also be noted here that effective preaching must ultimately lead people to encounter God and experience him personally in their lives, thus bringing spiritual vitality.

However, I have some points of difference with this viewpoint. First, as Gibson points out, the advocates of the NH think that all the books in the Bible can be preached through a particular method – a narrative method – which undermines the complexities and different types of genres in Scripture,[282] which is untenable. Second, although experience is important, if the emphasis on the preacher-listeners' role in mutually generating an experience through preaching is considered equivalent to written revelation – the word of God – then we elevate the human factors to being equally authoritative to the source of God's word or even eclipsing God's word, and it remains a rightful concern for many, including me. Third, the role of the Holy Spirit in preaching is not clearly spelled out in the NH. Fourth, the authority of the word of God in preaching is under attack, because in their effort to accommodate sources that engage with the listeners, the sufficiency of the Scripture is belittled.

6.7 Evaluation of Stott and Keller and a Response to the Critique against Expository Preaching

In this section we will do two things. We will evaluate Stott and Keller's theology and method of preaching and respond to the critiques made by some evangelicals as to expository preaching.

---

281. Wilson, "New Homiletic," 401.

282. Gibson, "Critique of the New Homiletic," 480. *Contra*, some critique that the expository preaching method also reduces all genres to one way of sermon construction, based on idea development or a three-point sermon, without considering the uniqueness of other genres, like narratives and poetry.

It is true that some expository sermons are boring when they major in exegesis without application. Such sermons are not only simplistic but unbiblical, because God's words must address human problems. However, in light of Stott's and Keller's theology of preaching, these accusations are not convincing, because none of them are sufficiently serious enough to abandon this approach. Perhaps these critiques had been directed against bad expository preaching rather than expository preaching itself. Below are the core theologies of preaching as formulated by Stott and Keller, neatly depicting and defending the accusations levelled against them.

Stott's locus of authority in preaching is God (the revealed Scripture), not human beings. However, Stott clearly lays out the role of "church teachers" (pastors and preachers) who have experienced and accepted Jesus Christ as Lord and Saviour to unravel the slightly closed Scripture. Then, Stott is strong in his emphasis on "double-listening." Far from prohibiting preachers from engaging with the various sources available in the society (through aesthetic expression in the form of pictorial images) to theologise and sermonise, as Barth is perceived by some as doing,[283] Stott strongly encourages preachers to be attentive to the cries, crises, cultures, and climate of the society they live in and to address its felt needs. Further, Stott carefully balances rationality, experience, orthodoxy, and being listener-centric. Over and above all these, Stott is immovable in his belief that man, a finite and limited creature of God, can never be a worthy dispenser of God's word or a transforming agent in listeners' lives without the consuming presence and role of the Holy Spirit. Among other factors, Stott's theology of preaching that seriously emphasises "double-listening" rebuts the accusation of Buttrick that expository preaching cages God and his work in historical narratives.[284]

For Keller too, the locus of authority for preaching is the written revelation of God, the Holy Scripture, not human-located experiences nor the human preacher with his dynamic personality and rhetoric. He affirms that the authority is God, but also spells out the responsibility of the preacher who has to do the exegesis, develop the sermon, and gauge the cultural situation of

---

283. Karl Barth asserts that a preacher must not "expound or present the truth of God aesthetically in the form of a picture, an impression, or an aesthetic evocation of Jesus Christ . . . If God himself wills to speak his truth, preachers are forbidden to interfere with any science or art of their own"; Barth, *Homiletics*, 47–48.

284. Buttrick, *Homiletics*, 18.

the listener to make the sermon relevant. Moreover, he agrees that a preacher must be consciously sensitive to the listeners' situations and context, which is another strength that emerges from Keller's understanding of expository preaching. Keller is particularly strong on the preacher's responsibility to unravel the deep hidden social worldviews and cultural baggage that conflict with the truth of the gospel. Keller is committed to penetrating and challenging otherwise invisible and culturally accepted worldviews.

Thus, looking at the various elements which Stott and Keller have laid out, expository preaching is not boring, irrelevant, or insensitive to people's experience as some have asserted. Further, as argued above, if expository preaching is sensitive to the contexts and real-life situations of people, then every text of the sermon will have a different implication and application according to the needs of the listeners. As such, the sermon will not become predictable but relevant. Moreover, it endorses the authority of the Scripture and spells out the role of human beings in this endeavour. Furthermore, their theology and method have comprehensively and effectively answered all the critiques levelled against expository preaching.

6.8 Recommendation of Expository Preaching for the Baptist Churches of Imphal

In the Baptist churches of Imphal, although topical preaching is more popular and frequently employed by the pastors and preachers, we discovered that not many churches have experienced spiritual vitality through this method, although there had been some few exceptions as we have discussed above, due to the presence of some pastors with charisma. So, it will be inappropriate to recommend this method to the churches on the ground of its dependence on exceptions.

However, regarding the expository method of preaching, it was found during the field survey that some of the senior pastors who confessed to not having charisma,[285] and some pastors who had joined the ministry towards the end of the period of research,[286] found the members growing in the knowledge of the Scripture as they employed the expository method. Their experience

---

285. Cf. 4.3.3.4.1.
286. Cf. 4.3.1.5.

reveals that even without charisma, oratory skill, and advanced capability, the expository preaching method can still make a visible impact.

Moreover, from what we have heard from Stott and Keller, expository preaching is not an impossible and complex task which only experts and professionals can carry out. At the most, it demands more time and discipline, and perhaps some basic training courses[287] for pastors, as they explore this new dimension and method of preaching. Although this method remains to be tested and employed in the majority of the pulpits of the Baptist churches of Imphal, it is a method we can recommend.[288]

6.9 Conclusion

In this chapter, we set out to answer the question, what is the best practice that could happen here? Towards that end, we surveyed two biblical books: Malachi and 1 Corinthians and analysed how Malachi and Paul dealt with the people of God in their unique spiritually lethargic situations and contexts. We then saw how both addressed their respective issues homiletically and how their approaches could be helpful for the Baptist churches in Imphal. We also evaluated the role and importance of charisma in both topical and expository preaching, a discussion arising from the previous chapter. After this, we deliberated on the theology and method of expository preaching by Stott and Keller, the two representative homileticians of this method. Then we listened to some of the critiques levelled against expository preaching by the NH school of thought and other evangelical homileticians. After this, a response and appraisal was made of the critiques of the NH. Then, as we evaluated the method and theology of expository preaching as endorsed by Stott and Keller, we simultaneously responded to the criticisms levelled against this school of preaching effectively. Although the advantage of expository preaching is enormous and we have recommended its usefulness and viability in the pulpits of the Baptist churches of Imphal, we have also mentioned some challenges of this homiletical method and the fact that this method remains largely untested.

---

287. We will talk about pragmatism, the issue of "What to do?" in the next chapter.
288. To know the homiletical-theological position of the researcher, see Appendix 1 (The Spectrum of Preaching).

CHAPTER 7

Pragmatic Task

7.1 Introduction

The preceding chapter on normative task addressed the question, what is the best practice that could happen here?[1] In this current chapter, we will strategize concerning the pragmatic task, which is the last of the four steps in the Practical Theology methodology we are employing in this research work.[2] In light of the descriptive data emerging from the people surveyed, its interpretation and the normative discussion in the previous chapters, this chapter will be guided by the question, "How might we respond in ways that are faithful and effective?"[3] The research findings inform us that, apart from some positive impact of good preaching on spiritual lives, the people also perceived a relationship between the negative impact of bad preaching and nominalism prevalent among some members of the Baptist churches of Imphal.

During the field research, some of the church members offered their opinions on several issues that could help in addressing the problem of nominalism in the church in the context of preaching. We will refer to them, develop their ideas, and make some recommendations to revitalise the pulpit and preaching ministry so as to bring about change,[4] which is to combat nominalism in the church.

---

1. Osmer, *Practical Theology*, 4.
2. Osmer, 173.
3. Osmer, 4, 10.
4. Osmer, 176, 10.

7.2 Discussions and Recommendations to Revitalise the Preaching Ministry in Order to Combat Nominalism

Here we will develop the comments already made by the church members on what they think will help a pastor's preaching ministry to combat nominalism. Although the discussion will begin from what the participants suggested, it will end with some recommendations arising out of our engagement with the issues.

7.2.1 Love the Word of God[5]

Some participants felt that a pastor or preacher must love and value the word of God far above other skills and activities the pastor loves doing in the pulpit, like entertaining people. They thought that the utmost concern of the pastor must be to seek the enlightenment of the people's minds with the word of God. They were convinced that if God's word is properly taught to the people, they can endure various existential tribulations. These participants claimed that going back to the basic doctrines of the Scripture and consistently nurturing the people with the biblical gospel, will not only sustain their spirituality, but rejuvenate and shield them from spiritual lethargy and nominalism.[6]

A logical corresponding question that could be raised then is, how far do pastors value the word of God? This takes us to the recommendation in relation to the issue of the theology of preaching (i.e. seek to first understand the theology of preaching before the methodology of preaching).

Over and above all other things, a pastor and preacher must come to terms with what God says and what the Scripture witnesses to the importance of speaking God's word. Stott is right when he said that the theology of preaching precedes the methodology of preaching,[7] because the form of preaching will be lifeless without anchoring on what God's word itself says about what God's word does. Clarity and conviction on what the Scripture says about his spoken word will drive pastors and preachers, with a renewed authority and urgency, and make them mount the pulpit to preach "as a dying man to

---

5. Unlike the original category, here the sub-heading has been divided into two components for convenience. The next one is "Preach the Biblical Gospel"; cf. 4.3.3.4.1.

6. Cf. 4.3.3.4.1.

7. Stott, *Between Two Worlds*, 92.

dying men."[8] It is true that emphasis must be given to learning homiletics, but merely acquainting themselves with techniques will not make them effective preachers. This is because a sound theology of preaching must lie at the root of the preaching enterprise – our personal understanding of God and his authoritative Word shapes our own preaching.[9] Although there are several truths about the theology of preaching we can derive from Scripture,[10] for our purpose, we will confine our discussion to just two of them. I recommend that pastors seek to understand and be convicted that God's word gives life and God's word and preaching build and grow the church.

7.2.1.1 Pastors Must Seek to Understand and Be Convicted That God's Word Gives Life

The Bible unambiguously begins with the statement, "In the beginning, God created . . ." in Genesis 1:1 and links it with, "then God said" in Genesis 1:3, to show that God's act of creation was through his spoken word.[11] It is clear from the creation narrative that everything God created before Adam and Eve was through his life-giving spoken word. In fact, if we look closer, even when God made human beings, God first spoke, "Let Us make man in Our image" (Gen 1:26) before he actually made male and female. In another creation account in Genesis 2:18, we also find God speaking, "It is not good for the man to be alone; I will make him a helper suitable for him," and then he made a woman from the "rib which he had taken from the man" (Gen 2:22). So, whatever God created was inseparable from his speech. His word brought forth life!

Then in the gospel account according to John in the NT, we find the prologue starting with "In the beginning was the Word and the Word was with God and the Word was God" (John 1:1), which evokes the creation narrative, and in John 1:3, he links whatever had been created by God in Genesis 1:1 to this Word who was in the beginning, and introduces this Word as Jesus in John 1:14. The Scripture clearly witnesses to the life-giving power of God's

---

8. Baxter, *Poetical Fragments*, 40 (https://libquotes.com/richard-baxter/quote/lbp7f7m); (cf. *Reformed Pastor*, Ch. 3, Sec. 1.2, for a similar expression); Green, "Very Brief Account," viii.

9. Stott, *Between Two Worlds*, 92–93.

10. For example: from God, Jesus, Holy Spirit, the Bible, church, history, the preacher and others.

11. When God made Adam (man) and Eve (woman), he made them with his hands, but he blew his breath into them, so that they became living beings. God speaks with his breath and so we can argue that when God created Adam and Eve, his breath is his speech.

spoken word; that his deeds and his words cannot be dichotomised, "that the two belong indissolubly together."[12] This is clearly demonstrated when Isaiah wrote that God's word will not fall to the ground without inevitably accomplishing its purpose (Isa 55:10–11).

The implication of the argument made above for preaching is huge – that God's word creates. As God spoke light into existence in Genesis 1:3, Jesus the Word of God also spoke stillness into the turbulent sea of Galilee[13] and life into the corpse of Lazarus.[14] Thus Darrell W. Johnson logically argues, "when the living God speaks, something always happens," and "when the preacher speaks God's speech, God speaks," "therefore, when the preacher speaks God's speech, something always happens."[15] In the vision of Ezekiel in chapter 37, we see how this is being played out. The prophet, by obeying God's word, spoke to the dry bones and was shocked to see the bones rattling, the sinews joining, the flesh growing, and the skin covering them. Then Ezekiel spoke to the four winds as God commanded him to, and he saw breath coming into lifeless bodies (Ezek 37:7–8, 9). Reflecting on this vision, Johnson asserts that it is not because of a preacher's skill of persuasive speech nor the "responsiveness of the dry bones," but because of the "nature of the word" that the decayed bones came to life.[16] The Bible confirms that "the word of God is living and active"[17] and in this light, Johnson expounds, "the word of God not only informs, it performs, it transforms."[18]

Therefore, as pastors and preachers prepare their sermons and stand to preach, they must be excited with the conviction that God's word is going to perform something new, hopeful that someone's broken and decayed life in

---

12. Stott, *Between Two Worlds*, 95.
13. Mark 4:35–40.
14. John 11:41–44.
15. Johnson, *Glory*, 10. *Contra*, there could be some people who question the validity of this phrase, "something always happens," although they may agree with the statement "something may happen sometimes." It is true that although the word of God has the capacity to bring life every time, the human heart, like the three other types of soils in the parable of the sower (Mark 4:1–9), can become inhospitable for the word of God to take root and grow. Johnson, *Glory*, 33–52. *Contra*, in Heb 1:3, we find that the word of God sustains everything. We see here the timelessness of God's sustaining power. In other words, something continues to happen. Cf. Johnson, *Glory*, 28–29.
16. Johnson, 25.
17. Heb 4:12.
18. Johnson, *Glory*, 25; cf. Dever and Gilbert, *Preach*, 24–30.

the congregation,[19] irreversible by any human power and authority, is going to receive a new lease of life. It is perceivable that if pastors and preachers in the Baptist churches of Imphal firmly hold on to this conviction, their valuation of the worth and authority of the word of God and their confidence in speaking God's word will change. Consequently, when the listeners listen to a sermon preached with this kind of conviction and passion, their attitude and receptivity may change for the better. Therefore, I recommend that pastors seek to understand and be convicted that God's word gives life before they mount the pulpit to preach any sermon.

7.2.1.2 Pastors Must Seek to Understand and Be Convicted That God's Word and Preaching Builds and Grows the Church

Stott argues that God's word brought the church into existence, as it had the universe. The church is not an agency to be relegated to antiquity, but God "maintains and sustains it (the Church), directs and sanctifies it, reforms and renews it through the same Word."[20] Stott is right because, historically, the church, the body of Christ, came into being after the apostles proclaimed God's word to the people.[21]

Even in the OT, we find that God's word and his call on Abraham brought life and made him the father of God's people,[22] and his obedience to God's call justified him.[23] The prophets Isaiah and Jeremiah also appealed to the people of God, to listen and obey God's word and repent, but the peoples' disobedience brought disaster upon Israel.[24] In fact, the people "went backward and not forward,"[25] for which act of disobedience they suffered exile.[26] Thus, obedience to God's word brought life, and disobedience to it brought about tragic consequences.

---

19. Here, the focus is more on metaphysics: spiritual, psychological, and emotional life. But in God's sovereign will and purpose, we cannot discount the possibility of physical healing.

20. Stott, *Between Two Worlds*, 109.

21. Acts 2:14, 41.

22. Gen 12; Gen 22; cf. Stott, *Between Two Worlds*, 110.

23. Gen 15:1–6; 22:15–18; Stott, 110.

24. Isa 1:2, 10, 19, 20; 42:18–25; 43:8; 48:17–19, 22; Jer 7: 24; 7: 23–26; cf. Jer 25:3–7; 32:33; 35:12–16; 44:1–6. There are other prophets who also made the same call to the people, but suffice it is to say that these two prophets represent our case adequately. Cf. Stott, 112–13.

25. Jer 7:24.

26. 2 Chr 36:15, 16.

In the NT, we find God's word coming to the people through the gospels and the epistles.[27] Stott accurately expounds that through the various writers of the NT, Jesus "instructs, admonishes, rebukes and encourages them, gives them promises and warnings, and appeals to them to listen, to believe, to obey, and to hold fast until he comes." It is also true that through God's faithfully expounded word, he "quickens, feeds, inspires, and guides his people."[28] Thus, we find evidence from Scripture that the church was given birth, sustained, and nurtured by God's word.

P. T. Forsyth boldly stated in the opening lines of his book, *Positive Preaching and the Modern Mind*, "It is, perhaps, an overbold beginning, but I will venture to say that with its preaching Christianity stands or falls."[29] We can argue from history that the sturdiness of the health of God's people lies "on their attentiveness to his Word."[30] While O. C. Edwards argues that preaching had helped accomplish mission movements of the church in history,[31] D. Martyn Lloyd-Jones claims, "The decadent periods and eras in the history of the Church have always been those periods when preaching had declined."[32] Stott also links "the low level of Christian living" to the "low level of Christian preaching" and asserts that "the pew is a reflection of the pulpit. Seldom if ever can the pew rise higher than the pulpit."[33] Dr. E. C. Dargan then validates the above arguments in his two-volume *History of Preaching*, covering the years of church history between AD 70 and 1900:

> Decline of spiritual life and activity in the churches is commonly accompanied by a lifeless, formal, unfruitful preaching, and this partly as cause, partly as effect. On the other hand, the great revivals of Christian history can most usually be traced to the work of the pulpit, and in their progress they have developed and rendered possible a high order of preaching.[34]

---

27. 1 Thess 2:13; 2 Thess 3.
28. Stott, *Between Two Worlds*, 113.
29. Forsyth, *Positive Preaching*, 3.
30. Stott, *Between Two Worlds*, 113.
31. Edwards, *History of Preaching*, 828–29.
32. Lloyd Jones, *Preachers and Preaching*, 24.
33. Stott, *Between Two Worlds*, 115.
34. Dargan, *History of Preaching*, 13. It is true that the role of preaching is absolutely vital, but there are others who may attribute revivals to the work of prayer also. So to single out

Thus, if pastors and preachers realised the enormity of this implication, they would not take their role lightly, because a malnourished church will breed spiritual disease. It is true that "if the Church is to flourish again, there is no greater need than a recovery of faithful, powerful, biblical preaching."[35] Therefore, I recommend that pastors must understand and be convicted that the preaching of God's word builds and grows the church.

7.2.2 Preach the Biblical Gospel Faithfully[36]

Another endorsement arising from the participants is the need to preach a biblical[37] gospel to address nominalism, although a few members are perceived to have taken offense when their pastors went back to the basics of the Christian faith – the birth, death, and resurrection of Jesus Christ. Perhaps these few listeners felt offended in wrongly thinking that Christians who are senior in age must move away from the elementary topics of sin and salvation, not realising that these subjects form the core of the Christian faith.[38]

The idea of the biblical gospel was described in different ways by the participants; while some take it as the whole counsel of God, some consider it as dealing with "creation, sin, and re-creation in Christ."[39]

What then constitutes a biblical gospel?[40] Are the ideas suggested by the participants exclusive and unrelated or are they facets of one common concept? We can argue that although they may not be able to articulate the idea succinctly, their opinions lead to the same thing, because the truth of the Bible is holistic, organic, and dynamic in nature; its message cannot be torn apart, as disjointed planks of wood, for every aspect is inseparably related.

In our discussion of the gospel, we concluded that the gospel is about the holy and sovereign act of God reconciling the world of sin and broken relationships through what Christ has done on the cross and his resurrection.[41] In

---

only preaching could be an overstatement. Cf. Waugh, *Flashpoints of Revival*, 3–40; Bartleman, *Azusa Street, passim*; Ward and Wild-Wood, *East African Revival, passim*.

35. Stott, *Between Two Worlds*, 116.

36. Cf. 7.2.1.

37. The adjective "biblical" is important because it clarifies that the good news is from the Bible and not any other type of good news.

38. Cf. 4.3.3.4.1.

39. Cf. 4.3.3.4.1.

40. A debate on what constitutes the gospel is discussed under 1.8.2 and 5.6.4.2.

41. Cf. 4.3.3.4.1; 5.6.4.2.

the light of that, I recommend that instead of preaching legalistic, moralistic, motivational, and inspirational sermons on what we should do and how we should live, pastors and preachers must instead preach what God has done in Christ, that we cannot do anything good and cannot live in this world of sin without the love of God, the saving grace of Christ, and the empowering and enabling presence of the Holy Spirit in our lives.

Perhaps some of the pastors and preachers' inadequate engagement with the gospel or their stereotyped gospel presentation[42] has made the people perceive its message to be irrelevant for their complicated lives today.[43] The gospel also tells us how we must live on earth as salt and light, having received God's salvation. It also teaches us how God operates in our world today, how he intervenes in our personal, societal, and churches' lives, although it may all seem mundane and routine. The gospel also warns us that the stakes are high and eternal if we disobey and ignore God's voice in our temporal existential decisions. It is therefore recommended that in a situation where people are overwhelmingly becoming spiritually shallow and nominal, a biblical gospel must be preached regularly in the churches.

7.2.3 Preach as a Shepherd with Love to God's People

Some pastors acknowledged that showing partiality among the members would be disastrous for the pastor's preaching ministry. Some of the listeners narrated that favouritism by some pastors made their sermons ineffective and unappetising. The participants were unanimous in their assertion that love is the soil in which a pastor's sermon must grow. They felt that if the pastors do not have genuine love, their advanced homiletical skill and profound preparation and delivery will fail to achieve its purpose.[44] A reasonable question is then, why do pastors and preachers preach without love. To engage with this question we will draw some lessons from the imagery of a shepherd as Jesus exposited.[45]

---

42. Jesus Christ came to die for sinners and if you believe and repent, you will go to heaven.

43. A section of Timothy Keller's talk "Gospel Shaped-Life" addresses how one can bring out the gospel message from different Bible texts for various issues of life; Keller, *Gospel-Shaped Life*.

44. Cf. 4.3.3.4.2.

45. John 10:11–15.

The Bible commands Christians to love one another as Christ loved them.[46] Beyond that, a pastor is expected to love his congregation,[47] "as Christ also loved the church and gave Himself up for her"[48] by purchasing her "with His own blood."[49] In the conversation between Christ and Peter, Peter was commanded to "Tend my (Christ's) lambs" (John 21:15), "Shepherd my (Christ's) sheep" (vs. 16) and "Tend my (Christ's) sheep" (vs. 17), in response to his confession that he loved Christ.[50] Christ, the "Chief Shepherd"[51] and the "great Shepherd"[52] expects every human under-shepherd of his flock to love them, and Peter exhorts that God's shepherds must feed God's people with great enthusiasm and affection.[53] But why are there accusations that some pastors feed God's word to his people without enthusiasm and love? There could be many factors for this to happen, but one possible reason could be that the pastors consider themselves as hirelings rather than as shepherds.

A shepherd and a hireling are different, as Christ carefully contrasted the two. He explained that hirelings are self-centred and only after self-enhancement, and so in the face of danger, sacrifice, and potential personal loss, they will abandon the sheep and flee. The truth is that they may not be concerned about the health and welfare of the sheep even during normal times. On the other hand, Jesus describes himself as "the good shepherd" who "lays down His life for the sheep" (John 10:11) and the good[54] shepherd who knows his own and his own know him (John 10:14). Jesus here describes the supreme love of the shepherd demonstrated by his supreme sacrifice. Consequently, a good shepherd has "an intimate knowledge" of his sheep, "sacrifices" and provides good "leadership," gives "protection and care" to the sheep,[55] feeds

---

46. John 13:34; 1 John 3:11, 18; 4:12–13; 1 Cor 16:14; Eph 4:2–3; 1 Pet 3:8–9; 4:8; Rom 13:8; Lev 19:18.

47. 1 Tim 1:5.

48. Eph 5:25. Paul here exhorts husbands to love their wives, but we can also argue that the theological implication extends to pastors to love Christ's church, as he gave himself up for her.

49. Acts 20:28.

50. John 21:15–17.

51. 1 Pet 5:4.

52. Heb 13:20–21.

53. 1 Pet 5:2.

54. Even shepherds can become selfish and self-seeking, so Jesus had to qualify himself as the "good" shepherd. See Tidball, *Builders and Fools*, 137.

55. Stott, *Between Two Worlds*, 116.

his flock with the most nourishing food, guides his sheep from going astray, guards his sheep from predators, and heals his sheep whenever they get injured and wounded.[56]

On the other hand, Paul vividly elucidates the futility of feeding God's flock (preaching) without love. He argues that even if he speaks or preaches "with the tongues of men and angels, but does not have love," then he will "become a noisy gong or a clanging cymbal."[57] Paul here rubbishes the entire enterprise of preaching in the context of the absence of love as its primary motive.[58] Similarly, Thomas Becon poignantly expresses the tragedy of preaching God's word without having a good shepherd's heart:

> As there cannot be a greater jewel in a Christian commonwealth than an earnest, faithful, and constant preacher of the Lord's Word, so can there not be a greater plague among any people than when they have reigning over them blind guides, dumb dogs, wicked wolves, hypocritical hirelings, popish prophets, which feed them not with the pure wheat of God's word, but with the wormwood of men's trifling traditions.[59]

In the light of what we have discussed above, it is clear that there is no alternative for pastors but to love their people genuinely to gain the right to be heard. Many members come to church expecting to hear a new revelation from God's word for their existential situation. But their ears and hearts will be blocked if the pastors are not genuine in their relationship with the members, even before they open their mouths to preach. To love is to demonstrate with one's actions and not necessarily to verbalise with one's words alone. If pastors desire to address the spiritual lethargy and nominal situation of the members, it is recommended that they must seek to love them before they enter the pulpit, and upon entering the pulpit, they must preach with love and urgency. Love is the soil where a pastor's preaching will invariably thrive.

---

56. Volbeda, *Pastoral Genius*, 79–85; cf. Tidball, *Skilful Shepherd*, 31; Tidball, *Builders*, 135.

57. 1 Cor 13:1.

58. In 1 Cor 13, Paul is talking about the indispensability of love, although God may have gifted different people with different spiritual gifts (1 Cor 12:28–29). So it is not particularly of preaching that Paul is speaking, although it could be theologically argued that the roles of "apostles," "prophets," and "teachers" involve preaching, as Paul's life demonstrated.

59. Becon, *Demands*, 598.

7.2.4 Pastors Should Be Humble, Prayerful, and Preach in the Power of the Holy Spirit, because They Hold the Key

A person with the virtue of humility is attractive.[60] One participant expressed that a preacher must not be arrogant but humble.[61] Similarly, another participant, without downplaying the importance of theological education and homiletical skills, argued that for the sermons to have deep and long-lasting impact and to address nominalism, they must stem out of a good prayer life,[62] an act that displays one's dependence on the power of the Holy Spirit[63] for the sermon's impact.[64]

We cannot make a general sweeping statement here, that the pastors of the Baptist churches in Imphal do not pray or depend on the work of the Holy Spirit; however, there could be some of them who do not pray, because of which some participants raised the issue. The Bible clearly teaches the role which the Holy Spirit plays in preaching, including the following: he gives the preacher the appropriate word during difficult times,[65] he enables one to proclaim "Jesus is Lord,"[66] he leads a preacher to a specific place to preach,[67] and he empowers the preacher.[68] Moreover, a preacher must cultivate the "humility of dependence,"[69] and must realise that ineffectiveness in preaching happens due to pride.[70] Thus, the Holy Spirit, prayer, and humility hold the key.

---

60. For Baxter, "meekness and condescension must mark" a preacher, and humility precedes sobriety; Baxter, *Reformed Pastor*, 30, 41.

61. Cf. 4.3.4.5.2.

62. Baxter claims that a pastor "does not preach heartily to his people who does not pray for them . . . we must prevail with God to mend both us and them, or else we are likely to be very unsuccessful in our work"; Baxter, *Reformed Pastor*, 30.

63. Before preachers preach in public they must "first employ themselves in holy exercises" and preach "as if possessed of the Holy Spirit" because only he changes the "carnal heart"; Baxter, 31, 88.

64. Cf. 4.3.3.4.3.

65. Matt 10:19–20.

66. 1 Cor 12:3.

67. Acts 11:15.

68. 1 Cor 2:4. The role of the Holy Spirit in preaching has been discussed in the previous chapters, so we will not elaborate here. Cf. 6.4.1.1; 6.4.2.1.

69. Stott, *Between Two Worlds*, 328.

70. Stott, 329–30.

Although it is true that preaching is both a divine and a human event,[71] it is clear that if our preaching is going to bring any lasting change, in the final analysis, it would be because of the Holy Spirit, the "unction from above" that touches, changes, and builds faith, and not because of any human skill.[72] It must therefore be reinforced that it is only God's Spirit who "convicts, converts, and changes."[73] Human arrogance and pride have no place in the divine economy.

To depend on the Holy Spirit is to acknowledge one's own limited ability, and at the same time, it gives an overwhelming confidence that through him something will happen, which the preacher in his own accord cannot perform. This realisation and hope come because of the preacher's posture of prayer, wherein a higher power intervenes and changes the status quo, like the jars of water mystically turned into wine.

I recommend that the pastors in the Baptist churches of Imphal evaluate where they stand in terms of their dependence on God, their own prayer lives, and their opinion about the power and relevance of the Holy Spirit in preaching before they attend any seminar or workshop on preaching.

7.2.5 Pastors Should Preach to the Believers' Context

Another important subject raised by the participants is the issue of relevance. They are of the opinion that preaching on global concerns without engaging with the existential issues relevant to the listeners' lives is worthless.[74] Unless pastors and preachers in the Baptist churches seek to know what and where the specific ailments of the people lie and treat them accordingly, mere textual expositions and generic applications may not help the cause of the people and revitalise their spirituality.[75] Below, we recommend some ways to help preachers address believers' contexts in their preaching.

It is recommended that, while preparing their sermons, pastors think of people who are not like themselves. There is an inherent tendency to interpret and apply the Scripture by operating from a default mode, influenced

---

71. Stott, *Contemporary Christian*, 211–12.
72. Lim, *Power in Preaching*, 21.
73. Lim, 21.
74. Cf. 4.3.3.4.4.
75. Cf. 4.3.3.4.4.

by one's particular context. To think of people who are not like oneself would mean taking into account factors like gender, age, and health issues; education and exposure; employment, work-related stress and income; marital status and family issues, children and grandchildren; tradition, culture, and worldviews; sociopolitical and economic situations of the society and others. After considering all these factors, one must consciously labour with how the interpreted text can be applied to these people in their specific situations. It is understandable that every sermon may not address every member's situation, but a conscious effort in the long run should aim to cover everybody's needs.

7.2.6 Pastors Should Put Personal Integrity above Their Sermon

The other important issue the participants raised is that of integrity. They claimed that a pastor's sermon is only as good as his personal life. Perhaps in a human society where people see rampant double-standard lives, they look for somebody as an anchor, to reassure themselves that the high ideals of Scripture are realistic and achievable. From mostly empty political speeches and promises[76] to news of deceit and scams in the marketplace, people generally feel trapped, not knowing whom to trust. So, when people come to the church and listen to the sermons, they may keenly observe the pastor's personal life to see if he can be trusted.[77]

In the light of what we have discussed about the negative impact of bad preaching,[78] the idea of integrity is complex and cannot be boxed in one singular idea. However, for a pastor who must preach regularly, his pulpit moment will be either vindicated or condemned by what he has spoken and how he has lived before the people sitting in the pews and standing in the courtyards. The incarnational concept of Jesus, being perfectly divine and perfectly human, exemplifies how pastors also must embrace soundness of speech and wholeness of conduct in their lives. Therefore, it is recommended that this virtue be held above the pastor's sermon itself, because if the vessel is soiled, the entire contents put into it will become unattractive and inedible.

---

76. Often politicians are understood to be those who do not keep their word and who are therefore untrustworthy.
77. Cf. 4.3.3.4.5.
78. Cf. 5.4.2.

7.2.7 The Church Should Provide Formal and Non-Formal Preaching Training for Their Pastors

On the practical front, some pastors acknowledged that the pastors of the Baptist churches in Imphal need more preaching training to build the church, because according to them, the rise and fall of the church arguably lies in the hands of the pastors.[79] This is also in accord with Mingthing's recommendation in his research, that we need to train our pastors and leaders in preaching in the theological colleges run by the Baptist churches of MBC and CBCNEI.[80] Although we have seen some initiatives on informal pastors' training in preaching already, we are yet to see a vibrant and systematic preaching training both in the non-formal and formal setting, especially with a vernacular medium of instruction as recommended by Mingthing, with or without certification. The formal setting means theological colleges and vocational training centres, and the non-formal setting would include seminars and retreat programmes (of varying length) with possible multiple cycles with or without any certification, in a local church context or by an organisation or even through a formal institution.

It was found in the survey that some of the pastors in the Baptist churches have not been to a theological college to be trained before they took up their pastoral responsibilities.[81] There might have been pastors who are exceptional orators and critical thinkers among them. Although it is not a spiritual requirement nor is it mandatory for every pastor to go through such a formal theological training programme to qualify as a pastor, the advantage of it cannot be undervalued. Proper training will give the pastors a holistic learning experience. In a formal training set-up, an individual can be adequately trained and oriented on several other theological subjects, including the basic science and art of preaching, in a systematic way for a longer period, depending on the curriculum[82] of the institution or the knowledge and experience of the concerned instructor.

---

79. Cf. 4.3.4.5.1.

80. Cf. notes 245, 255–56.

81. Cf. 4.3.1.2.2.

82. For example, some of the basic subjects could be: theology and history of preaching; how to handle the word (matters of exegesis, hermeneutics, genres and sermon structure); the world (engaging with the listeners' culture and tradition, worldviews and underlying philosophies); text to sermon (basic steps in sermon preparation); how to handle the self (issues concerning homiletics: voice, gesture, delivery and others) and the listeners (issues concerning

A few issues could be discussed here concerning formal training on preaching. After firmly grounding themselves on the theology of preaching, the students can then explore a variety of preaching methods, although they may develop a liking for a certain method. This will help them to adapt their methods in different preaching contexts. A longer training duration will also enable the individuals to digest and soak in their learning experiences and then apply and experiment with them either in the classroom context or a likeminded informal peer group setting. Further, the art of preaching is often caught rather than taught, therefore one can learn much by hearing how the teachers and fellow students preach in the seminary chapel throughout the year. If the church leadership is farsighted and intentional enough in building the church's spirituality, it would do them good to prepare their potential pastors by sending and supporting them financially to be trained in a theological college.

On the other hand, the purpose of the informal grassroot training programme is for on-the-job training purposes, for pastors who are already serving in the church, without former training (formal or informal) or those who want to join church ministry but cannot go to a theological college for training. Here, the subjects covered may not be as detailed as in a theological college setting, but repetition is the key. After attending the seminar or workshop (for example, Level-1), they would be required to come back after having implemented whatever they have learned, over a period of six to twelve months in their churches. After this, they would come back again to be trained for the next level (for example, Level-2), and this cycle would continue until they have completed the course of training.[83] In some cases, some of these trainees go on to become the vernacular trainers themselves for the other pastors.[84]

---

imagination and illustration, application, creativity and others); and methods (expository, topical, narrative, and others).

83. This is the model "Langham Preaching" follows around the world. "How Langham Preaching Works."

84. Langham Preaching believes in the multiplication of preaching trainers in the indigenous language. See, "How Langham Preaching Works."

Below is an illustration of how equipping preachers in a non-formal training programme can help build up individuals, the church, and the community.⁸⁵

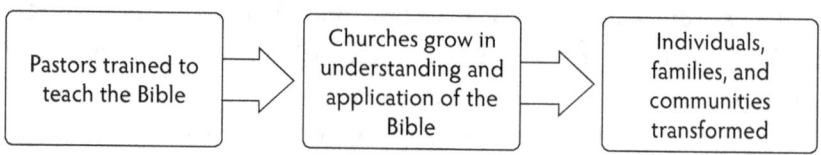

Figure 11: Equipping Preachers Has an Exponential Impact

Instead of preaching Sunday after Sunday without exposure to either formal or non-formal training programmes, it is recommended that pastors attend non-formal training programmes even if they cannot go to a formal theological college or vocational training centre. Such training programmes like that will help them learn about how to handle the word of God properly and win the attention of the listeners, which would positively impact the church's spirituality.

7.2.8 Pastors Must Extend Their Preaching Ministry beyond the Pulpit

One pastor shared his experience of needing to repeat his sermons in the homes of individuals who have not attended church on a particular Sunday, to avoid a lapse in understanding the next sermon in the series. Although such a practice may be suitable for his context, it may not be practical in churches with many members.⁸⁶ However, several participants were unanimous in their belief that preaching transcends mere pulpit ministry on a Sunday and therefore pastors must look out for every opportunity to preach on weekdays too. Moreover, many rightly felt that pastoral care and home visits ably assist the preaching ministry,⁸⁷ because they help connect the pastor with the

---

85. "Equipping Preachers Has an Exponential Impact." The other way to put this argument is, "When we have unhealthy pastors and unhealthy churches, unhealthy societies have nothing to rein in their disease." See, "Embracing Brokenness."

86. Cf. 4.3.4.5.3.

87. Baxter advocates a systematic approach to home visits for the sake of catechising. The purpose of his advocacy for home visits may be a little different, but the principle of meeting

personal life and struggles of the people and prepare them to come back to the church to listen to the pastor's preaching.[88]

The pulpit alone is not a pastor's preaching space, nor Sunday the only day for God's word to impact people's lives, as some of the participants have rightly elaborated.[89] It is therefore recommended that pastors take the time and make efforts to engage with the members throughout the week and not detach themselves until the next Sunday sermon. This will benefit both the pastor and the members in terms of mutual understanding, sermonic application, and better receptivity.

7.2.9 Deacons[90] Must Play a Pro-Active Role in the Pastor's Preaching Ministry

Several participants believed in the positive role deacons must play to make sure the pastor is faithful in preparing and delivering sermons. They argued that the deacons must be involved and alert to encourage pastors or gently remind them of their responsibility whenever necessary. They believed it would raise the standard of a pastor's preaching.[91] Moreover, they must be involved in the preaching ministry of the church, along with the pastor, by screening which guest speakers to give the pulpit to and whom to decline.

It is recommended that the deacons, without patronising the pastor and becoming authoritarian despots, must be pro-active to find out if the pastors' administrative and managerial responsibilities are distracting from their time of sermon preparation, and if possible, even to shoulder these responsibilities together to free the pastor to study and prepare the sermon.[92] Although it is the pastor who must prepare and deliver the word of God, in the absence of good preaching in the church, the deacons cannot remain indifferent and wash their hands as Pontius Pilate did to claim his innocence and to

---

the church members and the need to know their situations remain the same; Baxter, *Reformed Pastor*, 67.

88. Cf. 4.3.4.5.3.

89. Cf. 4.3.4.5.3.

90. In other church contexts, they would be the elders or lay leaders who have responsibility for the spiritual oversight of the church.

91. Cf. 4.3.4.5.4.

92. Cf. 4.3.4.5.4.

symbolically demonstrate his non-partisan approach to the crucifixion of Jesus Christ.[93]

Moreover, it is recommended that the deacons must work with the pastor as his homiletical advisory team, to annually plan out the sermon series for the year, by helping the pastor see the existential situation, needs and struggles, cultural prejudices, society, culture, and worldviews of the people. Accordingly, the pastor can plan what books of the Bible to preach from in order to address the problems of the people.[94]

Further, it is recommended that the deacons must evaluate the sermons of pastors periodically by affirming what they have done well and encouraging them on where to do better. Such exercises would elevate the pastor's sermons because the sermons would become more relevant and meet the people where they are. Besides, in a situation where the pastor may be new to a particular church, the deacons' feedback could help the pastor discern what subjects, doctrines, and books the congregation have never been taught before or need revisiting after a long time.

7.3 Conclusion

In this chapter, based on the recommendations of the participants on what they think will help a pastor's preaching ministry to combat nominalism, we have engaged with and developed their ideas towards several pragmatic steps. These pragmatic recommended steps which have been discussed in detail are:

i. Pastors must seek to understand and be convicted that God's word gives life.
ii. Pastors must seek to understand and be convicted that God's word and preaching builds and grows the church.
iii. Pastors should preach the biblical gospel faithfully.
iv. Pastors should preach as a shepherd with love for God's sheep.
v. Pastors should be humble and prayerful, and preach in the power of the Holy Spirit, because they hold the key.
vi. Pastors should preach to the believers' context.

---

93. Matt 27:24.

94. Cf. Lama, who talks about the importance of knowing the multi-layered contexts and situations of the people to preach effectively in India's North East; 2.2.2.

vii. Pastors should put personal integrity above their sermon.
viii. The church should provide formal and non-formal preaching training for the pastors.
ix. Pastors must extend their preaching ministry beyond the pulpit.
x. Deacons must play a proactive role in the pastor's preaching ministry.

CHAPTER 8

Conclusion

8.1 Introduction

The current research work[1] explored the impact of preaching on the spiritual lives of the people in the Baptist churches of Imphal. To examine this topic, several research questions were formulated. The primary research question was, "What do people perceive to be the effects of preaching on the spiritual life of the members of the Baptist churches of Imphal, 2000–2015?" There were also six subsidiary questions.[2]

8.2 Summary

The researcher employed the qualitative research methodology, with an eclectic design; a combination of phenomenological approach and the four steps of Osmer's Practical Theology. To collect the data, the researcher employed semi-structured interviews and open-ended questions for the questionnaires. A total of twenty participants were interviewed, including pastors, church leaders, and church members. The researcher identified six pastors and three church members for the purposive sampling, then the snowball sampling method helped in identifying other participants. As for the questionnaire, a total of thirty questionnaires were despatched for the pilot survey work, out

---

1. "An examination of preaching in the Baptist churches of Imphal city, 2000–2015, and its impact on the spiritual life, with special reference to nominalism."
2. Cf. 1.8.2.

of which fifteen of them were returned. Subsequently, after reworking them, a total of 170 questionnaires were sent out to the members of fifteen churches, out of which seventy questionnaires were returned.

The literature review unit established the theoretical framework of the research work, and was categorised under three broad headings: The Effect of Preaching; Nominalism; and Nominalism and Preaching.

The research also explored the arrival of Christianity, church growth, and the preaching movement in Manipur, discussing both the contribution of the missionaries and the roles of the indigenous preachers. It traced the effect of Christian preaching on the church growth of Manipur during the first half and the second half of the twentieth century, especially analysing the homiletical focus of the MBC leadership in various eras.

In the next chapter, "Description of the Data," the researcher "bracketed" his bias and prejudices, and described what the participants felt, experienced, and thought about their personal spiritual lives and the situation of their churches, after having listened to the preaching of the pastors and preachers in their churches during the research period.

The subsequent chapter, "Interpretation of the Data," interpreted the positive and negative impact of preaching among the church members and the society. Although the empirical research yielded much information and was documented in the descriptive chapter, our engagement in this chapter was primarily guided by the research questions[3] in relation to the literature review.

The chapter "Normative Task" examined the issue of spiritual lethargy by referring to Malachi and 1 Corinthians and saw how they addressed the problem homiletically. We argued they did so by means of prophetic and expository preaching.

In addition, since the participants recommended expository preaching to combat nominalism, we explored John Stott and Timothy Keller's theology and methodology of preaching. We also explored the advantages and challenges of expository preaching, and analysed some critiques levelled against expository preaching by the New Homiletic school and other evangelical thinkers. This was followed by our own recommendation of the expository preaching method for the Baptist churches in Imphal to combat nominalism.

---

3. Cf. 1.8.

In the chapter "Pragmatic Task," we developed the suggestions of the participants, and made some recommendations to strengthen the preaching ministry to combat nominalism.

8.3 A Critical Self-Evaluation and Critique

In this section, a brief self-evaluation and critique will be made on some of the strengths and weaknesses of the whole research project.

8.3.1 Weaknesses

First, it was identified that the situation of the churches of the Meitei and tribal communities have different challenges. While the Meitei community has more seekers and new believers, the tribal community has more believers who were born into a Christian family. It is felt that the interview and questionnaire questions could have been nuanced differently, as both groups of people have their unique set of challenges and experiences. The researcher felt that his questions were more generic[4] and therefore needed more precision in such a context.

Second, instead of dispatching questionnaires written in English to the Meitei community, it would have served the purpose better had they been translated into *Meiteilon* (Manipuri language) for some church members who were not comfortable with English-language questionnaires.

Third, it was discovered that once the questionnaires were distributed to the church members, a specific date for collection was preferable, without an extension of deadline. Although a few participants benefited from the deadline extension, perhaps more questionnaires would have been returned had the deadline not been extended, because some of the participants had misplaced the questionnaires.

Fourth, a case study approach would have been a good option because it would have helped the researcher to speak to several people from the same church and diagnose their issues better. Doing research of this nature with several churches is difficult, as one or two samples of interviews from each church may not necessarily give a holistic picture of the church under investigation, although their experiences may be genuine.

---

4. Cf. Appendices 2 and 9.

Fifth, the researcher is of the view that the sample size could have been larger. But this remains a debatable issue because as mentioned above, there are people who think that even lesser interviews (without questionnaires) than what the current research had, would have sufficed for the PhD programme.[5]

Sixth, some of the questions could have been more simply worded. Perhaps the reason why some did not answer directly and could not explain their thoughts was because the questions were not simple enough for them and they could not easily understand what the researcher was asking.

Seventh, the selection of participants for the semi-structured interview through the snowball sampling method brought some disadvantages, although it began with a purposive sampling method. All the pastors in the Baptist churches in Imphal who formed the primary interviewees were male and they suggested more males than females. Moreover, despite attempts to include some female voices, it could not be done because some women preferred to respond in the questionnaire form. There were several female participants who responded actively and positively in the questionnaire data collection and their inputs were rich. However, it must be acknowledged that more gender representation would have further enriched the research work and perhaps there would have been some variations in the responses and findings.

If the researcher were to do this all over again, he would try to avoid these shortcomings. However, despite having pointed out some inadequacies, the researcher made every attempt to be faithful to the eclectic research design which was chosen for this work and made every attempt to maintain academic integrity. Below we will discuss some strengths of this research work.

8.3.2 Strengths

First, apart from Mingthing's MTh thesis in 1977 that explored how preaching had developed the church (among the Tangkhul tribe in Manipur)[6] and how preaching had impacted the members' spiritual lives from a quantitative research viewpoint among lay Catholics,[7] none according to my research had examined the effect of preaching in members' spiritual lives, by employing a

---

5. Cf. 1.14.1.5.
6. Cf. 2.2.3.2.
7. Cf. 2.2.3.1.

qualitative and practical theological approach. This current research engages with and follows up on Mingthing's work, but its scope covers various other tribes in Manipur. This research therefore fills that gap and explores the effect of preaching on the spiritual lives of the members. Hopefully, this work will trigger an interest in the study of preaching among future researchers from the North East of India, particularly from Manipur.

Second, apart from Kengoo's MTh thesis in 2007 that brought to light the problem of nominalism among the youth in MBC,[8] the researcher unfortunately has not come across any other academic work that engaged with nominalism within the MBC. As discussed in the literature review, Kengoo proposed an emphasis on discipleship to address the issue. Moreover, Pongen also discussed nominalism among the Ao churches in Mokokchung, Nagaland, by giving a pastoral theological response. We also found that Edre explored the phenomenon of nominalism in the context of church membership among the Bunia churches in DR Congo. But none have discussed how to counter nominalism from a homiletical point of view as this research has done. Further, it is an in-depth study of fifteen churches and is inclusive of both the clergy and laity from the Baptist churches in Imphal.

Third, Mingthing talked about the issue of preaching on church development, while Kengoo dealt with nominalism; however, no one had studied nominalism from a preaching point of view. Hence, this research bridges the gap between the two and raises a new concern on their relationship, within MBC. In fact, as the literature review evidenced, this research could provide an impetus for a new discussion on this field.

Fourth, the issue of nominalism within MBC is an "open secret."[9] During the research, the participants openly shared their experiences and perceptions on the issue. Subsequently, the views of the people have enriched the academic discussion on the subject and have led to an attempt to describe and define nominalism from a contextual viewpoint by building upon the earlier discussions of the Lausanne movement.

Fifth, this research has helped in identifying the prevalent methods of preaching in the Baptist churches, along with their strengths and weaknesses.

---

8. Cf. 2.4.1.5.

9. Secret because people avoided its discussion, and open because many people are aware of its existence.

Hence, this can help pastoral trainers plan and prepare their materials and curricula better.

Sixth, this research opens up the opportunity for pastors to make an honest and critical self-assessment of their own preaching ministry in order to grow as a preacher.

Seventh, it brought to light how the resistant majority community (Meitei), who had once been repulsive to the Christian faith and community, have become more open after seeing change in the lives of derelicts, alcoholics, drug addicts, immoral people, and others in society through the preaching and pastoral ministry. Although for some this openness is still covert, restrained, and measured, a gradual movement is seen.

Eighth, this research engaged with Malachi and 1 Corinthians and observed how Malachi and Paul combated spiritual lethargy and nominalism in their own contexts through prophetic and expository preaching and drew lessons on how the pastors of the Baptist churches could do the same.

Ninth, this research engaged with some homileticians who espoused the expository method of preaching and made a case to employ this method as recommended by several participants in the Baptist churches in Imphal, as a response to counter nominalism.

Tenth, as Eddie Gibbs of the Lausanne movement mentions that his remark (churches have become "an incubator of nominality" due to bad preaching) should act as a stimulus to the discussion of nominalism and preaching, this research evaluated their relationship from the MBC churches' context and found that bad preaching can lead churches to become incubators of nominalism and recommended ten steps to combat it homiletically.

8.4 Contribution to the Field of Practical Theology

Here are some of the findings[10] of the research that examined the impact of preaching on the spiritual lives of the members of the Baptist churches in Imphal, 2000–2015, and the contribution of the research to the church and the field of practical theology.

---

10. For more see 8.3.2; others are in chapter 4.

8.4.1 Baptist Churches in Imphal

The research began with the purpose statement to explore if the pastors, church leaders, and members in the fifteen Baptist churches in Imphal are aware of the effect of preaching on the spiritual lives of the people. The findings have established that these two variables are invariably interconnected. Further, it also found that they are aware of the presence of nominalism in the churches. Consequently, this research has recommended ten steps for the Baptist churches in Imphal to combat it homiletically and they have the potential of being transferred to other contexts that are facing a similar challenge of nominalism.[11]

8.4.2 Practical Theology

(1) The research revisited the understanding of nominalism as discussed by the Lausanne movement, and redefined it from the contextual viewpoint, shaped by the findings of the research.

(2) The research began with the possibility of contributing to a functional theory, subject to the findings of the research, that preaching a clear expository and biblical gospel will impact the spiritual lives, ethics, and commitment of the people positively, thus combating nominalism. The findings proved the assumption to be correct that nominalism could be combated if there is more systematic expository preaching in the churches.

8.5 Further Recommendations for Future Research

For further research on this subject, I recommend that consideration be given to the following issues:

- A survey on the historical significance of effective preaching for revival movements.
- A historical enquiry on the impact of preaching on seekers coming from the majority community (Meitei) in Manipuri society.

---

11. Cf. 7.2 and 7.3.

- A critical historical mapping of homiletical methods employed in the Baptist churches from the time of the pioneering missionaries to the contemporary period.
- A critical assessment of the role of preaching in mitigating, building, and restoring communal harmony and reconciliation between tribes and communities divided by ethnic conflicts in Manipur.
- An exploration of the role of narrative preaching in a society marked by oral tradition and culture to combat nominalism.

8.6 Summary and Conclusion

This chapter summarised the entire research work, briefly depicting what and how the research was done in different stages. We also made a critical self-evaluation and critiqued the current research work, assessing its weaknesses and strengths. Finally, based on what the researcher encountered and experienced during the research period, some recommendations for future research have been proposed.

APPENDIX 1

The Spectrum of Preaching

1. Introduction

Preaching was a vibrant topic for discussion in the past as well as in the present. Any attempt to define preaching is an almost impossible task, because of the existence of various schools of thought favouring different methods of preaching in different contexts.[1] In this section, instead of defining what preaching is, an attempt will be made to describe and categorise the various viewpoints of preaching in a spectrum, shown in figure 12 on pages 328 and 329.[2] These are viewpoints and not eras in history.

I will survey the views of various homileticians and theologians of preaching and after all the viewpoints are discussed, I will locate myself under one of them. The primary question in focus here is, "What is preaching?"[3] Although this topic could be taxonomised under various headings, the present survey will be done under the following headings: Preaching is – Individual experience-driven communication; Text-driven communication; Context-driven communication; and Contextually applied theodrama. In each of the

---

1. G. Isaiah has compiled various definitions on preaching. Cf. Isaiah, *Preach the Word*, 20–21.

2. Figure 12 highlights the spectrum of preaching; a spectrum provides more flexibility, against a taxonomical arrangement which is more rigid.

3. There is a project called "Homiletical Theology Project" at the Boston University School of Theology under David Schnasa Jacobsen, PhD. Albeit its usefulness to the field of homiletics addressing various "theological intersections," it does not directly relate to my work, as mine surveys the spectrum (viewpoints) of preaching answering the question, what is preaching? "Homiletical Theology Project."

viewpoints, the theological position of two representative homileticians or theologians of preaching will be analysed. The main purpose of this section is to make a theoretical epistemic base to understand homileticians' diverse perceptions on what preaching is.

Before the discussion begins on the first viewpoint on preaching – preaching as individual experience-driven communication – a brief background study of the Enlightenment era will illuminate this viewpoint and some others as well. The Enlightenment ideology prided itself on the supremacy of reason above faith and questioned the rationale of the "ultimate reality."[4] Rationalists like Immanuel Kant believed that,

> *Enlightenment is mankind's exit from its self-incurred immaturity. Immaturity* is the inability to make use of one's own understanding without the guidance of another. *Self-incurred* is this inability if its cause lies not in the lack of understanding but rather in the lack of the resolution and the courage to use it without the guidance of another.[5]

This period dealt a devastating blow to the authority of the church, as the scriptural truth which is "eternal, unchanging, and authoritative" was questioned, as though "Christian truth was . . . something which could be subject to critical investigation as if it were a work of art."[6] As far as preaching is concerned, it is argued that "any part of the Scripture that presented problems . . . original sin, eternal punishment, or predestination" was avoided, citing the problem of "authenticity."[7] It was also revealed that most of the sermons in

> this school took to "moral preaching." Sometimes they changed the language of the Bible in order to make it more rational. For conversion or regeneration, they spoke of amendment of life; for

---

4. Larsen, *Company of the Preachers*, 346 (emphasis original).

5. Kant, "Answer to the Question," 58 (emphasis original). It must also be said here that the tradition of giving authority to reason started way back during the time of Spinoza and Descartes who "had ceased to presuppose revelation and had begun to depend on human reason alone"; see Edwards, "History of Preaching," 212.

6. Byrne, *Religion and Enlightenment*, x. Christian truth should be critically investigated, questioned, and deliberated, but cannot be treated like an art piece crafted by an artist and critiqued with subjective opinions.

7. Schmidt, *What Is Enlightenment*, 7; see also Larsen, *Company of the Preachers*, 328; Birstsch, "Christian as Subject," 317–26.

justification of forgiveness on condition of repentance; for the Holy Spirit, of the exercise of the higher reason; for the atonement of Christ, of the spirit of sacrifice which He has taught us by His example, and so on.[8]

Although preaching in this era was against Christian orthodoxy, not all protestant preachers were guilty, though the numbers were small.[9] There were two ways Christians reacted to the onslaught of the Enlightenment ideology – the liberal modernist and conservative modernist viewpoints. While liberal modernists adjusted their theological position against the assault of the enlightenment ideology, conservative modernists reacted against the adjusted theological position of the liberal modernists as well as against the enlightenment ideology. We begin with the liberal modernist viewpoint – Preaching as individual experience-driven communication.

2. Preaching as Individual Experience-Driven Communication

A theology of preaching that is "individual experience-driven" considers revelation as individual "experiential expressivism."[10] In this viewpoint, preaching is seen as an individual human event where the preaching style leans towards humanistic affiliations. Its locus of authority in preaching is universal individual experience. Regarding the nature of the preaching event, it is human communication focused on universal morals. Below are two theologians of preaching we will engage with.

2.1 Friedrich Schleiermacher (1768–1834)

Alister McGrath states that the liberal modernism period began when people like Friedrich Schleiermacher found the need to "relate Christian faith to the human situation . . . amidst a growing realization that Christian faith and theology alike required reconstruction in the light of modern knowledge."[11]

---

8. Ker, *Lectures on the History of Preaching*, 247.

9. Preachers like Charles Simeon and Charles Spurgeon were some outstanding exceptions during this era.

10. This expression is credited to George Lindbeck; Lindbeck, "George Lindbeck on Postliberal," 67.

11. McGrath, *Christian Theology*, 101; see also Forsyth, *Positive Preaching*, 210.

So by "reacting against the aridity of reason," people began to lean towards the "epistemological significance of human feelings and emotion."[12] For Schleiermacher, "feeling" is another name for religion; as he states, "feeling of absolute dependence, we call *aesthetic* Religion."[13] On preaching, he states that it is "chiefly the utterance and presentation which have a directly rousing effect,"[14] awakening in a listener "the immediate religious self-consciousness."[15] Self-consciousness is at the centre point of Christianity, as he argues, "for as self-conscious individuals we can only have the God-consciousness."[16] On the role of the Holy Spirit in preaching he states more generally, "The Holy Spirit can never be inactive, and therefore can never be tied in its [sic] activities to definite times; rather it moves each believer to do whatever comes to hand" even "with religious influence and communication."[17] He also believes that preachers communicate "the Ministry of God's Word" through "the attitude of spontaneity . . . by self-communication" to the listeners who "maintain chiefly the attitude of receptivity."[18]

Schleiermacher's effort to defend the reasonableness of the Christian faith during the onslaught of the Enlightenment period is admirable. As human beings, made of flesh and blood, we cannot discount the importance of our experience and feelings, and Schleiermacher laboured hard to connect Christian theology and preaching with our existential experiences because he felt that is the context in which we could truly understand God and his love. Although his contributions are widely accepted by many, I differ with his viewpoints for several reasons.

Critiquing Schleiermacher, Daniel Blanche concedes that "it is terrifying" to see that Schleiermacher believes that the "preacher has a stronger consciousness of God than the other members of the congregation" given the fact that "the preacher and the congregants all stand on a continuum with Christ."[19] Second, Blanche critiques Schleiermacher's recommendation

---

12. McGrath, 96.
13. Schleiermacher, *Christian Faith*, 42; cf. Christian, *Friedrich Schleiermacher*, 29.
14. Schleiermacher, 87.
15. Schleiermacher, 87.
16. Schleiermacher, 719.
17. Schleiermacher, 614.
18. Schleiermacher, 611.
19. Blanche, "Schleiermacher and Preaching."

to preach the Bible and one's "own inner experience"; that for him, "it is not the Christ recorded in the Bible who really matters; it is the Christ present in the preacher's own heart that is important."[20]

Evaluating Schleiermacher, first, although he acknowledges the role of the Holy Spirit in a believer's life in general, he does not specify how the Holy Spirit causes the "rousing effect" while preaching. Moreover, although Schleiermacher says that preaching must aim at awakening in the congregants an "immediate religious self-consciousness," he again does not clearly spell out the role of the Holy Spirit,[21] which then makes preaching more of a human effort. Second, his understanding of preaching as aiming to achieve a "rousing effect" in the listeners seems too shallow and short-sighted – emotions can be deceptive. Third, he projects preachers as more God-conscious than listeners and the preaching task as the effort of human beings sharing their experiences,[22] not the word of God. This conviction poses the danger of canonising human experience no matter how spiritual they may be, because ultimately, the source of revelation is not from human experience but the Scripture alone.

2.2 Rudolf Bultmann (1884–1976)

Rudolf Bultmann served as the professor of New Testament (NT) at Marburg University. His contribution to the study of the New Testament is epochal, especially with reference to the hermeneutical methods of "presupposition" and "demythologizing." Jeffrey Jon Richards recommends that to understand Bultmann's preaching better, an engagement with his hermeneutics will be helpful.[23] Here for our purpose, we will discuss an aspect of his hermeneutics – demythologising. Bultmann argues that,

---

20. Blanche, "Schleiermacher and Preaching."

21. There are two schools of thought with two extreme views about Schleiermacher's view on the Holy Spirit. The first group is supported by people like B. Holm who argue that Schleiermacher depreciated the role and concept of the Holy Spirit; see Holm, "Work of the Spirit," 100. The second group believed that Schleiermacher emphasised heavily the concept of Holy Spirit, although not obviously; see Barth, *Dogmatics in Outline*, 66.

22. Peter did share his experience on the Day of Pentecost and the disciples also did the same in Acts 15, but the difference is that while Peter and the disciples shared what they experienced in relation to the power they received through their relationship with God and his Holy Spirit, Schleiermacher's focus is only on the human existential experience bereft of God's power.

23. Richards, "Hermeneutics and Homiletics," 35.

to de-mythologize is to reject not Scripture or the Christian message as a whole, but the world-view of Scripture, as the world-view of a past epoch . . . retained in Christian dogmatics and in the preaching of the church. To de-mythologize is to deny that the message of the Scripture and of the Church is bound to an ancient world-view which is obsolete.[24]

Bultmann rejects as corrupted the cosmological three-storied worldview of the Bible (earth, heaven, and hell) and argues that preaching based on it is scandalous and unscientific and therefore objectionable to modern listeners.[25] He argues that preaching about miracles is unacceptable because reason cannot explain its phenomenon. Simply put, he argues that the Bible operates with the "ancient world-view" which is "mythological," whereas, modern man is directed by a "scientific" temperament.[26] Bultmann explains that demythologising is simply separating the kernel of God's word from the husk of mythology, influenced by a "by-gone world-view."[27] He also clarifies that demythologizing is not "rationalising the Christian message" for the "incomprehensibility of God lies not in the sphere of theoretical thought but in the sphere of personal experience."[28] Elaborating his existential argument, Bultmann says that God must be understood not in "what God is in himself, but how he acts with men," as in a human relationship with friends where the experience of "love and faithfulness" is experienced. It is this mystery, says Bultmann, that "faith is interested" in and preaching must address.[29]

On faith, Bultmann says that it is "both the demand of and the gift offered by preaching. Faith is the answer to the message."[30] On preaching, Bultmann says that it is a "personal address. It is authoritative address, the address of the Word of God,"[31] "true Christian preaching is . . . the call of God through the mouth of man" that "demands belief. It is its characteristic paradox that

---

24. Bultmann, *Jesus Christ*, 35.
25. Bultmann, "New Testament and Mythology," 3; cf. Bultmann, *Jesus Christ*, 36.
26. Bultmann, *Jesus Christ*, 37–38.
27. Bultmann, 43.
28. Bultmann, 43.
29. Bultmann, 42–43.
30. Bultmann, 40–41.
31. Bultmann, "General Truths."

in it we meet God's call in human words."[32] Ronald E. Sleeth also says that for Bultmann, "the salvation-occurrence was in the act of preaching and only there."[33]

Sleeth elucidates, "Bultmann's understanding of preaching as God's Word spoken in the mouth of the preacher is followed naturally by what is now called Word-Event theology." That, when the word of God is preached, an "Event" is created, "not about the Christian faith, but the Christian faith itself. That is, preaching is not talking about the Gospel, it is the Gospel."[34] As such, for Bultmann, "preaching is not the simple communication of facts . . . reporting of a discovery," not "teaching or instruction,"[35] not doctrinal enlightenment, nor ethical and therapeutic treatment.[36] Rather, "Preaching means a declaration which speaks directly to the hearer and challenges him to a specific reaction." Christian preaching then is a declaration of the "*kerygma*, the heralding or *evangelion*, the message . . . *the call of God*"[37] for the people to respond in obedience based on their existential reality.[38]

Then Bultmann asks, what "content" does the message "consist" of? He asks, if "true Christian preaching would be the *communication of a historical fact*?"[39] He avers that simply preaching the "story of Jesus' life and deeds" would be just giving a "historical report." But "a genuine preaching preaches, 'Jesus Christ is Lord,' . . . It means not basing one's life on what is temporary"[40] but eternal, and placing before the listener the choice to respond.[41]

---

32. Bultmann, "Preaching: Genuine and Secularized," 237. As the idea of spectrum suggests flexibility, Bultmann leans towards a "divine-human" event in preaching. More of this concept will be discussed in the fourth category.

33. Sleeth, "Bultmann," 154. See Franz Peerlinck, *Rudolf Bultmann also Prediger*, n.p.

34. Sleeth, 155.

35. Bultmann, "Preaching," 236.

36. Bultmann, 240.

37. Bultmann, 236; see also Bultmann, *Existence and Faith*, 168; Ladd, "What Does Bultmann Understand," 91.

38. Bultmann, "Preaching," 238.

39. Bultmann, 240.

40. Bultmann, 241; see also Ashcraft, *Rudolf Bultmann*, 44–45.

41. Bultmann, "Preaching," 242.

On the role of the Holy Spirit in preaching, Bultmann says that he is the "Spirit in whose working Jesus' revelation is continued," that a preacher proclaims in his power.[42]

Bultmann's contribution to the church and preaching is immense. He is held in great esteem by many because of his effort to make the biblical truth palatable to modern readers and in making theology focus on existential realities. However, he is not without his detractors. Below are some critiques of his hermeneutics that directly influence his theology of preaching.

Bultmann is critiqued by Clark Pinnock for "twisting the Scriptures to bring them into line with his own extrabiblical presuppositions." Kerygma is forced "to become what his secular worldview requires it to be," without first accepting it as "factual and true independently." Pinnock also argues that one cannot interpret and preach the New Testament "purely" in an "existentialist manner."[43] Miller and Grenz also critique Bultmann that instead of "proclaiming" Christ's accomplishment in biblical history "in the ministry, cross, and resurrection of Jesus Christ, Bultmann defined it in terms of what individuals experience in their own personal confrontation with existence," which in reality has no substance.[44] On the historical Jesus, D. A. Carson, Douglas J. Moo, and Leon Morris argue that Bultmann has peeled off much of the mysterious and supernatural elements which are incomprehensible to the human mind from the NT "until there was almost nothing left."[45]

Bultmann's understanding of the word of God and the role of the Holy Spirit in preaching is laudable, although a deeper clarification on the role of the Holy Spirit in what he does in the listeners and the spoken word is needed. Along with some good contributions, there are areas where Bultmann's hermeneutics is problematic. First, although Bultmann clearly issues a disclaimer that demythologising is not rationalising the Christian message and doing away with the mystery element in Christian faith, he leaves room for doubt by his view that modern man does not accept miracles and anything that does not fall in line with reason and science. Second, Bultmann prioritises the need to engage with human experience above the claims of the

---

42. Bultmann, *Gospel of John*, 560.
43. Pinnock, *Tracking the Maze*, 115.
44. Miller and Grenz, *Introduction to Contemporary*, 51–52.
45. Carson, Moo, and Morris, *Introduction to the New Testament*, 51; cf. Greidanus, *Modern Preacher*, 33; Toon, *End of Liberal Theology*, 192.

historicity of the word of God, a sequence that should have been reversed, given that Scripture is a revelation from God. Third, although he does not say that Jesus never existed in history, his unwillingness to link the Christ of faith to the Jesus of history and his effort to demythologise the historicity of Jesus's birth, death, and resurrection by calling them myths sinks the very basis of his preaching, because one cannot have the fruits of faith, love, and salvation without the roots of incarnation – Christ's gruesome atoning death and his miraculous resurrection.

3. Preaching as Text-Driven Communication

The theology of preaching in this section is the other response against the Enlightenment and one that disagrees with the liberal modernist viewpoint. A preaching theology that puts revelation or the word of God as the authority in preaching and gives little or no attention to the context would come under the conservative modernist category. Below is a brief background.

This category's philosophical background would consider "revelation as information." Harold Lindsell, one of the voices of this theological framework argues that God has revealed himself completely through the Bible and that it is the "sourcebook" of all "information."[46] In this category, preaching would be seen as a divine event where the preaching style would lean towards being more deductive and text driven, and the locus of authority in preaching being revelation. As far as the nature of the preaching event is concerned, in this category, preaching is viewed as a divine communication, where exegesis plays a prominent role without or little emphasis on application. There are several homileticians who would fit under this:

3.1 Karl Barth (1886–1968)

Knowing Karl Barth's context, where he lived, and how he theologised will be helpful in analysing his theology of preaching. Barth learned his theology under the great liberal theologians – Friedrich Schleiermacher and Wilhelm Hermann – but later became the leading voice against them.[47]

---

46. Lindsell, *Incomparable Word*, 130–32.
47. Rogers and McKim, *Authority and Interpretation*, 406.

Barth was antagonistic to the Enlightenment ideology and the liberal modernist theology that truncated the orthodox Christian theology. Moreover, he was against Hitler and his ideology. Barth saw Hitler as the product of a liberal church which no longer had the capacity to oppose evil.[48] And so Barth's theology in general and his theology of preaching in particular is a welcome correction to the liberal theological position.

For Barth, the locus of authority in preaching is revelation. Richard Lischer also states that "the centrality of revelation in Barth's theology means that preaching is a divine activity."[49] Barth says, "Preaching must conform to revelation." This means that "in preaching we do not repeat or transmit the revelation of God by what we do" because "the event of preaching is God's own speaking."[50] Further, he argues,

> when the gospel is preached, God speaks: there is no question of the preacher revealing anything or of a revelation being conveyed through him . . . Revelation is a closed system in which God is the subject, the object and the middle term . . . if Christ deigns to be present when we are speaking, it is precisely because the action is God's, not ours.[51]

Further, he says that preaching is not to "expound or present the truth of God aesthetically in the form of a picture, an impression, or an aesthetic evocation of Jesus Christ . . . If God himself wills to speak his truth, preachers are forbidden to interfere with any science or art of their own."[52] He also argues, "Preaching is not a neutral activity, nor yet a joint action by two collaborators. It is the exercise of sovereign power on the part of God and obedience on the part of man."[53] Further, Barth says that "Preaching is the Word of God which he himself has spoken" and that "when a man preaches . . . We are carried beyond human thinking to God, who utters the first and the last word. God cannot be enclosed in any human concept . . . God will make himself heard;

---

48. Gorringe, *Karl Barth*, 121.
49. Lischer, *Theories of Preaching*, 338.
50. Barth, *Homiletics*, 47.
51. Barth, *Preaching*, 12–14.
52. Barth, *Homiletics*, 47–48.
53. Barth, *Preaching*, 16.

he it is who speaks, not man."⁵⁴ Clearly disregarding human personality, he says that if a preacher gives the "congregation a clever conceptual picture, even though it be arrived at by serious and intensive exegesis, it will not be Scripture itself that speaks."⁵⁵ On the role of the Holy Spirit in preaching, Barth clearly expounds, "Living preaching is preaching which is awakened and activated by the witness of the Holy Spirit, challenging from within the community which has heard His witness, and summoning the community itself to a fresh hearing of His witness."⁵⁶

Karl Barth must be appreciated for his theology of preaching that revelation or the word of God is the supreme authority in preaching. His belief that preaching is primarily God's event is valuable because without that high view of preaching, it could descend into another form of human-based communication. Therefore, Barth's effort to minimise the role of the preacher was an intentional effort to move away from the liberal modernist theology, which elevated the human element to disproportionate heights. And in so doing, he was trying to maximise who God is and what God can do. Moreover, Barth's recognition of the Holy Spirit working both in the preacher and the listener during preaching is commendable. However, his viewpoints are not without detractors. Other voices will first be heard before I give my thoughts.

Clement Welsh⁵⁷ contends that this "high" view of revelation in Barth "is haunted by the ghosts of many unanswered questions concerning the authority of scriptures" and so "it raises worrisome questions about mistaking man's voice for God's voice."⁵⁸ Welsh suggests that a preacher "must give to the creation (i.e. to the phenomena of human life) the same exegetical care that he would give a passage of Scripture."⁵⁹ Endorsing this comment, John Stott maintains that preaching that is insensitive to the context is the "*ex cathedra*"

---

54. Barth, 9–10.
55. Barth, *Homiletics*, 49.
56. Barth, *Church Dogmatics*, vol. 4, 127.
57. He was once the "Director of Studies and Warden of the American College of Preachers in Washington DC." See, Stott, *I Believe in Preaching*, 61.
58. Welsh, *Preaching in a New Key*, 102–3. Alister McGrath points out that Paul Tillich critiqued Karl Barth's theology on the ground that Barth is attempting to "drive a wedge between theology and culture"; McGrath, *Christian Theology*, 103.
59. Welsh, *Preaching in a New Key*, 109–10. *Contra*, we are aware of Barth's famous statement that a preacher must in his preaching connect "between the problem of human life on the one hand, and the content of the Bible on the other"; see Bush, "Preaching," 168. Divergent opinions about Karl Barth demonstrate the complexity of the Barth brand even in homiletics.

type of "preaching which is divorced from worldly reality, answers the wrong questions, and discourages responsible thinking in the congregation."[60]

We find that Karl Barth's position minimises the human role in preaching. It also minimises human intelligence in the preparation of the sermon because he is against imagination and creativity in preaching.

3.2 John F. MacArthur Jr. (1939–)

There are homileticians like Graeme Goldsworthy who consider preaching to be "essentially the practice of explaining the meaning of a passage of Scripture."[61] His view is well represented by John F. MacArthur Jr. Arguing from the perspective of Scripture's inerrancy, he states, "The message began as a true word from God and was given as truth because God's purpose was to transmit truth. It was ordered by God as truth and was delivered by God's Spirit in cooperation with holy men who received it."[62] Then, on the nature of the sermon to communicate this truth, MacArthur asks, "if God's message began true and if it is to be delivered as received, what interpretative processes necessitated by changes of language, culture, and time will ensure its purity when currently preached? The answer is that only an exegetical approach is acceptable for accurate exposition."[63] He elaborates,

> Inerrancy demands an exegetical process and an expository proclamation. Only the exegetical process preserves God's Word entirely, guarding the treasure of revelation and declaring its meaning exactly as He intended it to be proclaimed. Expository preaching is the result of the exegetical process. Thus, it is the essential link between inerrancy and proclamation. It is mandated to preserve the purity of God's originally given inerrant Word and to proclaim the whole counsel of God's redemptive truth."[64]

---

60. Stott, *I Believe in Preaching*, 62. For more discussion, see Lischer, *Company of Preachers*, 395.
61. Goldsworthy, *Preaching the Whole Bible*, 120.
62. MacArthur, "Mandate of Biblical Inerrancy," 21.
63. MacArthur, 21.
64. MacArthur, 26.

He reiterates by saying, "I assert that expository preaching is really exegetical preaching and not so much the homiletical form of the message."[65] MacArthur is here re-defining his own understanding of exposition of the Scripture where the homiletical feature of listener-sensitivity is undermined.

The viewpoint of MacArthur honours the written revelation (word of God) as inerrant and the supreme authority in preaching, which must be appreciated. Preaching which does not find its source in the living water will wither and crumble. However, his viewpoint is also not without difficulties. Below are some voices that critique his viewpoint.

In MacArthur's zeal to present a high view of Scripture by primarily focusing on what the Bible says, there are people like Ben E. Awbrey and R. Keith Willhite who observe that he does not give equal and adequate emphasis to the listeners' situation – on how people will appropriate the sermonic truths in their real-life experiences.[66] As such, MacArthur's position undermines the contemporary hearing of the word of God, the liveliness of Scripture, and its multiple applicability to different ages in the preaching event . Although MacArthur lives far away from the conservative modernist period, his text-driven approach in preaching brings him under this viewpoint.

Critiquing the homileticians in this viewpoint, Buttrick argues, "Perhaps, biblical preaching has been paralysed by Barthian fears of cultural accommodations" and therefore has been confined to just reciting "Scripture to churchly faith." This has led "biblical preaching" to tell a "biblical story replete with oodles of biblical background, a 'holy history,' but has not permitted God to step out of the biblical world into human history." Further he argues, "The God of the biblical preaching has been a past-tense God of past-tense God-events whose past-tense truth ('original meaning') may be *applied* to the world, while God remains hidden within a gilt-edged book." So, without allowing God and his word to engage and speak to the contemporary issues of society and the world at large, Buttrick calls it "simply unbiblical."[67] In the same way, Craddock argues that a sermon can become an "unbiblical" sermon even when it "buries itself in the text, moves through it phrase by phrase"

---

65. MacArthur, 22.
66. Awbrey, "Critical Examination," 17. See also Willhite, "Audience Relevance."
67. Buttrick, *Homiletics*, 18.

but "never comes up for air" because then "it fails to achieve what the text achieves,"[68] that is, meeting the needs of the listeners.

I believe that a sermon that only buries itself in the air-tight chamber of exegesis will suffocate in it. As much as it must walk in the streets of Scripture,[69] it must also walk in the streets of the real world where people live and try to make sense of their lives. God's word for people then must be made relevant for God's people now; otherwise, preaching will lose its meaning. In the light of the arguments made above, I find this viewpoint's theology of preaching too rigid. Although this category faithfully defends the orthodox Christian truth, I will not identify with it because it is deficient in sermonic application and imagination and undermines the role of the human preacher.

4. Preaching as Context-Driven Dialogical Monologue

A preaching theology that is context-driven and the belief that context is king, with the conviction that listeners must also participate in the preaching event through an inductive, dialogical, and narrative approach falls in the New Homiletic school of thought, which could be associated with the post-modern period. In this viewpoint, the effort to preach is mostly of human origin. The role of the preacher is to engineer a preacher-listener collaboration, so as to make sermons engaging and appealing to the listeners. Although one could trace the roots of this school of thought to the modernist liberal approach in preaching that elevates human experience, this school is more complex in its makeup and the divergent branches of the New Homiletic make it difficult to pinpoint one method to represent it. So the general term "context-driven dialogical monologue" will represent this school of thought. While it emphasises human experience, it accepts the post-modern critique of liberal modernism by emphasising particular rather than universal experiences. This is a key feature of postmodernity – a rejection of grand narratives and universals and a celebration of particulars and diversity. We will now examine the preaching theology of one of the forerunners of this viewpoint, Fred Craddock.

---

68. Craddock, *Preaching*, 28.
69. This idea is attributed to Gardner Taylor; see Holmes, "Enabling the Word," 77.

4.1 Fred Craddock (1928–2015)

Fred Craddock argues that preaching should emphasise the work aspect of preaching,[70] the listener-centric dimension of preaching. He argues, "in them is some deserved judgment against a church that gives recitations, lifeless words cut off from the hearts and minds of those who speak and those who listen."[71] About the text, Craddock states,

> In this encounter with the text, the Word of God is not simply the content of the tradition, nor an application of that content to present issues, but rather the Word of God is the address of God to the hearer who sits before the text open to its becoming the Word of God. Most importantly, God's Word is *God's Word* to the readers/listeners, not a word about God gleaned from the documents.[72]

Craddock's primary interest is focusing on the "mode of proclamation that is relevant to the present speaker-hearer relationship."[73] Thus, to address the "fundamental weakness in traditional preaching, its monological character," Craddock says that an alternative method, the dialogical method is in place because it increases preaching's impact because of the interaction between the preacher and the listener "in the proclamation of the Word."[74] He argues, "embracing the dialogical principle requires a radical assessment of one's role as a preacher . . . effective preaching calls for a method consistent with one's theology because the method is message; form and content are of a piece."[75] Craddock also disapproves of a sermon that has "logical development, clear argument, thorough, and conclusive treatment," but rather prefers a sermon that goes along with the listeners.[76]

Craddock's call for a change in the method of preaching that moves towards spontaneity and the sermon as a journey rather than a fixed and written

---

70. Craddock, *As One without Authority*, 6.
71. Craddock, 6.
72. Craddock, 114.
73. Craddock, 17.
74. Craddock, 18.
75. Craddock, 18.
76. Craddock, 27.

manuscript[77] deserves appreciation, for who likes to listen to a sermon that is monotonous and painfully predictable? But there are some voices that disagree with his position. Critiquing this viewpoint, Charles L. Campbell laments that the outcome of robust New Homiletic activity has not impacted and sparked life in the mainline protestant churches in America. Rather, he says that it is during this period of homiletical "resurgence" that they felt something still "lacking in their preaching."[78] Campbell observes that "new theories" brought nothing new to the life of the church. Though there may have been some serious concern with the health of the church, pastors recognised that life-giving vitality was missing in their preaching. Campbell argues, "They've [the pastors] tried inductive preaching, story preaching, dialogue sermons, and homiletical plots" but these "new methods" have not changed the status quo.[79] Further, he says that "amid the myriad books, articles, and conferences," many preachers have not articulated what the problem is, nor have they understood the "direction for the future."[80]

4.2 David G. Buttrick (1927–2017)

David G. Buttrick was another important homiletician in this category. For him, "sermons happen in consciousness," and so his approach to homiletics is known as a phenomenological approach.[81] He advocated the concept of sermonic "moves,"[82] and "plot" as against the traditional approach in propositional preaching which is guided by logical and analytical outlines.[83] He says, "sermons are a movement of language from one idea to another, each idea being shaped in a bundle of words. Thus, when we preach, we speak in formed modules of language arranged in some patterned sequence. These modules of language we will call 'moves.'"[84] Moreover, he endorses the importance of rhetoric in making sermonic moves effective.[85] Speaking out against

---

77. Craddock, 27.
78. Campbell, *Preaching Jesus*, xi.
79. Campbell, xi.
80. Campbell, xii.
81. Buttrick, *Homiletics*, xii.
82. Buttrick, 23.
83. Buttrick, 15.
84. Buttrick, 23.
85. Buttrick, 28.

the traditional method of preaching in point form, he argues that "the word 'point' is peculiar; it implies a rational, at-a-distance pointing at things, some kind of objectification" and the idea that there are "fixed truths."[86] However he says, "good preaching involves the imaging of ideas – the shaping of every conceptual notion by metaphor and image and syntax."[87]

Although Buttrick endorses the authority of Scripture in preaching, he recognises its authority only in the context of a preacher deriving "contemporary meaning" and not because it is "a text on a page of the Bible."[88] For Buttrick, the Scripture is authoritative in terms of its "symbolic logic" and not because of the historicity of the events, including the resurrection of Christ.[89] And so, he says, "such stories may not be preached in a here-is-what-actually-happened historical style."[90] For him, "the locus of authority" for preaching is "*faith-consciousness*" where one is repeatedly "brought before the cross of Christ by means of a remembered gospel message," and not because the gospel is a "body of fixed objective truth."[91] On the enterprise and theology of preaching, Buttrick considers human preaching as "*commissioned by the resurrection*" and "*a continuation of the preaching of Jesus Christ.*"[92] Second, "*In our preaching, Christ continues to speak to the church, and through the church to the world.*"[93] Third, "*The purpose of preaching is the purpose of God in Christ, namely the reconciliation of the world.*"[94] Fourth, "*Preaching evokes response: The response to preaching is a response to Christ, and is, properly, faith and response.*"[95] Fifth, "*Preaching is the 'Word of God' in that it participates in God's purpose, is initiated by Christ, and is supported by the Spirit with community in the world.*" On the other hand, Buttrick avers that "Preaching must be described as a human activity that draws on human understanding

---

86. Buttrick, 23.
87. Buttrick, 27.
88. Buttrick, 376.
89. Buttrick, 399–402.
90. Buttrick, 399.
91. Buttrick, 247.
92. Buttrick, 449 (emphasis original).
93. Buttrick, 451 (emphasis original).
94. Buttrick, 452 (emphasis original).
95. Buttrick, 453 (emphasis original).

and employs human homiletical skills that can be learned."[96] On the relationship between preaching and Scripture, he makes the affirmation that "We must not say that preaching from Scripture is requisite for sermons to be the Word of God" for "it is possible to preach the Word of God without so much as mentioning Scripture."[97] Further, on the role of the Holy Spirit, he claims, "the presence of the Spirit is not self-evident but is, indeed, an article of faith – of *homiletic* faith. Wherever there is faith in Jesus Christ, the Spirit is with community and with speakers to community."[98]

Buttrick's approach and method of preaching has several advantages. First, it is true that a sermon moves "from one idea to another" by using language or words. A preacher who has a good grasp of language or rhetoric is, humanly speaking, more spontaneous and accessible to the listeners. Second, on the aspect of "imaging of ideas" in preaching, we appreciate Buttrick's desire to simplify and engage the listener's imagination in preaching and not remain only in the cerebral and abstract logical realm.

However, Buttrick's approach is not without criticism. First, in his emphasis on bringing contemporary significance of the Scripture to the listeners, he denies the propositional and the "fixed objective truth" of the revealed word of God. In doing so, he makes the word of God stoop down to human subjectivism by not maintaining an objective standard for all humanity. Second, for him the Scripture is authoritative in terms of its "symbolic logic," thus compromising the historicity of the Christian faith and the revealed word of God. Third, on his theology of preaching, our preaching is certainly commissioned by the resurrected Christ and not the event of resurrection alone, and we do not continue to preach like Jesus Christ, rather we preach Jesus Christ himself. Fourth, it is true that preaching is "supported by the Spirit," but how he supports the preacher and listeners is not clearly spelled out. Buttrick's argument implies that it is not easily identifiable whether the Spirit is absent during a boring sermon or active during a lively and spontaneous sermon. Moreover, although Buttrick believes that preaching is an enterprise where Christ speaks to the church, his statement that it is "a human activity" questions the definitive role and function of the Holy Spirit. Fifth, in his effort

---

96. Buttrick, 456 (emphasis original).
97. Buttrick, 458.
98. Buttrick, 457.

to make sermons listener-centric and culturally relevant by putting other sources at par with the Scripture, Buttrick compromises the sufficiency and authority of the Scripture.

On the summary of the section under context-driven dialogical monologue, which is technically the New Homiletic (NH), I agree with Scott M. Gibson that there are several advantages. For example, "Induction is arguably the way in which the parables and some sermons chronicled in the New Testament were preached."[99] Further, it must be acknowledged that the NH draws our attention back to the importance of human experience and the use of language in engaging human imagination. It must be also noted here that effective preaching must ultimately lead people to encounter God and experience him personally in their lives, thus bringing spiritual vitality.

However, there are some differences I have with this viewpoint explaining why I will not associate myself with it. First, as Gibson points out, the advocates of the NH "underplay the nonnarrative passages of Scripture 'to narrow the communicational range of preaching to a single method'"[100] which is untenable. Second, although experience is important, if the emphasis on the preacher-listener's role in co-creating the "sermonic experience" is considered equivalent to written revelation, we elevate the human factors to being equally authoritative to or even eclipsing the source of God's word. Third, the role of the Holy Spirit is not clearly spelled out. Fourth, the authority of the word of God in preaching is under attack, because, in their effort to accommodate sources that engage with listeners, the sufficiency of Scripture is minimised.

5. Preaching as Contextually Applied Theodrama

This viewpoint believes in the rootedness of preaching in the authority of the written revelation (Scripture), the responsibility of the human preacher, the need to make preaching engaging and attractive to the listeners, the indispensable role of the Holy Spirit, and sensitivity to the felt needs and life-situations of the listeners.

A theology of preaching that is as sensitive to the experience and context of the listeners as it is convinced in the authority of the written word of God

---

99. Gibson, "Critique of the New Homiletic," 480.
100. Gibson, 480.

as supreme in the preaching event could be termed "contextually applied theodrama" and falls under the "critically post-modern category."[101] Both Hans Urs Von Balthasar and Kevin J. Vanhoozer used this term "theodrama" to demonstrate God's redemptive action and a person's grateful response: a divine-human affair.[102] In this work, Vanhoozer's perspective on "theodrama" will be employed. By "theodrama," he means the "divine communication and the church's communicative action."[103] He also contends that "theology involves both what God has said and done for the world and what we must say and do in grateful response."[104]

In this viewpoint, preaching is seen as a "divine-human event"[105] and expository preaching[106] is the style of preaching it believes in. While its locus of authority is written revelation, the nature of the preaching is a divine-human communication that is contextually applied. It is a "divine-human event" because first, God is the initiator – both as the one who first revealed by speaking invisible things into existence and the one who still speaks into human situations. On the other hand, as God used human authors with their unique personalities and locations in history to write down what he revealed to them for his purpose, God uses human preachers to collaborate with him to bring his living word to the people. In this viewpoint, there is an intentional focus on the experiences and life-situations of the congregants, and therefore it attempts to build a bridge to contemporise Scripture which was written in another context for the listeners today. For our purpose here, two homileticians who hold to this viewpoint will be examined.[107] After hearing from each of them, the voices of some critics will be heard and then a final analysis will be made.

---

101. This category is named so because the homileticians who represent it are critical of post-modernism. They believe that the text has an objective meaning.

102. Vanhoozer, *Drama of Doctrine*, 37–38. Von Balthasar, *Theo-Drama*, 1–6.

103. Vanhoozer, 74.

104. Vanhoozer, 37–38.

105. Stott, *I Believe in Preaching*, 60.

106. Stott calls it biblical preaching as well. Stott, *Between Two Worlds*, 116.

107. These two homileticians have already been discussed in the main thesis when we analysed their methodology and theology of preaching in the "Normative Chapter." But we need to mention them here again to give a big picture of the spectrum of preaching.

5.1 John R. W. Stott (1921–2011)

On preaching as a divine event, John Stott declares that the "locus of authority" in preaching "resides only in God . . . and not at all in us who quote them [Scriptures] today."[108] He also affirms that the origin of every sermon which the preacher preaches is from God and nowhere else. He argues that "in the ideal sermon it is the Word itself which speaks, or rather God in and through His Word."[109] On the other hand, Stott is very clear on the importance of the human role in preaching, which is therefore a human event as well:

> Here, then, is the biblical case for biblical exposition. It consists of two fundamental convictions, namely that God has given us in Scripture a text which is both inspired (having a divine origin and authority) and to some degree closed (difficult to understand). Therefore, in addition to the text, he gives the church teachers to open up the text, explaining it and applying it to people's lives.[110]

Elaborating on the human dimension in preaching, Stott brings up the issue of a preacher's experience with God that will empower his preaching. He says, "by 'experience,' I do not mean experience of the preaching ministry or experience of life in general, necessary as these are to the preacher. I mean rather a personal experience of Jesus Christ Himself. This is the first and indispensable mark of the Christian witness (preacher)."[111]

He says that expository preaching cannot be stereotyped as "a verse-by-verse explanation of a lengthy passage of the Scripture," rather it points to "the content of the sermon (biblical truth)." He clarifies,

> The expositor pries open what appears to be closed, makes plain what is obscure, unravels what is knotted and unfolds what is tightly packed . . . Whether it is long or short, our responsibility as expositors is to open it up in such a way that it speaks its message clearly, plainly, accurately, relevantly, without addition, subtraction or falsification. In expository preaching, the biblical

---

108. Stott, *I Believe in Preaching*, 58.
109. Stott, *Preacher's Portrait*, 30.
110. Stott, *Contemporary Christian*, 211–12.
111. Stott, *Preacher's Portrait*, 70–71.

text is neither a conventional introduction to a sermon on a largely different theme, nor a convenient peg on which to hang a ragbag of miscellaneous thoughts, but a master which dictates and controls what is said.[112]

On the importance of context in preaching, Stott talks about bridge-building between the world of the text and the world of the listeners. Stott advises that a preacher must, before preaching, "seek to enter into the other person's world of thoughts and feeling" so that he may rightfully "contextualise the gospel." For this to happen, Stott says that "double listening" is vital. He then says preaching stands

> between the Word and the world, with the consequent obligation to listen to both. We listen to the Word in order to discover ever more of the riches of Christ. And we listen to the world in order to discern which of Christ's riches are needed most and how to present them in their best light.[113]

On the role of the Holy Spirit, Stott says that a preacher must cultivate the "humility of dependence"[114] and reveals that ineffectiveness in preaching happens due to pride.[115] Human preachers are "finite, fallen, frail, and fallible creatures" and the "words we speak in human weakness the Holy Spirit carries home by his power to the mind, heart, conscience, and the will of the hearers."[116] It is not in the power of the human preacher to bring to life and transform the "spiritually and morally blind, deaf, dumb, lame, and even dead or imprisoned by Satan . . . Only Jesus Christ through his Spirit can . . . wake up the conscience, enlighten the mind, fire the heart, move the will, give life to the dead, and rescue slaves from Satan."[117]

---

112. Stott, *Between Two Worlds*, 126. To learn more about the value of systematic exposition, see 4.3.2.2 and 4.3.2.3. For further discussions on expository preaching see Chapell, *Christ-Centered Preaching*, 57; Keller, *Preaching*, 32; Lamb, *Dynamics of Biblical Preaching*, 16; Bromiley, "Preface to Homiletics," 14; Old, *Reading*, 11, Fullerton, Orrick, and Payne, *Encountering God*, 19–34.

113. Stott, *Contemporary Christian*, 110–11.

114. Stott, *I Believe in Preaching*, 328.

115. Stott, 329–30.

116. Stott, 334.

117. Stott and Scharf, *Challenge of Preaching*, 89.

5.2 Timothy Keller (1950-)

According to Timothy Keller, preaching is "engaging with the authoritative text" and "not your opinion."[118] He argues that when a preacher preaches the Scripture, he is speaking "the very words of God,"[119] that, preaching biblically involves making "clear the meaning of the text in its context – both in its historical time and within the whole of Scripture."[120] Further, he declares,

> Expository preaching grounds the message in the text so that all the sermon's points are in the text, and it majors in the text's major ideas. It aligns the interpretation of the text with the doctrinal truths of the rest of the Bible. And it always situates the passage within the Bible's narrative, showing how Christ is the final fulfillment of the text's theme.[121]

Moreover, he says that "in the end, preaching has two basic objects in view: the Word and the human listener . . . Sound preaching arises out of two loves – love of the Word of God and love of people."[122] On the human dimension and effort in preaching Keller says,

> Understanding the biblical text, distilling a clear outline and theme, developing a persuasive argument, enriching it with poignant illustrations, metaphors, and practical examples, incisively analysing heart motives and cultural assumptions, making specific application to real life – all of this takes extensive labor.[123]

On the role of the Holy Spirit, Keller says, "the sermon's differing impact on individuals was due to the work of God's Spirit,"[124] that, the "difference between good preaching and great preaching lies mainly in the work of the Holy Spirit in the heart of his listeners as well as the preacher."[125] Keller says

---

118. Keller, *Preaching*, 20.
119. Cf. 1 Pet 4:11.
120. Keller, *Preaching*, 20.
121. Keller, 32.
122. Keller, 14.
123. Keller, 11.
124. Keller, 10
125. Keller, 11.

that this is so because the Holy Spirit ultimately holds the key to all the secrets of "God's wise plans."[126]

5.3 Critiques and Rebuttals

However, expository preaching in general is not without any counter viewpoints. Some of that critique will be discussed below, followed by some homileticians' defence. Then I will provide seven reasons why I choose to locate myself under this viewpoint.

Calvin Miller says, "Many people secretly felt that this 'expository' style of preaching was boring, but nobody would say so out loud for fear of being branded as a liberal."[127] According to Jerry Vines and Jim Shaddix, many accuse expository preaching of "dullness,"[128] "irrelevancy," "monotony," "spiritlessness," "formlessness" and "detail overload."[129] They agree that people "dislike *poor* expository preaching," though not expository preaching in itself.[130]

It is true that some biblical sermons are boring when they major in exegesis without application. Such sermons are not only simplistic but unbiblical, because God's words must address human problems. However, in the light of the theology of preaching under the "contextually applied theodrama" viewpoint, these accusations are not convincing because none of them are sufficiently serious as to abandon this contextually applied theodramatic approach.

Below are the core theologies of preaching as formulated by the homiletical theologians of this viewpoint, neatly depicting and defending the accusations levelled against them.

First, Keller believes that the locus of authority for preaching is the written revelation of God, the Holy Scripture, not human-located experiences nor the human preacher with his dynamic personality and rhetoric. Although the authority is God, he also spelled out the responsibility of the preacher who had to do the exegesis, develop the sermon, and gauge the cultural situation of the listener to make the sermon relevant to the listeners. Moreover, a preacher

---

126. Keller, 11.
127. Miller, *Preaching the Art*, 20.
128. Vines and Shaddix, *Power*, 55; Charles agrees that many term expository preaching "boring"; Charles, *On Pastoring*, n.p.
129. Vines and Shaddix, *Power*, 55–58.
130. Vines and Shaddix, *Power*, 53; cf. Appendix 1, sections 3.2 and 4.

must be consciously sensitive to the listeners' situations and contexts, which is another strength that emerges from Keller's understanding of preaching. Keller is particularly strong on the preacher's responsibility to unravel the deep hidden social worldviews and cultural baggage in conflict with the truth of the gospel. Keller's commitment to penetrate and challenge the otherwise invisible and culturally accepted worldviews aligns with the viewpoint of "contextually applied theodrama." Looking at the various elements Keller has laid out, expository preaching is not "boring," or "simplistic," and cannot be called a "cheating" endeavour as some have claimed.

Second, Stott's locus of authority in preaching is God (the revealed Scripture), not men. However, Stott clearly lays out the role of "church teachers" (pastors and preachers) who have experienced and accepted Jesus Christ as Lord and Saviour to unravel the slightly closed Scripture. Stott is very strong in his emphasis on "double-listening." Far from prohibiting preachers from engaging with various sources in society to theologise and sermonise, as Barth is perceived by some as doing,[131] Stott strongly encourages preachers to be attentive to the cries, crises, cultures, and climate of the society they live in and address their felt needs. Further, Stott neatly balances all the viewpoints – rationality, experience, orthodoxy, and listener-centredness, which is exemplary and therefore praiseworthy. Over and above all these, Stott is immovable in his belief that man, a finite and limited creature of God, can never be a worthy dispenser of God's word and be a transforming agent in the listeners' lives, without first experiencing a personal encounter with Christ and the consuming presence and role of the Holy Spirit. Among others, Stott's theology of preaching that seriously believes in "double-listening" rebuts the accusation of Buttrick that expository preaching chains God and his work to historical narratives.

6. Evaluation: Seven Advantages of the Contextually Applied Theodramatic Viewpoint

These seven points, representing the contextually applied theodramatic view, critically draw in the positive elements from all the other three viewpoints. My view on preaching falls under this viewpoint.

---

131. Barth, *Homiletics*, 47–48.

i. The contextually applied theodramatic view properly pays attention to *what* preaching is (theology) before it turns its attention to *how* preaching is to be effective (methodology).
ii. The contextually applied theodramatic view intentionally and correctly adopts God and his written word as the primary locus of authority. God's revelation is acknowledged as the crucial source of truth among all the human voices we encounter. God speaks. He is still the communicative God.
iii. The contextually applied theodramatic view correctly identifies preaching as an event in which both God and humans act. It recognises the important place for human beings (preacher and listeners) in the event of preaching. It recognises the place for the unique personality of the preacher and the importance of his character which must be "like Jesus'" (in his surrender to God's will and the power of the Holy Spirit) if he is to speak "on behalf of God." It also recognises the context of the listeners – their experiential needs and their locatedness in terms of their culture, language, place, etc., and consequently their choice for an expository, inductive, narrative, apologetical approach in preaching.
iv. The contextually applied theodramatic view recognises its primary goal as the systematic unpacking of a given scriptural text. However, it embraces the importance of connecting the world of the biblical text to that of contemporary listeners by the discipline of "double-listening." As such, the dual goal of textual faithfulness and contextual sensitivity is accomplished.
v. The contextually applied theodramatic view properly makes space for the necessity of the work of the Holy Spirit for a divine effect to happen in human lives. Nevertheless, it shows how some responsibility remains upon the preacher to make the preaching creative, lively, and engaging, so that preaching does not become "boring" to the listeners.
vi. The contextually applied theodramatic view believes that the word of God is not merely the "springboard" but the "swimming pool" in which the preacher must remain for the whole duration of the sermonic period, with the main points of the sermon developing

like a "rose from its bud."[132] In this way, it maintains a sermonic unity and continuity – be it in a narrational form or an outline form.

vii. The contextually applied theodramatic view is open to the inductive method of preaching (starting with the context) so long as the source of preaching's authority is revelation.

7. Conclusion

The purpose of this chapter was to answer the question, what is preaching? Towards that end we described and categorised the various viewpoints of preaching (not eras in history) in a spectrum. They are: Individual experience-driven communication; Text-driven communication; Context-driven communication; and Contextually-applied theodrama. We discussed and analysed each of these viewpoints, through the prism of two of their prominent homileticians or theologians of preaching. After which, I located myself under the category of the "Contextually applied theodrama" by giving seven reasons as distinct advantages of this viewpoint, and thus my preference for it.

---

132. Lowry, *Homiletical Plot*, 8.

Preaching is...	Individual experience-driven communication	Text-driven communication
Background philosophy	Liberal Modernism (revelation as individual experiential expressivism)	Conservative Modernism (revelation as information)
Preaching is seen as a...	Individual human event	Divine event
Style	Experiential	Deductive
Locus of Authority in Preaching	Universal individual experience as the supreme authority in preaching	Revelation as the supreme authority in preaching
Nature of the Preaching Event	Human communication focused on universal morals	Divine communication (exegesis with no or little application)
	Names of Theologians of Preaching	**Names of Theologians of Preaching**
	Johann Lorenz Mosheim (1693–1755) Hugh Blair (1718–1800) Friedrich Schleiermacher (1768–1834) Paul Tillich (1886–1965) Phillips Brooks (1835) Rudolf Bultmann (1884–1976)	Karl Barth (1886–1968) Graeme Goldsworthy (1934–) John F. MacArthur Jr. (1939–) John Piper (1946–) Peter Adam (1946–) Phillip D. Jensen (c. 1946–)

Figure 12: A Spectrum of Theology of Preaching

Context-driven dialogical monologue	Contextually applied theodrama
Post-Modernism (community experience as the source of ideas for preaching)	Critically Postmodern (revelation as information and sensitive to experience)
Human community event	Divine-human event
Inductive/Dialogical/Narrative (New Homiletic)	Expository
Human Context/Life situation as the supreme authority in preaching	Revelation as the supreme authority in preaching and context is relevant
Mainly human communication on life situations	Divine-human communication that is contextually applied
Names of Theologians of Preaching	**Names of Theologians of Preaching**
Harry Emerson Fosdick (1878–1969) H. Grady Davis (1890–1960) R. E. C. Browne (c. 1906–c. 1965) David G. Buttrick (1927–2017) Fred Craddock (1928–2015) Eugene Lowry (1933–) Thomas Long (1946–) Abraham Kuruvilla (c. 1955–)	Jonathan Edwards (1703–1758) Charles Spurgeon (1834–1892) John Stott (1921–2011) Sydney Greidanus (1935–) Michael Quicke (1950–) Gaddala Isaiah (c. 1940–2010) Timothy Keller (1950–) Ramesh Richard (c. 1952–) Kevin Vanhoozer (1957–)

APPENDIX 2

Open-Ended Research Questionnaire

Dear Participants,

I am Mr. R. T. Johnson Raih, from Oinam Hill Baptist church, under Poumai Naga Baptist Association (PNBA), and currently pursuing my PhD (Preaching) at South Asia Institute of Advanced Christian Studies (SAIACS). My research topic is "An Examination of Preaching in the Baptist Churches of Imphal City, 2000–2015, and Its Impact on the Spiritual Life, with Special Reference to Nominalism." The research is guided by the main question, "What are the effects of preaching on the spiritual life of the members of the Baptist churches of Imphal city 2000–2015?" This particular period is chosen to engage with the contemporary situation of the church, where primary data collection may be more feasible. The main focus of this research is to investigate the church members' spiritual, experiential interpretation on the effect of preaching in their churches.

This research is significant because academically, it engages a current homiletical discussion on the relationship between preaching and spirituality, both spiritual vitality and nominalism. Moreover, many people may not have done such an investigation among the Imphal Baptist churches under Manipur Baptist Convention (MBC) so far. Second, it is important because it will encourage pastors and preachers to re-examine their preaching – both in terms of form and content. Third, this research will enable the pastoral trainers to identify areas where pastors and preachers need to be trained. The contribution you make in this research will immensely benefit my study towards identifying the effect of preaching on people's spirituality. If this research is properly done, we will better understand preaching's impact on our ethical behaviour and the exercise of spiritual disciplines in the society, marketplace, and the family. So, this questionnaire is designed to gather vital information needed for the research.

Hence, I request your help in filling it up. Whatever you provide would remain anonymous without any hint to trace its source and it will be used exclusively for academic work. To make this research work authentic, I plead for your honesty. In case there is something that I must hear from you which will benefit the research work, please do not hesitate to contact me. I sincerely value your participation in my research work. May God bless you!

Sincerely,
Sd/-
R. T. Johnson Raih (PhD Student)

College Address:

363, SAIACS
Dodda Gubbi Cross Road
Kothanur Post, 560077
Bangalore, Karnataka

INFORMED CONSENT FORM

Dear Participant,

I am a student at South Asia Institute of Advanced Christian Studies (SAIACS) Bangalore, doing my PhD in Preaching, under the Pastoral Theology and Counselling department. As a requirement for my PhD degree, I am writing a dissertation on the title, "An Examination of Preaching in the Baptist Churches of Imphal City, 2000–2015, and Its Impact on the Spiritual Life, with Special Reference to Nominalism." I am required to carry out my research in fifteen Baptist churches in Imphal. Therefore, with the permission of your local church authority, I approach you to kindly help me in my endeavour by becoming one of the participants in responding to my questionnaire. The following facts need to be mentioned so that you are aware of what you are getting into.

Confidentiality

The information gathered from you will be treated with utmost respect and confidentiality and it will only be used for academic purpose alone. Your identity will remain anonymous and protected. While quoting any information you have given, you will be referred to with a different name.

Refusal/Withdrawal

You are free to withdraw from the research at any point of the research journey and also refuse the inclusion of any information you've given in the research, should you reconsider your decision.

Discomfort and Risks

In the course of this research, I expect minimal risks but there may be moments of discomfort because it will ask the participant to probe deeper into their own personal spiritual life. It may also be inconvenient for some to be "honest and blunt" while expressing their experiences, linking the preaching they've heard to the spiritual condition they are in. However, it is not without any benefits.

Benefits

Being a participant of this research could help you trigger memories on how God's word touched your life in the past. For some, it could help you to evaluate the effectiveness of your own preaching ministry in relation to impacting the spirituality of your listeners.

Signature of Participant and Date

_____   _____

Gender	Numbers	Percentage
Female		
Male		
Age Group		
20–30 | 31–40 | 41–50 | 51–60 | 61–70 | 71 & above	Total	
Marital Status		
Single | Married | Widow | Widower | Divorcee | Others	Total	
Educational Qualification		
Under-Graduate | Graduate | Post-Graduate | Above Post-Graduate | Any Other	Total	
Profession		
Teacher | Govt. Employee | Lecturer/Prof | Student | Christian Mission Worker | Retired | Doctor | Businessman | NGO | Engineer | Unemployed | Others	Total	
Number of years living in Imphal		
1–5 | 6–10 | 11–15 | 16 and above	Total	
Number of years in the current church between 2000–2015		
1–5 | 6–10 | 11–15 | 16 and above	Total	

Introductory and Practical Questions:	
No.	Questions
1.	How many pastors are there in your church? *One	Two	More than Two*
2.	Approximately, how many people preach in your church, in a calendar year? *One	Two to Five	Six to ten	Ten and above	Twenty and above	Fifty and above*
3.	What types of sermon structures (narration; expository; topical etc.) are preached in the churches? *Narration	Expository	Testimonial	Topical	Textual	Others*
4.	What is the duration of each sermon? *Less than 30 Minutes	30 Minutes	30–45 Minutes	More than 45 Minutes*
5.	In your opinion, what type of preaching do you think exists in the pulpits of the Baptist churches in the city of Imphal? *Narration	Expository	Testimonial	Topical	Mix up	Traditional	Others*
Peaching and Spiritual Vitality:	
1.	What do you think makes a good sermon?
2.	What types of sermon bring satisfaction and what types of sermon disappoint you? Why?
3.	In your opinion, what kind of preaching can bring spiritual vitality?
4.	Does listening to preaching consistently lift you up spiritually?
5.	Has your interest in reading the Bible increased because of the preaching you've heard? Why?
6.	How would you describe a person who demonstrates having a life of spiritual vitality?
7.	How far is there an adequate understanding of God's word in your church?
8.	How can a sufficient understanding of God's word protect believers from being spiritually stagnant and nominal?
9.	What are the central themes in the Bible that are prominent in your church?

Preaching and Spiritual Nominalism:	
No.	Questions
1.	As the global church today faces the problem of nominalism, is it a concern for your church too?
2.	How would you describe a nominal Christian?
3.	In your opinion what are the factors that may be associated with the growth of nominalism in the church?
4.	In your opinion can bad preaching incubate spiritual stagnation? Please elaborate?
5.	Do you think not knowing God's word properly can lead a person to dichotomise/separate between sacred (Sunday lifestyle) and secular (Monday to Saturday lifestyle), thus leading to compromise and nominalism? Explain.
Preaching and Spiritual Impact:	
1.	How would you describe the focus or goals of the sermons you have heard in your church?
2.	After you hear the preaching on a regular basis, do you feel energised, stimulated, secured, excited or depressed, discouraged, unfulfilled? Please elaborate.
3.	Do you look forward to attending the next church service and listen to the preaching? Kindly elucidate.
4.	How have your life's practices changed in the society/ world/ family, as a result of listening to sermons, in terms of ethical behaviour and the exercise of spiritual disciplines?
5.	What changes do you see (or you don't see) in the society as a result of Christians having listened to preaching in the church?
6.	How far can you see change in the lives of the believers as you preached in six months? (For pastors and preachers)
Any other questions	
1.	Is there anything you think I should've asked or you would like to add?

APPENDIX 3

Some Other Ways to Address Nominalism

The views of several members on how to address nominalism have been mentioned in the thesis. Some additional information from the data is given below.

1. Disciple Making, Mentoring, and Church Planting

Pastor Patrick thought that individual members who did not know the word of God clearly through the sermon needed individual attention. He observed that many members walked into and out of the church without any sense of seriousness and focus in life because he could not disciple them and give them his time; moreover, he had been unable to mentor his deacons and let them do the job. He argued, "If we do not invest and disciple the youth today, then, when they become rebellious, we will not have future church leaders." Thus, he continued, "It is very important to invest in disciple making. Therefore, the pastor should not only be preaching to win souls, but to make disciples."[1]

Pastor Luther also shared his strategy to combat nominalism. He claimed that in the past, he preached according to societal needs. But now he applies the "First Principles church-based theological education" and he sees the members and church leaders showing interest in this approach. He clarified that this approach is all about multiplying. He elaborated,

---

1. Kumar strongly endorsed this view.

I will have a six-member team and then each member in the team will have another team and this is how disciples make discipleship work in the church. As a pastor, I will also have to form another team from the grassroots. So, it is like following the Paul–Timothy example, finding and building the next leadership level. So, this is a very important tool to combat nominalism.[2]

2. Regular Bible Study

Pastor Oliver is a staunch believer in the role of a regular and systematic Bible study to confront and address nominalism in the families and churches within the Baptist family. He conducts an annual event[3] where they meet for three to four days at a stretch and study the Bible under a theme each year. For example, once they chose the theme "The Cross" and studied it: "What is the cross? How did it come? What is its meaning? How should a Christian relate to the cross?" Then he remarked, "When people get to know the cross deeper, they can bear life's problems and difficulties better."

Bijoy argued, "We talk of dawn prayer, sub-committees, and building projects but we cannot do without regular Bible study." In a Bible study, "It will not be just a monologue but a dialogue and conversation, where questions and doubts can be clarified. This can contribute to the growth of one's spiritual life."[4]

---

2. Pastor Mark also expressed the same view.

3. As he does not have an assistant pastor, it is difficult to conduct a weekly Bible study with the number of responsibilities he shoulders as a pastor.

4. Kenneth echoed this claim; Pastor Tomba argued for the need of a Bible study for the pastors in the city of Imphal.

APPENDIX 4

List of Some Theologically Trained MBC Leaders[1]

1. V. S. Phanitphang, LTh (Diploma in Theology) in 1930, and in 1950–1951 he went for another course at Serampore College.
2. Rev. Th. Kotha, GTh from ABTS, 1955.
3. Rev. R. V. Mashangthei, GTh from ETC (then Assam Baptist Theological Seminary/ABTS), in 1956.
4. Rev. N. Rungsung, BD, from Serampore College in 1963.
5. Rev. Champhang Jajao, BD in 1964 from Senate of Serampore, and STM in 1982 from Andover Newton Theological College, Boston, USA.
6. Rev. K. Hepuni Mao, BTh in 1964, from Senate of Serampore College.
7. Rev. Th. Thangmi, GTh from Hindustan Bible Institute and College in 1969.
8. Rev. Dr. Tuisem A. Shishak, PhD from State University of New York, Buffalo, in 1973.
9. Rev. Ramkhun Pamei, BD in 1970 and MA in Theology in 1974 from Northern Baptist Theological Seminary, Chicago, USA.
10. Rev. Sumkholen Serto, MDiv from Andover Newton Theological Seminary, Boston, USA in 1970.
11. Rev. Songkhopao Gangte, BD, UBS, in 1971.
12. Rev. R. L Tennyson, BD, from Serampore College in 1975.
13. Ms. Aram Pamei, BD, from Union Biblical Seminary (UBS) in 1975, and ThM in Korea in 1983.
14. Rev. Dr. Hawlngam Haokip, BD from Serampore College in 1977 and DMin in 1980 from Southern Baptist Theological Seminary, Louisville, KY, USA.

---

1. Zeliang, *History of Manipur*, 207–75. The list is based solely on Zeliang's book and has been arranged chronologically. Many theological students belonging to MBC, graduate every year around world, but no source of this kind seems to be available. This is primarily a list of the MBC leaders, but at best, it serves as a sample.

15. Rev. K. Mahangthei, BD from Leonard Theological College, Junailpur in 1977.
16. Rev. S. Prim Vaiphei, ThM from Fuller Theological Seminary Pasadena, California, USA, in 1979.
17. Rev. Peter Kashung, BD from UBS in 1980 and Master of Sacred Theology at Dallas Theological Seminary, USA in 1989.
18. Rev. Asong Leivon, BD from ETC in 1983.
19. Rev. R. R. Lolly, MTh in South Korea in 1983.
20. Rev. James Dhale, MA (Mission), from Reformed Theological Seminary, USA in 1983.
21. Rev. Hokey, BD in 1984 from Eastern Theological College (ETC) under Serampore University.
22. Rev. Dr. J. M. Ngul Khan Pau, BD in 1985 from UBS and DMiss from Western Seminary in 1995.
23. Rev. L. Timothy Phaomei, MA in Christian Leadership (MCL) in the Northwest Baptist Seminary, WA, USA in 1988.
24. Rev. Vumthang Sitlhou, BD in 1988 from ETC, and ThM from ACTS, Seoul, Korea in 1998.
25. Rev. Dr. Banner Makan, MDiv and DMin from International Theological Seminary, Pasadena, CA, USA in 1988 and 2004 respectively.
26. Rev. Longam Chara, BD, from ETC in 1989.
27. Rev. T. P. Mordecai, BD, from ETC in 1989.
28. Rev. Ngaranmi M. Risom, BD from Serampore College in 1978 and MTh from Seoul, South Korea in 1989.
29. Rev. Dr. Jonathan H. Thumra, DTh in Religion and Society, from United Theological College (UTC), Bangalore in 1992.
30. Rev. Dr. Mangkhosat Kipgen, DTh from Senate of Serampore in 1992.
31. Rev. Khupza Go, MTh from UTC, in 1995.
32. Rev. Stephen Touthang, BD, from UBS in 1996.
33. Mrs. Roselyn Serto, BD, from Aizawl Theological College in 1998.
34. Rev. Dr. Mathanmi Zimik, DMiss. from Western Seminary, Portland, USA in 2000.
35. Rev. Dr. L. Kholi, ThD from Presbyterian College and Theological Seminary, Seoul, South Korea in 2001.
36. Rev. Dr. Kim (Vaiphei) Haokip, pursuing PhD from Oxford, England in 2005.[2]
37. Rev. Ningwon Woleng, BTh.
38. Rev. Piano Pani; MTh from UTC.

---

2. It is reported that she has completed her studies.

APPENDIX 5

Political Map of Manipur in the Context of Global Map[1]

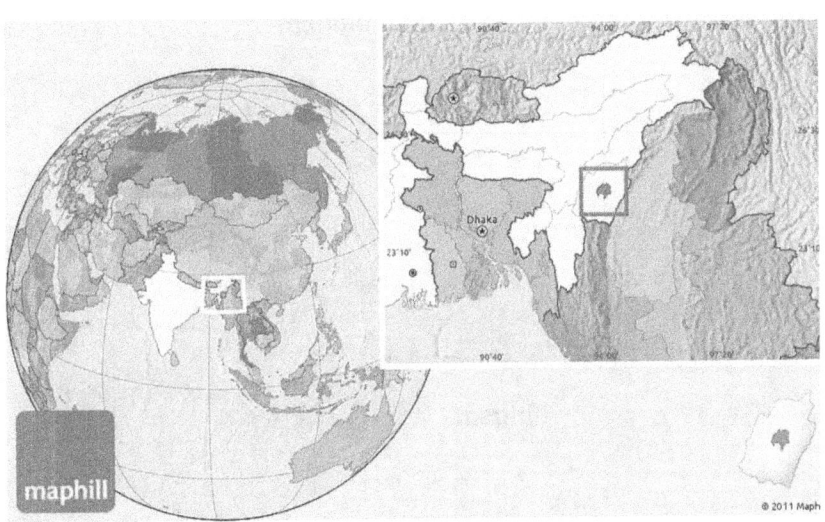

---

1. Political Location Map of Imphal. Image © Maphill / CC BY-ND. http://www.maphill.com/india/manipur/imphal/location-maps/political-map/highlighted-country/, accessed 13 October 2019.

APPENDIX 6

A Political Map of India[1]

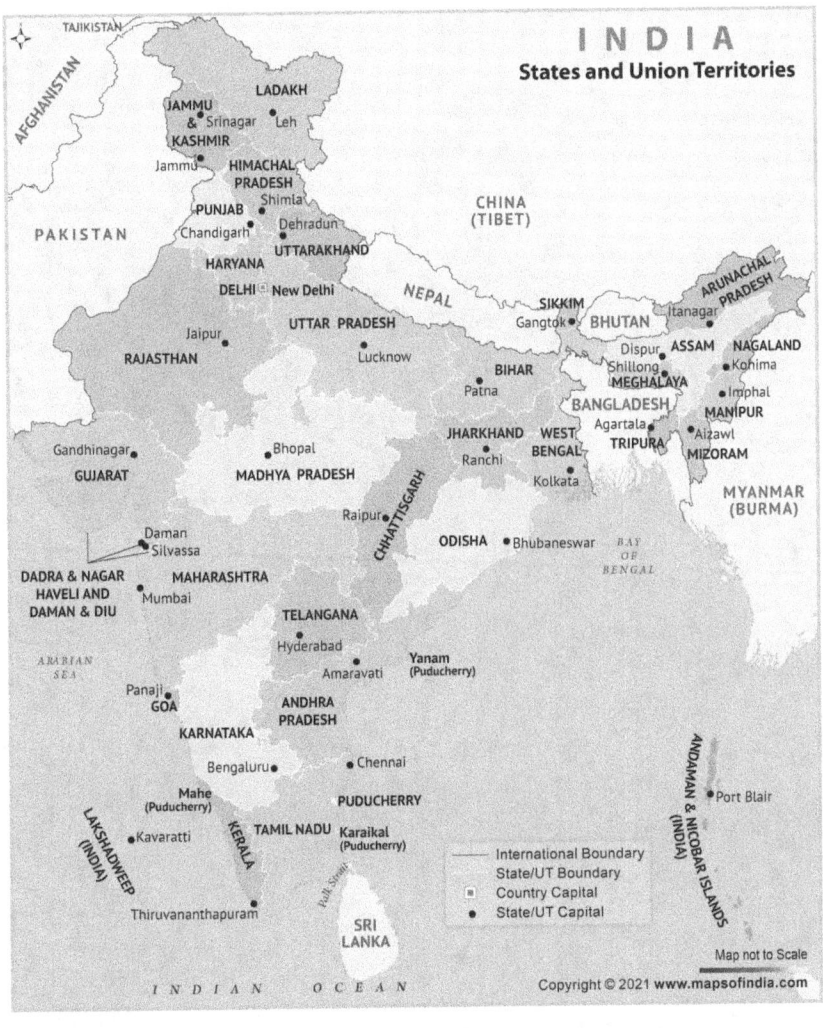

1. Copyright © 2021 www.mapsofindia.com, used by permission.

APPENDIX 7

Manipur Map[1]

---

1. Copyright © 2021 www.mapsofindia.com, used by permission.

APPENDIX 8

Imphal Map[1]

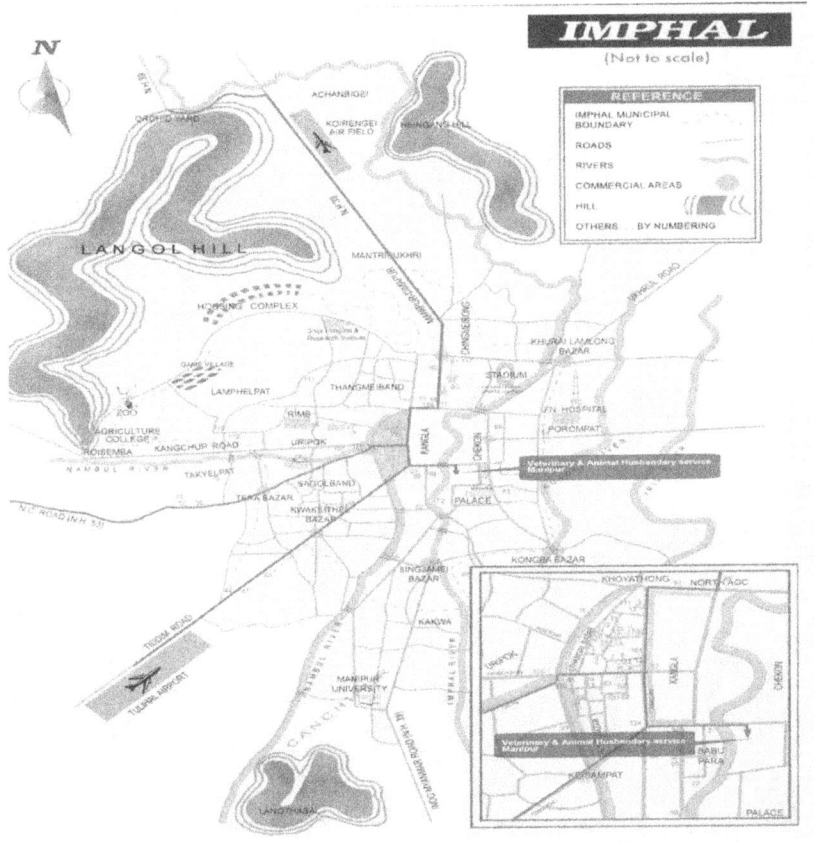

---

1. Image taken from https://vetymanipur.nic.in/guide.html, accessed 13 September 2021.

APPENDIX 9

Semi-Structured Interview Questions

Name _____

Code _____

Thesis Topic

"An Examination of Preaching in the Baptist churches of Imphal city, 2000–2015, and Its Impact on the Spiritual Life, with Special Reference to Nominalism."

Main Research Question

"What are the effects of preaching on the spiritual life of the members of the Baptist churches of Imphal, between 2000–2015?"

Introductory Questions

1. How many pastors are there in your church?
2. Approximately, how many people preach in your church, in a calendar year?
3. What types of sermon structures (narration; expository; topical, testimonial, etc.) are generally being preached in the churches?
4. What is the duration of each sermon?
5. In your opinion, what types of preaching do you think exist in the pulpits of the Baptist churches in the city of Imphal?

6. Based on your experience of having listened to different sermons in your local church, what are the types of preaching (both content and form) you can list down?
7. What do you think makes a good sermon?

Preaching and Spiritual Vitality

1. Some people say that "biblical gospel" must be preached to bring spiritual vitality. What do you think comprises "biblical gospel"?
2. In your opinion, is there a relationship between preaching and spiritual vitality? Give reasons.
3. To what extent are you aware of the effect of preaching on the spiritual life of a listener?
4. Does listening to preaching consistently feed your spiritual passion?
5. Has your interest in reading the Bible increased because of the preaching you've heard? Why?
6. In what way can preaching contribute to the spiritual vitality or spiritual lethargy of the listener?
7. How would you describe a person who demonstrates having a life of spiritual vitality?
8. Basing on the types of preaching listed above, in your opinion, what types of preaching bring about spiritual vitality and what types of preaching incubates spiritual stagnation, even nominalism?
9. What types of sermon bring satisfaction and what type of sermons disappoint you? Why?
10. In your opinion what is the main authority in preaching (Warm experience or good delivery or vivid illustration or faithfulness to the text?) and why?
11. How far is there an adequate understanding of God's word in your church?
12. How can a sufficient understanding of God's word transform the spiritual life of the members and prevent Christians from becoming spiritually stagnant?

13. What are the central themes or theology in the preaching you have heard in your church?

Preaching and Spiritual Nominalism

1. As the global church today faces the rampant problem of Christian spiritual stagnation, even nominalism, in what way do you think this problem is a concern for your church too?
2. When do you think a Christian becomes nominal and how would you describe such a person?
3. In your opinion what are the factors that may be associated with the growth of nominalism in the church?
4. How acceptable is the claim perceived to be that Christian nominalism thrives when the "biblical gospel" is not preached clearly?
5. In your opinion, is there a relationship between preaching and nominalism? Give reasons.
6. In the city of Imphal, where the preaching ministry is considered vibrant, how relevant is it to discuss about the relationship between preaching and nominalism?
7. To what extent can an insufficient understanding of God's word in the preaching event lead to spiritual stagnancy and practices that breed nominalism?
8. Do you think that a right understanding of God's word in the preaching event but a wrong lifestyle influenced by various worldviews influence a lifestyle that breed nominalism? And if so, can you briefly elucidate?

Preaching and Its Impact on the Listeners

1. How would you describe the focus or goals of the sermons you have heard in your church?
2. After you hear the preaching on a regular basis, do you feel energised, stimulated, secured, excited or depressed, discouraged, unfulfilled? Please elaborate.

3. Do you look forward to attending the next church service and listen to the preaching? Kindly elucidate.
4. How has your practice changed in the society/world/family, as a result of listening to sermons, in terms of ethical behaviour and the exercise of spiritual disciplines?
5. How do other people live their lives in the society/world as an outcome of regularly listening to the preaching in the churches?
6. What changes do you see (or you don't see) in the society as a result of Christians having listened to preaching in the church?
7. If there seems to be change in the society, what could be the reason for that? Moreover, if there seems to be no change in the society, what could be the reason for that?
8. In what way do you think an insufficient understanding of God's word directly or indirectly contribute to a dichotomy between sacred and secular, thus leading to a lifestyle that breeds nominalism?
9. How far can you see change in the lives of the believers as you preached in six months?

APPENDIX 10

Pilot Survey Questionnaire

Thesis Topic:

"An Examination of Preaching in the Baptist churches of Imphal city, 2000–2015, and Its Impact on the Spiritual Life, with Special Reference to Nominalism."

Main Research Question:

"What are the effects of preaching on the spiritual life of the members of the Baptist churches of Imphal, between 2000–2015?"

Practical Questions

1. How many pastors are there in your church?

_____

_____

2. Approximately, how many people preach in your church, in a calendar year?

_____

_____

3. How many camps (e.g., Youth; Parents; Women and Men) and conferences are conducted in the church annually?

_____

_____

4. What types of sermons structures (narration; expository; topical etc) are preached in the church?

5. What is the duration of each sermon?

Experiential-Reflective Questions

1. To what extent do you think the pastors, church leaders and members in the Baptist churches of Imphal city are aware of the effect of preaching on the spiritual life of a listener?

2. As the global church today faces the rampant problem of Christian spiritual stagnation, even nominalism, in what way do you think this problem is a concern for your church too?

3. In your opinion what are the factors that may be associated with the growth of nominalism in the church?

4. Some people think that "biblical gospel" must be preached to bring spiritual vitality. What do you think comprises "biblical gospel"?

5. How acceptable is the claim perceived to be that Christian nominalism thrives when the "biblical gospel" is not preached clearly?

6. In your opinion, is there a relationship between preaching and spiritual vitality? Give reasons.

7. In your opinion, is there a relationship between preaching and nominalism? Give reasons.

8. Does listening to preaching consistently feed your spiritual passion?

9. After you hear the preaching on a regular basis, do you feel energised, stimulated, secured, excited or depressed, discouraged, unfulfilled? Please elaborate.

10. Do you look forward to attending the next church service and listen to the preaching? Kindly elucidate.

11. Have your interest in reading the Bible increased because of the preaching you've heard? Why?

12. How have your practice changed in the society/ world/ family, as a result of listening to sermons, in terms of ethical behaviour and the exercise of spiritual disciplines?

13. What changes do you see (or you don't see) in the society as a result of Christians having listened to preaching in the church?

Theological-Reflective Questions

1. What types of preaching in your opinion, bring about spiritual vitality and what types of preaching incubates spiritual stagnation, even nominalism?

2. What types of sermon bring satisfaction and what type of sermons disappoint you? Why?

3. In the city of Imphal, where the preaching ministry is considered vibrant, how relevant is it to discuss about the relationship between bad preaching and nominalism?

4. In your opinion what is the main authority in preaching (warm experience or good delivery or vivid illustration or faithfulness to the text?) and why?

5. What do you think makes a good sermon?

6. How far is there an adequate understanding of God's word in your church?

7. How can a sufficient understanding of God's word transform the spiritual life of the members and prevent Christians from becoming spiritually stagnant?

8. To what extent can an insufficient understanding of God's word in the preaching event lead to spiritual stagnancy and practices that breed nominalism?

9. Who do you think is responsible for the insufficient understanding of God's word in the church, if it is there? Explain.

_____

_____

10. In what way do you think an insufficient understanding of God's word directly or indirectly contribute to a dichotomy between sacred and secular, thus leading to a lifestyle that breeds nominalism?

_____

_____

11. Do you think that a right understanding of God's word in the preaching event but a wrong lifestyle influenced by various worldviews influence a lifestyle that breed nominalism? And if so, can you briefly elucidate?

_____

_____

12. What are the central themes or theology in the preaching you have heard in your church?

_____

_____

APPENDIX 11

Pilot Survey Interview Questions

Name _____

Code _____

Thesis Topic

"An Examination of Preaching in the Baptist churches of Imphal city, 2000–2015, and Its Impact on the Spiritual Life, with Special Reference to Nominalism."

Main Research Question

"What are the effects of preaching on the spiritual life of the members of the Baptist churches of Imphal, between 2000–2015?"

Questions

1. How many pastors are there in your church?
2. What types of sermon structures (narration; expository; topical, testimonial etc) are generally being preached in the churches?
3. In your opinion, what types of preaching do you think exist in the pulpits of the Baptist churches in the city of Imphal?
4. What do you think makes a good sermon?
5. Some people say that "biblical gospel" must be preached to bring spiritual vitality. What do you think comprises "biblical gospel"?

6. In your opinion, is there a relationship between preaching and spiritual vitality? Give reasons.
7. In what way can preaching contribute to the spiritual vitality or spiritual lethargy of the listener?
8. In your opinion what is the main authority in preaching (warm experience or good delivery or vivid illustration or faithfulness to the text?) and why?
9. As the global church today faces the rampant problem of Christian spiritual stagnation, even nominalism, in what way do you think this problem is a concern for your church too?
10. In your opinion what are the factors that may be associated with the growth of nominalism in the church?
11. In the city of Imphal, where the preaching ministry is considered vibrant, how relevant is it to discuss about the relationship between preaching and nominalism?
12. To what extent can an insufficient understanding of God's word in the preaching event lead to spiritual stagnancy and practices that breed nominalism?
13. How would you describe the focus or goals of the sermons you have heard in your church?
14. How do other people live their lives in the society world as an outcome of regularly listening to the preaching in the churches?
15. What changes do you see (or you don't see) in the society as a result of Christians having listened to preaching in the church?
16. If there seems to be change in the society, what could be the reason for that? Moreover, if there seems to be no change in the society, what could be the reason for that?

APPENDIX 12

General Challenges to the Spirituality of the Members

Some of the general challenges to the spirituality of the members in the Baptist churches of Imphal are mentioned here, in addition to what is mentioned in the text.[1]

1. Challenge of Confronting Corruption and Bribery

Pastors find it hard to confront their members who do not consider it a problem to conduct their lives as the world does, with corruption and bribery. Without any critical and Scripture-based discernment, many members follow the tide of the corrupt society, thereby seriously damaging Christian testimony, spirituality, and missions to the unbelieving world. Pastor Oliver described this situation almost with a confused look:

> Nowadays, it is very unfortunate or fortunate, I don't know (he laughs), when we visit the church members, church members openly say to us, "Pastor, we paid 10 lakhs[2] already (as bribery), but we don't get any job. Pray for us." It is very difficult for a pastor to respond to this. Some will say, "Pastor, we don't have money but we borrowed money to give 3 lakhs to that Minister but, now the result is negative, we are not qualified for that post.

---

1. Cf. 4.3.6.
2. Around one million US dollars.

Our money is also gone, and we don't know where and how to get it back. Please pray for us." Some of the members share, "Pastor, we paid only Rs. 10 lakhs (for a government job), the result is out, we are selected. Please come and offer thanksgiving prayers for us in the thanksgiving ceremony." So, there are these issues of buying jobs, getting fake certificates, and sitting for the examinations on behalf of others. We have seen such church members, but when they come to church, they behave as good people, they sometimes seem more spiritual than the pastor. But when we observe their lives carefully, they are not biblical; they have dual identity, or dual face. So, when they go home or to the office, they do everything the world is doing.

He confessed that even after many years of listening to sermons, there is hardly any change on this front in the lives of his congregation.

2. Honesty Issue in Job Placement after Being Employed

Another issue that the church must face is regarding honesty in job placement after receiving the government employment order. Pastor Oliver was cautious not to point his finger at his members before he clarified the reality of the circumstances surrounding them. The common accusation is that many government primary and council teachers do not go to the allocated place of posting but rather appoint a substitute teacher, by paying them around one-tenth of the total salary. He says this is a common practice among his own tribesmen. Instead of accusing them as "sinful people," like some preachers do, he reasons that the situations should be analysed first before one passes judgement on them.

For example, Pastor Oliver shared that there had been a situation when one of the girls who went to her place of posting did not "find the village nor the school." In another case, when the appointed teacher went to the village, they found "cows in the schools," but no students. Pastor Oliver asked, "The truth is, in the government record, the school is there, but the school does not function in reality. So, whom do we blame?" In other cases, when the appointed teachers went to the village school, excited to teach the students, the village chief told them,

> You go back, don't worry about this. We will work here. In our village, we have so many unemployed boys and girls. You should help them. You stay in your home, no problem, I will employ those of my villagers who have passed their 10th or 12th grade, but who are unable to continue further studies. Every month, we will deduct Rs. 3000 or Rs. 4000, you do other things, this will solve the village unemployment problem.

Then pastor Oliver asked, "Who is to blame there? That is peacefully negotiated. Whether that is spiritual or not, they have settled the matter peacefully." Then he said, "But there are people who do not go to their respective posting location intentionally and keep substitute teachers. For those people, it is a sin. But for others, we have to look into various aspects like the government, the MLA (Minister of the Legislative Assembly), underground groups, village chief, the school infrastructure, etc."[3] His remarks came with the rider that we cannot just make a categorical statement about an issue and ignore other related issues that influence it.

3. Presence of Sick People in the Church

Pastor Samuel shared some of the responses of the church members regarding church attendance and spirituality during the ministry of the previous pastor of the church. The members expressed to him that

> in the past, there was no holistic preaching. There were several factions among the members – one group focused on a healing ministry with the pastor;[4] another group which was comprised of rich and influential members abstained from attending the church to avoid contact with sick people in the church, as several sick people came from various parts of Manipur because of the healing ministry of the pastor; there was another group

---

3. Pastor Samuel also shared that even his church members do the same thing.
4. Under the previous pastor's leadership, they had a healing centre in the church, where several sick people were housed, and a prayer and healing ministry was carried out.

who were lazy and blamed others for everything, and still there was another group who strategised to control and overtake the leadership in the church.

Kamal remembers that

> for several years, many people refused to attend the church because they felt that the dingy church was contaminated with various communicable diseases. But with the new church building, new furniture, and new pastor who preaches textual sermons, and who enlightens us on what Jesus said and taught, there is more church attendance; also, our confusion on if human authors crafted the gospel was dispelled when the pastor taught us the contexts of what Jesus said and did.

4. Conflict of Interest between Pastor and the Deacons

Expressing disappointment in the nature of the relationship between pastors and deacons in the Baptist churches, Pastor Peter made the following comments. Although he appreciated the value of the democratic principle exercised in the Naga society and its governance, he regretted that in the Baptist church set-up, a pastor's vision can be obstructed, in the guise of the democratic principle, by the deacon board. Further, Pastor Peter remarked that as the pastors are financially weak, they are unable to take their stand, "they are helpless, the rich deacon or member controls the pastor." He confessed,

> We become puppet pastors. Even now, I myself am a puppet pastor, a rubber stamp. I can do nothing on my own, since I am very poor. If I stop, I may even die of hunger, although this is not a good thing to say before people and God. So, we follow the one who is rich and influential. If I myself (an outspoken pastor) am in this condition, what will be the condition of the other pastors? By virtue of age, education and experience, I am also a qualified pastor in our society, but when it comes to influential people and rich people, when they say, do this or that, I have to simply say "yes" and follow.

5. Conflict of Theology between Prayer Warriors and Pastors

Prayer warriors play an important role in several Baptist churches by sensitising the members to be spiritually inclined to the Holy Spirit and follow the will of God. Pastor Matthew agreed that these prayer warriors (or some call them freestyle evangelists) "do have good influence in our society." But most of the time, they strum the emotional strings of the people, so that they will repent from their sins and wayward lifestyles, but such an impact does not last.

The nature of the prayer warriors' modus operandi conflicts with that of the pastors. Pastor Samuel confessed that depending on the prayer warriors is disastrous for one's personal faith because, instead of turning one's heart to Jesus in faith and deepening their personal prayer life, people tend to depend on the prayer warriors, "as if Jesus directly descended and taught the prayer warriors, whereas we the pastors are not, and when pastors preach and teach, the people feel as though they are merely listening to stuff from the newspaper" and not a message from God. In a way, "our dependence on the prayer warriors is like that of the Roman Catholics depending on the Pope and Fathers."

Some feel that the more influential self-styled evangelists are "responsible in leading people away from knowing the right doctrine to a weak prosperity theology doctrine." Pastor Samuel admitted, "We the pastors also have to be blamed because we are very weak in our Bible knowledge," and so when we cannot counter their blackmail, "If you don't do this, you will have an accident or you will become like this, etc." which comes "like flood water, people become so scared." The challenge for the pastors is that "our society likes them" because they claim "to receive God's revelation and have on some occasions healed people."

Pastor Matthew revealed that many of the prayer warriors do not preach intimidating things from the pulpit but do so only when they visit homes where they warn or blackmail the family according to their context and existential situation, which is disastrous to the emotional balance of the people. Pastor Samuel thinks that this situation has the potent ability to break up the local church as many people are unable to disagree with or confront the prayer warriors.

Bibliography

"9 Beautiful Union Territories of India." *Walk Through India*. Accessed 13 November 2019. http://www.walkthroughindia.com/attraction/9-beautiful-union-territories-of-india/.

Achtemeier, Elizabeth. *Nahum to Malachi: Interpretation: A Bible Commentary for Teaching and Preaching*. Louisville: Westminster John Knox Press, 2012.

———. *Preaching from the Minor Prophets*. Cambridge: Eerdmans, 1998.

———. *The Old Testament and the Proclamation of the Gospel*. Philadelphia: Westminster Press, 1973.

Adams, Jay E. "Theology of Powerful Preaching: Nine Beliefs at the Heart of Biblical Preaching." In *The Art and Craft of Biblical Preaching: A Comprehensive Resource for Today*, edited by Haddon Robinson and Craig Brian Larson, 33–35. Grand Rapids: Zondervan, 2005.

Adams, Larry. *Revelation: A Fresh Perspective*. Bloomington: WestBow Press, 2014.

Adam, Peter. *Hearing God's Words: Exploring Biblical Spirituality*. Series Editor, D. A. Carson. Downers Grove: InterVarsity Press, 2004.

———. *The Message of Malachi*. BST. Edited by J. A. Motyer. Downers Grove: InterVarsity Press, 2013.

———. *Speaking God's Words: A Practical Theology of Preaching*. Leicester: InterVarsity Press, 1996.

Addo, Ebenezer Acheampong. *The Principles of Transformation*. Bloomington: Xlibris, 2015.

Ahuja, Ram. *Research Methods*. New Delhi: Rawat Publications, 2001.

Akhui, Z. A. S. *A Short Account of Tangkhul Naga Culture*. Imphal: Tarun Printing, 1973.

Allen, Leslie C. *A Theological Approach to the Old Testament: Major Themes and New Testament Connections*. Eugene: Cascade, 2014.

Allen, Ronald. *Preaching the Topical Sermon*. Louisville: Westminster John Knox Press, 1992.

Arnald, Richard. *A Critical Commentary on Such Books of the Apocrypha*. London: Bowyer, 1760. https://www.google.co.in/books/edition/A_Critical_Commentary_on_Such_Books_of_t/TlwwxQEACAAJ?hl=en.

American Baptist Foreign Mission Society. *Ninety-Eighth Annual Report* (1912).

AM of the ABMU: Report, 1895.

Anderson, John S. "Manipur State-Kangpokpi." *CBCA*, 1954.

———. "Manipur Annual Report 1954." *CBCAM*, 1955.

Arksey, Hilary, and Peter T. Knight. *Interviewing for Social Scientists: An Introductory Resource with Examples*. London: SAGE, 1999.

Arokianathan, S. *Tangkhul Folk Literature*. Mysore: Central Institute of Indian Languages, 1982.

Ashcraft, Morris. *Rudolf Bultmann*. Waco: Word Books, 1972.

Athyal, Saphir P. "Southern Asia." In *Towards the 21st Century in Christian Mission: Essays in Honor of Gerald H. Anderson*, edited by Robert T. Coote and James M. Phillips, 59–61. Grand Rapids: Eerdmans, 2000.

Auerbach, Carl F., and Louise B. Silverstein. *Qualitative Data: An Introduction to Coding and Analysis*. New York: New York University Press, 2003.

Awbrey, Ben E. "A Critical Examination of the Theory and Practice of John F. MacArthur's Expository Preaching." ThD diss, New Orleans Baptist Theological Seminary, 1990.

Azon, P. "Christianity and Transformation in Nagaland." In *Transform North East India: Revitalise the Church and Community*, edited by T. Hawiphal, 49–58. Guwahati: TNEI2020, 2016.

Bacon, Ernest W. *Spurgeon: Heir of the Puritans*. Arlington Heights: Christian Liberty Press, 1996.

Baker, Sarah Elsie, and Rosalind Edwards. "How Many Qualitative Interviews Is Enough? Expert Voices and Early Career Reflections on Sampling and Cases in Qualitative Research." *NCRMRP*. Accessed 13 June 2018. http://eprints.ncrm.ac.uk/2273/4/how_many_interviews.pdf.

Baldwin, Joyce G. *Haggai, Zechariah, Malachi*. Downers Grove: InterVarsity Press, 1972.

———. *Haggai, Zechariah, Malachi: An Introduction and Commentary*. TOTC. Edited by D. J. Wiseman. Leicester: Inter-Varsity Press, 1984.

Balthasar, Hans Urs von. *Theo-Drama: Theological Dramatic Theory*. San Francisco: Ignatius Press, 1988.

Barclay, John M. G. "Thessalonica and Corinth: Social Contrasts in Pauline Christianity." *JSNT* 15, no. 47 (1992): 49–74.

Barentsen, Jack. *Emerging Leadership in the Pauline Mission: A Social Identity Perspective on Local Leadership Development in Corinth and Ephesus*. Eugene: Pickwick, 2011.

Barnett, Paul. *The Message of 2 Corinthians*. BST. Edited by John R. W. Stott. Downers Grove: InterVarsity Press, 1988.
Barrett, C. K. "The Place of Eschatology in the Fourth Gospel." *ET* 59 (1947–48): 302–5.
Barth, Karl. *Church Dogmatics Study Edition 1: The Doctrine of the Word of God*. Edited by G. W. Bromiley and T. F. Torrance. New York: T&T Clark, 2010.
———. *Church Dogmatics: The Doctrine of Reconciliation*. Edited by G. W. Bromiley and T. F. Torrance. Translated by G. W. Bromiley. Vol. 4.2. London: T&T Clark, 2004.
———. *Dogmatics in Outline*. New York: Harper & Row, 1959.
———. *Homiletics*. Translated by Geoffrey W. Bromiley and Donald E. Daniels. Louisville: Westminster John Knox Press, 1991.
———. *The Preaching of the Gospel*. Translated by B. E. Hooke. London: SCM, 1963.
Bartleman, Frank. *Azusa Street: An Eyewitness Account to the Birth of the Pentecostal Revival*. New Kensington: Whitaker House, 1962.
Baur, Ferdinand Christian. "Die Christuspartei in der korinthischen Gemeinde, der Gegensatz der petrinischen und paulinischen Christentums in der ältesten Kirche, der Apostel Petrus in Rom." *Tübinger Zeitschrift für Theologie* 4 (1831): 61–206.
———. *Paul, the Apostle of Jesus Christ: His Life and Works, His Epistles and Teachings*. Two volumes. Peabody: Hendrickson, 2003.
Baxter, Richard. *Poetical Fragments*. Gregg International, 1971.
———. *The Reformed Pastor*. Lafayette: Sovereign Grace, 2000.
Becon, Thomas. *The Demands of the Holy Scripture*. Three volumes. London: Religious Track Society, 1563.
"Beginning of Ukhrul Station (1897), The." In *History of Christianity in Manipur: Source Materials*. Compiled by Elungkiebe Zeliang. Guwahati: CLC, 2005.
Benner, David G. *Care of Souls: Revisioning Christian Nurture and Counsel*. Grand Rapids: Baker Books, 1998.
Best, Ernest. *Second Corinthians*. Louisville: Westminster John Knox Press, 1987.
Bloor, Michael. "Techniques of Validation in Qualitative Research: A Critical Commentary." In *Context and Method in Qualitative Research*, edited by G. Miller and R. Dingwall, 37–50. London: SAGE, 1997.
Birstsch, Gunter. "The Christian as Subject." In *The Transformation of Political Culture: England and Germany in the Late Eighteen Century*, edited by Eckhart Hellmut, 317–26. Oxford: Oxford University Press, 1990.
Blanche, Daniel. "Schleiermacher and Preaching." *Shiny Ginger Thoughts*. Accessed 17 April 2018. http://danielblanche.blogspot.in/2018/01/schleiermacher-and-preaching.html.
Bloesch, Donald. *The Reform of the Church*. Grand Rapids: Eerdmans, 1970.

Bonhoeffer, Dietrich. *The Cost of Discipleship.* New York: Simon & Schuster, 1995.

Boyd, Carolyn Oiler. "Phenomenology: The Method." In *Nursing Research: A Qualitative Perspective*, 3rd ed., edited by P. L. Munhall, 93–122. Sudbury: Jones & Bartlett, 2001.

Bretton, Henry L. *The Power of Money: A Political-Economic Analysis with Special Emphasis on the American Political System.* New York: New York University Press, 1980.

Brierley, Peter. *Leaders Briefings No 8, Nominalism Reconceived – The Phenomenon of the 1990s.* London: Christian Research, 1997.

———. "Numbering the Nominals." In *They Call Themselves Christian: Papers on Nominality Given at the International Lausanne Consultation on Nominalism*, edited by Heather Wraight, 69–88. London: Christian Research, 1999.

Bromiley, Geoffrey W. "Preface," *Homiletics*, by Karl Barth. Translated by Geoffrey W. Bromiley and Donald E. Daniels, 13–15. Louisville: Westminster John Knox Press, 1991.

Brooks, Phillips. *Lecture on Preaching: Delivered before the Divinity School of Yale College.* New York: E. P. Dutton & Company, 1878.

———. *On Preaching.* New York: Seabury Press, 1964.

Brown, Harold. *Rationality.* Problems of Philosophy series. London: Routledge, 1990.

Bruce, F. F. "Paul on Immortality." *SJT* 24 (1971): 457–72.

Brown, R. *Statistics Account of Manipur.* New Delhi: Mittal Publication, 2001.

Browne, E. Harold. *Julian's Reply to the Lord Bishop of Ely: Christ's Influence on History.* London: Hamilton, Adams & Co., 1871.

Brueggemann, Walter. *Spirituality of the Psalms.* Minneapolis: Fortress Press, 2002.

Brunner, Emil. "The Significance of the Old Testament for Our Faith." In *The Old Testament and Christian Faith: A Theological Discussion*, edited by Bernhard W. Anderson, 243–64. New York: Herder & Herder, 1969.

Bryman, Alan. *Social Research Methods*, 4th ed. Oxford: Oxford University Press, 2012.

Bultmann, Rudolf. *Existence and Faith.* Translated by Schubert Ogden. London: Hodder & Stoughton, 1960.

———. "General Truths and Christian Proclamation." In *History and Hermeneutic*, edited by Robert Walter Funk, 153–62. Vol. 1. Translated by Schubert M. Ogden. Tübingen: Mohr Siebeck, 1967.

———. *The Gospel of John: A Commentary.* Translated by G. R. Beasley-Murray. Philadelphia: Westminster Press, 1971.

———. *Jesus Christ and Mythology.* New York: Charles Scribner's Sons, 1958.

———. "New Testament and Mythology." In *Kerygma and Myth,* edited by Hans Werner Bartsch, 1–44. New York: Harper & Row, 1961.

———. "Preaching: Genuine and Secularized." In *Religion and Culture: Essays in Honor of Paul Tillich,* edited by Walter Leibrecht. Translated by Harold O. J. Brown, 236–42. New York: Harper & Bros., 1959.

Bush, L. Russ, and Tom J. Nettles. *Baptists and the Bible.* Nashville: B&H, 1999.

Bush, Michael D. "Preaching." In *The Westminster Handbook to Karl Barth,* edited by Richard E. Burnett, 168–70. Louisville: Westminster John Knox Press, 2013.

Buttrick, David. *Homiletics: Moves and Structures.* Philadelphia: Fortress Press, 1987.

———. "On Doing Homiletics Today." In *Intersections: Post-Critical Studies in Preaching,* edited by Richard L. Eslinger, 88–104. Grand Rapids: Eerdmans, 1994.

Byrne, James M. *Religion and the Enlightenment: From Descartes to Kant.* Louisville: Westminster John Knox Press, 1996.

Calvin, John. *Twelve Minor Prophets*: Zechariah and Malachi, vol. 5. Edinburgh: T&T Clark, 1849.

Cameron, Helen. "How to Study the Local Church." In *Studying Local Churches: A Handbook,* edited by Helen Cameron, Philip Richter, Douglas Davies, and Frances Ward, 35–42. London: SCM Press, 2005.

Cameron, Helen, and Catherin Duce. *Researching Practice in Ministry and Mission: A Companion.* London: SCM Press, 2013.

Cameron, Julia. "John Stott: Preacher and Writer Who Exerted a Colossal Influence on Evangelical Christianity." *Independent.* Accessed 23 August 2019. https://www.independent.co.uk/news/obituaries/john-stott-preacher-and-writer-who-exerted-a-colossal-influence-on-evangelical-christianity-2327834.html.

Campanini, Massimo. "Abu Hamid Muhammad al-Ghazali." In *Muhammad in History, Thought, and Culture: An Encyclopedia of the Prophet of God,* edited by Coeli Fitzpatrick and Adam Hani Walker. Vol. 1. Oxford: ABC-CLIO, 2014.

Campbell, Charles L. *Preaching Jesus: New Directions for Homiletics in Hans Frei's Postliberal Theology.* Grand Rapids: Eerdmans, 1997.

Carson, D. A. *A Model of Christian Maturity: An Exposition of 2 Corinthians 10–13.* Grand Rapids: Baker Books: 2007.

———. "Teaching the Whole Bible." In *The Art and Craft of Biblical Preaching: A Comprehensive Resource for Today,* edited by Haddon Robinson and Craig Brian Larson. Grand Rapids: Zondervan, 2005.

Carson, D. A., Douglas J. Moo, and Leon Morris. *An Introduction to the New Testament.* Grand Rapids: Zondervan, 1992.

Chafer, Lewis Sperry, and John F. Walvoord. *Major Bible Themes.* Grand Rapids: Zondervan, 1974.

Chapell, Bryan. *Christ-Centered Preaching*. Grand Rapids: Baker Books, 2015.

Chapman, Alister. "Evangelical or Fundamentalist." In *Evangelicalism and Fundamentalism in the United Kingdom during the Twentieth Century*, edited by David Bebbington and David Ceri Jones, 192–208. Oxford: Oxford University Press, 2013.

Chapman, C. L. *Rightly Dividing the Word of Truth*. Bloomington: Trafford Publishers, 2010.

Charles, H. B., Jr. *On Pastoring: A Short Guide to Living, Leading, and Ministering as a Pastor*. Chicago: Moody Publishers, 2016.

Chase, Randal S. *Old Testament Study Guide, Pt. 1: Genesis to Numbers*. Washington: Plan & Precious Publishing, 2010.

Chester, Tim, and Marcus Honeysett. *Gospel-Centred Preaching*. Epsom: Good Book Company, 2014.

Childers, Eric. *College Identity Sagas*. Eugene: Pickwick Publications, 2012.

Christian, C. W. *Friedrich Schleiermacher*, edited by Bob E. Patterson. Waco: Word Books, 1979.

Chung, Paul S. *Karl Barth: God's Word in Action*. Eugene: Cascade Books, 2008.

Ciampa, Roy E., and Brian S. Rosner. *The First Letter to the Corinthians*. The Pillar New Testament Commentary. Nottingham: Apollos, 2010.

Clark, E. W. *Naga Mission and Church Record*. Valley Forge: ABFMS, 2 July 1894.

Clines, D. J. *Ezra, Nehemiah, Esther*. NCBC. London: Marshall, Morgan & Scott, 1984.

Collins, Raymond F. *First Corinthians*. Collegeville: Liturgical Press, 1999.

Cotton, Henry. "Introduction." In *The Five Books of Maccabees in English: With Notes and Illustrations*, edited by Henry Cotton, xi–xxxviii. Oxford: Oxford University Press, 1832.

Coutsoumpos, Panayotis. *Paul, Corinth, and the Roman Empire*. Eugene: Wipf & Stock, 2015.

Craddock, Fred B. *As One without Authority*. St. Louis: Chalice Press, 2001.

———. *Preaching*. Nashville: Abingdon, 1985.

Creswell, John W. *Qualitative Inquiry and Research Design: Choosing Among Five Traditions*, 3rd ed. New Delhi: SAGE, 2013.

———. *Research Design: Qualitative and Quantitative Approaches*. Thousand Oaks: SAGE, 1994.

———. *Research Design: Qualitative, Quantitative, and Mixed Methods*. New Delhi: SAGE, 2014.

Crossroads International. "Indigenous Missions: The Changing Face of Missions." Accessed 17 October 2017. http://www.crossroadsinternational.org/news/missions-full-circle.

Crotty, M. *The Foundations of Social Research: Meaning and Perspective in the Research Process*. Thousand Oaks: SAGE, 1998.

Crouch, Mira, and Heather McKenzie. "The Logic of Small Samples in Interview-based Qualitative Research." *SSI* 45, no. 4 (2006): 483–99.

Crozier, G. G. *Educational Report from Manipur,* December 1929, 1 (Cyclostyled).

Cully, Iris V. *Education for Spiritual Growth.* San Francisco: Harper & Row, 1984.

Curry, F .F. "Kangpokpi - M.E. School." *CBCA,* 1953.

Dahl, N. A. "'Do Not Wonder': Jn 5:28–29 and Johannine Eschatology Once More." In *The Conversation Continues,* edited by R. Fortna and B. Gaventa, 322–36. Nashville: Abingdon Press, 1990.

Danesi, Marcel. *Popular Culture: Introductory Perspectives.* 2nd ed. New York: Rowman & Littlefield, 2012.

Dargan, Edwin C. *A History of Preaching.* Vol. 1. Grand Rapids: Baker Books, 1974.

Davies, Douglas. "Why Study the Local Church?" In *Studying Local Churches: A Handbook,* edited by Helen Cameron, Philip Richter, Douglas Davies, and Frances Ward. London: SCM Press, 2005.

Davis, Henry Grady. *Design for Preaching.* Philadelphia: Fortress Press, 1958.

Decker, Bert, and Hershael W. York. *Preaching with Bold Assurance: A Solid and Enduring Approach to Engaging Exposition.* Nashville: B&H, 2003.

Dena, Lal. *Christian Mission and Colonialism: A Study of Missionary Movement in North East India with Special Reference to Manipur and Lushai Hills, 1894–1947.* Shillong: Vendrame Institute, 1988.

deSilva, David A. *Introducing the Apocrypha: Message, Context, and Significance.* Grand Rapids: Baker Academic, 2004.

"Districts in Manipur." *Manipur Government Website.* Accessed 6 September 2018. https://manipur.gov.in/?page_id=619.

Dockery, Daniel L. "The Theology of Scripture as a Decisive Factor in Homiletical Theory and Methodology: A Comparative Analysis of David G. Buttrick and John R. W. Stott." PhD diss., Southeastern Baptist Theological Seminary, 2010.

Doughty, W. L. *John Wesley the Preacher.* London: Epworth Press, 1955.

Downs, F. S. *The Mighty Works of God: A Brief History of the Council of Baptist Churches in North East India: The Mission Period 1836–1950.* Gauhati, Assam: CLC, 1971.

Dozo, Phuveyi. "A Unique Role of the Nagas in Christ." In *In Search of Praxis Theology for the Nagas.* New Delhi: CNBC, 2003.

Drummond, Lewis A. *Spurgeon: Prince of Preachers.* Grand Rapids: Kregel, 1992.

Dunn, James D. G. *Jesus, Paul, and the Gospels.* Grand Rapids: Eerdmans, 2011.

Ebeling, Gerhard. *Theology and Proclamation: A Discussion with Rudolf Bultmann.* London: Collins, 1966.

———. *Word and Faith.* Philadelphia: Fortress Press, 1963.

Edre, Enosh Anguandia Adia. "Christian Nominalism within Church Membership: A Case Study of the Church in the Town of Bunia in the Democratic Republic of Congo." PhD diss., South Africa Theological Seminary, 2015.

Edwards, O. C., Jr. *A History of Preaching*. Vol. 1. Nashville: Abingdon, 2014.

———. "History of Preaching." In *Concise Encyclopedia of Preaching*, edited by William H. Willimon and Richard Lischer, 184–227. Louisville: Westminster John Knox Press, 1995.

Eijnatten, Joris Van. "Reaching Audiences: Sermons and Oratory in Europe." In *The Cambridge History of Christianity: Volume VII, Enlightenment, Reawakening and Revolution 1660–1815*, edited by Stewart J. Brown and Timothy Tackett, 128–46. Cambridge: Cambridge University Press, 2006.

Ekstrand, D. W. "The Intertestamental Period and Its Significance upon Christianity." *The Transformed Soul*. Accessed 18 September 2019. http://www.thetransformedsoul.com/additional-studies/spiritual-life-studies/the-intertestamental-period-and-its-significance-upon-christianity.

Elazar, Gideon. "Nominalism: Negotiating Ethnic and Christian Identity in Contemporary Yunnan." *MAS* 53, no. 5 (2019): 1415–49.

Ellis, E. Earle. *Prophecy and Hermeneutic in Early Christianity: New Testament Essays*, WUNT 18. Tubingen: Mohr Siebeck, 1978.

"Embracing Brokenness." *RREACH*. Accessed 3 October 2019. https://rreach.org/portfolio-items/gprocongress-highlights.

"Equipping Preachers Has an Exponential Impact." *Langham Partnership*. Accessed on October 2019. https://langham.org/what-we-do/langham-preaching/.

Eslinger, Richard L. *The Web of Preaching*. Nashville: Abingdon, 2002.

Etter, John W. *The Preacher and His Sermon: A Treatise on Homiletics*. Dayton: United Brethren Publishing, 1883.

Fan, Lizhu, and James D. Whitehead. "Spirituality in a Modern Chinese Metropolis." In *Chinese Religious Life*, edited by David A. Palmer, Glenn Shive, and Philip L. Wickeri, 13–29. Oxford: Oxford University Press, 2011.

Fedorak, Shirley A. *Pop Culture: The Culture of Everyday Life*. Toronto: University of Toronto Press, 2009.

Feltham, Trevor. *Deep Spiritual Thoughts*. Bloomington: WestBow Press, 2015.

Fiedler, Klaus. *The Story of Faith Missions: From Hudson Taylor to Present Day Africa*. Oxford: Regnum Press, 1994.

Foreign Department. *Secret Proceedings*, Nos. 24–28, January 1895.

Forsyth, P. T. *Positive Preaching and the Modern Mind*. Grand Rapids: Baker Books, 1980.

Foster, Richard J. *Streams of Living Water: Celebrating the Great Traditions of Christian Faith*. New York: Harper Collins, 2017.

Friedrich, G. "To Proclaim Good News." In *Theological Dictionary of the New Testament Abridged in One Volume*. Edited by Gerhard Kittel and Gerhard Friederich, 233–39. Translated by Geoffrey W. Bromiley. Grand Rapids: Eerdmans, 1985.

Fuchs, Ernst. *Studies of the Historical Jesus*. London: SCM, 1964.

Fuller, Charles W. *The Trouble with "Truth through Personality": Phillip Brooks, Incarnation, and the Evangelical Boundaries of Preaching*. Eugene: Wipf & Stock, 2010.

Fullerton, Ryan, Jim Orrick, and Brian Payne. *Encountering God through Expository Preaching: Connecting God's People to God's Presence through God's Word*. Nashville: B&H Academic, 2017.

Galdamez, Michael Raymond. "Worldview Preaching in the Church: The Preaching Ministries of J. Gresham Machen and Timothy J. Keller." PhD diss., Southern Baptist Theological Seminary, 2012.

Garvie, A. E. *The Christian Preacher*. New York: C. Scribner's Sons, 1923.

Gerkin, Charles. *The Living Human Document: Re-Visioning Pastoral Counseling in a Hermeneutical Mode*. Nashville: Abingdon, 1984.

Getz, Donald, and Stephen J. Page. *Event Studies: Theory, Research and Policy for Planned Events*, 3rd ed. London: Routledge, 2016.

Gibbs, Eddie. *In Name Only: Tackling the Problem of Nominal Christianity*. Wheaton: Bridge Book, 1998.

———. "Introduction and Literature Review." In *They Call Themselves Christians: Papers on Nominality Given at the International Lausanne Consultation on Nominalism*, edited by Heather Wraight. London: Christian Research, 1999.

Gibson, Scott M. "Critique of the New Homiletic: Examining the Link between the New Homiletic and the New Hermeneutic." In *The Art and Craft of Biblical Preaching*, edited by Craig Brian Larson and Haddon Robinson, 476–81. Grand Rapids: Zondervan, 2005.

Gibson, Scott M., and Matthew D. Kim, eds. *Homiletics and Hermeneutics*. Grand Rapids: Baker Academic, 2018.

Gilbert, Greg. *Preach: Theology Meets Practice*. Nashville: B&H, 2012.

Gnana, Robinson. "Homiletics Today vs. Biblical Homiletics." In *Preaching in the 21st Century: Towards a New Homiletics*, edited by Vinod Victor and Amritha Bosi Perumalla, 58–64. Delhi: ISPCK, 2013.

Goldsworthy, Graeme. *Preaching the Whole Bible as Christian Scripture*. Grand Rapids: Eerdmans, 2000.

González, Justo L., and Catherine Gunsalus González. *Liberation Preaching: The Pulpit and the Oppressed*. Nashville: Abingdon, 1993.

Gorringe, Timothy J. *Karl Barth: Against Hegemony*. Oxford: Oxford University Press, 1999.

Gottwald, N. K. *The Hebrew Bible: A Socio-Literary Introduction*. Philadelphia: Fortress Press, 1985.

Goulder, Michael. *Paul and the Competing Mission in Corinth*. Peabody: Hendrickson, 2001.

Grady, Michael P. *Qualitative and Action Research: A Practitioner Handbook*. Bloomington: Phi Delta Kappa Educational Foundation, 1998.

Graffy, Adrian. *A Prophet Confronts His People: The Disputation Speech in the Prophets*. AnBib 104. Rome: BIP, 1984.

Grand Canyon University. "Strength and Limitations of Phenomenology." *CIRT*. Accessed 27 June 2018. https://cirt.gcu.edu/research/developmentresources/research_ready/phenomenology/strengths_limits.

Green, Jay. "A Very Brief Account of the Life of Richard Baxter." In *Reformed Pastor*, edited by Richard Baxter. Lafayette: Sovereign Grace, 2000.

Greidanus, Sidney. *The Modern Preacher and the Ancient Text*. Grand Rapids: Eerdmans, 1996.

———. *Preaching Christ from the Old Testament: A Contemporary Hermeneutical Method*. Grand Rapids: Eerdmans, 1999.

Groenwald, Thomas. "A Phenomenological Research Design Illustrated." *IJQM* 3, no. 1 (2004): 42–55.

Groeschel, Benedict J. *Spiritual Passages*. New York: Crossroad, 1983.

Guest, G., A. Bunce, and L. Johnson. "How Many Interviews Are Enough? An Experiment with Data Saturation and Variability." *Field Methods* 18, no. 1 (2006): 59–82.

Haak, Carl. "Spiritual Lethargy." Protestant Reformed Churches in America. Accessed 12 August 2019. http://www.prca.org/resources/sermons/reading/reformed-witness-hour/item/3272-spiritual-lethargy.

Hafemann, Scott J. *Paul's Message and Ministry in Covenant Perspective: Selected Essays*. Eugene: Cascade Books, 2015.

Hage, Maarten. *A Stakeholders Concern: Towards an Economic Theory on Stakeholder Governance*. Assen: Van Gorcum, 2007.

Hale, Tom, and Steve Thorson. *Applied Old Testament Commentary: Applying God's Word to Your Life*. Colorado Springs: David C. Cook, 2007.

Hammersley, M. *Taking Sides in Social Research*. London: Routledge, 2000.

Haokip, Jangkholam. *Can God Save My Village? A Theological Study of Identity Among the Tribal People of North-East with a Special Reference to the Kukis in Manipur*. Carlisle: Langham Monographs, 2014.

Haokip, T. Ngulkhomang. "Spread of Christianity and Its Impact on the Hill Tribes of Manipur." MPhil thesis, North-East Hill University, 2004.

Harmon, Dan. *Charles Haddon Spurgeon*. Uhrichsville: Barbour Publishing, 2013.

Harris, Murray J. *The Second Epistle to the Corinthians*. NIGTC. Grand Rapids: Eerdmans, 2005.

Hart, C. *Doing a Literature Review: Releasing the Social Science Research Imagination*. London, SAGE, 1998.

Hattaway, Paul. *From Head-Hunters to Church Planters: An Amazing Spiritual Awakening in Nagaland*. Downers Grove: InterVarsity Press, 2006.

Hatzaw, H. S. *Christianity in Manipur*. Central Lamka Churachandpur, Manipur: H. Hang Za Kam, 2003.

Hawkins, Steve. *From Legal to Regal: Religion to Royalty*. Lake Mary: Creation House, 2013.
Hayes, Richard B. *First Corinthians: Interpretation*. Louisville: Westminster John Knox Press, 2011.
Hazelip, Harold, and Ken Durham. *Becoming Persons of Integrity*. Grand Rapids: Baker Books, 1988.
Hedlund, Roger E. *World Christianity: South Asia*. Vol. 3. Monrovia: MARC, 1980.
Heidegger, Martin. *Being and Time*. Translated by Joan Stambaugh. Albany: SUNY Press, 2010.
Heitink, Gerben. *Practical Theology*. Grand Rapids: Eerdmans, 1999.
Hellmut, Eckhart, ed. *The Transformation of Political Culture: England and Germany in the Late Eighteenth Century*. Oxford: Oxford University Press, 1990.
Herzog, Jonathan P. *The Spiritual-Industrial Complex: America's Religious Battle against Communism in the Early Cold War*. Oxford: Oxford University Press, 2011.
Hill, Andrew E. *Malachi: A New Translation with Introduction and Commentary*. London: Doubleday, 1998.
Hill, Samuel Payton. "Jesus Christ and Him Crucified: The Christocentric Preaching Instinct of Timothy Keller." PhD diss., Southern Baptist Theological Seminary, 2018.
Hminga, Chhangte Lal. "The Life and Witness of the Churches in Mizoram." DMiss diss., Fuller Theological Seminary, 1976.
Hokey, S. K. "General Secretary Report." *Manipur Baptist Convention Annual Report 1993*. Imphal: MBC, 1994.
———. "General Secretary Report." *Manipur Baptist Convention Annual Report 1995*. Imphal: MBC, 1997.
Holloway, Immy. *Basic Concepts for Qualitative Research*. Hoboken: Wiley-Blackwell, 1997.
Holm, B. "The Work of the Spirit: The Reformation to the Present." In *The Holy Spirit in the Life of the Church*, edited by P. Opsahl. Minneapolis: Augsburg, 1978.
Holmes, Zan. "Enabling the Word to Happen." In *Power in the Pulpit: How America's Most Effective Black Preachers Prepare Their Sermons*, edited by Cleophus J. LaRue, 74–82. Louisville: Westminster John Knox Press, 2002.
Home Missionary, The. Vol. 45. New York: American Home Missionary Society, 1873.
"Homiletical Theology Project." *Boston University School of Theology*. Accessed 28 January 2020. https://www.bu.edu/homiletical-theology-project/.
Hopewell, James. *Congregation: Stories and Structures*. London: SCM Press, 1987.
Horsley, Richard A. *1 Corinthians*. Nashville: Abingdon, 1998.

———. "Gnosis in Corinth: 1 Corinthians 8: 1–6." In *Christianity at Corinth: The Quest for the Pauline Church*, edited by Edward Adams and David G. Horrell, 119–28. Louisville: Westminster John Knox Press, 2004.

"Pneumatikos-Psychikos: Distinction of Spiritual Status among the Corinthians." *HTR* 69 (1976): 269–88.

"How Langham Preaching Works." *Langham Partnership*. Accessed 3 October 2019. https://langham.org/what-we-do/langham-preaching/.

Hrangkhuma, Fanai. "Mizo Spirituality." In *Witness to Christ in North East India*, RECS, Vol. 31, edited by Marina Ngursangzeli and Michael Biehl, 399–408. Oxford: Regnum, 2016.

———. "Mizoram Transformational Change: A Study of the Processes and Nature of Mizo Cultural Change and Factors That Contributed to the Change." PhD diss., Fuller Theological Seminary, 1989.

Hsieh, Hsiu-Fang, and Sarah E. Shannon. "Three Approaches to Qualitative Content Analysis." *QHR* 15, no. 9 (Nov. 2005):1277–88.

Hussell, Lewis P. *A Commentary on Amos, Ezra, Esther, Haggai, Nehemiah*. Bloomington: AuthorHouse, 2013.

Husserl, Edmund. *Ideas: General Introduction to Pure Phenomenology*. London: Routledge, 2014.

———. *Phenomenology and the Crisis of Philosophy*. Translated by Quentin Lauer. New York: Harper Torchbooks, 1965.

———. *Phenomenology and the Foundations of the Sciences*. Translated by Ted E. Klein and William E. Pohl. London: Martinus Nijhoff Publishers, 1980.

Hutson, Curtis. *Great Preaching on Soul Winning*. Murfreesboro: Sword of the Lord Publishers, 1989.

Hycner, R. H. "Some Guidelines for the Phenomenological Analysis of Interview Data." In *Qualitative Research*, Vol. 3, edited by A. Bryman and R. G. Burgess, 143–64. London: SAGE, 199.

Irwin, William. "Philosophy as/and/of Popular Culture." In *Philosophy and the Interpretation of Pop Culture*, edited by William Irwin and Jorge J. E. Gracia, 41–63. New York: Rowman & Littlefield, 2007.

———. "Philosophy Engages Popular Culture: An Introduction." In *Philosophy and the Interpretation of Pop Culture*, edited by William Irwin and Jorge J. E. Gracia, 1–18. New York: Rowman & Littlefield, 2007.

Isaiah, Gaddala. *Preach the Word*. Tiruvalla: Christava Sahitya Samithi, 2004.

Issler, Klaus. "Practicing the Elements of Spiritual Formation." In *Foundations of Spiritual Formation: A Community Approach to Becoming Like Christ*, edited by Paul Pettit, 124–254. Grand Rapids: Kregel, 2008.

Iyadurai, Joshua. *Transformative Religious Experience: A Phenomenological Understanding of Religious Conversion*. Chennai: MCISR, 2017.

Jensen, Phillip D. "Preaching That Changes the Church." In *When God's Voice Is Heard: The Power of Preaching*, edited by David Jackman and Christopher Green, 137–48. Leicester: Inter-Varsity Press, 2003.

Johnson, Alan F. *1 Corinthians*. NTCS. Downers Grove: IVP Academic, 2004.

Johnson, Darrell. *The Glory of Preaching: Participating in God's Transformation of the World*. Downers Grove: IVP Academic, 2009.

Johnson, George D. *What Will a Man Give in Exchange for His Soul?* Harrisburg: Light of the Saviour Ministries, 2011.

Jones, Douglas Rawlinson. *Haggai, Zechariah and Malachi: Introduction and Commentary*. London: SCM, 1962.

Jones, Ilion T. *Principles and Practices of Preaching*. New York: Abingdon, 1956.

Joshi, S. C. *Manipur: The Jewel of India*. New Delhi: Akansha Publishing, 2002.

"Jubilee in Manipur (1898), The." In *History of Christianity in Manipur: Source Materials*. Compiled by Elungkiebe Zeliang. Guwahati: CLC, 2005.

Kabui, Gangmumei. *Anal: A Transborder Tribe of Manipur*. New Delhi: Mittal Publications, 1985.

Kaiser, Walter C., Jr. *The Christian and the Old Testament*. Pasadena: William Carey Library, 1998.

———. *Malachi: God's Unchanging Love*. Eugene: Wipf & Stock, 1984.

———. *Preaching and Teaching from the Old Testament: A Guide for the Church*. Grand Rapids: Baker Academic, 2003.

Kant, Immanuel. "An Answer to the Question: What Is Enlightenment?" In *What Is Enlightenment? Eighteenth-Century Answers and Twentieth-Century Questions*, edited and translated by James Schmidt, 58–64. Los Angeles: University of California Press, 1996.

Kasbekar, Asha. *Pop Culture India!: Media, Arts, and Lifestyle*. Oxford: ABC-CLIO, 2006.

Kashung, Shangpam. "Impact of Christianity on the Tangkhuls of Ukhrul Town, Manipur." PhD diss., North Eastern Hill University, 2012.

Keating, Thomas. *The Heart of the World*. New York: Crossroad, 1981.

Keller, Timothy. "The Gospel-Shaped Life." TGC. Accessed 14 January 2020. https://www.youtube.com/watch?v=-mu_CLg2Nfo.

———. *Preaching: Communicating Faith in a Sceptical Age*. London: Hodder & Stoughton, 2015.

———. *The Reason for God: Making Sense of God and the Prodigal God*. London: Hodder & Stoughton, 2016.

Kengoo, Ringphami. "Effective Strategies for Discipling the Nominal Baptist Youth of the Manipur Baptist Convention." ThM thesis, Torch Trinity Graduate School of Theology, 2007.

Kensit, D. A. "Rogerian Theory: A Critique of the Effectiveness of Pure Client-Centred Therapy." *CPQ* 13, no. 4 (2000): 345–42.

Kent, Grenville J. R., Paul J. Kissling, and Laurence A. Turner. "Introduction." In *Reclaiming the Old Testament for Christian Preaching*, edited by Grenville J. R. Kent, Paul J. Kisslin,g and Laurence A. Turner, 11–12. Downers Grove: IVP Academic, 2010.

Ker, John. *Lectures on the History of Preaching*. New York: Armstrong, 1889.

Kindell, Alexandra, and Elizabeth S. Demers. *Encyclopedia of Populism in America: A Historical Encyclopedia*, vo.l 2. Oxford: ABC-CLIO, 2014.

Klein, Christopher. "Queen Victoria's Diamond Jubilee." *History*. Accessed 5 March 2019. https://www.history.com/news/queen-victorias-diamond-jubilee.

Konghar, Wungnaoting. "A Word of Welcome and Introduction." In *MBC Quasquicentenary Celebration Souvenir*, 9–10. Guwahati: Manipur Baptist Convention, 2019.

Kosygin, Laishram. *Wetlands of North East India: Ecology, Aquatic Bioresources and Conservation*. New Delhi: Akansha Publishing, 2009.

Kreitzer, Larry Joseph. *Jesus and God in Paul's Eschatology*. London: Bloomsbury, 2015.

Kruger, D. *An Introduction to Phenomenological Psychology*, 2nd ed. Cape Town: Juta, 1988.

Kumar, Dnyanesh. "What Are the Role and Functions of Sub-Divisional Officer (India)?" *Preserve Articles*. Accessed 6 December 2018. http://www.preservearticles.com/2011100514628/what-is-the-role-and-functions-of-sub-divisional-officer-india.html.

Kumar, Suresh Singh. *People of India: Manipur*. Kolkata: Anthropological Survey of India, 1998.

Kvale, S. *Doing Interviews*. Edited by Uwe Flick. London: SAGE, 2007.

———. *Interviews: An Introduction to Qualitative Research Interviewing*. Thousand Oaks: SAGE, 1996.

Ladd, George E. "What Does Bultmann Understand by the Acts of God?" *JETS* 5 (Summer 1962): 91–97.

Lalsawma. "The Shaking of Foundations in Mizo Society." *Mizoram Today* 1, no. 2 (1975): 13–17.

Lamb, Jonathan. *The Dynamics of Biblical Preaching*. Carlisle: Langham Preaching Resources, 2016.

———. *Integrity: Leading with God Watching*. Nottingham: Inter-Varsity Press, 2006.

Langdridge, Darre,n and Gareth Hagger-Johnson. *Introduction to Research Methods and Data Analysis in Psychology*. Harlow: Pearson, 2013.

Larsen, David L. *The Company of the Preachers*. Grand Rapids: Kregel, 1998.

Larson, Craig B., ed. *Prophetic Preaching*. Peabody: Hendrickson, 2012.

Lauer, Quentin. "Introduction." In *Phenomenology and the Crisis of Philosophy*, edited by Edmund Husserl. Translated by Quentin Lauer. New York: Harper Torchbooks, 1965.

———. *Phenomenology: Its Genesis and Prospects*. New York: Harper, 1958.

Lawmkunga, P. C. *Welcome to Mizoram: A Candid and Holistic Presentation on Mizoram and Its People*. Aizawl: Lengchhawn Press, 2017.

Leonard, Bill J. "Preaching in Historical Perspective." In *Handbook of Contemporary Preaching*, edited by Michael Duduit, 21–36. Nashville: B&H, 1992.

Lewis, Jonathan. *World Mission: An Analysis of the World Christian Movement*, 2nd ed. Pasadena: William Carey Library, 1994.

Liankhohau, T. *Social, Cultural, Economic and Religious Life of a Transformed Community: A Study of the Paite Tribe*. New Delhi: Mittal Publications, 1994.

Lieblich, Amia., Rivka Tuval-Mashiac,h and Tamar Zilber. *Narrative Research: Reading, Analysis and Interpretation*, ASRMS Vol. 47. New Delhi: SAGE, 1998.

Lim, Johnson T. K. *Power in Preaching*. New York: University Press of America, 2002.

Lincoln, Yvonna S., and Norman K. Denzin. *Collecting and Interpreting Qualitative Materials*, 4th ed. Thousand Oaks: SAGE, 1998.

Lindbeck, George. "George Lindbeck on Postliberal Approaches to Doctrine." In *The Christian Theology Reader 1.34*, edited by Alister McGrath, 55–58. 2nd ed. Malden: Blackwell, 2001.

Lindquist, Lareau. *Glory, Glory, Glory: Focussing on the Glory of God*. Xulon Press, 2010.

Lindsell, Harold. *The Incomparable Word*. Wheaton: Victor Books, 1977.

Lisam, Khodam Singh. *Encyclopedia of Manipur: Volume 2*. New Delhi: Kalpaz Publications, 2011.

Lischer, Richard, ed. *The Company of Preachers: Wisdom on Preaching, Augustine to the Present*. Grand Rapids: Eerdmans, 2002.

———. *The Preacher King: Martin Luther King, Jr. and the Word That Moved America*. Oxford: Oxford University Press, 1995.

———. *Theories of Preaching: Selected Readings in the Homiletical Tradition*. Durham: Labyrinth Press, 1987.

Litfin, Duane. *St. Paul's Theology of Preaching: The Apostle's Challenge to the Art of Persuasion in Ancient Corinth*. Downers Grove: InterVarsity Press, 2015.

Lloyd-Jones, D. Martyn. *Preaching and Preachers*. Grand Rapids: Zondervan, 2011.

Lodico, Marguerite G., Dean T. Spauding, and Katherine H. Voegtle. *Methods in Educational Research: From Theory to Practice*. San Francisco: Jossey-Bass, 2010.

Long, Michael G. *Against Us, But for Us: Martin Luther King, Jr. and the State*. Macon: Mercer University Press, 2002.

Longman, Tremper, III, and David E. Garland, eds. *The Expositor's Bible Commentary: Proverbs–Isaiah*, revised 2nd ed. Grand Rapids: Zondervan, 2008.

Lopez, Rene A. "Is Faith a Gift from God or a Human Exercise?" *BS* 164 (July–Sept. 2007): 259–76.

Loritts, Bryan. "Grace-full Prophetic Preaching." In *Prophetic Preaching*, edited by Craig Brian Larson, 41–46. Peabody: Hendrickson, 2012.

Lowry, Eugene L. *The Homiletical Plot: The Sermon as Narrative Art Form*. Atlanta: Westminster John Knox Press, 1980.

———. *The Sermon: Dancing the Edge of Mystery*. Nashville: Abingdon, 1997.

Luikham, T. *A Short History of the Manipur Baptist Christian Golden Jubilee – 1948*. Ukhrul, Manipur: North East Christian Association, 1975.

MacArthur, John F., Jr. "The Mandate of Biblical Inerrancy: Expository Preaching." In *Preaching: How to Preach Biblically*, edited by John MacArthur Jr., 17–26. Nashville: Thomas Nelson, 2013.

Machen, J. Gresham. *Christianity and Liberalism*. Grand Rapids: Eerdmans, 2009.

Mackrell, Paul. "1857 Day of Humiliation, The." *Evangelical Times*. Accessed 29 May 2018. https://www.evangelical-times.org/24594/the-1857-day-of-humiliation-spurgeons-sermons/.

Mandryk, Jason. *Operation World*, 7th ed. Colorado Springs: Biblica, 2010.

Manipur Baptist Convention. *Annual Report 2000–2001*. Imphal: MBC, 2000.

———. *Minutes of the 110th EC, CC*. Imphal, November 22–24, 1990.

———. *Minutes of the 11th AA*. Hnatham BC, March 11–14, 1992.

———. *Minutes of the 19th AA*. CBA Centre Church, New Checkon, Imphal, March 10–12, 2000.

"Manipur Religion Census 2011." *Census 2011*. Accessed 11 September 2018. https://www.census2011.co.in/data/religion/state/14-manipur.html.

Markquart, Edward F. *Quest for Better Preaching*. Minneapolis: Augsburg, 1985.

Martin, Dale B. *The Corinthian Body*. New Haven: Yale University Press, 1999.

Mason, Mark. "Sample Size and Saturation in PhD Studies Using Qualitative Interviews." *Forum: Qualitative Social Research* 11, no. 3 (Sept. 2010). Accessed 19 July 2021. https://www.qualitative-research.net/index.php/fqs/article/view/1428/3028.

Mason, Nettie Purssell. "'These Seventy-five Years': An Historical Sketch of Mission Work in Assam." *ABMC of the ABFMS*, 1911.

Mathai, Samuel. "Would God Transform India? Would We See India in a Mass Conversion?" In *Mission Mandate II*, edited by Ezra Sargunam, 333–36. Chennai: Mission Educational Books, 2006.

Mathewson, Steven D. "Verse-By-Verse Sermons That Really Preach." In *The Art of and Craft of Biblical Preaching: A Comprehensive Resource for Today*, edited by Haddon Robinson and Craig Brian Larson. Grand Rapids: Zondervan, 2005.

———. "What Makes Textual Preaching Unique?" In *The Art and Craft of Biblical Preaching: A Comprehensive Resources for Today*, edited by Haddon Robinson and Craig Brian Larson, 412–17. Grand Rapids: Zondervan, 2005.

"Max Weber's 'The Protestant Ethic and the Spirit of Capitalism.'" *Bartleby Research*. Accessed 29 June 2018. https://www.bartleby.com/essay/Max-Webers-The-Protestant-Ethic-and-the-P3XP74ZTC.

McClure, Barbara J. *Moving beyond Individualism in Pastoral Care and Counseling: Reflections on Theory, Theology and Practice*. Eugene: Cascade Books, 2010.

McComish J. F., R. Greenberg, and K. L. Easton. "Avoid Common Pitfalls in Qualitative Data Collection and Transcription." *Qualitative Health Research* 10 (2000): 703–8.

McDonald, B. Glazier. *Malachi: The Divine Messenger*, SBLDS 98. Atlanta: Scholars, 1987.

McDuie-Ra, Duncan. "Borders, Territory, and Ethnicity: Women and the Naga Peace Process." In *Border Politics: Social Movements, Collective Identities, and Globalization*, edited by Nancy A. Naples and Jennifer Bickham, 95–119. New York: New York University Press, 2015.

McGavran, Donald A. *Understanding Church Growth*, edited by C. Peter Wagner. Grand Rapids: Eerdmans, 1990.

McGrath, Alister E. *Christian Spirituality*. Oxford: Blackwell, 1999.

———. *Christian Theology: An Introduction*. 2nd ed. Oxford: Blackwell, 1997.

———. *The Christian Theology Reader*. 2nd ed. Malden: Blackwell, 2001.

McKim, Donald K., and Jack Rogers. *The Authority and Interpretation of the Bible: An Historical Approach*. Eugene: Wipf & Stock, 1999.

McMillan, Wendy. "Theory in Healthcare Education Research: The Importance of Worldview." In *Researching Medical Education*, edited by Jennifer Cleland and Steven J. Durning, 15–24. Oxford: Wiley Blackwell, 2015.

McQuilkin, Robertson. "Spiritual Formation through Preaching (part 2)." *PreachingToday.com*. Accessed 9 December 2017. http://www.preachingtoday.com/skills/thespirituallifeofthepreacher/200010.8html.

Merleau-Ponty, Maurice. *Husserl at the Limits of Phenomenology*. Evanston: Northwestern University Press, 2002.

Merrill, Eugene H. *Haggai, Zechariah, Malachi: An Exegetical Commentary*. LaVergne: Biblical Studies Press, 2003.

———. *Phenomenology of Perception*. Translated by C. Smith. London: Routledge, 2012.

Meyer, Daniel. *Witness Essentials: Evangelism That Makes Disciples*. Downers Grove: IVP Connect, 2012.

Millar, Gary, and Phil Campbell. *Saving Eutychus*. Sydney: Mattias Media, 2013.

Miller, Calvin. *Preaching the Art of Narrative Exposition*. Grand Rapids: Baker Books, 2006.

Miller, E. L., and Stanley J. Grenz. *Introduction to Contemporary Theologies.* Minneapolis: Fortress Press, 1998.

Miller, Stephen. *Nahum-Malachi.* HOTC. Nashville: B&H, 2004.

Miller, W. L., and B. F. Crabtree, eds. *Doing Qualitative Research: Research Methods for Primary Care.* Vol. 3. Newbury Park: SAGE, 1992.

Milner, Joseph. *The History of the Church of Christ: From the Days of the Apostles, Till the Famous Disputation between Luther and Miltitz, in 1520.* Edinburgh: Peter Brown & Thomas Nelson, 1836.

Milward, Alan S. *War, Economy and Society, 1939–1945.* Berkeley: University of California Press, 1979.

Mingthing, Y. L. "The Role of Preaching in the Development of the Church among the Tangkhul Nagas of Manipuri." MTh thesis, United Theological College, 1977.

Montague, George T. *First Corinthians.* Grand Rapids: Baker Academic, 2011.

Moody, D, L. *"The Gospel Awakening": Comprising the Sermons and Addresses, Prayer Meeting Talks and Bible Readings of the Great Revival Meetings conducted by Moody and Sankey.* St. Louis: Scammell & Co., 1878.

Moran, Dermot. *Introduction to Phenomenology.* London: Routledge, 2000.

Morris, Linus J. *The High Impact Church.* Thousand Oaks: Christian Associates International, 1993.

Mosheim, Johann Lorenz. *Institutes of Ecclesiological History, Ancient and Modern.* Vol. 1. New Haven: A.H. Maltby, 1832.

Moustakas, Clark. *Phenomenological Research Methods.* New Delhi: SAGE, 1994.

Mouton, Johann, and H. C. Marais. *Basic Concepts in the Methodology of the Social Sciences.* Pretoria: Human Sciences Research Council, 1990.

Moyon, Mono. "Manipur State Convention." *CBCA,* 1952.

Mr. Truth Episode 1, *Dreamz Unlimited.* Accessed 16 November 2019. https://www.youtube.com/watch?v=moiEen2FSM0.

Munck, Johannes, ed. "The Church without Factions: Studies in 1 Corinthians 1–4." In *Paul and the Salvation of Mankind,* 135–67. London: SCM, 1959.

Murray, D. F. "The Rhetoric of Disputation: Re-examination of a Prophetic Genre." *JSOT* 38 (1987): 95–121.

Musschenga, A. W. "The Many Faces of Individualism." In *The Many Faces of Individualism,* edited by Albert W. Musschenga and Anton van Harskamp, 3–24. Virginia: Peeters, 2001.

MBCCCI. *Souvenir: Manipur Baptist Convention Centre Church Imphal, Diamond Jubilee Celebration,* edited by Priya N. Shimray. Imphal: MBCCCI, 2015.

Nag, S. *India and North East India: Mind Politics and the Process of Integration 1946–1950.* New Delhi: Regency Publications, 1998.

Narendra Singh. "Religious Landscape in Manipur." Accessed 11 September 2018. http://epao.net/epSubPageExtractor.asp?src=manipur.Manipur_and_Religion.Religious_Landscape_in_Manipur_Part_1_By_RK_Narendra.

Nee, Watchman. *The Spiritual Man*. Anaheim: Living Stream Ministry, 1992.

"Need for a United Voice." *World Council of Churches*. Accessed 3 June 2018. https://www.oikoumene.org/en/press-centre/news/201cthere2019s-need-for-a-united-voice201d-says-new-wcc-member-council-of-baptist-churches-in-northeast-.

Newman, William M., and Stuart A. Wright. "The Effects of Sermons among Lay Catholics: An Exploratory Study." *RRR* 22, no. 1 (1980): 54–59.

Nogalski, J. D. *Redaction Process in the Book of Twelve*. Berlin: De Gruyter, 1993.

North East Cornerstone TV. "Nominalism in Christianity: Social Impact Commentary, Nagaland Episode 4/ Kohima." YouTube video, 33.19, 12 July 2017. Accessed 24 January 2018. http://tojsiabplay.com/watch?v=-p4Vf1Rce7Y.

Norton, Mary Beth, Carol Sheriff, David W. Blight, Howard P. Chudacoff, Fredrik Logevall, and Beth Bailey, eds. *A People and a Nation: A History of the United States, Brief Edition*. Stamford: Cengage, 2015.

Nuh, V. K. *Revive Us Again*. Kohima: CNBC Research Department, 1998.

———. *Struggle for Identity in North East India: A Theological Response*. Delhi: Spectrum Publications, 2001.

———, ed. "Theological Reflection on Nominalism in Naga Churches Today." In *In Search of Praxis Theology for the Nagas*, 116–30. New Delhi: CNBC, 2003.

Nunthara, C. *Mizoram: Society and Polity*. New Delhi: Indus Publishing, 1996.

Nystrom, Maria, Karin Dahlberg, and Nancy Drew. *Reflective Lifeworld Research*. Sweden: Professional Publishing, 2008.

Oden, Thomas C. *John Wesley's Teachings Volume 4: Ethics and Society*. Grand Rapids: Zondervan, 2014.

Old, Hughes Oliphant. *The Reading and Preaching of the Scriptures in the Worship of the Christian Church: The Biblical Period*. Vol. 1. Grand Rapids: Eerdmans, 2002.

Olford, Stephen, and David Olford. *The Secret of Soul Winning*. Nashville: B&H, 2007.

Olson, Roger E. *The Journey of Modern Theology*. Downers Grove: IVP Academic, 2013.

O'Reilly, Karen. *Ethnographic Methods*, 2nd ed. London: Routledge, 2005.

Orendorff, Aaron. "The Gospel According to N. T. Wright." *The Drama of Dogma*. Accessed 18 January 2020. http://dramaofdogma.blogspot.com/2010/05/gospel-according-to-n-t-wright_08.html.

Osmer, Richard R. *Practical Theology: An Introduction*. Grand Rapids: Eerdmans, 2008.

Ott, Craig. "Introduction." In *The Mission of the Church*, edited by Craig Ott, ix–xxxiv. Grand Rapids: Baker Academic, 2016.

Page, Stephen J., and Donald Getz. *Event Studies: Theory, Research and Policy for Planned Events*, 3rd ed. London: Routledge, 2016.

Pamei, Ramkhun. "Manipur Baptist Convention Report," *CBCNEI*, 1976.

———. "Report on Manipur Baptist Convention 1978," *CBCNEI*, 1979.

Parratt, John. *Wounded Land: Politics and Identity in Modern Manipur*. New Delhi: Mittal Publications, 2005.

"Pastoral Office." In *The Wesleyan-Methodist Magazine for the Year*. Vol. 14, 3rd Series. London: J. Mason, 1835.

Pathshala. "Interpretation of Qualitative Data." YouTube video, 28:09. Accessed 18 June 2019. https://www.youtube.com/watch?v=XkhJyrq8Ui4&t=528s.

Patton, Michael Quinn. *Qualitative Research and Evaluation Methods*. New Delhi: SAGE, 2002.

"PC Lawmkunga to Relieve from Chief Secretary on Oct 1." *Imphal Times*. Accessed 6 September 2018. http://www.imphaltimes.com/news/item/3791-pc-lawmkunga-to-relieve-from-chief-secretary-on-oct-1.

"Peace Trust Kanyakumari." Accessed 28 May 2018. http://peacetrustkanyakumari.blogspot.com/p/founder-president.html.

Pearson, Birger. *The Pneumatikos-Psychikos Terminology in 1 Corinthians*. SBL Dissertation Series 12. Atlanta: Scholars Press, 1973.

Peerlinck, Franz. *Rudolf Bultmann als Prediger*. Hamburg: H. Reich Evangelischer Verlag, 1970.

Perkins, Pheme. *First Corinthians*. Grand Rapids: Baker Academics, 2012.

Perry, Marvin. *Western Civilization: A Brief History, Volume 2: Since 1600*. Boston: Cengage Learning, 2016.

Peshkin, Alan. "The Nature of Interpretation in Qualitative Research." *ER* 29, no. 9 (2000): 5–9.

Petersen, David L. *Zechariah 9–14 and Malachi*. TOTL. Louisville: Westminster John Knox Press, 1995.

Pettigrew, William. *Annual Report Manipur*, 1921 (Cyclostyled).

———. "The Beginning of Ukhrul Station (1897)." *The Baptist Missionary Magazine* 77, no. 9 (1897): 526.

———. *Evangelistic, Educational and Literature Report, December 1931*, Nos. 2 & 4 (Cyclostyled).

———. *Evangelistic Report from Manipur, December 1923,* No. 1 (Cyclostyled).

———. "The Jubilee in Manipur (1898)." *The Baptist Missionary Magazine* 78, no. 1 (1898): 25.

———. "My Twenty-Five Years 1897–1922 at Ukhrul Mission School," Appendix 1. In *Rev William Pettigrew (A Pioneer Missionary of Manipur)*. Imphal: Pettigrew Centenary Celebration Committee, Fraternal Green Cross, 1996.

———. "Manipur." *ABMC of the ABFMS*, 1917.

———. "Manipur Mission in the Early Years (1899)." In *The Assam Mission of the ABMU*, 1899.

Phanitphang, V. "Field Report – Manipur – 1954." *CBCAM*, 1955.

———. "Manipur Baptist Convention Report." *CBCNEI*, 1963.

———. "Manipur Field Report." *CBCNEI*, 1967.

———. "Report of Manipur Baptist Convention – 1969." *CBCNEI*, 1970.

Phillips, Estelle M., and D. S. Pugh. *How to Get a PhD: A Handbook for Students and Their Supervisors*. New Delhi: UBS Publishers' Distributors, 2000.

Phillipson, Michael. "Phenomenological Philosophy and Sociology." In *New Directions in Socio-logical Inquiry*, edited by P. Filmer, M. Phillipson, D. Silverman, and D. Walsh, 119–64. Cambridge: MITP, 1972.

Pinnock, Clark H. *Tracking the Maze*. San Francisco: Harper & Row, 1990.

Piper, John. *The Future of Justification: A Response to N. T. Wright*. Wheaton: Crossway, 2007.

Pongen, Imsungnungsang. "Nominalism among Christians with Special Reference to Selected Ao Baptist Churches in Mokokchung Town: A Pastoral Theological Response." MTh thesis, South Asia Institute of Advanced Christian Studies, 2008.

"Population by Religious Communities." *Census India*. Accessed 11 September 2018. http://censusindia.gov.in/Census_Data_2001/Census_data_finder/C_Series/Population_by_religious_communities.htm.

"Population of Manipur." *Statistics Times*. Accessed 11 September 2018. https://statisticstimes.com/population/population-of-manipur.php.

Poulton, John. *A Today Sort of Evangelism*. London: Lutterworth, 1977.

Poxon, Stephen J. *Through the Year with John Wesley: 365 Daily Readings from John Wesley*. Oxford: Monarch Books, 2017.

Prasain, Ganga Prasad, and Elangbam Nixon Singh. *Industrial Sickness in Manipur: Causes and Remedies*. New Delhi: Concept Publishing Company, 2012.

Pudney, John. *John Wesley and His World*. New York: Charles Scribner's Sons, 1978.

Qualben, Lars P. *A History of the Christian Church*. Eugene: Wipf & Stock, 2008.

Quicke, Michael J. *360-Degree Leadership: Preaching to Transform Congregation*. Grand Rapids: Baker Books, 2006.

Raih, R. T. Johnson. "A Critical Reading of Van Tillian Apologetics for Evangelism, Especially in the Poumai Naga Context." MTh thesis, Mysore University, SAIACS, 2015.

———. "The Mighty Acts of God." In *MBC Quasquicentenary Celebration Souvenir*. Guwahati: Manipur Baptist Convention, 2019.

Randolph, David James. *The Renewal of Preaching*. Philadelphia: Fortress, 1969.

Rauschenbusch, Walter. *Christianity and the Social Crisis*. New York: Macmillan, 1924.

———. *Christianizing the Social Order*. New York: Macmillan, 1912.

Reiners, Gina M. "Understanding the Differences between Husserl's (Descriptive) and Heidegger's (Interpretive) Phenomenological Research." *Journal of Nursing and Care* 1, no. 5 (2012). DOI: 10.4172/2167-1168.1000119.

Report of the Resolution Committee of the 22nd MBC Annual Assembly, 2003.

Rice, John R. *The Golden Path to Successful Personal Soul Winning*. Murfreesboro: Sword of the Lord Publishers, 1989.

Richard, Ramesh. *Preparing Expository Sermons: A Seven-Step Method for Biblical Preaching*. Grand Rapids: Baker Books, 2005.

Richards, Jeffrey Jon. "Hermeneutics and Homiletics of Rudolf Bultmann and Dietrich Bonhoeffer in the American Discussion." PhD diss., Philipps-University Marburg, 2008.

Richter, Patti. "Teaching Former Head-Hunters." *TGC*. Accessed 2 January 2018. https://www.thegospelcoalition.org/article/teaching-former-head-hunters/.

Ridley, D. *The Literature Review: A Step-by-Step Guide for Students*. London: SAGE, 2008.

Ritschl, Dietrich. *A Theology of Proclamation*. Richmond: John Knox, 1960.

Robertson, William. *The Works of William Robertson: The History of Scotland*. London: Cadell & Davies, 1812.

Robinson, Haddon W. *Biblical Preaching: The Development and Delivery of Expository Messages*. 2nd ed. Grand Rapids: Baker Books, 2001.

———. "Dramatic Expository Preaching." In *The Art and Craft of Biblical Preaching: A Comprehensive Resource for Today*, edited by Haddon Robinson and Craig Brian Larson, 405–06. Grand Rapids: Zondervan, 2005.

Rogers, Jack, and Donald K. McKim. *The Authority and Interpretation of the Bible: An Historical Approach*. Eugene: Wipf & Stock, 1999.

Rojek, Chris. *Pop Music, Pop Culture*. Cambridge: Polity Press, 2011.

Rongpi, Solomon, "The Challenge of Nominalism." In *Transform North East India: Revitalise the Church and Community*, edited by T. Hawiphal, 94–96. Guwahati, Assam: TNEI2020, 2016.

Ronrang, Molem. *Emergence and Growth of Baptist Churches among the Tangsas of Arunachal Pradesh*. Guwahati: Saraighat Printers, 1997.

Rubin, Allen, and Earl Babbie. *Essential Research Methods for Social Work*. 2nd ed. Belmont: Brooks/Cole, 2010.

Roy, Joyotirmoy. *History of Manipur*. Imphal: Imphal East Light, 1973.

Sadala, M. L. A., and R. de C. F. Adorno. "Phenomenology as a Method to Investigate the Experiences Lived: A Perspective from Husserl and Merleau-Ponty's Thought." *JAN* 37, no. 3 (2003): 282–93.

Saldana, Johnny. *The Coding Manual for Qualitative Researchers*. Thousand Oaks: SAGE, 2013.

———. *Fundamentals of Qualitative Research: Understanding Qualitative Research*. Oxford: Oxford University Press, 2011.

Sangma, Milton, S. *A History of American Baptist Mission in North-East India (1836–1950)*, Vol. 1. Delhi: Mittal, 1987.

Schaeffer, Francis. *True Spirituality*. London: Hodder & Stoughton, 1972.

Scharf, Greg R. "John Stott: Preaching That Listens to the Word and the World." In *A Legacy of Preaching*, Vol. 2, edited by Benjamin K. Forrest, Kevin L. King, Bill Curtis, and Dwayne Milioni, 339–53. Grand Rapids: Zondervan, 2018.

Schleiermacher, Friedrich. *Christian Faith*. Edited by H. R. Mackintosh and J. S. Stewart. Edinburgh: T&T Clark, 1999.

Schmidt, James. *What Is Enlightenment? Eighteenth-Century Answers and Twentieth-Century Questions*. Edited and translated by James Schmidt. Berkely: University of California Press, 1996.

Schuller, Eileen. *Post-Exilic Prophets MOBS 4*. Wilmington: Michael Glazier, 1988.

Seamands, John T. *Tell It Well: Communicating the Gospel across Cultures*. Chennai: Mission Educational Books, 2000.

Select Committee. "Great Britain: Parliament House of Commons." *Fourth Report from the Select Committee on Colonization and Resettlement (India)*. England: Her Majesty's Stationery Office, 1858.

Sen, Sipra. *Tribes and Castes of Manipur: Description and Select Bibliography*. New Delhi: Mittal Publications, 1992.

Shaddix, James L., and Jerry Vines. *Power in the Pulpit: How to Prepare and Deliver Expository Sermons*. Chicago: Moody Publishers, 2017.

Shapiro, Jeremy J., and Valerie Malhotra Bentz. *Mindful Enquiry in Social Research*. Thousand Oaks: SAGE, 1998.

Shimray, U. A. "Naga Population Scenario and Immigration." *A Monthly Journal: The Legacy* 4, no. 5 (2006): Ukhrul, CENTSHIRED.

"Short View of the History, and the Present State of Christianity in South India, A." *The Christian Examiner* 5 of vol. 2 (Sep.–Oct. 1825).

Sim, J. "Collecting and Analysing Qualitative Data: Issues Raised by the Focus Group." *JAN* 28, no. 2 (1998): 345–52.

Singh, A. Prafullo Kumar. *Elections and Political Dynamics*. New Delhi: Mittal Publications, 2009.

Singh, Manpreet Singh. "The Soul Hunters of Central Asia." *Phora*. Accessed 29 January 2018. http://www.thephora.net/forum/showthread.php?p=1341329.

Singh, R. K. Narendra. "Impact of NRC Updating (Assam) on Manipur: A Dynamics of Migration." In *Kangla Lanpung* 12, no. 1, edited by Ningthou Lancha. Imphal: Lourembam Ranjit, 2018.

Sitlhou, Vumthang. "Annual Report of the General Secretary," 2004.

Skoglund, John E. "Towards a New Homiletic." *PSB 60* (Fall 1967): 57.

Sleeth, Ronald E. "Bultmann and the Proclamation of the World." *PSB* 2, no. 2, (1979): 153–62.

Smith, Fred Sr. *Leading with Integrity: Competence with Christian Character*. Minneapolis: Bethany House, 1999.

Smith, George Adam. *Works on the Prophets: The Books of Zephaniah, Nahum, Habakkuk, Obadiah, Haggai, Zechariah, Malachi, Joel, Jonah*. Vol. 2. London: Harper & Brothers, n.d.

Smith, Keller Miller. *Social Crisis Preaching: The Lyman Beecher Lectures 1983*. Macon: Mercer University Press, 2004.

Smith, Kevin Gary. *Writing and Research: A Guide for Theological Students*. Carlisle: Langham Global Library, 2016.

Smith, John. *The Missionary Appeal to British Christians on Behalf of Southern India*. London: Hamilton, Adams & Co., 1841.

Smith, Jonathan A., Paul Flowers, and Michael Larkin. *Interpretive Phenomenological Analysis: Theory, Method and Research*. New Delhi: SAGE, 2009.

Snaitang, O. L. "Christianity and Change among the Hill Tribes of Northeast India." In *Christianity and Change in North East India*, edited by Tanka Bahadur Subba, Joseph Puthenpurakal, and Shaji Joseph Puykunnel, 146–57. New Delhi: Concept Publishing, 2009.

Solo, Jonah M. "Captain the Rev. William Pettigrew." In *Souvenir: Phungyo Baptist Church, Ukhrul 1901–2001 Centenary Celebration 26th to 29th September 2002*, edited by David L. Shimray. Ukhrul: Phungyo Baptist Church, 2002.

Spurgeon, Charles Haddon. *The Complete Works of C. H. Spurgeon, Vol. 5: Sermons 225–285*. Fort Collins: Delmarva Publications, 2013.

———. *Lectures to My Student*. 2nd Series. London: Passmore & Alabaster, 1877.

———. *The New Park Street Pulpit*. Vol. 6. Grand Rapids: Baker, 1994.

———. "The Present Crisis." In *The Metropolitan Tabernacle Pulpit*, Vol. 25. Pasadena: Pilgrim Publications, 1972.

———. *The Soul Winner*. Grand Rapids: Eerdmans, 1984.

Stevens, Paul. *2 Corinthians: Finding Strength in Weakness*. Downers Grove: IVP Connect, 2001.

Stokes, George. *The History of the Church of Christ, Previous to the Reformation, Vol. 2: During the Early and Middle Ages*. Stamford Street, London: W. Clowes & Sons, 1840.

Stott, John R. W. *Balanced Christianity*, 3rd ed. Downers Grove: InterVarsity Press, 2014.

———. *Basic Christianity*, 2nd ed. Downers Grove: InterVarsity Press, 1972.

———. *Between Two Worlds*. Grand Rapids: Eerdmans, 1982.

———. "The Biblical Basis for Evangelism." In *Let the Earth Hear His Voice: International Congress on World Evangelicalism*, Lausanne, Switzerland, Official Reference Volume, edited by J. D. Douglas. Minneapolis: World Wide Publications, 1975.

———. *The Contemporary Christian: An Urgent Plea for Double Listening*. Leicester: Inter-Varsity Press, 1992.

———. *Evangelical Truth: A Personal Plea for Unity, Integrity and Faithfulness*. Carlisle: Langham Global Library, 2003.

———. "Foreword." In *Integrity: Leading with God Watching*, by Jonathan Lamb. Nottingham: Inter-Varsity Press, 2006.

———. *God's Word for Today's World*. Carlisle: Langham Preaching Resources, 2015.

———. *I Believe in Preaching*. Mumbai: GLS Publishing, 2014.

———. *Issues Facing Christians Today*. 4th ed. Grand Rapids: Zondervan, 2011.

———. "The Lausanne Covenant: Exposition and Commentary." *Lausanne 1974 Documents* (Lausanne Movement). Accessed 17 May 2018. https://www.lausanne.org/content/lausanne-1974-documents.

———. *The Living Church: Convictions of a Lifelong Pastor*. Downers Grove: InterVarsity Press, 2007.

———. *The Preacher's Portrait: Five New Testament Word Studies*. Grand Rapids: Eerdmans, 2017.

Stott, John R. W., and Christopher J. H. Wright. *Christian Mission in the Modern World*. Downers Grove: InterVarsity Press, 2015.

Stott, John R. W., and Greg Scharf. *The Challenge of Preaching*. Carlisle: Langham Preaching Resources, 2011.

Sunukjian, Don. "The Biblical Topical Sermon." In *The Art and Craft of Biblical Preaching: A Comprehensive Resource for Today*, edited by Haddon Robinson and Craig Brian Larson, 421–23. Grand Rapids: Zondervan, 2005.

Suttle, Tim. *An Evangelical Social Gospel?: Finding God's Story in the Midst of Extremes*. Eugene: Cascade Books, 2011.

Swingewood, Alan. *A Short History of Sociological Thought*. New York: St. Martin's, 1984.

Swinton, John, and Harriet Mowat. *Practical Theology and Qualitative Research*, 2nd ed. London: SCM Press, 2016.

Taylor, Richard A., and E. Ray Clendenen. *Haggai, Malachi*. Nashville: B&H, 2004.

Terry, R. B. *A Discourse Analysis of First Corinthians*. Dallas: Summer Institute of Linguistics, 1995.

Thanzauva, K. *The Theology of Community: Tribal Theology in the Making*. Aizawl, Mizoram: Research & Development of AICS, 2004.

Theissen, Gerd. *The Social Setting of Pauline Christianity: Essays on Corinth*. Philadelphia: Fortress Press, 1982.

Thiselton, Anthony C. *The First Epistle to the Corinthians*. NIGTC. Grand Rapids: Eerdmans, 2000.

———. "The New Hermeneutics." In *A Guide to Contemporary Hermeneutics: Major Trends in Biblical Interpretation*, edited by Donald K. McKim, 78–110. Grand Rapids: Eerdmans, 1986.

———. "Realised Eschatology at Corinth." In *Christianity at Corinth: The Quest for the Pauline Church*, edited by Edward Adams and David G. Horrell, 107–18. Louisville: Westminster John Knox Press, 2004.

———. "Realised Eschatology at Corinth." *NTS* 24, no. 4 (1978): 510–26.

Tidball, Derek. *Builders and Fools: Leadership the Bible Way*. Nottingham: Inter-Varsity Press, 1999.

———. *Skilful Shepherd: Explorations in Pastoral Theology*. Nottingham: Apollos, 1997.

Tillotson, John. *The Works of the Most Reverend Dr. John Tillotson, Lord Archbishop of Canterbury*. London: Ware, 1743.

Tisdale, Leonora Tubbs. *Prophetic Preaching: A Pastoral Approach*. Louisville: Westminster John Knox Press, 2010.

Toon, Peter. *The End of Liberal Theology*. Wheaton: Crossway Books, 1995.

Torrey, Joseph. *General History of the Christian Religion and Church: Volume 2*. London: Crocker & Brewster, 1855.

Tozer, A. W. *The Dangers of a Shallow Faith: Awakening from Spiritual Lethargy*. Ventura: Regal, 2012.

"Tribes of Manipur." *Tribal Research Institute*. Accessed 6 September 2018. http://trimanipur.res.in/masters/Title.aspx?ref=tribes_of_manipur.

"Tribute to Dr. I. Ben Wati, A." *Pathien Thucha*. Accessed 10 March 2018. http://pathienthu.in/a-tribute-to-dr-i-ben-wati/.

"Tribute to the Rev. Dr. I Ben Wati (1920–2012)." *WEA*. Accessed 10 March 2018. https://dev.worldea.org/news/3381/wea-pays-tribute-to-the-rev-dr-i-ben-wati-1920-2012/.

Troeger, Thomas H. *Imaging a Sermon*. Nashville: Abingdon, 1990.

Troxel, Ronald L. *Prophetic Literature: From Oracles to Books*. Chichester: Wiley-Blackwell, 2012.

"Ukhrul Field Report for 1911." In *History of Christianity in Manipur: Source Materials*. Compiled by Elungkiebe Zeliang. Guwahati: CLC, 2005.

University of Glasgow. "Coding Qualitative Data for Categories and Themes." YouTube video, 08:56. Accessed 8 November 2019. https://www.youtube.com/watch?v=YP3yAX5w6x8.

Urquhart, Cathy. *Grounded Theory for Qualitative Research: A Practical Guide*. New Delhi: SAGE, 2013.

Vaiphei, Th. Lamboi. *Advent of Christian Mission and Its Impact on the Hill-Tribes in Manipur*. Imphal: Frontier Mission Society, 1997.

Vanhoozer, Kevin J. *The Drama of Doctrine: A Canonical Linguistic Approach to Christian Theology*. Louisville: Westminster John Knox Press, 2005.

———. *Is There a Meaning in This Text?* Grand Rapids: Zondervan, 1998.

Verhoef, Pieter A. *The Books of Haggai and Malachi*. TNICOT. Grand Rapids: Eerdmans, 1993.

"Vision." *LICC*. Accessed 10 March, 2019. https://www.licc.org.uk/about/.

Vines, Jerry, and James L. Shaddix. *Power in the Pulpit: How to Prepare and Deliver Expository Sermons*. Chicago: Moody Publishers, 2017.

Volbeda, Samuel. *The Pastoral Genius of Preaching*. Grand Rapids: Zondervan, 1960.

"Walter Rauschenbusch." In *20 Centuries of Great Preaching: An Encyclopedia of Preaching*, edited by Clyde E. Fant Jr. and William M. Pinson Jr., 125–72. Vol. 7. Waco: Word Books, 1971.

Ward, Frances. "Methodological Approaches: Practical Theology." In *Studying Local Churches: A Handbook*, edited by Helen Cameron, Philip Richter, Douglas Davies, and Frances Ward. London: SCM Press, 2005.

Ward, Kevin, and Emma Wild-Wood, eds. *East African Revival: History and Legacies*. Surrey: Ashgate Publication, 2012.

Warren, Timothy S. "Can Topical Preaching also Be Expository?" In *The Art of and Craft of Biblical Preaching: A Comprehensive Resource for Today*, edited by Haddon Robinson and Craig Brian Larson, 418–20, Grand Rapids: Zondervan, 2005.

———. "Topical Preaching on Theological Themes." In *The Art of and Craft of Biblical Preaching: A Comprehensive Resource for Today*, edited by Haddon Robinson and Craig Brian Larson, 431–33. Grand Rapids: Zondervan, 2005.

Wati, I. Ben. "Music of Ten Thousand Hills: The Story of Nagaland and Its Church." In *Whither Evangelicals? The Evangelical Movement in India*, edited by Ben Wati, 34–39. New Delhi: EFI, 1975.

Waugh, Geoff. *Flashpoints of Revival: History's Mighty Revivals*. California: Createspace Independent Publishing, 2009.

Wax, Trevin. "Interview with N. T. Wright – Responding to Piper on Justification." *TGC*, January 13, 2009. Accessed 18 January 2020. https://www.thegospelcoalition.org/blogs/trevin-wax/interview-with-nt-wright-responding-to-piper-on-justification/.

———. "The Justification Debate: A Primer." *Christianity Today*, June 2009. Accessed 18 January 2020. http://www.christianitytoday.com/ct/2009/june/29.34.html?start=2.

"WEA Pays Tribute." *WEA*. Accessed 10 March 2018. http://worldea.org/news/4027/wea-pays-tribute-to-the-rev-dr-i-ben-wati-1920-2012.

Weber, Max. *The Protestant Ethic and the Spirit of Capitalism*. Translated by Talcott Parsons. London: Routledge, 2000.

Weitzman, Eben A. and Matthew B. Miles. "Choosing Software for Qualitative Data Analysis: An Overview." *CAM* 7, no. 2 (1995): 1–5.

Wellman, Sam. *John Wesley: The Horseback Preacher*. Uhrichsville: Barbour, 2000.

Welman, Chris, S. J. Kruger, and Fanie Kruger. *Research Methodology for the Business and Administrative Sciences*. Johannesburg: International Thompson, 1999.

Welsh, Clement. *Preaching in a New Key: Studies in the Psychology of Thinking and Listening*. Philadelphia: United Church Press, 1974.

Wendland, Ernst R. *Prophetic Rhetoric: Case Studies in Text Analysis and Translation*. Maitland: Xulon Press, 2009.

Werelius, W. R. "Evangelistic Report." *ABMC Report*, 1936.

———. "Kangpokpi," *ABMC Report*, 1936,

Wesley, John. *The Journal of the Rev. John Wesley, A.M., Sometime Fellow of London College, Oxford, Vol. 2 of 4 Volumes*. London: Wesleyan Conference Office, 1869.

———. *The Miscellaneous Works of the Rev. John Wesley*. Vol. 1. New York: J & J Harper, 1828.

———. *The Works of the Rev. John Wesley*. Vol. 1. London: Conference-Office, 1809.

Westerhoff, John H., III, and John D. Eusden. *The Spiritual Life: Learning East and West*. New York: Seabury, 1982.

Wiersbe, Warren. "Phillips Brooks: A Preacher of Truth and Life." In *Phillips Brooks: The Joy of Preaching*, 5–22. Grand Rapids: Kregel, 1989.

Wilkerson, Bryan. "Trends in Sermon Series." In *The Art and Craft of Biblical Preaching: A Comprehensive Resource for Today*, edited by Haddon Robinson and Craig Brian Larson. Grand Rapids: Zondervan, 2005.

Willhite, Keith. "Audience Relevance and Rhetorical Argumentation in Expository Preaching: A Historical-Critical Comparative Analysis of Selected Sermons of John F. MacArthur Jr., and Charles R. Swindoll, 1970–1990." PhD diss., Purdue University, 1990.

Willhite, Keith, and Scott M. Gibson, eds. *The Big Idea of Biblical Preaching*. Grand Rapids: Baker Books, 1998.

Willig, Carla. *Qualitative Interpretation and Analysis in Psychology*. Maidenhead: Open University Press, 2012.

Wilson, Andrew J. *The Warning-Assurance Relationship in 1 Corinthians*. Tubingen: Mohr Siebeck, 2017.

Wilson, Paul Scott. "New Homiletic." In *The New Interpreter's Handbook of Preaching*, edited by Paul Scott Wilson, Jana Chiders, Cleophus J. LaRue, and John M. Rottman, 398–401. Nashville: Abingdon, 2008.

Winks, Robin W. *World Civilization: A Brief History*, 2nd ed. San Diego: Collegiate Press, 1993.

Windsor, Paul. "What Is Preaching?" In *Text Messages: Preaching God's Word in a Smartphone World*, edited by John Tucker, 1–17. Eugene: Wipf & Stock, 2017.

Wogaman, J. Philip. *Speaking the Truth in Love: Prophetic Preaching to a Broken World*. Louisville: Westminster John Knox Press, 1998.

Woodbridge, Noel. "The EDNA Model for Doing Research in Practical Theology: A Biblical Approach." *JSATS* 17, no. 3 (2014): 89–121.

Woodfin, Yandall. "A Theology of Preaching: A Search for the Authentic." *SJT* 23, no. 4 (1970): 408–19.

Wraight, Heather, ed. "Foreword: The Consultation." In *They Call Themselves Christian: Papers on Nominality Given at the International Lausanne Consultation on Nominalism*. London: Christian Research, 1999.

———. "Varieties of Nominality." In *They Call Themselves Christians: Papers on Nominality Given at the International Lausanne Consultation on Nominalism*. London: Christian Research, 1999.

Wright, Christopher J. H. *Sweeter than Honey: Preaching the Old Testament*. Carlisle: Langham Preaching Resources, 2015.

Wright, David I. *From Patriarchs to Prophets: A Poetic Anthology of the Old Testament*. Bloomington: WestBow Press, 2011.

Wright, N. T. *Justification: God's Plan and Paul's Vision*. Downers Grove: InterVarsity Press, 2009.

———. *The Resurrection of the Son of God: Christian Origin and the Question of God*. Vol. 3. London: Fortress Press, 2003.

———. *Simply Good News*. New York: HarperCollins, 2015.

———. *What Saint Paul Really Said*. Grand Rapids: Eerdmans, 1997.

Wright, Stuart A., and William M. Newman. "The Effects of Sermons among Lay Catholics: An Exploratory Study." *RRR* 22, no. 1 (1980): 54–59.

Younis, Eamon. "Chapter 32 – The Enlightenment." Accessed 28 May 2018. http://eamonyounis.blogspot.in/2017/04/chapter-32-enlightenment.html.

Zawngia. "Christianity in Mizoram." In *Transform North East India: Revitalise the Church and Community*, edited by T. Guwahati Hawiphal. Assam: TNEI2020, 2016.

Zeliang, Elungkiebe. *A History of the Manipur Baptist Convention*. Imphal, Manipur: Manipur Baptist Convention, 2005.

Langham Literature, with its publishing work, is a ministry of Langham Partnership.

Langham Partnership is a global fellowship working in pursuit of the vision God entrusted to its founder John Stott –

to facilitate the growth of the church in maturity and Christ-likeness through raising the standards of biblical preaching and teaching.

Our vision is to see churches in the Majority World equipped for mission and growing to maturity in Christ through the ministry of pastors and leaders who believe, teach and live by the word of God.

Our mission is to strengthen the ministry of the word of God through:
- nurturing national movements for biblical preaching
- fostering the creation and distribution of evangelical literature
- enhancing evangelical theological education

especially in countries where churches are under-resourced.

Our ministry

Langham Preaching partners with national leaders to nurture indigenous biblical preaching movements for pastors and lay preachers all around the world. With the support of a team of trainers from many countries, a multi-level programme of seminars provides practical training, and is followed by a programme for training local facilitators. Local preachers' groups and national and regional networks ensure continuity and ongoing development, seeking to build vigorous movements committed to Bible exposition.

Langham Literature provides Majority World preachers, scholars and seminary libraries with evangelical books and electronic resources through publishing and distribution, grants and discounts. The programme also fosters the creation of indigenous evangelical books in many languages, through writer's grants, strengthening local evangelical publishing houses, and investment in major regional literature projects, such as one volume Bible commentaries like the *Africa Bible Commentary* and the *South Asia Bible Commentary*.

Langham Scholars provides financial support for evangelical doctoral students from the Majority World so that, when they return home, they may train pastors and other Christian leaders with sound, biblical and theological teaching. This programme equips those who equip others. Langham Scholars also works in partnership with Majority World seminaries in strengthening evangelical theological education. A growing number of Langham Scholars study in high quality doctoral programmes in the Majority World itself. As well as teaching the next generation of pastors, graduated Langham Scholars exercise significant influence through their writing and leadership.

To learn more about Langham Partnership and the work we do visit **langham.org**

www.ingramcontent.com/pod-product-compliance
Lightning Source LLC
Chambersburg PA
CBHW061703300426
44115CB00014B/2546